European Economic Integration and Sustainable Development

European Economic Integration and Sustainable Development

Institutions, Issues and Policies

Robert Barrass and Shobhana Madhavan

McGRAW-HILL BOOK COMPANY

London · New York · St Louis · San Francisco · Auckland
Bogotá · Caracas · Lisbon · Madrid · Mexico· Milan
Montreal · New Delhi · Panama · Paris · San Juan · São Paulo
Singapore · Sydney · Tokyo · Toronto

Published by
McGRAW-HILL Book Company Europe
Shoppenhangers Road, Maidenhead, Berkshire SL6 2QL, England
Telephone 01628 23432
Fax 01628 770224

British Library Cataloguing in Publication Data

Barrass, Robert
   European Economic Integration and Sustainable Development: Institution, Issues, Policies
   I. Title II. Madhaven, S.
   337.142

ISBN 0–07–707836–5

Library of Congress Cataloguing-in-Publication Data

Barrass, Robert, (date)
   European economic integration and sustainable development: institutions, issues, policies / Robert Barrass and
Shobhana Madhavan.
      p.   cm.
   Includes bibliographical references.
   ISBN 0–07–707836–5 (pbk: alk. paper)
   1. European Union. 2. European Union countries – Economic policy. 3. Europe–Economic integration. I. Madhavan,
S. (Shobhana) II. Title.
HC240.B296 1996   95–47472
337.1′4–dc20   CIP

McGraw-Hill
A Division of The **McGraw·Hill** Companies

12345   CL   99876

Typeset by Computape (Pickering) Ltd, North Yorkshire
and printed and bound in Great Britain at Clays Ltd, St Ives plc
Printed on permanent paper in compliance with ISO standard 9706

CONTENTS

LIST OF ABBREVIATIONS

ACP	Africa, Pacific and Caribbean
CAP	Common Agricultural Policy
CEE	Central and Eastern Europe
CEN	Comité européen de normalisation
COREPER	Committee of Permanent Representatives
DG	Directorate General
EAGGF	European Agricultural Guidance and Guarantee Fund
EBRD	European Bank for Reconstruction and Development
EC	European Community
ECB	European Central Bank
ECSC	European Coal and Steel Community
ECU	European Currency Unit
EEA	European Economic Area
EEC	European Economic Community
EFTA	European Free Trade Area
EIA	Environmental Impact Assessment
EIB	European Investment Bank
EMS	European Monetary System
EMI	European Monetary Institute
EMU	Economic and Monetary Union
ERDF	European Regional Development Fund
ERM	Exchange Rate Mechanism
ESF	European Social Fund
ESC	Economic and Social Committee
ESCB	European System of Central Banks
EU	European Union
Euratom	European Atomic Energy Community
FIFG	Financial Instrument for Fisheries Guidance
GATT	General Agreement on Tariffs and Trade
GDP	Gross Domestic Product
GNP	Gross National Product
IGC	Inter Governmental Conference
LIFE	*L'instrument financier pour l'environnement*
LU	Livestock Unit
MCA	Monetary Compensation Amount
MFA	Multi Fibre Arrangement
MFN	Most Favoured Nation

NCI   New Community Instrument
OECD   Organisation for Economic Cooperation and Development
PHARE   Poland and Hungary: Aid for Reconstruction of Economies
PPP   Polluter Pays Principle
TEN   Trans European Network
VAT   Value Added Tax
VER   Voluntary Export Restraint
WTO   World Trade Organization

PREFACE

The two main intentions of this book are, first, to dispel misunderstanding and incomprehension about European institutions and their activities; and, second, to respond to a growing appreciation of the importance of European integration, and its influence on our lives.

Increasing 'Euro-awareness' has been reflected in higher education, with the development of courses focusing on European issues. We have perceived a need for material to support such courses; indeed, the original concept of this book arose from the final-year courses on European integration in the Business and Social Studies degrees at the University of Westminster. These degrees have modular structures, so courses may include students from a variety of specialisms; therefore teachers have to ensure the coherence of their courses at an advanced undergraduate level, without being able to assume a uniform degree of specialized knowledge on the part of the course participants.

Our aim is to explain and analyse the economic issues arising from European integration, in a manner that is accessible to readers who may not necessarily regard themselves as economics specialists. We seek to cut through the 'fog' which so often obscures European issues, and to enable readers to make sense of—and detect the nonsense in—media coverage of European issues, whether it concerns crises in negotiations between governments, threats to traditional British sausages, or butter mountains and wine lakes.

More fundamentally, we seek to enable readers to appreciate the economic and political forces which influence the long-term development of European integration, and the agenda for policy-making at European level. The book necessarily has an economic perspective, simply because the European Community's *raison d'être* is defined in economic terms; but it is not an economics book, at least not in the conventional sense. We have included some formal analysis to supplement the verbal explanation of economic integration, but we do not presuppose more than an elementary knowledge of economics.

The main argument of the book can be briefly summarized as follows. Economic integration requires a legal and institutional framework; the European single market has widened and deepened the Community policy agenda; and concerns over sustainability of development call for a policy response at Community level.

In presenting readers with the relevant basic information, we have to a great extent drawn upon European Community documentation, so that the information given is as close as possible to first hand. We have sought to explain in accessible terms how the European institutions work, how policies are formulated, the reasons for specific policy measures, and—importantly—how they operate. Our objective is to give a balanced and factually accurate account. Although a certain degree of complexity is unavoidable, readers will be rewarded with insights into the workings of important and often mysterious institutions and processes; and, as an incidental benefit, these insights will, we hope, enhance the entertainment value of inaccurate media stories.

We seek, above all, to give a 'feel' for the policy process in action; and we emphasize the legal, institutional, and political dimensions of the Community's economic role. The institutional material goes beyond the recital of formal powers, to consider evolving interrelationships between the Community and member states (with an explanation of the much cited subsidiarity principle), and also between the various institutions of the Community. We give particular emphasis to Community law, as a powerful force for integration even in the face of obstruction by national governments; in our judgement, this has not been given sufficient emphasis in existing books (other than legal texts) on the European Community.

We emphasize the fundamental purposes of the European Community, with reference to long-term economic and political developments. Specific policy areas are discussed with reference to the objectives set out in the founding Treaties. This highlights the essential aims of Community intervention, and demonstrates a coherence that might not otherwise be apparent in the role played by the Community.

Economic cohesion is one of the main themes, and enters into every chapter. As we see it, controversies over the deepening, and widening, of the Community are both a manifestation and a consequence of deeper forces in the real economy. Thus, for example, both monetary union and enlargement to the east depend on the degree of convergence that can be achieved between European economies.

We cover the implications of the single market in the broadest sense, and in particular the impetus that it has given for policy-making at Community level. Development of the single market, including the move towards a single currency, essentially involves completion of the task that the Community originally set for itself in the 1950s. We can anticipate that in the future there will be an increasing role for the Community as the originator of policies.

This in turn implies that the policy response to new pressures and challenges must be sought at Community as well as national level. We are concerned principally with longer-term developments rather than transitory crises, and specifically with the evolving agenda for sustainable development, which has potentially far-reaching implications for economic policies. Sustainable development has become a major preoccupation in international relations—as was exemplified by the 1992 World Conference on Environment and Development—and it has an increasingly significant influence on policies in a wide range of areas. In addition to the Community's environmental policy, we identify transport and agriculture as key policy areas in this context, and show how new concerns have led beyond the original emphasis on economic integration.

We are of course very conscious that, even by the time of publication, a work such as this is unavoidably somewhat out of date. At the time of writing, in early 1995, the European Union is in the process of adjustment to the Maastricht Treaty and to the addition of three new member states; the 1996 intergovernmental conference is in prospect, but the course of the negotiations, and their outcome, is very much a matter of speculation. Nevertheless, we do not foresee any *fundamental* changes in the economic policy framework established by the European Community. As we stress throughout the book, the single market is the core of the economic integration process, and—notwithstanding the various 'opt-outs' in the Maastricht Treaty—there are limits to 'à la carte' participation in the single market. There may be more radical changes in arrangements for political and defence co-operation (at present covered by the 'intergovernmental' pillars of the Maastricht Treaty), but these are outside the scope of the present book; we would only say that in our judgement politics in the long run usually follows economic interests.

Finally, a note on terminology. We have sought to minimize the Eurojargon, but where its use is unavoidable we explain its meaning in intelligible terms. We distinguish between

European 'Union' and 'Community', notwithstanding a tendency for the former to subsume the latter in popular usage. When discussing the institutions of economic integration, we have used the expression 'European Community'. This is not to be pedantic: it is, rather, to take proper account of a fundamental distinction, which figured prominently in the Maastricht negotiations, between a supranational institutional structure and a system of intergovernmental co-operation.

Terminology and source material used in this book

The term 'European Community' is used with reference to the legal entity established by the 1951 Paris Treaty and the 1957 Rome Treaties, and to the institutional structures, legislation, and policies based on these Treaties, as subsequently amended.

In general the term 'European Union' is used with reference to the 1992 (Maastricht) Treaty on European Union, or as a geographical expression with reference to the Member States and their territory.

References to the European Union and European Community denote the membership (numbering 15 states) from 1 January 1995, unless otherwise specified or unless a reference is made to the EC at a specific date; in the latter case the membership is normally as it was at that date.

The Treaty establishing the European Community (as it is now known) is referred to as the 'EC Treaty', unless the reference predates the 1992 EU Treaty, in which case the Treaty is referred to as the 'EEC Treaty'. References to Treaty Articles are cited as [Article number] EU, EC, ECSC, or Euratom.

The Commission established under the Treaties (which is also called the 'High Authority' in the ECSC Treaty) is referred to throughout as the 'European Commission', the name that was adopted following the 1992 Maastricht Treaty on European Union.

Amendments to the Treaties by the 1986 Single European Act and the 1992 Treaty on European Union are dated from the completion of the ratification process (1987 and 1993 respectively).

Unless stated otherwise, the legislation cited in the text was enacted exclusively under the EC Treaty (or its predecessor, the EEC Treaty), and was adopted solely by the Council. Explicit references are given for legislation under the ECSC and Euratom Treaties (including measures enacted in conjunction with the EC (EEC) Treaty), and for legislation adopted by the Commission or jointly by the Council and Parliament.

Sources are listed at the end of each chapter for references cited in the text. The listing is in the following order: general works, Community legislation (Regulations, Directives, Decisions), European Commission documents, Court judgments, legal actions. Where necessary, the listing is subdivided according to these categories.

The authoritative publication for Community legislation is the *Official Journal of the European Communities* 'L' series; the *Official Journal* 'C' series contains legislative Proposals and other material relating to Community legislation and policies. Legislation is cited by the type of act (Regulation, Directive, etc.) and the reference number, and the published sources are given as follows: *Official Journal* [year] [L or C][issue number]/[page number].

The Commission publishes a large amount of material—legislative Proposals and background material, Communications, Reports and White and Green Papers—in the COM document series. References in the text are cited as COM[(year)][number], and the title and date are given in the list of references at the end of each chapter.

Judgments of the European Court of Justice are cited according to the official case reports in the European Court Reports (ECR) series. References in the text are cited as Case (or Opinion) [number]/[year], and any page references relate to the ECR report. The list of references at the end of each chapter cites the case report as follows: [[date]] ECR [page number]. Legal actions pending before the Court are referred to by case number, and listed with the entry in the *Official Journal*.

Monetary amounts are generally expressed in ECUs, the precursor of the European Community currency. At the time of writing (in Summer 1995), exchange rates made the ECU worth approximately 0.82 pounds sterling, 1.87 German marks, and 1.26 US dollars.

Robert Barrass and Shobhana Madhavan

ACKNOWLEDGEMENTS

We would like to thank a number of people who have helped us in writing this book. Frances Stevens, while being a very close friend, has also been our mentor and critic: we are immensely grateful for her interest and encouragement in all our intellectual endeavours over many years. Brian O'Connell helped us to put European economic issues in perspective, and his general comments proved invaluable. We would like to thank Richard Whitman for his critical reading of the entire manuscript and for his comments which have greatly improved the book. Michael Browne helped us to reinforce our understanding of certain aspects of European Community transport policy, and Rolf Sprenger has done likewise for environmental policy.

For advising us on the finer aspects of word processing we would like to thank Johanne Bignell. We also wish to thank Nic Zafiris and Len Shackleton for their support and encouragement.

Thanks are also due to library staff of the University of Westminster, the European Commission, the European Parliament and the Westminster European Depository Library.

INTRODUCTION
SETTING THE SCENE

In the public consciousness, the European Union is generally acknowledged to be important, but it is also seen as remote and often obscure. For most citizens of its member states, political issues centre on the national or regional level: so, for instance, elections to the European Parliament can resemble a series of national elections, with the outcome strongly influenced by the performance and popularity of governments in member states.

The prospect of closer European integration has often attracted suspicion. The Maastricht Treaty on European Union, concluded in 1992, underwent a frequently tortuous process of ratification in the member states. The Treaty was initially rejected by referendum in Denmark, amid allegations that it would involve an unacceptable compromise to national sovereignty, thus (for example) prejudicing the ability of member states to maintain high environmental standards above the European 'norm'. In France the Treaty was only narrowly supported by a referendum in which many of the issues were not relevant to the content of the new Treaty—one prominent example was the future of agricultural subsidies, which would be determined under existing Treaty arrangements, irrespective of the fate of the Maastricht Treaty.

Amidst such confusion, there is a need for clarification, which is the main purpose of this book. First of all, what is the European Union? The answer is a hybrid organization, part of which is designed to facilitate political co-operation between governments of the 15 member states, while the other part—the European Community—itself has some of the attributes of a nation state. (Technically, it is characterized as a supranational institution.) The relationship between the Union and the Community, and the structure of the Treaties that established them, are explained in Chapter 1.

The subject of this book is the European Community, rather than—and as distinct from—the European Union. The European Community is the economic component of the Union: its main purpose is to realize the benefits of European economic integration. The integration process has led the Community to assume policy responsibilities which cannot be satisfactorily discharged by the member states.

The Community was established to integrate the economies of its member states within a single market system. It has a legal identity which is distinct from that of its member states, and enacts legislation which overrides any conflicting provisions in national laws; in this vital respect, the Community is unlike other international organizations (including the other components of the European Union).

The Community began as a response to economic and political pressures in the aftermath of the Second World War. European countries had suffered severe economic damage, and were facing the beginning of the East–West division which was to last for four decades. There was also a consciousness of the lessons of the 1930s, when nationalistic economic policies had led to the Great Depression which preceded the outbreak of war. The founders of the Community sought to promote economic reconstruction through co-operation, and to this end they were prepared to share their national sovereignty within a supranational Community.

The years since the Community's foundation have seen both a 'deepening' and a 'widening' of the integration process. The former was highlighted by Treaty amendments in 1986 which sought, successfully, to accelerate progress towards a single market, and by the 1992 Maastricht Treaty on European Union, which established the framework for a common Community currency. The 'widening' of the Community has led to an extension of its policy responsibilities, and to the enlargement of its membership. There is now a major challenge to prepare the way for membership of countries in central and eastern Europe. The governments of member states are due to meet in 1996 to consider possible further amendments to the EU Treaty; monetary unification and enlargement of the Community are likely to figure as key issues in these discussions.

The fundamental economic purpose of the Community is to gain from freedom of movement of goods, services and factors of production. To this end it was necessary to eliminate barriers between member states which prevented goods being obtained from the lowest-cost sources, and which did not allow labour and capital to go where they could be employed most productively. Removal of these barriers yields benefit to the Community's citizens, provided that economic integration in the Community generates trade, rather than merely diverting it from non-Community countries. The factors that motivate economic integration, in general and in the particular circumstances of the Community, are explored in Chapter 1.

The Community is a political as well as an economic entity. As such it is not easy to categorize: there are some of the attributes of a federal system, such as the United States, but at the same time it still has many of the features of a conventional international organization. The Council, comprising representatives of member states, remains the most powerful body— although the *individual* power of national governments has diminished with the evolution of the Community, member states *collectively* remain dominant. The Commission (the main executive body) makes proposals for legislation, and the Parliament may suggest amendments and—in some instances—must give its assent. However, important decisions ultimately require the assent, often by unanimous agreement, of the member states in the Council. The interplay between the institutions, and the formulation and implementation of Community law, are discussed in Chapter 2.

In the process of economic integration, the Community has developed a legal framework for a single market linking the economies of member states. This has entailed the removal of barriers to movement between member states for goods, services, labour and capital, which has necessitated legislation to harmonize national regulations and product standards. Adjustment to the single market, and the realization of its benefits, will require both economic restructuring and the development of infrastructure: the Community has adopted measures to assist this process, concentrating on the less prosperous regions. Policies for the single market are discussed in Chapter 3.

The proper functioning of the single market also requires that markets operate in a competitive manner. The Community competition rules are designed to prevent anti-competitive practices and abuse of a dominant position in the market; there are also provisions to regulate (and if necessary prohibit) mergers that inhibit competition. The Commission has powers to control subsidy payments by national governments, and to ensure that payments to state-owned industries are not disguised subsidies. Community competition rules and their implementation are discussed in Chapter 4.

The Community has long-standing arrangements for the co-ordination of economic and monetary policies of member states. A framework has been established to take the process further to economic and monetary union with a single currency. A single market with multiple currencies is something of a paradox, and exchange of currencies—and risks of exchange rate movement—are an impediment to trade. Nevertheless, the single currency raises important issues, concerning national sovereignty, economic adjustment and the future course of economic policy. These issues are addressed in Chapter 5.

Economic integration has led the Community into new policy areas. National policy measures have in many instances become inappropriate or inoperable, and Community intervention is often needed to protect the integrity of the single market. In the area of social policy, a concern for an economic 'level playing field' has come into conflict with the UK's opposition to further measures on the grounds that employment will be damaged: the result is the UK's 'opt out' from much of the Community's developing social legislation. Chapter 6 examines the implications of this, and also Community intervention, linked to the single market, in various fields including industrial policy, culture, public health, education and training, and consumer policy.

In parallel with the Community's movement towards economic integration, other changes were occurring which would lead to significant reorientation of its policies. A growing perception of environmental crisis led to the inauguration of a Community environmental action programme in 1974. Concerns to safeguard the quality of life, in a broad sense, were reflected in a new emphasis on sustainable development, both in the framework for Community policy and in measures brought forward by the Commission. The evolution of Community policy in the direction of sustainable development is examined in Chapter 7.

To promote sustainable development, all Community policies are required to take account of the environmental dimension. Transport is one of the key sectors in this context, since it is an important source of various environmental impacts, from local to global in scale. Accordingly, policies for sustainable development must give a high priority to action to modify these impacts. Transport also has great importance for the single market, both as a major sector of the economy and also with reference to the communications infrastructure that is needed to make economic integration a reality. The various transport issues arising from the single market and from the new concerns for 'sustainable mobility' are discussed in Chapter 8.

In many respects, the most 'high profile' policy area has been, and continues to be, agriculture. There is a long history of intervention in agricultural markets, predating the Community's Common Agricultural Policy which superseded and integrated various national policy mechanisms. The Community's original objective was to secure its food supplies, and to facilitate orderly structural change in the agricultural sector. The first of these has been largely achieved, but at great cost, both to the Community budget, and in terms of environmental degradation. There is now a need to reorientate agricultural policies towards sustainable development, and to recognize that agricultural support is not generally the most cost-effective way to secure the viability of rural communities. These issues are considered further in Chapter 9.

As a result of the integration process, the Community has become a major economic entity in its own right, while at the same time the world economy has undergone profound changes. Economic activity has become increasingly globalized, with massive increases in international trade and capital movements, which will be further stimulated by the conclusion of the GATT Uruguay Round negotiations, in which the Community took a leading part. In 1989 a dramatic transformation began in eastern Europe with the collapse of the Communist regimes, followed in 1991 by the break-up of the Soviet Union. Policies to secure sustainable development have become a major factor in international relations, highlighted by the 1992 World Conference on Environment and Development. The Community's response to these developments, and its role in international economic policy, are discussed in Chapter 10.

PART
ONE

ORIGINS, FUNCTIONS AND INSTITUTIONS

The European Community is unique: it has a legal identity distinct from those of its member states, and it has the power to enact legislation that overrides national laws. The Community has an executive body independent of national governments, and a legislature directly elected by the citizens of the member states.

The foundation of the Community is a set of treaties between sovereign states. These states evolved from the process of nation building which—in various forms—preoccupied Europe for several centuries. Many were formed with the conscious purpose of national unification—Germany and Italy in the nineteenth century, and before them France and the United Kingdom; others achieved independence from imperial powers—Finland, Greece, Ireland and the Netherlands.

So—paradoxically—the consolidation of nation states was closely followed by the development of a supranational structure that circumscribed national sovereignty. The foundation of the European Community constituted a recognition that the model of the sovereign state inherited from the nineteenth century was of limited value in the mid-twentieth century.

Sovereignty may imply freedom for a nation; but in international relations the unconstrained exercise of sovereignty can lead to anarchy, and preclude mutually beneficial co-operation between countries. This was vividly demonstrated in the great depression of the 1930s, when countries raised tariffs to protect their industries, and in the process accelerated the collapse of world trade. There followed the even greater disaster of the Second World War. The imperatives of postwar recovery, in a divided Europe, gave a powerful stimulus for international co-operation. This period saw the establishment of many international bodies, including the United Nations, the International Monetary Fund and the Organisation for Economic Cooperation and Development.

Against this background, the European Community came into existence. Whatever its subsequent difficulties and shortcomings, the Community has clearly been a success as a focus for economic integration in Europe: its membership has grown from the original 6 to 15 states, with many non-member countries aspiring to join.

THE EUROPEAN COMMUNITY AND ITS ECONOMIC CONTEXT

The origins of the European Community (and, by extension, of the European Union) lie in a Treaty concluded in 1951 between six countries. This Treaty established an institutional framework for economic co-operation and for the development of common policies. There was at that time an imperative need to restore economies ravaged by war, and to ensure that postwar reconstruction was not hampered by rivalries between European countries. A beginning was made in 1951 with the (then) key industrial sectors, coal and steel; the scope of the Community was subsequently broadened to provide the basis for the evolution of a single market, in which goods, services, capital and labour could circulate across national frontiers.

The Community has benefited its members: this is shown not only by economic calculations of growth in trade, but also by the eagerness of countries to join when political constraints on their membership have been removed. Interest in the Community has been stimulated by a growing awareness of the limitations of policy-making at national level, and by the realization that individual European countries cannot aspire to the importance that some of them enjoyed on the world stage a hundred years ago. On the other hand collectively, through the Community, the countries can be very influential, as the world economy becomes increasingly globalized, with massive growth in international trade and investment. The Community has a vital role, as the world's largest economic entity, in influencing the international response to these developments.

The process of integration within a single market has had the effect of 'deepening' the Community, and shifting responsibilities for policy-making from national to Community level. This phenomenon has been manifested in successive Treaty revisions, which came into effect in 1987 and 1993, to extend the scope of economic policy-making and (with the Treaty on European Union) to formalize political co-operation.

1.1 THE EUROPEAN UNION AND THE EUROPEAN COMMUNITY

The European Union (EU) is a unique entity, comprising for some purposes a group of nation states, but also including a supranational organization with the power to make (and enforce) its own body of law. The EU is founded on a set of treaties between its 15 member states, providing a framework for co-operation between national governments and also establishing an economic organization with a legal identity in its own right. This combination of international co-operation and supranational law-making is distinctive, and thus difficult to categorize in terms of formal models of international relations.

1.1.1   The Treaty foundations

The Union was formed by the Treaty on European Union (the EU Treaty), signed at Maastricht in the Netherlands in February 1992; following ratification by the participating countries, this Treaty eventually came into effect in 1993.

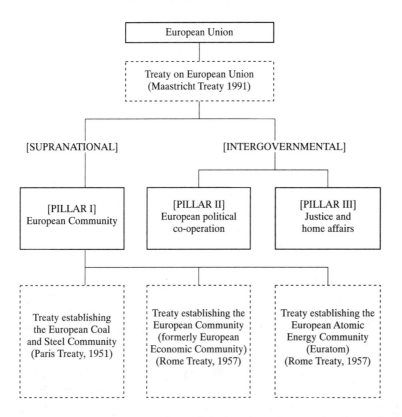

Figure 1.1   The European Union and the European Community: Treaty foundations

The EU Treaty (see Fig. 1.1) has three substantive elements, or 'pillars'. Two of these 'pillars' provide for political co-operation between governments, on foreign and security policies, and on justice and home affairs. This is essentially a mechanism for co-ordination of policies that are formulated and implemented by national governments. Any legislation required to implement agreed policies (for example laws to combat illegal immigration or international fraud) is enacted by national legislatures (or in some circumstances by the European Community); treaties and agreements with countries outside the Union are concluded by national governments; and any disputes over the application of legislation are normally resolved by national courts without reference to the Union. In short, for political purposes the Union is no more than its member states: it has no separate legal identity.

The European Community, the other 'pillar' of the EU, is very different. Its objectives are defined in economic rather than political terms, and it has a 'legal identity' (Article 210 EC) and a supranational structure, with the capacity to enact and implement laws. This element of the Union predates the EU Treaty by many years.

The European Community was established by a set of treaties in 1951 and 1957 (see Fig. 1.1).

All three treaties were concluded between the same six countries: France, Germany, Italy, and the Benelux countries (Belgium, Luxembourg and the Netherlands). Membership increased from 6 to 15 by 1995, as additional member states became parties to the three treaties (see Table 1.1).

Table 1.1   Membership of the European Community

Founder members	Subsequent members (year of accession)	
Belgium	Denmark (1973)	Austria (1995)
France	Ireland (1973)	Finland (1995)
Germany	United Kingdom (1973)	Sweden (1995)
Italy	Greece (1981)	
Luxembourg	Portugal (1986)	
Netherlands	Spain (1986)	

The European Community is more than a body for co-ordinating national policies: it has an existence in law which is distinct from the legal systems of its member states, and as such has some of the features that normally characterize a nation state.

Among these is a Court of Justice, which is the final arbiter of European Community law, and which can overrule provisions of national law where these conflict with Community law. The Court has defined the unique character of the European Community as follows:

The Community Treaties established a new legal order for the benefit of which the states have limited their sovereign rights, in ever wider fields, and the subjects of which comprise not only the Member States but also their nationals. The essential characteristics of the Community legal order which has thus been established are its primacy over the laws of member states and the direct effect of a whole series of provisions which are applicable to their nationals and to the member states themselves.

(Opinion 1/91, p. 6102)

This is contrasted with a conventional international organization based on intergovernmental agreement, which 'merely creates rights and obligations between the contracting parties and provides for no transfer of sovereign rights to the intergovernmental institutions which it sets up'.

The three 'pillars' of the European Union share a common institutional structure, with the Council of Ministers representing the member states, the Commission (designated by the EC Treaty as an executive body and the proposer of legislation), and a directly elected Parliament. However, between the intergovernmental provisions and the EC Treaty, the roles of these institutions differ significantly. When acting on foreign policy or justice and home affairs, the Council is pre-eminent; the Commission is 'fully associated' with its activities, while the role of the Parliament is limited to asking questions, making recommendations and being informed (on foreign policy) or consulted (on justice and home affairs). The Court of Justice may have jurisdiction only where the Council so decides. Under the EC Treaty (and the ECSC and Euratom Treaties), the Commission has a vital responsibility as 'guardian' of the Treaties, the Parliament has a major role in the legislative process, and the Court of Justice ensures that the law is observed. (The functions of these institutions under the EC Treaty are discussed further in Chapter 2).

1.1.2   Intergovernmental conferences and negotiation of the Treaties

All three pillars of the European Union have been established by Treaties negotiated between the member states at intergovernmental conferences (IGCs); major revisions of the Treaties are also preceded by an IGC. Like all international agreements between sovereign powers, the conclusion and revision of these Treaties requires the unanimous accord of the contracting parties.

The procedure for convening an IGC is formalized in the EU Treaty (Article N). Proposed treaty amendments may be submitted to the Council by member states or the Commission; the Council then decides (in consultation with the European Parliament) whether to summon an IGC.

Up to 1995 there have been five IGCs. The first two of these led to establishment of the Community by the Paris and Rome Treaties in 1951 and 1957 respectively; the third revised the Treaties by the 1986 Single European Act; while the two subsequent IGCs, on political and monetary union, led to the 1992 Treaty on European Union. Preparations are now in hand for a further IGC to review the EU Treaty, as provided for in Article N of that Treaty.

1.1.3   Models of international organization

Political scientists (for example Pentland 1973) have developed a number of models of institutional co-operation and development, driven either by political, or technological and economic, change. Developments may, depending on the model, lead to increased co-operation between sovereign states, or to a shift of power to supranational institutions. In terms of organizational structures, a contrast can be drawn between *ad hoc* co-operation between nation states for specific defined purposes (a *pluralist* or *functionalist* model), and a system with supranational institutions which have their objectives defined in general terms, and which are empowered to take action as required by specific circumstances (a *federalist* or *neo-functionalist* model). The various models may be represented in a simplified form as shown in Table 1.2. Political and technological/economic motivations are not mutually exclusive, and the distinction between them in the table is essentially a matter of emphasis. The 'political' model is concerned primarily with the constitutional relationships between institutions. In contrast, the 'economic/ technological' model focuses on the functions that institutions perform, and on the effects of changing functional requirements. In practice, both types of motivation are important influences on the development and functioning of institutions for co-operation across national frontiers.

Table 1.2   Models of international organization

Motivation	Type of organization	
	Nation states	Superstate
Political	*Pluralism*: a Community of sovereign states	*Federalism*: a federation of states
Technological and economic	*Functionalism*: a transnational network of organizations performing specific tasks	*Neo-functionalism*: a supranational state

Elements of all of these models can be found in the EU Treaty. The intergovernmental provisions for political co-operation are principally a manifestation of pluralism; and in so far as activities are co-ordinated between countries (for example, exchange of information between law enforcement agencies), there are elements of functionalism.

In the case of the European Community matters are less clear cut. The Community can be seen from a pluralist/functionalist perspective, essentially as a group of nation states, or, in a federalist/neo-functionalist analysis, as a developing 'super state'.

In the model of the Community as a group of nation states, *pluralism* involves co-operation which does not in any way compromise national sovereignty, so that the Community is nothing more than a series of treaties between member states. From the *functionalist* perspective, international co-operation is a pragmatic and piecemeal response to technological imperatives, and to increasing globalization of economic and environmental problems.

In these terms, membership of the Community would merely denote agreement to take common action in certain defined areas; while these areas may be more extensive than for other international organizations, the difference is seen as only a matter of degree. From this viewpoint, there is no fundamental difference between the Community and other organizations based on international treaties, such as NATO or the United Nations—or indeed the other 'pillars' of the European Union.

The 'super-state' model represents an opposite extreme. *Federalism* would depict the Community as a framework for a 'United States of Europe', on the lines of the United States of America, with a separate tier of government above those of member states. From the *neo-functionalist* perspective, the interaction of economic interests is a driving force which shifts loyalties to new centres, and which is liable to render the nation state obsolete. The Community in this scenario is an entity distinct from the sum of its member states. Its legitimacy derives from the people of the Community, as opposed to their governments, and power is shared with, rather than devolved from, national governments.

These models are of course idealized representations, constructed for analytical purposes. They also express, or at least imply, philosophical positions concerning sources of power and political legitimacy. Neither model fully represents the complex reality of the European Community, although elements of both can be seen in the functioning of the Community.

1.2   THE BEGINNINGS OF THE EUROPEAN COMMUNITY

The origins of the European Community can be properly understood only with reference to the economic and political context of Europe in the late 1940s, in the aftermath of the Second World War. The European nations were in a state of chronic economic weakness, exhausted by war; Germany was divided into military occupation zones administered by the 'four powers', the United States, France, the United Kingdom and the Soviet Union; and Europe was the focal point as the 'cold war' between rival power blocks began. Moreover, there were strong memories of the depression of the 1930s, when countries raised tariffs to protect their industries from import competition, seeking to insulate their economies from recession. The result of these so-called 'beggar my neighbour' policies was a collapse in world trade, and a general reduction of prosperity.

Against this background, increased co-operation between the countries of western Europe appeared to offer considerable economic and political benefits, which would outweigh any disadvantages associated with a loss of national sovereignty. Accordingly, the six founder members of the European Community (see Table 1.1) set about negotiations to establish institutional structures for economic co-operation, which led to the Treaties that founded the

Coal and Steel Community in 1951, and the Economic Community and Euratom in 1957. The principal objective at that time was the establishment of a common market; and this called for a degree of co-ordination of policy-making on the part of the Community's member states.

1.2.1 Economic and political conditions in postwar Europe

The European Community was to some extent the product of its times. With an urgent need for reconstruction and a return to prosperity, countries could ill afford to stand on national sovereignty if closer co-operation offered a path to accelerated economic recovery. Indeed, as a matter of historical speculation, it is conceivable that in less extreme circumstances the European Community might never have come into existence, or might have taken a very different form.

In any event, economic and political conditions in the aftermath of the Second World War were in many respects very different from those that prevail in Europe today. Former combatants faced the task of postwar recovery and the start of the 'cold war' in a divided Europe and a divided Germany. Although the founders of the European Community were not lacking in idealism, they also saw its creation as a pragmatic response to these circumstances.

So the development of the Community can be properly understood only with reference to the changing historical context. The Community is—even now—primarily an economic organiza-tion, with a limited political role and no overt military function. Moreover, it is clear that powerful economic forces have provided the impetus for continuing development and expansion of the Community. Nevertheless, realization of the economic gains from closer integration has depended upon the strength of political motivation: political conditions have often favoured economic co-operation, although in some instances political constraints may have run counter to the overall economic interest of the Community. For example, in 1966 national—as distinct from Community—interests were reasserted when the planned extension of decision-making by majority vote was effectively blocked, in the so-called 'Luxembourg compromise' (see Sec. 2.3.1).

Two main political issues had an immediate bearing on the economic integration of western Europe:

1. the so-called 'German question'—the political and economic role of a divided Germany in postwar Europe;
2. the position of western Europe *vis-à-vis* the two 'superpower' blocs.

There was a general anxiety to avoid a repetition of the two world wars, in which Europe had been the main battlefield, and the principal sufferer. At the same time, the postwar division of Germany was recognized as a potential source of political instability—this was vividly demonstrated by the Soviet blockade of Berlin in 1949. It was feared that a weak and disunited western Europe would be ill equipped to resist any threat from the East—and, clearly, the West would be much stronger if West Germany were to be included as a full partner. Accordingly, the Federal Republic of Germany was formed in 1949 out of the British, French and US military occupation zones. (The Soviet zone later became the German Democratic Republic, which was eventually absorbed in the Federal Republic in 1990.)

At the end of the war, European countries—some of which had been among the prewar great powers—found themselves in a state of military, political and economic weakness. The vacuum created by this catastrophic decline was filled by two 'superpowers', the United States and the Soviet Union. While Europe remained the scene of great power confrontation, fuelled by the clash of rival ideologies, the leading roles were taken by non-European countries. The

Europeans were forced into a subordinate, dependent role. Many of the countries of western Europe depended on aid from the United States—under the Marshall Plan—to reconstruct their economies; while eastern Europe was dominated, politically and economically, by the Soviet Union.

Economic considerations reinforced the political impetus for European co-operation. The period between the world wars had seen increases in protectionist policies, which had led to a dramatic decline in world trade; this is illustrated by a study of five European countries (Denmark, Italy, Norway, Sweden and the United Kingdom) showing that the ratio of trade (imports + exports) to gross national product declined from 43.7 per cent in 1905–14 to 35.7 per cent in 1925–34 (Grassman 1980).

Protectionist tendencies had became particularly acute during the great depression of the early 1930s. Countries sought individually to mitigate the impact of the depression by raising barriers to trade adopting policies that have been described as 'beggar my neighbour'. A notable example was the 1930 increase in US tariffs following the Smoot–Hawley Act; at around the same time there were tariff increases in European countries, including France, Italy, Spain and Switzerland (Kindleberger 1987: 123–4). In a subsequent round, in the period October 1931–March 1932, tariffs and other trade barriers were raised by the United Kingdom, Denmark, Sweden, the Netherlands, France, Belgium and Luxembourg. Between 1929 and 1932, world trade contracted by some 60 per cent (Kindleberger 1987: 169–70).

The dollar shortage   Before the Second World War, the countries of western Europe had been able to finance their imports from the rest of the world without undue difficulty. Although there was usually a deficit in trade with the United States, this was offset by 'invisible' earnings (from sources such as shipping, banking, insurance and tourism), investment income, and exports from other countries which were importers of European manufactures.

The Second World War resulted in a severe cost to Europe's economy, with loss of productive capacity and damage to infrastructure. The productivity of labour was undermined by exhaustion and under-nutrition, and mass movements of population led to economic disruption. These problems persisted after the war, and were compounded by natural adversity—an exceptionally cold winter in 1946–47, and a drought the following summer.

Economic recovery required substantial investments, but the European countries lacked the means to finance expenditure on the scale required. Consequently the *dollar shortage* became a central concern of economic policy in western Europe. To pay for the war there had been a substantial liquidation of foreign investments, which reduced investment income far below its prewar level; postwar disruption also reduced Europe's 'invisible' earnings, while political tensions threatened exports from colonial territories.

In contrast to Europe, the United States emerged from the war economically strong (although politically it was to be challenged by the Soviet Union). In the late 1940s the USA was producing nearly one-half of the world's manufactured goods (Foreman-Peck 1983: 270), and was by a very large margin the dominant power in the world economy. To speed its reconstruction, Europe needed imports from the USA—but at the same time, it lacked the means to pay for these imports. As *The Economist* of 31 May 1947 observed, 'The whole of European life is being overshadowed by the great dollar shortage. The margin between recovery and collapse throughout western Europe is dependent at this moment upon massive imports from the United States' (quoted in van der Breugel 1966: 56).

Marshall aid   The problem of the dollar shortage was eased by US aid to Europe, which began on an *ad hoc* basis and was subsequently institutionalized under the European

Recovery Programme (the *Marshall Plan*), which ran from 1948 to 1952. An important feature of the Plan was its requirement that the participating European countries should themselves decide on priorities and mechanisms for the allocation of assistance. This was done through a newly constituted international body, the Organisation for European Economic Co-operation (OEEC), founded in April 1948 (the forerunner of the Organisation for Economic Co-operation and Development—OECD). The OEEC assessed national programmes for production and exports in order to decide the allocation of aid under the Marshall Plan. The total amount of Marshall aid provided between 1948 and 1952 was approximately $12 bn: most of this was spent on raw materials and semi-manufactured products ($3.4 bn), and on food, animal feed and fertilizers ($3.2 bn); other significant items were machinery, equipment and vehicles ($1.8 bn) and fuel imports (($1.6 bn) (Hogan 1987: 414–15).

1.2.2   The impetus for European co-operation

While postwar European co-operation was stimulated in part by a desire to avoid the mistakes of the past, there was also a strong positive motivation to build for the future, based on a realization that co-operation represented the key to peace and prosperity. In this spirit many international organizations were founded—including the United Nations, the World Bank, the International Monetary Fund and the OECD.

In western Europe it became apparent that the freedom of action for individual nation states was very constrained. European countries were in no position to afford a repetition of prewar economic policies, and it became apparent that the small scale of national economies (in comparison with that of the United States) constituted a potential impediment to postwar reconstruction. If individual states, pursuing their own economic policies, sought to maintain their economies as separate entities, they would be obliged to maintain barriers to trade with other European countries. The result, on a European scale, would be fragmentation of economic activity. Scarce resources could be mobilized more effectively if these barriers were lowered—but this in turn would require initiatives to secure co-ordination in economic policies.

The economic and political impetus for European co-operation led to two specific initiatives, originating with French proposals for:

- a European Defence Community (EDC);
- a European Coal and Steel Community (ECSC).

The EDC was an ambitious proposal for an integrated military structure; it failed, largely because it would have required a degree of political integration that was not feasible—and which was not envisaged in the proposal (Willis 1965: 158). This episode demonstrates that a potential benefit from closer integration is not in itself sufficient: there must also be a political will to realize the benefit (see Box 1.1).

1.2.3   The European Coal and Steel Community Treaty

The 1951 Treaty establishing the European Coal and Steel Community was the first institutional step towards the development of a common market in western Europe; it predates by six years the establishment of the European Economic Community. Coal and steel were seen as basic industries, and as key sectors of the economy which had been of considerable strategic significance during the Second World War. Thus it was an economic and political priority to

> **BOX 1.1**
>
> **The European Defence Community: why it was proposed, and why the proposal did not succeed**
>
> A proposal for a European Defence Community (EDC) was advanced in October 1949 by the French Prime Minister René Pleven. In the aftermath of the Second World War a high priority was given to avoidance of the mistakes of the past. There was some support in the Council of Europe for the Extension of European integration to defence. Just as the ECSC sought to develop a mutual economic interdependence, the EDC was designed to bring about military integration. This would remove the capacity for armed conflict between the countries of western Europe, so that there could be no repetition of the Second World War.
>
> Co-operation in the defence of western Europe was given urgency by the tension between the USA and its allies and the Soviet bloc, which led to the 'cold war'. The USA was concerned that its European partners should assume a larger share of the defence burden, and to this end strongly advocated the rearmament of Germany. However, this was liable to disturb sensitivities in countries that had recently suffered invasion by German forces. The EDC was seen as an alternative to the creation of a separate German army, whereby German soldiers could nevertheless be enlisted in the defence of western Europe.
>
> The German response to the EDC proposal was on the whole positive, since it was seen as a means of recovering elements of sovereignty which were still restricted by the postwar allied occupation. However, the French Parliament failed to ratify the EDC agreement: the benefit of neutralizing German military power was outweighed by the prospect of compromising France's Great Power status through the loss of the French army.
>
> The EDC proposal ultimately failed because political circumstances were not sufficiently favourable. This provides a vivid demonstration of the dependence of European integration on the existence of strong imperatives and political will.
>
> Military co-operation did proceed, but between separate national armed forces, primarily within the framework of the North Atlantic Treaty Organisation (NATO), which had a much wider membership than the proposed EDC. Defence issues were also discussed in the Western European Union (comprising the six European Community founder members and the United Kingdom, later joined by Spain and Portugal). Some forty years after the EDC proposal, the concept of integrated military forces was revived, with the establishment of small-scale joint Franco-German army and navy units. This piecemeal 'bottom-up' approach is much less ambitious than the EDC proposal: it remains to be seen whether more extensive integration will eventually follow.

speed the integration process, in order to strengthen the economy, and to secure the future peace, of western Europe.

Postwar economic recovery began with national coal and steel industries heavily protected by barriers to trade. However, European countries could now ill afford the costs of self-sufficiency. Moreover, there was a fear that as production increased the steel industry would become dominated by national cartels—as it had been in the 1920s and 1930s.

The first postwar international institution for the coal and steel industries was concerned specifically with the reconstruction and redevelopment of the industries in Germany, which was then under four-power military occupation. The International Authority for the Ruhr (IAR) was created at the London Conference in 1948, and inaugurated the following year. The IAR had the following responsibilities with respect to industry in the Ruhr (Willis 1965: 20):

- control of coal, coke and steel production

- division between German consumption and exports
- prevention of discriminatory market practices.

The ECSC was eventually established by the 1951 Paris Treaty for a period of 50 years (so the ECSC will cease to exist in 2002). The Treaty provided for a common market in coal and steel, with free trade between member states, unobstructed by tariff barriers or other forms of discrimination. The immediate objective was to promote rationalization of the coal and steel industries, with increased competition between the industries in member states; this would in turn lead to modernization of production, development of export markets and improved living standards. In the longer term, its founders saw the ECSC as the forerunner of the European Community, and a first step towards a united Europe with a large internal market.

The ECSC introduced the institutional structure which (with certain modifications) continues in the present-day European Community (see Chapter 2). The executive body, the High Authority (the precursor of the European Commission), was given responsibility for ensuring that the objectives of the Treaty were attained; its members were appointed by national governments, through their representatives in the Council of Ministers. The ECSC Treaty (unlike the subsequent EEC and Euratom Treaties) also gives the High Authority (Commission) the principal responsibility for enactment of legislation—although all important legislation is subject to the unanimous assent of the Council of Ministers.

At a policy level, the Treaty provisions established a framework both for planning and for liberalization. The High Authority was empowered to use financial instruments (loans financed by production levies) to promote restructuring and investment, to fix maximum and minimum prices and (subject to the assent of the Council of Ministers) to draw up production programmes and to impose production quotas. These 'management' provisions coexisted with measures to facilitate the operation of market forces: the High Authority was empowered to prohibit anti-competitive practices, and to control the provision of subsidies to the coal and steel industries by member states.

Although economic co-operation may offer substantial overall gains, often considerable restructuring is necessary if these gains are to be realized. This means in practice that high-cost, tariff-protected producers are liable to suffer, as they become exposed to competition from lower cost-imports. Hence the process has 'losers' as well as beneficiaries. This was indeed the case with the ECSC. The balance of potential competitive advantage is apparent in the structure of French–German trade in coal and steel prior to the establishment of the ECSC Willis (1965: 93):

- German coal had a cost advantage of approximately 30 per cent (in terms of pithead prices).
- France exported low-quality iron ore, very little of which went to Germany.
- There was a small two-way trade in steel; France enjoyed a slight advantage, which was being eroded as the German industry recovered.

In France the ECSC proposal met with opposition from the producer interests most directly affected:

- The iron and steel industry and marketing associations were strongly opposed, since the ECSC would threaten the industry cartel.
- The chemical and engineering industry associations were also opposed, on similar grounds, fearing that it would be extended to their industries.
- Small and medium-enterprise associations feared that competition would put many small producers out of business.

The French industry federation supported the objectives of the ECSC, but feared that it would be excessively bureaucratic and interventionist. The French planning system was unpopular in some industry circles: while the extension of its approach to a European level might have attractions in constraining foreign competitors, it would also tend to entrench and strengthen the planning system—and this was perceived as undesirable (Willis 1965: 94).

It was feared that a lowering of barriers to foreign competition would find French industry at a disadvantage:

- The ECSC would in the long run weaken France's competitive position in coal and steel; the attractions of cheaper coal imported from Germany would be outweighed by the prospect of German dominance of the steel industry.
- Social legislation was more extensive in France than in other countries, and consequently imposed heavier costs on industry; it was argued that removal of barriers to competition from imports should be dependent on a raising of standards (and hence costs) in other member states.

The early 1950s saw increasing economic co-operation in western Europe, both under the auspices of the ECSC and between enterprises in various economic sectors. There was a growing appreciation of the benefits of cross-border linkages for product development, market entry and exploitation of economies of scale. At the same time, there was a strong current of political support for a united Europe—and, in some quarters, for a 'United States of Europe'.

The failure of the European Defence Community showed the importance of broad political support for the success of supranational institutions. The ECSC was successful because it was concerned with specific economic problems which could be addressed through international action. (For this reason it has been cited in support of *functionalist* theories of international organization) (see Sec. 1.1.3). European governments therefore had to consider what institutional framework might be appropriate for further economic co-operation, leaving the way open for closer political union, but without forcing the pace beyond what was broadly acceptable.

1.2.4   The European Economic Community

An outline for treaties establishing the European Economic Community and the European Atomic Energy Community (Euratom) was set out in a 1955 memorandum by the governments of the Benelux countries, proposing a common market for western Europe, and integration of the electricity industries, nuclear energy and transport (Willis 1965: 242). The foreign minsters of the six founder members of the European Community (listed in Table 2.2) met at Messina in June 1955, and agreed in principle upon the objectives of a united Europe with common institutions, economic integration and harmonization of social policies. Intergovernmental discussions continued in Brussels until October 1955, with the participation of the six, the ECSC High Authority and the United Kingdom. The UK was unwilling to accept the principle of an economic community; it subsequently withdrew from the discussions, and sought to promote the concept of a looser free trade association (Küsters 1987: 95). This was the origin of the European Free Trade Association (EFTA), founded in 1960. Meanwhile, at their meeting in Venice in May 1956, the foreign ministers of the six decided to proceed to the conclusion of the Rome Treaties.

The eventual form of the European Economic Community was a compromise between differing visions, and in particular two conceptions of its role and functioning (Willis 1965: 246):

1. *economic liberalism*, emphasizing competitive markets, and free trade with non member states;
2. *economic management*, with interventionist measures such as support for research and development, and tariff and other external trade barriers to protect 'strategic' economic sectors.

In general terms, the first of these was associated with the Netherlands and Germany, and the second with France. More specifically, the positions of the individual countries were influenced by economic conditions and political concerns.

The *Benelux* countries (Belgium, the Netherlands and Luxembourg), already in a customs union since 1948, had few problems with the common market, and were strongly attracted by the economic advantages of larger markets for their exports.

Italy was also enthusiastic, having enjoyed strong economic growth in the postwar years; but there appears to have been only a limited appreciation of the obligations of membership, such as competition regulations and a common external tariff (van der Groeben 1987: 42).

Germany, for political and economic reasons, favoured an 'outward-looking' Community; there was a particular concern to mitigate the effects of the division of Germany, which led to special provisions, in a protocol to the EEC Treaty, whereby trade between (West) Germany and the (then) German Democratic Republic was treated as 'German internal trade'. (As a result, the GDR was sometimes described as a shadow member of the Community.)

German industry was, on balance, in favour of the Community, although there was anxiety to avoid disruption of trade. Non-Community countries in western Europe accounted for almost one-third of Germany's exports; it was feared that high Community tariffs might divert much of this trade to Community partners. Germany also had substantial trade with the Americas, and again there was a fear of a tariff-induced diversion, to French and Belgian colonial territories, principally those in Africa. The result of this diversion of trade would be a loss of export markets and increased prices of imports. For example, it was feared that exports of machine tools to Brazil would be threatened if Germany reduced its imports of Brazilian coffee (Willis 1965: 268). Similarly, there was concern in the mechanical engineering industry at risks to export markets in the UK, Scandinavia and Austria. In some other industries—such as agriculture, textiles, leather, soap—there was apprehension over the prospect of increased competition from imports from other Community countries, following the removal of tariff protection. The chemical industry was concerned that the Euratom Treaty would restrict access to US technology.

France supported the Euratom Treaty because it gave an impetus to research and development. There was less wholehearted support for the EEC Treaty, mainly owing to fears over industrial competitiveness following a reduction in trade barriers; in particular, there was concern that industry would be handicapped by costs stemming from France's relatively advanced social legislation. There were also economic difficulties associated with France's colonial involvements, with 20 per cent export subsidies and import levies to counter balance payments deficits, and to compensate for overvaluation of the franc, (van der Groeben 1987: 35). One of the main objectives of French policy was to spread the burden of its colonial commitments, which were reflected in levels of military expenditure and in the structure of its trade (over a quarter of which was with its colonial territories).

In the French agricultural sector opportunities were perceived for increasing exports, but there was also support for a policy of minimum prices to protect producers. The steel industry supported the EEC Treaty, because it would remove distortions between prices of steel (which were fixed under the ECSC) and prices of finished products. The car industry also favoured the

EEC, because of the protection that it would afford against non-Community competitors; in contrast, the mechanical engineering industry, with many small firms, was apprehensive at competition from larger producers with lower costs (Willis 1965: 249–66).

1.2.5   The Rome Treaties

The foundations of the European Community were completed with the two Rome Treaties of 1957 establishing the European Economic Community (the EEC), and the European Atomic Energy Community (EAEC—also known as Euratom). Unlike the ECSC [Paris] Treaty, the life of the Rome Treaties has no time limit.

Of the three 'parallel' Treaties (ECSC, EEC (now EC), and Euratom), the Euratom Treaty has proved by far the least significant. Its purpose was 'to contribute to the raising of the standard of living and to the development of relations with other countries by creating the conditions necessary for the speedy establishment and growth of nuclear industries' (Euratom Treaty, Article 1). The reference to 'other countries' was primarily to the United States: Euratom was seen as a device for securing access to American nuclear technology. There were three main reasons for Euratom's lack of success:

1. strong interdependence between civil and military nuclear programmes: France was determined to maintain the independence of its nuclear weapons programme;
2. a desire to retain national control over what appeared, at that time, to be the technologies of the future;
3. a failure of the high hopes for nuclear power as a low cost source of energy.

The Treaty establishing the European Community (previously the European Economic Community) forms the basis for most policies and legislation under the economic 'pillar' of the European Union; unlike the ECSC and Euratom Treaties, the scope of the EC Treaty is not restricted to specific sectors. The comparatively 'open-ended' nature of the EC Treaty may be seen as favouring the development of the Community as a 'supranational' entity, and thus lending support to a *neo-functionalist* perspective (see Sec. 1.1.3).

The original EEC Treaty set out to raise living standards and achieve closer relations between member states; these objectives were to be attained by economic integration to form a common market. Now usually known as the 'single market', this remains central to the role of the Community, and it is to a large extent the basis for the Community's wide-ranging policy responsibilities.

The effect of economic integration on the Community's policy agenda is examined in Sec. 1.5.2 and Sec. 1.5.3; but to appreciate why governments saw advantages in economic integration, with policy-making at a supranational level, it is necessary to examine the rationale for the integration process, and the benefits that the participants may derive.

1.3   THE BENEFITS OF ECONOMIC INTEGRATION

The central concern of the European Community from its inception has been to facilitate the removal of unnecessary barriers between member states: indeed, this is seen as the key to increased prosperity. Article 9 of the EC Treaty states that the Community is 'based upon a customs union'—within which trade is free of tariffs and other artificial barriers. Economic theory predicts that in some circumstances a removal of barriers to trade can have substantial benefits; and the European Community customs union represents a practical attempt to realize these benefits. The theoretical analysis of customs unions is presented below, together with a summary of the evidence of studies designed to measure the impact of removal of tariff barriers. Although for simplicity the analysis is presented solely in terms of tariffs, it should be recognized that there are many types of 'non-tariff' barrier, which are often less obvious, and hence more difficult to counter. Examples of these barriers include quotas, differences in tax structures, variations in product specifications, public procurement restrictions, and differing regulatory requirements. Genuinely free trade requires the elimination of all types of barrier—tariff and non-tariff alike.

1.3.1 The gains from free trade and the reasons for trade barriers

In principle all countries would benefit from the complete elimination of artificial barriers to international trade; each country would be enabled to achieve the greatest possible benefit from the resources available to it. However, in practice trade barriers are widespread, and indeed are maintained, for a variety of reasons, as a deliberate policy measure.

The gains from free trade   The benefits of free trade can be illustrated by a simple example. The United Kingdom, despite its climate, *could* be self sufficient in grapes—but at a heavy cost, in terms of higher prices and lower consumption; alternatively, grapes could be imported from countries with warmer climates, where they can be grown more cheaply. To pay for these imports, the UK must sell products (and services) which—in comparison with other countries—it is better able to supply.

Gains from trade are therefore the result of *specialization*. Countries can concentrate on types of economic activity for which they are particularly suited, while in other areas a shortfall in output can be met by imports. There can also be gains from increased competition between producers based in different countries, and a consequent widening of consumer choice; for example, the considerable two-way trade in cars between European countries enlarges market opportunities for producers and the buyers' choice between makes. Indeed, within the European Community much of the impact of trade liberalization has been felt in the growth of intra-industry trade, rather than inter-industry specialization (Sapir 1992: 1496–7), so that, while trade increased, geographical concentration of industries across the Community increased only to a limited extent.

Economic theory thus leads to the conclusion that free trade is to the mutual advantage of all participants. However, if this is self-evidently desirable, why then should any barriers to trade exist?

Reasons for trade barriers   The use of policy instruments involving trade barriers is logical if it affords some longer-term gain which offsets the short-term cost of forgoing the benefit of free trade. There are various circumstances in which trade barriers may be advantageous.

Exogenous shocks   Where an economy is subject to sudden changes which strain its capacity to adjust, trade barriers may moderate the effects of the change and afford 'breathing space' while the adjustment is made. The theoretical argument outlined above demonstrates that free trade is optimal in equilibrium *at a point in time*; but if the conditions for equilibrium change over time, the system cannot instantly accommodate to these changes. In economic terms, this inflexibility is manifested in a divergence between *short and long-run costs*; if there is limited scope for variation in costs in the short term, a reduction in price would be a rational response to a loss of competitiveness. This has two principal implications:

1. There will be a deterrent to investment in sectors that are vulnerable to such fluctuations, so that investors will demand a higher return to compensate for the additional risk. (This takes the form of a *risk premium* on investment returns.)
2. There will be a danger of more general economic disruption resulting from an instability of supply and prices of traded commodities.

Two prominent examples of such external 'shock' impacts are movements in the currency exchange rate and fluctuations in agricultural harvests. In these instances the European Community has sought to mitigate the effects of instability by measures such as the exchange rate mechanism (see Sec. 5.2.2) and agricultural price guarantees (see Sec. 9.1.1), which involve the management of markets, and hence limit the extent of free trade.

Structural change   The theoretical case for free trade assumes that each country has a given resource endowment and a given industrial and technological base, which determines the sectors of economic activity in which a country has a relative advantage compared with its trading partners. This does not explain how the existing pattern of advantage came about, or how it might be modified. In practice, countries can (and do) pursue policies that consciously aim to restructure economic activity, so that a sector that is currently uncompetitive in world markets may become competitive in the future. Another concern is to protect industries from disruption caused by a practice known as 'dumping' (see Sec. 10.2.3), whereby imports are sold at prices less than those charged in their home markets, or below their cost of production; this can be justified—in principle—as an adjustment to ensure that trade follows the true pattern of advantage.

Relative advantage   The argument for free trade may in some circumstances be inconsistent with policy objectives. The theoretical case for free trade, outlined above, implicitly assumes that nations have a common interest in seeking to maximize their aggregate welfare in *absolute* terms. This assumption may not always be correct. It is conceivable that countries may be more concerned with their *relative* advantage, and may seek to weaken their rivals by excluding them from access to markets; for example, colonial powers maintained tariff barriers which ensured privileged access to their colonies' raw materials, and which by the same token tended to limit the access to these materials of other industrial powers.

Strategic considerations   Free trade may also be thought undesirable for political reasons, particularly to avoid dependence on foreign sources for items that are of key importance in times of conflict. For example military procurement, particularly of technologically advanced products, is often restricted in order to avoid dependence on imports.

Where trade barriers exist, there are often formidable obstacles to their removal. Possibilities for rapid redeployment of resources are usually heavily constrained, and so it is conceivable that, in the short term, adjustment costs may to an extent outweigh the benefit from free trade. Even if there will eventually be an overall gain to the economy, the immediate costs of economic restructuring may be considerable, as contraction is forced on uncompetitive sectors. These costs—in the form of unemployment, bankruptcies and social disruption—are likely to be very apparent; the benefits from the expansion of other, more competitive, sectors may be less obvious. In such circumstances a phased liberalization of trade would be preferable to an immediate removal of trade barriers.

BOX 1.2
Free trade area, customs union and single market

	Tariff-free trade between member states?	Common tariffs on trade with non-members?	Movement of capital and labour unrestricted by exchange and immigration controls?
Free trade area	Yes	No	No
Customs Union	Yes	Yes	No
Single market	Yes	Yes	Yes

1.3.2 Regional free trade areas and customs unions

Global free trade represents a theoretical ideal; its attainment—or even approximation—is beset by practical difficulties (these are discussed in Sec. 10.2.2). Nevertheless, it may be possible to secure free trade between a group of countries, through the creation of a *regional free trade area*, or a *customs union*. Both of these entail the removal of barriers to trade between member states, but a customs union has the additional feature that all member states levy tariffs at the same rate on trade with non member states. The analysis that follows examines the effects of a customs union, although the analysis of a free trade area, and the conclusions to which it leads, are similar. (A *single market* represents a further stage still, with free movement of factors of production—see Box 1.2.)

Customs unions may appear to be a step in the right direction, on the grounds that some free trade is better than none. However this is not always the case: economic analysis shows that a partial liberalization of trade is not *necessarily* a step in the right direction, so that regional free trade in a customs union cannot be characterized simply as global free trade on a smaller scale. This is because a lowering of tariffs between members of the customs union has the effect (in relative terms) of *raising* the tariffs applicable to imports from non member states (assuming of course that other things remain the same). This may lead to a process of trade *diversion*, as trade between member states increases at the expense of imports from outside the customs union.

If a product can be supplied more cheaply from outside the customs union, it would be economically rational to import it. However in this case, the effect of lowering tariffs between members of the customs union (while maintaining tariffs on imports into the customs union) is to discriminate against the lower-cost producer. The net result is a switch from lower-cost to higher-cost suppliers—which is a move *away from* economic efficiency.

The technicalities of the economic analysis of trade creation and diversion are explained in more detail in Appendix 1.1 at the end of this chapter.

Conditions favouring the success of a customs union As a practical matter, the effect of a customs union depends upon the net result of trade creation, expansion and diversion. Its success is measured by the extent to which the removal of tariffs between member states actually increases the overall volume of trade. A number of conditions can be identified as conducive to success:

1. Traded goods and services should have a high price elasticity of demand. This in turn depends on the degree of substitutability between domestic and imported products. Countries whose products are close substitutes—and hence competitors—have scope to increase their penetration in each other's markets. In contrast, suppliers of complementary goods have less scope for increasing market penetration.

2. Trade should not be obstructed by other barriers, such as high transaction or transport costs. The removal of tariffs will have little impact if it does not lead to significant reductions in prices, and increased availability, of traded products. In this connection, it should be noted that some of the most formidable, and intractable, trade barriers are the so-called 'non-tariff barriers' (see Chapter 3).

3. Since gains from trade stem from specialization, countries will increase their output in sectors where they have a competitive advantage; and the gain will be amplified if costs of producing traded goods can be reduced. Hence the benefit of the customs union will be enhanced if the larger market permits the exploitation of hitherto unrealized economies of scale.

4. Industry in member states must be able to respond to the new opportunities that are offered by easier access to export markets. By the same token, countries face the challenge of managing the decline of those sectors in which they do not enjoy a competitive advantage. Successful adaptation calls for flexibility in the deployment of productive resources, stimulated where necessary by policy initiatives such as training programmes, measures to promote adaptation to new technologies, and infrastructure investment.

5. The larger the customs union, the greater the overall benefit to its member states (other things being equal). This is because trade between customs union countries displaces trade with non member states. The more countries that participate in the customs union, the lower will be the proportion of their total trade that can be affected by trade diversion. Formation of a large customs union may also lead to a change in relative prices of traded goods, so that there is a benefit from a favourable movement in the terms of trade.

1.3.3 Trade creation and diversion: the evidence

By 1968 all *tariff* barriers to trade had been abolished between the original six European Community member states (although many *non tariff* barriers were to persist—see the discussion of the single market programme in Sec. 3.1.2). The available evidence suggests that the removal of intra-Community tariffs gave rise to trade creation amounting to a substantial proportion of the Community's trade with non member countries, and that the trade diversion effect was appreciably smaller.

The estimated net increase in economic welfare that is directly due to trade creation and diversion (in terms of the gains and losses shown in Fig. A1.1) was fairly small—a fraction of 1 per cent of the Community's aggregate GNP—and a proportion of this, perhaps as much as 40 per cent, was offset by welfare losses owing to trade diversion arising from the Common Agricultural Policy. However the economies of scale effect (as shown in Fig. A1.4) appears to have been more substantial (Balassa 1974).

Several empirical studies have sought to estimate the trade creation and diversion effects of the elimination of tariff barriers. The results are summarized in Table 1.3, which shows the range and mean of estimates, in money terms and as a percentage of total imports.

The findings set out in Table 1.3 represent 'best estimates' from studies that have employed a

Table 1.3 Empirical estimates of creation and diversion of trade in manufactured products resulting from the European Economic Community, various years, 1967–1970

	Trade creation	*Trade diversion*
Range of estimates		
$bn	1.8–11.4	0.1–3.0
% of imports	5–29	0.2–8
Mean (unweighted)		
$bn	6.8	1.4
% of imports	15	3.5

Source: derived from Balassa (1974: 115, Table 5); and Davenport (1982: 227, Table 8.1) (by permission of Oxford University Press).

variety of methodologies. (These are surveyed in Davenport (1982) and Balassa (1974).) The fundamental problem of all such studies is that it is impossible to be certain what would have happened in the absence of the customs union. All the results quoted are based on 'normalized' estimates, which make allowance for the underlying upward trend in trade (which is independent of the changes brought about by the customs union). Various methods have been used to isolate the 'customs union effect'. These include:

- estimation of the change in trade net of a trend that is calculated assuming growth in imports *pro rata* with economic growth;
- estimation of import demand and export supply functions, giving a relationship between 'price' (with and without tariffs) and 'quantity' (volume of trade);
- estimation of the change in trade net of a trend that is calculated assuming growth in import penetration at the same rate as in countries outside the customs union;
- estimation of shares of imports from different sources as a function *inter alia* of relative prices; as these prices change, the structure of trade will also change.

1.3.4 Economic integration: achievements

The Community in its early years enjoyed major successes, both in the orderly reconstruction of its heavy industry, and in the elimination of tariff barriers between its member states. Testimony to this success is the interest shown by other European countries in becoming members of the Community. The most notable instance is the United Kingdom: the UK government, which had stood aloof in 1957, quickly changed its attitude, and applied for membership (unsuccessfully) in 1962.

The economic attraction of the Community has remained strong, although the rate of enlargement has been slowed by political factors. Countries freed from the constraints of totalitarian regimes (Greece, Spain and Portugal), cold war neutrality (Austria, Finland and Sweden) or communist systems (Poland and Hungary) moved rapidly to apply for Community membership.

The Community has grown, and changed, since its foundation; and the deepening of economic integration has presented new challenges. Meanwhile there have been fundamental economic and political changes on a world scale, and the response to these changes has increasingly been made at Community level. The following section considers the developments that have occurred in the economic context in which the Community operates, as Europe has moved from postwar reconstruction, through the East–West divisions of the cold war, and towards further integration and a wider membership in the years ahead.

1.4   THE CHANGING CONTEXT

When the Community was first established, Europe was divided by superpower dominated blocs, and member states' economies were recovering from the ravages of war. International trade and investment were constrained by tariff barriers and the non-convertibility of currencies. The vital sectors of the economy, afforded priority in economic co-operation, were heavy industry and agriculture. The population was less urbanized than now: agriculture was a major employer, while anxiety over the security of food supplies was a major influence on agricultural policy.

The present economic context is different in many ways. The European Community has enjoyed many years of sustained economic growth and political stability. Industrial structures have changed radically, with increased emphasis on light industry and the service sector. Agricultural self-sufficiency in most products has been more than achieved: attention is now focused on the budgetary costs of agricultural support, and the environmental effects of farming practices. The population has become more urbanized, leading to concerns over the future viability of rural communities.

Meanwhile, the Community has proceeded with economic integration, but it has also become more diverse, as its membership has enlarged. As a result, the interests and priorities of the member states are less homogeneous; for example, while the more prosperous countries are preoccupied with problems of economic success, and particularly the environmental consequences of economic development, the less prosperous are anxious to secure the full benefit of the single market.

Changes which have occurred in Europe since the Second World War are also manifested in the global economy. International trade and investment have increased, and tariff barriers have been lowered. The European Community, as a result of its integration into a single market, is now a major economic entity in its own right, and to a large extent is the conduit for its member states' influence on the global economic system.

1.4.1   The globalization of economic activity

In the years since the Community's foundation, economic integration has proceeded on a global scale. Transactions across national frontiers have become increasingly important: since 1970, while total world output has doubled worldwide foreign direct investment has quadrupled, and the value of exports has risen two and a half times (*The Economist*, 27 March 1993). The late 1980s saw a spectacular growth in trans-frontier direct investment, as is illustrated by Table 1.4.

Governments are less able to exercise control over the economy—a notable instance occurred in 1992, when the weight of speculative currency movements overwhelmed the UK government's efforts to maintain the exchange rate of the pound. Co-operation has developed in economic policy, institutionalized in the G7 grouping of the world's leading economic powers (the four largest EU countries, plus the USA, Canada and Japan; the Community is also represented at G7 meetings, by the Commission President).

Table 1.4 Outward direct investment flows as a percentage of GDP for the seven leading industrial nations, 1971–1990

	1971–5	1976–80	1981–5	1986–90
Canada	0.4	0.7	0.9	1.0
France	0.3	0.4	0.5	1.4
Germany	0.5	0.4	0.6	1.1
Italy	0.2	0.1	0.4	0.5
Japan	0.3	0.3	0.4	1.2
UK	1.8	2.1	2.0	3.7
USA	0.7	0.7	0.2	0.5

Source: © OECD (1992) *International Direct Investment: Policies and Trends in the 1980s.* Reproduced by permission of the OECD.

1.4.2 Structural change in the European economy

The period since the Second World War has seen far-reaching economic and social changes within Europe. Societies have become increasingly urbanized, economic interdependence has grown between countries and regions, and new technology has transformed economic activity in many areas. These developments have profoundly affected economic structures and patterns of employment.

Urbanisation   Over the three decades 1960–90, there was a substantial shift in population from rural to urban areas. The number of inhabitants in rural areas declined by more than one-fifth, while the urban population increased by one-third: by 1990 only one person in five lived in the countryside. The change was particularly marked in the 'peripheral' countries (Ireland, Greece, Portugal and Spain) where the urban population rose by approximately 75 per cent, and the proportion living in rural areas went down from more than half to under a third of the population. These countries were appreciably less urbanized than the rest of the Community, although the difference has become less pronounced over time: in the Community as a whole, the rural population declined from 31 per cent to 21 per cent of the total population between 1960 and 1990 (World Resources Institute 1990: Tables 16.1 and 17.2).

Changes in economic activity   When the Community was founded, agriculture and heavy industry were key sectors of the economy, in terms of employment, output and strategic importance. Since that time the development of new technologies and the rise of service industries have transformed the economy. Many workers today are employed in industries, and making products, that did not exist 50 years ago. The trends in employment are illustrated in Table 1.5: over the past two decades the proportion of the workforce employed in industry and agriculture has declined, while the proportion of the workforce employed in the service sector has risen to almost two-thirds of total employment in the Community.

As the economy has grown, expenditure on agricultural products has diminished as a proportion of total consumption. At the same time, productivity has risen dramatically in the agricultural sector—a striking instance of success in achievement of one of the Community's

Table 1.5 Structure of employment in the European Community, 1970, 1980, 1987 and 1991 (%)

	1970	1980	1987	1991
Agriculture	13.7	9.4	7.8	6.2
Industry	40.8	36.9	32.1	31.4
Services	45.6	53.6	60.1	62.4
Total employment	100.1	99.9	100.0	100.0

Note: These figures are for the 12 member states that constituted the European Community from 1986. Figures do not sum to 100 owing to rounding errors.
Source: European Commission (1992a: 86).

original objectives (set out in the EC Treaty, Article 39(1)(a)). This has led to declining agricultural employment (together with the trend towards greater urbanization), as on average fewer workers are needed to produce a given output.

In heavy industrial sectors the emphasis has switched from the benefits of economic co-operation to the management of decline. The economic importance of these sectors in the 1950s is shown by the priority given to economic co-operation in the coal and steel industries. (The 1951 ECSC Treaty predates by six years the foundation of the European Economic Community.) However, this importance is now greatly diminished. In the 12 member states that constituted the European Community in 1986, coal production, which amounted to almost 450,000 tonnes in 1962, was below 200,000 tonnes by 1990 (Eurostat 1986; 1993: Table 4.23). The number of mines producing hard coal (excluding those in Spain and Portugal) declined from 334 in 1975 to 107 in 1990 (a reduction of more than two-thirds), while personnel employed underground fell by more than a half between 1980 and 1990, from 350,000 to 150,000 (European Commission 1990).

The iron and steel industry has also experienced declining employment—as is shown in Table 1.6—and periodic crises, suffering from overcapacity and keen competition from newly industrializing countries.

Table 1.6 Employment in the European Community iron and steel industry, 1977, 1980, 1990

	1977	1980	1990
Employees ('000)	722	580	321
% of industrial workforce	1.92	1.57	0.98

Note: These figures are for the nine member states that constituted the European Community up to 1986.
Source: European Commission (1989 and 1992b)

Economic integration across national frontiers Economic activity has become increasingly integrated across the Community, a tendency that accelerated in the approach to the single market. The phenomenon is illustrated in Table 1.7, which shows that mergers, and other forms

Table 1.7   Collaboration involving major enterprises in the European Community, at national, community and international level 1984/5–1991/2 (%)

	Mergers*		All collaboration†	
	1984/5–1987/8	1988/9–1991/2	1984/5–1987/8	1988/9–1991/2
National	65	50	55	42
Community	23	34	19	31
International	12	16	26	27
Total	100	100	100	100

* Includes majority acquisitions.
† Mergers (including majority acquisitions), minority acquisitions and joint ventures.
Source: European Commission (1986–93).

of collaboration, between enterprises were to a growing extent crossing national frontiers. At the peak of merger activity, in 1988/9 there were 315 mergers (almost one per day) involving enterprises from different Community member states.

1.4.3   Cohesion of the European Community

The most obvious structural change in the Community has been its enlargement from the original 6 to 15 member states, with agreement on eventual membership for several states in eastern Europe. Enlargement has tended to increase the Community's diversity in various respects, including economic structures, social conditions and environmental circumstances.

In particular, divisions have arisen between the more and less prosperous member states— sometimes characterized as a 'north–south', or 'core–periphery' divide. This is reflected in the issues that are considered important: for example, the more prosperous, countries, such as Denmark, Germany and the Netherlands, have been concerned to alleviate the environmental pressures resulting from economic activity, while less prosperous countries of the periphery give high priority to infrastructure development and industrial growth.

Cohesion and successive enlargements of the community   In 1973 the original six member states were joined by three countries in northern Europe, one of which—the United Kingdom—was large and industrialized, and the other two—Denmark and Ireland—were small and agricultural. These new member states varied in levels of prosperity: Denmark is one of the Community's wealthier countries, while Ireland is among the poorest.

In the 1980s further enlargement saw three new member states from southern Europe: Greece, Spain and Portugal. Politically, and economically, these countries had been subject to illiberal regimes, with industry generally protected from import competition, and consequently ill equipped to compete in an open market. All three are among the less prosperous member states (see Table 1.8), and their economic structures are untypical of the Community: the percentage of the labour force employed in agriculture is over twice the Community average, and the proportions employed in the service sector are lower than in other member states. Consequently the pattern of agricultural output now has a very clear north–south divide, and

Table 1.8   Member states; gross domestic product per head, 1992

	GDP per head (ECU's)*	Index (EU = 100)
Luxembourg	20 538	131
France	17 646	113
Belgium	17 130	110
Austria	17 067	109
Denmark	16 812	108
Germany	16 777	107
Italy	16 497	106
Netherlands	16 061	103
Sweden	15 820	101
EU average	15 628	100
UK	15 422	99
Finland	13 853	89
Spain	12 121	78
Ireland	12 029	77
Portugal	10 532	67
Greece	7 851	50

* At current prices and purchasing power parities.
Source: derived from Eurostat (1994: Table 2.2).

Greece, Spain and Portugal account for a very high proportion of the Community's production of crops such as citrus fruits, grapes and olives.

The demise of the Soviet bloc ended the political constraints on Community membership for countries that had been non-aligned in the east–west division of Europe. Three such countries—Austria, Finland and Sweden—joined the Community in 1995. These countries are generally prosperous, and their integration is eased by long-standing trade links prior to membership.

As a result of these successive enlargements, the Community has become increasingly diverse. The original membership was a fairly homogeneous group of countries concerned primarily to develop a common market. The enlargement has increased the size—and the potential prosperity—of the Community's internal market; and the prospect of sharing in this prosperity was a powerful attraction to the newer member states. At the same time, Community membership has also intensified pressures for economic restructuring, particularly in the less prosperous regions.

Economic disparities   The EC Treaty (Article 130a) calls for action to strengthen economic and social cohesion and to reduce interregional disparities. A narrowing of disparities implies a rise in living standards in less prosperous regions towards levels prevailing elsewhere in the Community; and consequently these regions must have rates of economic growth above the Community average.

As is shown in Sec. 3.6 the Community's efforts in this respect, as measured by relative changes in GDP per capita, have not—thus far—been very successful. There is still a wide range of prosperity, as is evident from Table 1.8, which shows the least prosperous member states (Greece, Ireland, Portugal and Spain) coming well below the EU average. (These four countries have special provision for Community economic assistance under the Cohesion Fund—see Sec. 3.5.)

Indicators of cohesion   Cohesion, it should be emphasized, cannot mean uniformity, if only because of the wide geographical range of the Community, reflected in its economic, social and environmental diversity. Nor should comparisons between member states be restricted to narrowly defined economic indicators. The ultimate criterion must be the quality of life, within which is subsumed economic and other indicators.

This criterion is difficult to apply in practice because there is no objective index of a society's overall welfare. There are nevertheless indicators that might suggest that the countries with the highest GDP per capita do not necessarily enjoy the best quality of life in other respects.

For example, one such indicator is life expectancy. The highest level in 1989 was in the Netherlands (76.8 years), and the lowest, in Ireland (74 years). In general there was no significant correlation between economic prosperity and life expectancy: the rank correlation of life expectancy at birth in 1989 with GDP per capita was 0.15 (Standard Error 0.59); omitting Luxembourg, the figure was 0.42 (SE 0.62). Moreover, the trends in life expectancy do not show any evidence of increasing cohesion; on the contrary, over the 20-year period from 1970, the variance of life expectancy increased by almost 50 per cent (calculated from Eurostat 1991: 144–47, Table G15).

1.5   THE EUROPEAN COMMUNITY POLICY AGENDA

The European Community was from its inception designed to take economic integration well beyond the degree of co-operation required for membership of a customs union. The original Treaties state that the 'core' objective of the Community is to raise standards of living; and the development of a common market is the principal mechanism for achieving the objective (see Box 1.3). This remains the case, despite changes in terminology—the European Economic Community has become simply the European Community, and the 'common market' is usually referred to as the 'internal market' or the 'European single market'.

Thus, although the removal of intra-Community tariffs was a necessary precondition, it represented only a first step towards achievement of the Community's objectives. This is very clear from the EC Treaty, the preamble to which calls for 'an ever closer union between the

---

BOX 1.3

The original purpose of European economic integration

... to contribute ... through the establishment of a common market ... to economic expansion, growth of employment and a rising standard of living. (ECSC Treaty Article 2)

... by establishing a common market ... to promote throughout the Community a harmonious development of economic activities, a continuous and balanced expansion, an increase in stability, an accelerated raising of the standard of living and closer relationships between the states belonging to it.

(EEC Treaty Article 2)

... to contribute to the raising of the standard of living in the Member states ... (Euratom Treaty Article 1)

peoples of Europe'. These words suggest a continuing process of integration, which may follow the path illustrated, in a stylized form, in Box 1.4, moving from a free trade area to a federal system with supranational policy-making. The Community has now set its course for economic union, with provision for economic policy coordination and eventually a single currency; but in any case the single market in itself calls for a high degree of integration of the economies of member states, and the development of common policies in a wide range of areas.

BOX 1.4
Degrees of economic co-operation

Free trade area   Tariff-free trade between member states

Customs union   A free trade area with common tariffs on trade with non member states

Single market   A customs union with free movement of goods and services, and factors of production (labour and capital), facilitated by harmonization of policy measures

Economic union   A single market with harmonization of macroeconomic (fiscal and monetary) policies

Federalism   An economic union with supranational economic policy-making

---

The European single market, like all market systems, can operate only within a legal framework. The extent of regulation—the level of detail and the breadth of coverage—is frequently a matter of debate; but rules are necessary: for example, to specify product characteristics (particularly where these relate to safety or environmental protection), to ensure fair competition or to determine occupational qualifications. The European Community's institutions, and its legal system, exist primarily to ensure that freedom of movement is not obstructed, and that the rules necessary for the functioning of the single market are observed.

So the 1957 Treaty (then the EEC Treaty) included a framework for Community policies to complement freedom of movement. This originally comprised provisions relating to the promotion of competition, co-operation in economic and monetary policies, and social policies. The present Treaty (the EC Treaty) sets out an extensive policy agenda: those provisions directly concerned with the functioning of the single market are summarized in Box 1.5.

BOX 1.5
The European single market: essential requirements

- Elimination of customs duties and of quantitative restrictions on imports and exports, and all other measures having equivalent effect
- Common customs tariffs and a common commercial policy towards non member countries
- Abolition of obstacles to the free movement of persons, services and capital
- Measures to regulate entry and movement of persons in the internal market
- A system to ensure that competition is not distorted
- Approximation of the laws of member states to the extent required for the functioning of the common market.

The first two requirements are in a sense 'negative' objectives, inasmuch as they involve the elimination of restrictions on free movement, while the third entails the replacement of national trade policies by measures at Community level. The last requirement, approximation of national laws, has given rise to substantial transfers of policy responsibility from member states to the Community, and also considerable difficulties in the harmonisation of diverse national regulations (see Sec. 3.1.2).

1.5.1   The single market

In a single market there is free movement both of products and of the resources used to produce them—known as *factors of production*. The demand for these factors varies between countries as does their availability; consequently there is variation in their prices. This gives rise to incentives for factor mobility between countries, in the same way that there is an incentive to trade goods in markets where they can command the highest price.

Gains from factor mobility   The theoretical argument for free trade in goods can be applied to movement of labour and capital (see Appendix 1.1). Unrestricted mobility will permit the use of factors in locations where their productivity is greatest—and this is a precondition for efficiency in the use of productive resources. On the other hand, some producers benefit from restricted factor mobility—such as industries using capital that would otherwise be attracted away by higher returns available in other countries. However, in aggregate, there is an economic benefit from factor mobility, and hence there is no *economic* case for restrictions, except perhaps as a transitional measure to give the markets time to adjust to increased mobility. The argument for limitations on migration must therefore be made on social or political grounds.

The European Community framework for the single market   However, 'free trade' normally refers only to unrestricted movement of products (goods and services); defined in this way, it is compatible with controls on the mobility of factors of production. Indeed, countries generally seek to regulate the importation of labour and (in some instances) the export of capital; movement of labour is generally constrained by immigration controls, while many countries also maintain foreign exchange controls to restrict capital outflows.

The single market remains at the centre of European economic integration: and the growing importance of the European Community is due largely to the limitations of policy-making by individual countries within an integrated economic system. In a single market there can be no barriers to trade or restrictions on the transfer of productive resources between member states. Thus, products and services, labour and capital may be traded freely, without regard to national frontiers; and to this extent the economies of the member states are 'fused' within a single economic unit.

Nation states have for centuries maintained controls on movement across international boundaries; indeed, many would argue that such controls are a key element of national sovereignty. Frontier controls are used as a policy instrument:

1. to limit imports in order to protect a country's own industry from foreign competition
2. to prevent importation of products that do not conform to national standards
3. to control foreign exchange transactions in order to maintain the exchange rate for the national currency
4. to control the movement and employment of aliens.

The European Community's internal market is defined as 'an area without internal frontiers in which the free movement of goods, persons, services and capital is assured' (Article 7a EC). This precludes the use of frontier controls between member states for the purposes described above. In many instances, there are no alternative policy instruments available at national level that are consistent with membership of the Community. In such circumstances, the solution lies in the use of policy instruments on an agreed basis within the Community as a whole; for example:

- common standards for products and services
- industry policies to ensure fair competition
- regional and social policies to mitigate competitive disadvantages.

The Community has an institutional structure, described in Sec. 2.1, within which policies are formulated and implemented. The extent of the Community's responsibilities, and the powers of its institutions, remain matters of some controversy; but it should be emphasized that the Community, with its supranational institutions, is ultimately the creation of the member states themselves. The formation of the Community clearly had a political cost to the governments of member states, inasmuch as it diluted their sovereign power within their own territory; on the other hand, they gained by sharing in the decision-making of the Community.

The four freedoms   To achieve the benefits of a single market, it is necessary that all artificial barriers be removed between member states. For this reason, the EC Treaty includes a commitment to the 'four freedoms':

1. *Free movement of goods*   Customs duties (and any equivalent charges) are prohibited on trade between Community member states; member states must levy common tariffs on trade with non-member countries (Article 9). Quantitative restrictions on imports between member states, and all measures having equivalent effect, are prohibited (Article 30).
2. *Free movement of services*   Restrictions on the provision of services by citizens of member states across national frontiers are not permitted (Article 59).
3. *Free movement of workers*   Workers have the right to move between member states, and to reside in a Member State, for the purpose of employment. Discrimination between workers from Community member states is prohibited (Article 48). Restrictions on the establishment of self-employed persons in another Member State are also not permitted (Article 52).
4. *Free movement of capital*   Restrictions on the movement of capital between member states are prohibited (Article 73a).

1.5.2   The evolution of Community policies

The Community's movement towards a single market, together with the economic changes described above, have led to a deepening and also a broadening of the Community's policy responsibilities. As the relative importance of heavy industry has declined, the complexity of the economy has increased, with a shifting emphasis towards diverse products and services, many of them based on new technologies. Standards and—where appropriate—regulatory provisions had to be developed for new industries; and at the same time measures were needed to regenerate other industries.

Within the single market, the necessary action could in many instances be taken only at Community level, because national measures would be ineffective. A prime example is the provision of infrastructure necessary for economic integration: this must by definition follow Community, as distinct from national, priorities. Standards for new technologies are now set at Community level, where in the past member states might have set their own standards, which would then go through a process of harmonization; by the same token, measures to accelerate technological development are coordinated by the Community. Similarly, co-operation between member states in economic and monetary policy has led to Community policies, with an appreciation of the limits on freedom of action at national level.

More generally, integration has broadened the Community's role. In particular, the removal of frontiers, mobility of labour and citizenship of the European Union (Articles 7a, 48, and 8 EC), have extended the Community dimension in areas such as social policy, consumer protection, health and education.

The Community now has a major presence in the world, as the single market has developed against a background of growing interdependence in the global economy. With their economies integrated within a single entity, member states can no longer maintain economic relations on a purely individual basis with non-Community countries or within international organizations. Consequently, the Community has taken the lead in trade policy and international economic co-operation.

1.5.3 The Community policy agenda following the EU Treaty

Provisions for Community policies for agriculture and transport were included in the 'foundations of the Community' set out in the 1957 EEC Treaty (Titles II and IV respectively), and constituted the legal basis for the Common Agricultural Policy and the Common Transport Policy, which are discussed in Chapters 8 and 9. In 1987, following the Single European Act, new sections were introduced in the Treaty, relating to economic and social cohesion, research and technological development, and the environment.

The 1992 Maastricht Treaty on European Union extensively revised the EEC Treaty (and also renamed it the EC Treaty), bringing it within the framework of the 'three pillars' (see Sec. 1.1 above). The revised Treaty gave a formal legal basis for Community action in the areas of education and training, culture, public health, consumer protection, infrastructure development, industrial policy and development co-operation. The enlargement of the Community's areas of responsibility with successive Treaty revisions is described in Box 1.6.

In general, Community involvement in these areas did not begin with their introduction into the EC Treaty; for example, the Community concluded the first Yaoundé Convention (the forerunner of the Lomé Conventions) on development co-operation in 1963, and the first Community environmental action programme began in 1974. The Treaty revisions in one sense constitute an acknowledgement of policies already established; but it is nevertheless important for the future development of policies that the Community has a proper legal framework for action, setting out its areas of responsibility. It should also be emphasized that there is no question of the Community necessarily having *exclusive* responsibility in these areas: in many instances a problem is addressed at different levels—Community, national or local—using policy instruments appropriate to that level. (This accords with the subsidiarity principle—see Sec. 2.2.2.)

The Treaty also acknowledges that policy areas are not self-contained, and there are many complex interactions. For example, standardization of product specifications across the Community will facilitate trade across frontiers within the single market; but these specifications can also be important for environmental and consumer protection. In this context, there is a requirement that proposed legislation must 'take as a base a high level of protection' (Article 100a(3) EC). Moreover, the Treaty includes a number of provisions calling for an integrated approach, so that Community policies generally take account of dimensions relating to the environment, industry, consumer protection, public health and culture. Successful implementation of these provisions is essential for the achievement of the Community's broader objectives, which include (*inter alia*) 'a harmonious and balanced development of economic activities,

---

BOX 1.6
European Community policy areas

As listed in the Treaty establishing the European Community: Part Three, 'Community Policies'
I   Free Movement of goods
    1. The customs union
    2. Elimination of quantitative restrictions between member states
II   Agriculture
III   Free movement of persons, services and capital
    1. Workers
    2. Right of establishment
    3. Services
    4. Capital *and payments***
IV   Transport
V   Common rules on competition, taxation and approximation of laws
    1. Rules on competition
    2. Tax provisions
    3. Approximation of laws
VI   Economic and monetary policy
    1. Economic policy
    2. Monetary policy
    3. *Institutional provisions***
VII   Common commercial policy
VIII   Social policy, *education, vocational training and youth***
    1. Social provisions
    2. The European Social Fund
    3. *Education, vocational training and youth***
IX   *Culture***
X   *Public health***
XI   *Consumer protection***
XII   *Trans European networks***
XIII   *Industry***
XIV   Economic and social cohesion*
XV   Research and technological development*
XVI   Environment*
XVII   *Development co-operation***

*Added by the Single European Act in 1987
** Italics denote: added by the Treaty on European Union in 1993

---

sustainable and non-inflationary growth respecting the environment … the raising of the standard of living *and* quality of life' (Article 2 EC (emphasis added)).

1.5.4   Exemptions under the EU Treaty

The 1992 Treaty on European Union introduced the concept of an 'opt-out', such that legislation may not be applicable in certain member states. Before this, legislation pursuant to the EC Treaty (known then as the EEC Treaty) in principle applied equally to all member states. There were minor exceptions for territories of member states; for example, the Isle of Man participates in the customs union and the VAT system, but for other purposes is outside the Community. Also, Community legislation sometimes contained special provisions for specific member states, particularly where the costs of immediate compliance would be especially onerous; for example, Spain was permitted to set emission standards for power stations which were lower than in the rest of the Community, in order to accommodate economic growth (Directive 88/609, Article 5(3)). Nevertheless, the Community was essentially a unified legal order, and its legislative framework was fully applicable in all member states.

The EC Treaty now provides for a progression to a single currency for the Community, but Protocols attached to the Treaty permit Denmark and the UK to choose whether or not to participate in the new currency system. The practical effect of these exemptions remains unclear: if the remaining member states eventually move to a common currency, any advantages of monetary independence for Denmark and the UK would have to be weighed against the disadvantages of exclusion from decision-making in the monetary policy of the common currency group.

The Protocol on social policy provides a framework for an agreement between the member states, excluding the UK, under which legislation may be enacted by the other member states using the legislative processes and institutional structures of the Community. This legislation will not apply in the UK. The exemption has been politically controversial, because inferior social provisions might afford UK industry a cost advantage. (This issue is explored in Sec. 6.3.3.) The legal position is somewhat unclear, because the Social Protocol provides for legislation based on an intergovernmental agreement, making use of the Community's status as a source of law. In this sense there may be some similarities with the initial version of the Agreement on the European Economic Area, which would have established a body of law in parallel with, and overlapping, Community law: the Court of Justice held that this was inconsistent with the legal status of the Community (Opinion 1/91)) (see Sec. 1.1.1) and the Agreement was revised.

1.5.5   Political co-operation under the EU Treaty

The Treaty on European Union establishes a framework for political co-operation which includes provisions (outside the EC Treaty) on a common foreign and security policy (Title V) and on justice and home affairs (Title VI). Their essential purpose is the co-ordination of national policies on an intergovernmental basis; the Commission, although 'fully associated' with the Council of Ministers, does not play the supranational executive role which it has under the EC Treaty.

The origins of Title V lie in the practice of consultation between member states on foreign policy issues, which was formalized by the 1986 Single European Act. The Council presidency, which rotates among member states at six-monthly intervals (see Sec. 2.1.1), carries major responsibilities. The country holding the Council presidency is charged with implementation of common measures which are agreed by the Council, and in that capacity represents the Union in international forums (assisted by its predecessor and successor in the presidency).

There remain doubts as to the effectiveness of the intergovernmental process in foreign relations, where the ultimate policy instruments in foreign relations are military and economic. The Union for various reasons has had little success in coordinating military action. The EU Treaty stipulates that agreement on European Union defence policies 'shall not prejudice the specific character of the security and defence policy of certain member states' (Article J4(2)), and the difficulty of subordinating differing national interests to a common policy has been apparent ever since the failure of the ambitious 1949 proposal for a European Defence Community (see Box 1.1).

The use of economic instruments in foreign policy leads back to the EC Treaty. Goods and money circulate freely in the European single market, and the European Community has common policies with respect to trade with non member countries. The European Union has no capacity to legislate—so any economic sanctions must be implemented by legislation under the EC Treaty (Article 228a), which provides for measures to interrupt or reduce economic relations with a non member country.

Similarly, while immigration policy comes under the 'justice and home affairs' pillar of the EU Treaty, measures to implement the policy must be legislated by the Community, if there is to be free movement of people within the single market. The EC Treaty (Article 100c) provides for legislation on visa requirements for citizens of non member countries, and may apply to other matters as decided by intergovernmental agreement. Where Community legislation is not required, the EU Treaty (Article K.3(3)) provides for Conventions to be recommended for adoption by the member states; if all the members states agree, these Conventions may stipulate that the Court of Justice shall have jurisdiction to interpret their provisions and rule on any disputes.

This interlinkage between intergovernmental agreements and Community legislation is a recent legal innovation. It remains to be seen how it is viewed by the Court of Justice, especially in the light of the strong distinction the Court has previously made between the two (see Sec. 1.1.1 above). In particular, it is not clear how the exercise of any judicial functions with respect to intergovernmental Conventions will be compatible with European Community law.

1.6 THE EUROPEAN COMMUNITY IN CONTEXT: KEY POINTS AND ISSUES

The European Community's main purpose is to realize the benefits of integration of national economies within a single market. The Community originated in the particular circumstances following the Second World War; over subsequent decades economic and political integration has intensified, and has encompassed additional member states. Although created by a Treaty between nation states, the Community—uniquely among international organizations—has a legal existence that is distinct from its member states. Political—as opposed to economic—co-operation is formally outside the Community framework, and is conducted through inter-governmental agreements under the European Union Treaty.

In consideration of the progress of the Community (and of the European Union), the following issues can be identified:

1. The three-pillared structure of the European Union combines intergovernmental political co-operation and supranational economic integration: to what extent is it feasible or desirable to maintain this distinction?
2. What model more closely approximates the European Community: intergovernmental arrangements or supranationalism?
3. Economic gains and political commitment are necessary preconditions for international economic co-operation, and circumstances in the aftermath of the Second World War gave an impetus to the Community: why was the subsequent evolution of the Community an uneven process? Are present-day conditions favourable for the further development of the Community, in terms of an extension of its role or enlargement of its membership?
4. Acceptance of the case for free trade in principle tends to be accompanied by numerous qualifications in practice: how far should these qualifications influence policies for economic integration?

5. Although economic integration can be *on balance* advantageous, some economic sectors and regions are liable to be disadvantaged: how far can such adverse effects be tolerated? what strategies can be adopted to mitigate them?
6. The economy of western Europe has undergone profound structural change over the last 50 years: what are the implications for the process of economic integration, and the policies of the European Community?

References

Balassa, B. (1974) 'Trade creation and diversion in the European Common Market: an appraisal of the evidence', *The Manchester School*, **42**, 123–27.

Davenport, M. (1982) 'The economic impact of the EEC', in A. Boltho, *The European Economy: Growth and Crisis*, Oxford University Press, 252–7.

European Commission (1986–93) *Reports on Competition Policy* (annual), European Commission, Brussels.

European Commission (1989, 1992b) *Iron and Steel Yearly Statistics*, European Commission, Brussels.

European Commission (1990) *Energy Yearly Statistics*, Office of Official Publications, Luxembourg.

European Commission (1992a) *Employment and Unemployment*, European Commission, Brussels.

Eurostat (1986, 1993) *Basic Statistics of the Community*, Statistical Office, Luxembourg.

Eurostat (1991) *Demographic Statistics*, Statistical Office, Luxembourg.

Eurostat (1994) *Basic Statistics of the Community*, 31st edn, Statistical Office, Luxembourg.

Foreman-Peck, J. (1983) *A History of the World Economy: International Economic Relations since 1850*, Harvester Wheatsheaf, Hemel Hempstead.

Grassman, S. (1980) 'Long-term trends in openness of national economies', *Oxford Economic Papers*, **32**, 123–33.

Hogan, M. J. (1987) *The Marshall Plan: America, Britain and the Reconstruction of Western Europe 1947–52*, Cambridge University Press.

Kindleberger, C. P. (1987) *The World in Depression 1929–1939*, Penguin, Harmondsworth.

Küsters, H. J. (1987) 'The Treaties of Rome 1955–57', in R. Pryce (ed.), *The Dynamics of European Union*, Croom Helm, Beckenham, Kent.

OECD (1992) *International Direct Investment: Policies and Trends in the 1980s*, OECD, Paris.

Pentland, C. (1973) *International Theory and European Integration*, The Free Press, New York.

Sapir, A. (1992) 'Regional Integration in Europe', *Economic Journal*, 102, 1496.

van der Breugel, H. (1966) *From Marshall Aid to Atlantic Partnership*, Elsevier, Amsterdam.

van der Groeben, H. (1987) *The European Community. The Formative Years: the Struggle to establish the Common Market and the Political Union 1958–66*, Office for Official Publications of the European Communities, Luxembourg.

Willis, F. R. (1965) *France, Germany and the New Europe 1945–1963*, Stanford University Press.

World Resources Institute (1990) *World Resources 1990–91*, Oxford University Press.

Directive

Directive 88/609, on limitation of emissions into the air from large combustion installations, *Official Journal*, 1988 L336/1.

Opinion

Opinion 1/91, *Opinion on the European Economic Area Treaty*, [1991] ECR I-6084.

1.1

TRADE CREATION, DIVERSION AND EXPANSION: THE THEORY

The economic effect of a customs union can be shown in a simple example, in which there are two countries, A and B, and the rest of the world; country B is initially part of the 'rest of the world', but it subsequently joins country A in a customs union. For simplicity, the analysis is in terms of a single traded commodity, and it is assumed that there are no transport or transaction costs, and that all barriers to trade can be expressed in terms of tariffs.

Trade creation, diversion and expansion effects are illustrated in Fig. A1.1, which shows, for a hypothetical traded good, the relationship between the price of the good, the quantity demanded, and quantities supplied under different tariff regimes.

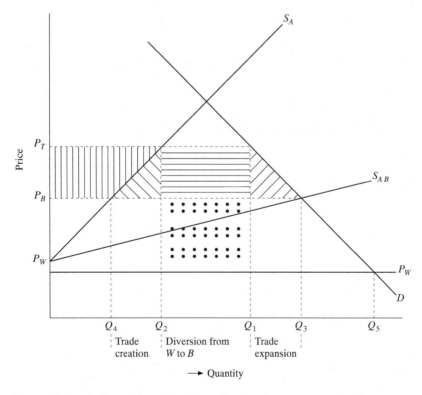

Figure A1.1   Trade creation, diversion and expansion

The demand in country A is given by the curve D; country A's supply curve is S_A. The world market price is P_W. (It is assumed that the world market is perfectly competitive, and that country A's demand accounts for only a small proportion of the world total, and hence has a negligible influence on the world market price: *in technical terms, the world supply to country A is infinitely price-elastic.*)

Trade subject to a tariff

If all imports into country A are subject to a tariff of $(P_T - P_W)$, the price to consumers in country A is initially P_T. At price P_T the industry in country A would supply Q_2, total consumption would be Q_1, with the balance $(Q_1 - Q_2)$ accounted for by imports from the rest of the world (at price P_W plus tariff, i.e. P_T).

A customs union

If country A joins in a customs union with country B, imports from B will no longer be subject to the tariff. The tariff-free supply of the good is then shown by the curve S_{AB}, which represents the aggregate amounts (depending on the level of price) that the industries in both A and B are prepared to supply to A's market. Imports from the rest of the world continue to be subject to the tariff, and so in the customs union it is cheaper to import (free of tariffs) from country B than from the rest of the world. The new market price in country A is P_B, and consumption increases from Q_1 to Q_3. The new level of demand (Q_3) is met by a combination of supply from country A (Q_4) (the quantity that A's industry is prepared to supply at price P_B), and imports from B $(Q_3 - Q_4)$. (This is the quantity that B is prepared to export to A at price P_B). Imports from the rest of the world cease, because their price after the tariff is levied (P_T) renders them uncompetitive following the formation of the customs union between A and B.

The effects on trade of countries A and B and the rest of the world

For this particular good, the customs union has:

1. increased international trade (from $(Q_1 - Q_2)$ to $(Q_3 - Q_4)$);
2. increased consumption in country A (from Q_1 to Q_3);
3. generated imports from country B $(Q_3 - Q_4)$;
4. eliminated imports from the rest of the world (which previously amounted to $(Q_1 - Q_2)$).

Some trade has been created, and some diverted from low-cost suppliers in the rest of the world, and also from high-cost suppliers in country A.

In terms of Fig. A1.1, the effects on international trade are measured as follows:

Gross increase in trade	$(Q_3 - Q_4)$
Minus Trade diversion	$-(Q_1 - Q_2)$
Equals Net increase in trade,	
comprising Trade creation	$=(Q_2 - Q_4)$
plus Trade expansion	$+ (Q_3 - Q_1)$

The effect on country B

The effect on the market in country B is illustrated by Fig. A1.2, which shows the supply and demand for the good in the tariff-protected market of country B. Before the customs union the market price in country B is P_B^0, the price at which the quantity of the good supplied equals the quantity demanded, Q_B^0 (with no imports or exports of the good). Following establishment of the customs union the price rises to P_B^1, at which price the quantity demanded in country B falls to Q_B^1, while the quantity supplied increases to Q_B^2; the difference between the two is accounted for by exports to country A, which are of course equal to country A's imports from country B. Thus, the quantity exported in Fig. A1.2 $(Q_B^2 - Q_B^1)$ is equal to the quantity imported in Fig. A1.1 $(Q_3 - Q_4)$.

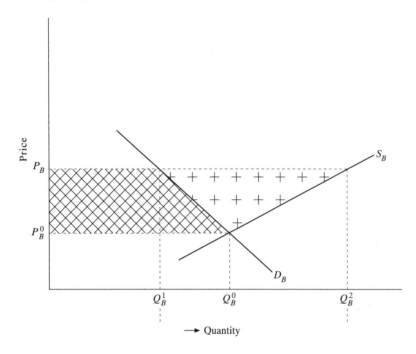

Figure A1.2 Impact of customs union in partner country

Gainers and losers

The changes in trade have benefits for some participants, and affect others adversely.
   The *Gainers* are:

- *consumers in country A*, who enjoy lower prices (P_B rather than P_T in Fig. A1.1)
- *producers in country B*, who have gained access to the country A market, and export $(Q_B^2 - Q_B^1)$ in Fig. A1.2

The *Losers* are:

- *producers in the rest of the world*, who have suffered the loss of an export market in country A amounting to $(Q_1 - Q_2)$ (Fig. A1.1) to competitors from country B

- *producers in country A*, who have lost some of their market $(Q_2 - Q_4)$ (Fig. A1.1) to imports from country B

However, this does not mean that *all* country A producers will lose. The analysis above is in terms of a single good; and for some other goods the pattern of gains and losses will be the converse of those shown above. The effect of the customs union will be to encourage member states to concentrate on supplying those goods for which their costs, *relative to those in other members of the customs union*, are lowest. Those country A producers that have such a cost advantage will gain, and country B producers lose, from tariff-free access to the market in country B.

The aggregate benefit of a customs union

Do the benefits to the gainers outweigh the disbenefits to the losers? Do customs unions increase aggregate economic welfare? Economic theory unfortunately offers no general answer to these questions: the outcome depends on the relative strength of the trade creation and diversion effects.

- Trade creation yields an economic benefit by switching supply from high-cost producers in country A to lower-cost producers in country B.
- Similarly, trade expansion yields an economic benefit by satisfying additional demand from consumers in country A.
- But trade diversion yields an economic *dis*benefit, by switching supply from a low-cost source (the rest of the world) to a high-cost source (country B).

In the case of the single-good illustration in Figs. A1.1 and A1.2, country A consumers gain because they can purchase the good at a lower price—and they buy more of the good. This gain is shown in Fig. A1.1 as an increase in consumer surplus (measured by the aggregate difference between the prices that consumers are willing to pay at each level of consumption—as shown by the demand curve D in Fig. A1.1—and the price they actually pay, which is reduced from P_T to P_B). The gain to consumers is shown in Fig. A1.1 by the aggregate of the shaded areas between P_T and P_B, equal to $(P_T - P_B) \times [Q_1 + \frac{1}{2}(Q_3 - Q_1)]$; note that $\frac{1}{2}(Q_3 - Q_1)$ is the area of the triangle shaded /// (this triangle is right-angled because the demand curve D is a straight line). However, some of this gain is simply due to others' losses:

- Country A producers lose the area shaded ||| (equal to $(P_T - P_B) \times [Q_4 + \frac{1}{2}(Q_2 - Q_4)]$)
- The government of country A loses tariff revenue—the area shaded $\equiv$ (equal to $(P_T - P_B) \times (Q_1 - Q_2)$)

The remaining *net* gain to country A consumers consists of the remainder of the increase in consumer surplus (as defined above) in Fig. A1.1:

- the area shaded \\\: $(P_T - P_B) \times \frac{1}{2}(Q_2 - Q_4)$
- the area shaded ///: $(P_T - P_B) \times \frac{1}{2}(Q_3 - Q_1)$

Against this gain must be offset the economic losses from trade diversion. Before the customs union country A purchased the good at the world price P_W; the difference between this and the country A price, P_T, accrued in tariff revenue to country A's government. A portion of this forgone revenue (represented by the area shaded $\equiv$) accrues to consumers; the remainder represents the cost of supply from a more expensive source. This loss from trade diversion is shown by

- the area shaded ⸬⸬⸬: $(P_B - P_W) \times (Q_1 - Q_2)$

There is also a welfare effect in country B: producers benefit from selling an increased quantity at a higher price. This gain is shown in Fig. A1.2 as an increase in producer surplus, measured by the aggregate difference between the prices at which producers are willing to supply a quantity of the good (shown by the supply curve S_B in Fig. A1.2) and the price they actually obtain in the market, which increases from P_B^0 to P_B). The gain to producers is shown in Fig. A1.2 by the aggregate of the two shaded areas between P_B and P_B^0; formally, this is measured as

$$(P_B - P_B^0) \times [Q_B^0 + \frac{1}{2}(Q_B^2 - Q_B^0)].$$

However some of this gain is at the expense of country B consumers, who lose consumers surplus shown by:

- the area shaded XXX: $(P_B - P_B^0) \times [Q_B^1 + \frac{1}{2}(Q_B^0 - Q_B^1)]$

Hence the *net* gain to country B producers is shown by:

- the area shaded $\begin{smallmatrix}+++\\+++\end{smallmatrix}$: $(P_B - P_B^0) \times \frac{1}{2}[(Q_B^0 - Q_B^1) + (Q_B^2 - Q_B^0)]$

The overall effect is determined by

- the gains from trade creation and expansion:
  - \\\ (Fig. A1.1)
  - *plus*
  - /// (Fig. A1.1)
  - *plus*
  - +++ (Fig. A1.2)
    +++
- *minus*
- the losses from trade diversion:
  - ⸬⸬⸬ (Fig 1.1)

The aggregate net effect of trade creation and diversion may be positive, zero or negative.

The overall outcome of the establishment of a customs union would thus be a combination of:

1. *trade creation*, as member states are encouraged to specialize in those areas of economic activity in which they have a cost advantage;
2. *trade diversion*, as tariffs confer a competitive advantage on higher-cost producers within the customs union;
3. *trade expansion*, as the removal of tariff barriers within the customs union leads to lower prices and thus stimulates demand.

The preceding illustration was simplified for the purpose of exposition, so that the customs union had only two members, trading in a single good. Where a customs union includes several member states, the trade creation and diversion effects may well vary considerably between countries, adding to the complexity of assessment of the ultimate impact. Furthermore, a customs union that becomes a significant presence in the world economy may affect the prices at which its members trade. (*Technically, this is referred to as a change in the terms of trade in favour of the customs union.*)

The previous analysis of countries A and B (Figs. A1.1 and A1.2) assumed that the price of imports from the rest of the world (i.e. countries outside the customs union) was constant (P_W in Fig. 1.1—*in technical terms, the elasticity of supply is infinite*). This implies that the markets in countries A and B are small in comparison to the world market, and so changes in the amounts which they import have no influence on the world market price. This assumption may be valid for imports into a single country, but is less plausible for a customs union with several members.

If the customs union leads to substantial trade diversion, its members' demand for imports from the rest of the world declines. The extent of the reduction in imports will depend upon the change in the world market price. This effect is illustrated in Fig. A1.3. The quantities that will be supplied in the world market at different levels of price are shown by the supply curve S_w. The aggregate customs union demand is shown by the curve ΣD: this represents the sum of quantities demanded in the customs union member states, *net of* the sum of the quantities supplied from within the customs union itself; prices are net of tariffs. The initial quantity demanded by the customs union is Q_0, at a world market price P_0.

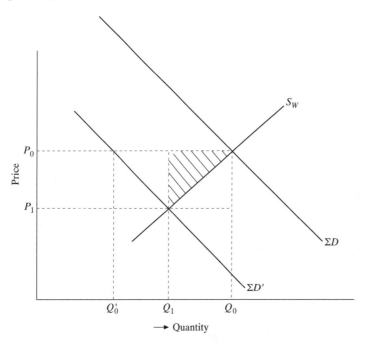

Figure A1.3 Impact of a large customs union which affects world market prices

If trade diversion leads to a reduction in demand, so that the customs union demand curve becomes $\Sigma D'$, the world market price is lowered to P_1, and the customs union imports quantity Q_1. (If the world market supply were infinitely elastic at price P_0, the quantity would be reduced to Q_0'.)

The lowering of the world market price has the effect of mitigating the diversion of trade, since the low-cost world producers are able to retain some sales which they would otherwise have lost. The reduction in price also changes the terms of trade, in favour of the customs union and against the rest of the world; thus, trade diversion has caused world producers to suffer a loss in welfare through a reduction in producer surplus. (This is shown in Fig. A1.3 by the area shaded \\\.)

Changes in the structure and volume of trade can also have an indirect influence on prices of traded goods if the costs of the goods are subject to *economies of scale*, so that producers' costs per unit of output decline as the scale of production increases. If efficient production requires a minimum level of output, and a single country is too small a market to absorb this output, there may be a gain from restructuring the industry within a customs union.

This is illustrated by Figure A1.4. Country A has a single producer of the traded good: average costs per unit of production are shown by the curve AC_A. These costs vary with output up to quantity Q_0, and the downward slope of the curve indicates that unit costs are declining up to Q_0, owing to economies of scale. Output Q_0 therefore denotes the *minimum efficient size* of producer.

Demand in country A is shown by D_A. It is assumed that the single producer has no other markets, so that country A is not an exporter of the good. In order to cover costs at price P_0, the supplier must sell a quantity of at least Q_0. However, country A's market is too small: if the producer supplied output Q_0 at price P_0, it would be possible to sell only Q_0', which is the quantity consumers are prepared to buy at price P_0 (given by the demand curve D_A). The producer can be viable with tariff protection, provided that the resulting price to the consumer is at least P_M. At this price, and with consumption Q_M (given by the demand curve D_A), the price of the good equals the average cost per unit (given by the cost curve AC_A). However, output Q_M is below the minimum efficient level (Q_0) and so the price charged to consumers exceeds the cost per unit at Q_0; the difference is measured by ($P_M - P_0$). The effect of the tariff is to keep out imports which might otherwise be supplied by producers at or above minimum efficient size, charging a price of P_0.

If country A joins in a customs union, the aggregate demand in all member states may be sufficiently large to permit the realization of economies of scale. If the customs union comprises

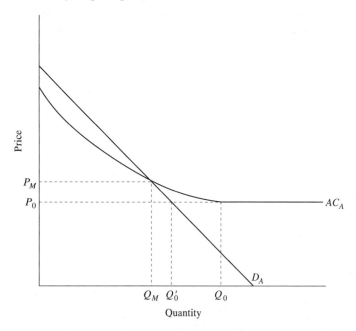

Figure A1.4 Realization of economies of scale within a customs union

N countries, and all members of the customs union have the same pattern of costs and demand as country A (as shown in Figure A1.4), the total size of the market at price P_0 would be $N \times Q_0'$. However the maximum number of producers that this market could support would be given by the aggregate demand for all countries in the customs union, divided by the level of output at minimum efficient size (Q_0), i.e.:

$$\frac{N \times Q_0'}{Q_0}$$

This is less than the number of countries in the customs union, N (since Q_0' is less than Q_0). Consequently there will need to be a restructuring following the inauguration of the customs union, with a reduction in the number of producers. Some producers will expand output up to, or beyond, Q_0; others will cease production altogether.

In this example the customs union is, on the whole, beneficial, since average costs of production are reduced (from P_M to P_0). The gain to consumers would depend on market conditions and tariffs before and after the customs union; other things being equal, the prospects for a competitive market structure would be better in a customs union with several producers than in a single country outside the customs union.

The gains from factor mobility are illustrated in Fig. A1.5. In this illustration there is a single factor of production, units of which are identical to one another (i.e. they are *homogeneous*); the initial availability of the factor is Q_A in country A and Q_B in country B. (It is assumed that the aggregate availability is fixed at ($Q_A + Q_B$).) The gain from employment of an additional unit of the factor (its *marginal productivity*) varies with the quantity of factor input (Q): this relationship is shown for countries A and B respectively by the curves MP_A (Fig. A1.5(a)) and MP_B (Fig. A1.5(b)). With no factor mobility between the two countries, the marginal productivity (employing quantity Q_A) in country A is P_A; in country B marginal productivity is higher, at P_B. If one unit of the factor were to move from country A to country B, its marginal productivity would increase from P_A to P_B; and there would be an incentive for movement to country B until marginal productivity in the two countries is equalized at P_C. At this point a quantity ($Q_A - Q_A'$) in Fig. A1.5(a) (equal to ($Q_B' - Q_B$) in Fig. A1.5(b)) has moved to country B, increasing the quantity of the factor in that country from Q_B to Q_B'. The overall gain from mobility is measured by the difference in marginal productivity for each unit of the factor, aggregated for all units moving to country B: this is shown in Fig. A1.5(b) by the area shaded $\equiv$ (equal to $\frac{1}{2}(P_B - P_A)(Q_B' - Q_B)$).

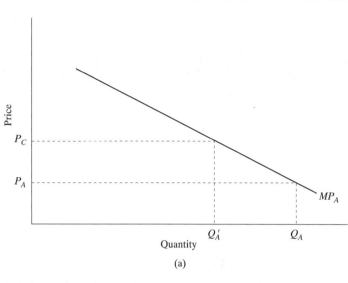

(a)

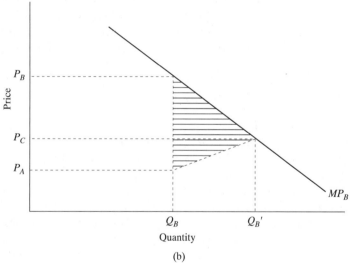

(b)

Figure A1.5   Gains from factor mobility: (a) Effect in country of emigration
(b) Effect in country of immigration

THE STRUCTURE AND INSTITUTIONS OF THE EUROPEAN COMMUNITY

The previous chapter showed how the European Community was created in the difficult economic and political circumstances following the Second World War. The principal motivation of the Community's founders was to increase prosperity through the development of a common market: this called for the removal of barriers to movement within the Community, and consequently required an institutional mechanism to co-ordinate policies in areas concerned with the functioning of the common market. The present chapter outlines the institutional structure of the Community, and analyses the role of the Community itself, and the part played by its institutions—the Council, the Commission and the Parliament—in decision-making. The chapter concludes with a discussion of the Community's legal system, and the implementation of Community law.

As a political entity, the European Community is difficult to categorize, in a world of sovereign nation states which co-operate through membership of numerous international organizations. It is in some respects unique, and even paradoxical: an international body with many of the attributes of a nation state. The Community has powers to enact legislation which is binding in all member states, an independent executive body with responsibility for implementation of legislative measures, and a judicial system in which members of the public may seek redress. The Community also has diplomatic relations with non member countries, and is a party to numerous bilateral and multilateral international agreements.

Yet it is not a nation state—at least, not as the term is currently understood. The Community has no elected government and no armed forces. Its framework is a series of Treaties between sovereign states, and national governments control its most powerful institution, the Council of Ministers. The Community's executive body, the Commission, is appointed by the Council. The elected Parliament has only limited powers over legislation and the Community budget. Foreign policy (apart from trade and development assistance) is a matter for intergovernmental co-operation between member states—and the Community as such has no formal role in defence matters.

2.1 THE INSTITUTIONAL STRUCTURE

Although there are three separate Treaties (and so, technically, three Communities), the main Community institutions are common to all three. There was from the beginning a single Court of Justice and a single European Assembly (the forerunner of the European Parliament). A single Commission (known in the original ECSC Treaty as the 'High Authority') and a single Council of ministers were established by the Brussels Treaty of 1965 (the 'Merger Treaty'). The powers and responsibilities of institutions and the form of legislation may nevertheless differ depending upon which treaty provides the legal basis for Community action.

2.1.1   The Council

The Community was created by a group of sovereign states, and its purpose was to provide an institutional framework to go beyond *ad hoc* co-operation between governments. The member states, collectively, have a decisive role in the Community's decision-making structure through the *Council of Ministers*, which consists of representatives of the member states. These are usually government ministers, and the foreign minister is normally the main representative. Other ministers meet regularly to discuss particular areas of policy, in specialized Council meetings. (These include internal market, economic and financial affairs, social affairs, industry, agriculture, environment, energy and transport Councils.) Representatives of the Commission attend meetings of the Council and its subordinate bodies.

Each member state has a permanent representation to the Community, headed by an official with the rank of ambassador. These officials come together in the *Committee of Permanent Representatives* (COREPER), which is responsible for preparation of the work of the Council and, in particular, for defining issues that require a political decision at ministerial level.

Initial discussion of legislative Proposals is undertaken by Council *working groups*, which consist of officials from permanent representations and experts from member states. There are many such groups, and participation depends upon the issues that are discussed.

The presidency of the Council rotates between member states at six-monthly intervals: the schedule of Presidencies is shown in Box 2.1. The presidency sets the agenda for the Council, and meetings at all levels—Council, COREPER and working groups—are chaired by delegates from the member state that holds the presidency; the national interests of that state are separately represented.

The *European Council* is the very highest level of decision-making within the Community (and for the European Union as a whole). It consists of the heads of state or government of member states, and the president of the Commission; meetings are held twice yearly, once under

---

BOX 2.1
European Union: council presidencies, 1995–2003

Year	Half	
	1st	2nd
1995	France	Spain
1996	Italy	Ireland
1997	Netherlands	Luxembourg
1998	UK	Austria
1999	Germany	Finland
2000	Portugal	France
2001	Sweden	Belgium
2002	Spain	Denmark
2003	Greece	

Source: Decision of 1 January 1995, determining the order in which the office of President of the Council shall be held, *Official Journal*, 1995 L1/220.

each presidency. The European Council is not normally concerned with the details of legislation; its function is rather to provide political impetus and lay down guidance for the development and policies of the Community (EU Treaty, Article D). Major issues addressed by the European Council since its inception in 1975 include direct elections to the European Parliament, the European Monetary System, reform of agricultural policy, accession of new states, the environment, and assistance to eastern Europe.

2.1.2 The Commission

The Commission is the Community's executive arm, and as such its role is in some respects analogous to that of a national government. The crucial differences are that the Commission is unelected, and its president has only a consultative role in the selection of other Commission members.

The Commission has two main areas of responsibility: the development and the implementation of Community legislation. Thus, the Treaties accord to the Commission:

1. the exclusive right to initiate formal Proposals for Community legislation;
2. the role of 'guardian' of the Treaties.

Organization of the Commission   The procedure for appointment of the Commission is laid down in Article 158 of the EC Treaty. The Commission president is nominated by common accord of the governments of the member states, after consulting the European Parliament. The governments, in consultation with the presidential nominee, then nominate the other members of the Commission. The Commission thus nominated is subject to a vote of approval by the Parliament, which votes for (or against) the Commission as a body (but does *not* vote on individual members).

Commissioners are enjoined to act in the interest of the Community and not to accept instructions from any national government: by the same token, member states must not seek to influence Commissioners in the performance of their duties (Article 157 EC).

Members of the Commission are therefore not representatives of their country or its government (this is the role the Council of Ministers); the only specification in the Treaties with respect to nationality is that each member state should have at least one, but not more than two, of the twenty Commissioners (Article 157 EC). In practice, two members are drawn from each of the larger countries (France, Germany, Italy, Spain and the UK), while the other countries each have one Commissioner; and close contact is usually maintained between Commissioners and the governments of their home countries.

Commissioners, like ministers in national governments, are allocated portfolios—specific areas of responsibility, subject to the overall collective responsibility of the Commission as a whole.

The Commission has its own support staff. Each Commissioner has a personal staff, known as a *Cabinet*, most (but not all) of whom are of the same nationality as the Commissioner. Responsibilities of Cabinets include assisting their Commissioners in their contributions to the work of the Commission, liaison with officials in other Commission services, and contact with other institutions, with member states and with the general public.

The Commission services are organized in 23 directorates general (DGs) and several other services (most of which support the work of the DGs); the services are listed in Box 2.2. The responsibilities of Commissioners do not necessarily coincide with those of DGs— a Commissioner's portfolio may cover areas that are the responsibility of more than one

BOX 2.2
The Commission services, 1994

Directorates General (DGs)

I	External economic relations
IA	External political relations
II	Economic and financial affairs
III	Industry
IV	Competition
V	Employment, industrial relations and social affairs
VI	Agriculture
VII	Transport
VIII	Development
IX	Personnel and administration
X	Audiovisual media, information, communication and culture
XI	Environment, nuclear safety and civil protection
XII	Science, research and development
XIII	Telecommunications, information market and exploitation of research
XIV	Fisheries
XV	Internal market and financial services
XVI	Regional policies
XVII	Energy
XVIII	Credit and investments
XIX	Budgets
XX	Financial control
XXI	Customs and indirect taxation
XXIII	Enterprise policy, distributive trades, tourism and co-operatives

Other services

Secretariat General	Publications Office
Inspectorate General	Informatics Directorate
Legal Service	Consumer Policy Service
Spokesman's Service	Euratom Supply Agency
Security Office	Humanitarian Office
Translation Service	Task Force for Human Resources, Education,
Interpreting and Conference Service	Training and Youth

DG, and a directorate general may report to more than one Commissioner for different areas of its work.

In addition to its role as the initiator of legislative Proposals, the Commission is also responsible, as the Community's executive body, for action to secure observance of the Treaties themselves and of Community legislation in the framework of the Treaties. Perhaps the Commission's most notable feature in this context is the small size of its support staff. There are approximately 13 000 Commission officials employed in areas immediately related to policy—and almost 20 per cent of their workload is concerned with translation and other language-related tasks. (In 1995 the Commission policy services had an establishment of 14 769 permanent posts, of which 1634 were for translators (European Parliament 1994b: 162).) This does not amount to a substantial bureaucracy—it is smaller than the staff of many government ministries in member states.

2.1.3 The European Parliament

The functions of the Parliament are analogous to those of a national legislature, in legislation, control of the budget, approval of international agreements and oversight of the executive. However, the European Parliament's powers are comparatively circumscribed, notwithstanding the enhancement of its position following the treaty amendments by the Single European Act in 1987 and the EU Treaty in 1993.

The Community has had a directly elected Parliament since 1979. The number of members from each member state (as specified in the Treaties) is shown in Table 2.1. Although the Parliament consists of 'representatives of the peoples' (Article 137 EC), representation is by no means uniform. Smaller countries are proportionately better represented, as is shown by the number of members per 1 million of the population: the lowest figure of 1.2 for Germany compares with 4.2 for Ireland and 15.4 for the smallest country, Luxembourg.

The procedure for electing members of the Parliament is governed by national provisions and varies between member states. All countries use some form of proportional representation, except for Britain (but not Northern Ireland), which has a 'first past the post' system with single-member constituencies. There is provision in the Treaties for the Parliament to draw up proposals for a uniform electoral procedure; the Council must then unanimously agree appropriate provisions to be recommended to the member states (Article 138(3) EC).

Table 2.1 Representation in the European Parliament, by member state

	Members*	% of total membership	Members per 1m population
Belgium	25	4.0	2.5
Denmark	16	2.6	3.1
Germany	99	15.8	1.2
Greece	25	4.0	2.4
Spain	64	10.2	1.6
France	87	13.9	1.5
Ireland	15	2.4	4.2
Italy	87	13.9	1.5
Luxembourg	6	1.0	15.4
Netherlands	31	5.0	2.0
Austria	21	3.4	2.7
Portugal	25	4.0	2.5
Finland	16	2.6	3.2
Sweden	22	3.5	2.5
United Kingdom	87	13.9	1.5
European Union	626	100.0	1.7

* The number of representatives of each member state is specified in the EC Treaty, Article 138.

Members of the Parliament sit in party, rather than national, groupings, and the main groups include members from several countries. The strength of the party groups by country in the European Parliament in 1995 (following the 1994 elections, and the 1995 enlargement) is shown in Table 2.2. Since the Community is not a parliamentary system of government, with an executive drawn from members of parliament, there is less intense party discipline than in many national parliaments; and members must also consider national interests. In this respect the Parliament may be more comparable to the Congress of the United States.

Table 2.2   The European Parliament: distribution of members by political group and by country, January 1995

	A	B	DK	FIN	FR	GER	GR	IR	IT	L	NL	PT	SP	SW	UK	Total
Socialists	8	6	3	4	15	40	10	1	18	2	8	10	22	11	63	221
Christian Democrats	6	7	3	4	13	47	9	4	12	2	10	1	30	6	19	173
Liberals	1	6	5	6	1			1	6	1	10	8	2	3	2	52
United Left			1	1	7		4		5			3	9	1		31
Forza Europa									29							29
Democratic Alliance					14		2	7				3				26
Greens	1	2		1		12		2	4	1	1			1		25
Radical Alliance		1			13				2				1		2	19
Europe of Nations			4		13							2				19
Independents	5	3			11				11						1	31
Total	21	25	16	16	87	99	25	15	87	6	31	25	64	22	87	626

Note: Representatives from the member states that acceded in 1995 (Austria, Finland and Sweden) were nominated by their national parliaments, pending European Parliament elections.

Source: European Parliament.

The Parliament has numerous committees to deal with particular areas of policy: these are listed in Box 2.3, which also shows the number of members on each committee in 1995. Proposals for consideration by the Parliament are normally referred to the appropriate committee for detailed consideration; a member of the committee is appointed *rapporteur*, with responsibility for preparing the report which the committee then agrees and submits to the Parliament in plenary session.

BOX 2.3
The European Parliament committees, January 1995*

Foreign Affairs, Security, and Defence Policy (61)
Agriculture and Rural Development (49)
Budgets (38)
Economic and Monetary Affairs and Industrial Policy (57)
Research, Technological Development and Energy (31)
External Economic Relations (28)
Legal Affairs and Citizens' Rights (26)
Social Affairs and Employment (47)
Regional Policy (40)
Transport and Tourism (39)
Environment, Public Health and Consumer Protection (50)
Culture, Youth, Education and the Media (39)
Development and Co-operation (37)
Civil Liberties and Internal Affairs (35)
Budgetary Control (27)
Institutional Affairs (45)
Fisheries (25)
Rules of Procedure, Verification of Credentials and Immunities (28)
Women's Rights (39)
Petitions (29)

* Numbers of members are given in parenthesis
Source: European Parliament.

2.1.4 Advisory bodies

The Community decision-making process includes advisory bodies representing economic and social interest groups in member states.

The Economic and Social Committee   This is a Community institution established under the EC Treaty (Article 193). It has 222 members, with a quota for each country; members are appointed by the Council, from lists provided by member states. The Committee comprises representatives of three groups: employers, employees and other interest groups; the 'other' category includes representatives from bodies such as consumer groups, the professions, organizations of small and medium-sized enterprises, environmental groups and scientific bodies. At a working level the Committee has nine sections, dealing with the principal areas covered by the EC Treaty, and may establish *ad hoc* subcommittees to deal with specific topics.

The Committee produces Opinions on Community issues: these may be following referrals from the Council or the Commission, or may be produced by the Committee on its own initiative. Opinions are adopted at plenary meetings of the full Committee, on the basis of a draft prepared by the relevant section. The EC Treaty requires that the Committee be consulted on legislative Proposals in the main areas of Community policy. Amendments proposed in its Opinions may be incorporated in revisions of Commission proposals, or adopted in legislation enacted by the Council. On average, the Committee delivers 120 Opinions per year.

The ECSC Treaty (Article 18) provides for a 'Consultative Committee', attached to the

Commission, with a role similar to that of the Economic and Social Committee: it may have between 72 and 96 members, comprising equal numbers of producers, workers, consumers and dealers from the coal and steel industries.

The Committee of the Regions   This Committee was established in 1993 by the EU Treaty. It has 222 members representing regional and local authorities in member states; members are appointed by the Council following nomination by member states (Article 198a EC). The Committee has a consultative role similar to that of the Economic and Social Committee; the EC Treaty specifies certain areas with a strong regional dimension where consultation is obligatory (see Appendix 2.1), but the Committee also has the right to issue Opinions in other areas if it feels that regional or local issues are important.

2.1.5   Specialized agencies

In addition to the institutions listed above, the Community is served by a number of specialized agencies, which cover a wide range of responsibilities. The *European Investment Bank* was created in 1958, and now has a key role in the financing of investments, and particularly infrastructure projects in less prosperous regions; the Bank uses its high credit rating to borrow at low rates of interest, and thus is able to lend at favourable rates. The *European Monetary Institute* co-ordinates monetary policy and is responsible for preparations for a Community currency and a European Central Bank (see Chapter 5). Other agencies serve the Community in a variety of ways: for example, *Europol* co-ordinates the activities of police forces, the *European Environment Agency* provides information on the state of the environment, and the *Agency for the Evaluation of Medicinal Products* is responsible for assessment of medicines and their approval for use. The development of many of these agencies was held back until the Council eventually agreed their locations late in 1993. The agencies and their locations are listed in Box 2.4.

2.2   THE ROLE OF THE COMMUNITY: THE SUBSIDIARITY PRINCIPLE

The Community institutions described above each play their part in the Community decision-making process, the Council representing national interests, the Commission initiating and implementing, the Parliament representing the peoples of the member states, and the Economic and Social Committee (and the ECSC Consultative Committee) and the Committee of the Regions giving advice.

Before examining the decision-making procedures in detail, consideration must be given to broader issues concerning the nature of the Community, in a world of legally sovereign nation states, and the criteria for defining the role of the Community and governments at national, regional and local level.

2.2.1   A 'superstate'?

How far have economic and political forces led the Community in the direction of a 'United States of Europe'? Some light may be shed on this issue by reference to the idealized models set out in Sec. 1.1.3. The Community as it actually functions has elements of both pluralism and federalism, and, while a case can be made that the Community is an embryonic 'superstate', there are also counter-arguments that it is merely a well developed framework for co-operation between nation states.

BOX 2.4
European Community specialized institutions

Institution	Location
European Investment Bank	Luxembourg
European Patent Office	Munich, Germany
Joint Research Centre	Ispra, Italy
European Foundations for Living and Working Conditions	Dublin, Ireland
European Environment Agency	Copenhagen, Denmark
European Training Foundation	Turin, Italy
European Veterinary and Plant Health Inspection Office	Dublin, Ireland
European Agency for the Evaluation of Medicinal Products	London, UK
European Monitoring Centre for Drugs and Drug Addiction	Lisbon, Portugal
European Monetary Institute	Frankfurt, Germany
European Trademark Office	Alicante, Spain
European Agency for Health and Safety at Work	Bilbao, Spain
Europol	The Hague, Netherlands
European Centre for the Development of Vocational Training	Thessaloniki, Greece*

*Moved from Berlin (see Article 1 of the Decision on the location of the seats of certain bodies and departments of the European Community and of Europol, *Official Journal*, 1993 C323/1).

The nation state/functionalist perspective emphasizes the crucial position of the Council of Ministers—although the Commission proposes, the Council disposes. No Community legislation can be enacted without the consent of the Council, and member states have extensive powers to veto proposed Community initiatives, since in many (but not all) instances the Council's decisions require a unanimous vote of the member states. More generally, vital national interests are acknowledged in the search for wide agreement on legislative proposals; and the need to respect such interests was formally agreed in the 1966 'Luxembourg compromise' (see Sec. 2.3.1), and in the 1993 Council Decision on qualified majority voting (see Sec. 2.5.2). It can thus be argued that in practice the sovereignty of member states remains intact, and the Community performs only those functions that are delegated to it by agreement under the Treaties or by subsequent legislation.

On the other hand, those who see the Community as an embryonic 'superstate', can point to its structure of supranational institutions. Specifically, the Commission and the European Parliament—bodies independent of national governments—have essential roles in the legislative process. Moreover, Community law overrides national law: adherence to the Treaties entails acceptance of Community legislation and the jurisdiction of the European Court of Justice, which can overrule decisions of national courts. Even in the Council national sovereignty is not absolute: in some important areas of legislation the Treaties provide for the Council to decide by qualified majority, rather than unanimity—so that member states do not have a general power of veto.

In practice, power within the Community is balanced between its institutions. As the creators of the Community, member states began from a position of strength, since they devised the framework for its decision-making processes. However, their action may also be construed as an admission of weakness, inasmuch as the Community, with its institutional structure, had a purpose which could not be adequately served by a looser form of co-operation. This implied an acknowledgement of the limitations of bilateral or multilateral agreements between sovereign states. Tension between Council, Commission and Parliament can be seen as an inherent feature of the Community's organizational structure, and the working relationships between institutions continue to develop in response to events and the challenges that arise from them.

Underlying these institutional tensions is the fundamental issue of the role of the Community itself. The founder member states created the Community for a purpose, i.e. in order to raise standards of living; and they evidently believed that the supranational structure of the Community offered advantages over bilateral co-operation between themselves. This means that in some circumstances the Community could act more effectively than its member states. Questions then arise: how are these circumstances to be defined? and what are the respective roles of the Community and of authorities in member states? Answers to these questions have been sought in the doctrine of *subsidiarity*.

2.2.2   Subsidiarity: defining the role of the Community

Subsidiarity has become standard Eurojargon. It has been extensively invoked in political debates concerning the future of the Community, in support of a variety of positions with respect to issues such as federalism and centralization.

Such debates impinge upon—and frequently obscure—some fundamental philosophical issues concerning the purpose of political institutions and the nature of sovereignty. It can be argued that for the individual citizen the important question is how the activities of these institutions can contribute to the quality of life. So governments at all levels (local, regional and national) and international organizations must justify their roles in the provision of services. From this perspective, sovereignty resides in the people, who may delegate powers to whatever institution is most appropriate, whether it be a local council, a national government, or a supranational authority.

Hence subsidiarity is a general philosophical principle, whereby individuals are supported *where necessary* by their families, their peers, the community, and various types of organization, both governmental and non-governmental. Individuals therefore delegate certain rights and responsibilities which can be exercised more effectively on their behalf. In political theory, this type of arrangement is characterized as a 'social contract' between the people and their rulers.

Organizations can delegate in a similar fashion. If there are tasks that cannot be performed satisfactorily by a municipality, responsibility may be assumed at the regional or national level of government; by the same token, policy measures should be taken at a supranational level where action at national (or lower) level will not yield satisfactory results.

It should be emphasized that subsidiarity as a principle is applicable at *all* levels. In the contest for power, national governments may seek rigorously to apply this principle in their relations with the Community, but not with local or regional governments; however, adherence to a principle, by its nature, requires consistency.

The Community and national governments   In the political context of relations between the Community and national governments, the subsidiarity principle establishes a presumption that, as far as possible, responsibility for policies and decision-making should be decentralized, unless centralization offers a significant advantage. The Commission has expressed its view of subsidiarity as meaning that 'decisions are taken as close as possible to the citizen' (COM(93)545, p. 1). Hence policy measures at Community level should be confined to those instances where action taken exclusively at local or national level would yield less satisfactory results.

Despite its frequent invocation in political debates concerning the Community, until recently the only formal legal basis for subsidiarity was in Article 130r of the EEC Treaty, relating to the environment, as follows:

The Community shall take action ... to the extent to which [Treaty] objectives ... can be attained better at Community level than at the level of the individual Member States.

The Treaty on European Union deleted the above provision, and introduced a general statement on the limits of Community action (Article 3b EC):

The Community shall act within the limits of the powers conferred upon it by this Treaty and of the objectives assigned to it therein.

In areas which do not fall within its exclusive competence, the Community shall take action, in accordance with the principle of subsidiarity, only if and in so far as the objectives of the proposed action cannot be sufficiently achieved by the Member States and can therefore, by reason of the scale or effects of the proposed action, be better achieved by the Community.

Any action by the Community shall not go beyond what is necessary to achieve the objectives of this Treaty.

Arguably the concept is expressed more clearly and succinctly by the Tenth Amendment to the Constitution of the United States, which reads as follows:

The powers not delegated to the United States by the constitution, nor prohibited by it to the states, are reserved to the states respectively, or to the people

or in the German Basic Law, which states that:

The exercise of governmental powers and the discharge of governmental functions shall be incumbent on the Länder in so far as this Basic Law does not otherwise prescribe or permit.

These legal provisions beg fundamental questions: What are the criteria for deciding the extent of the Community's role? And what form does Community intervention take? Substantial disagreements arise when these questions are addressed; and the points at issue are liable to be obscured by confusions over the meaning and interpretation of terms such as 'subsidiarity', in spite of (or possibly because of) the use of a common terminology.

One element of disagreement concerns the extent to which Community objectives can be achieved by co-operation between national governments, as opposed to initiatives at Community level. This is an issue that arises across the range of policy areas. For example, the completion of the Community's single market framework could have been achieved by various combinations of Community and national policy measures. At one extreme, a common market could operate purely through the mutual recognition by member states of national product standards; at the other extreme, the different national standards could be completely supplanted by detailed Community legislation. In practice, the Community has in recent years sought to follow a pragmatic middle course, pursuing harmonization of national standards to the extent necessary to achieve the economic benefits of the common market, and to ensure minimum standards for health, safety, environmental and consumer protection. (This approach was adopted in the Commission's programme for completion of the internal market—see Sec. 3.1.2.)

The Community and regional and local governments   The role of the Community and national administrations is also a matter of legitimate concern to lower levels of government within member states, particularly where there is a strong regional structure, as in Germany, Belgium or Spain. In those member states with a federal constitution, Community legislation often impinges on areas within the competence of a regional administration. Lower levels of government—such as the German Länder—engage in lobbying their national governments and also Community institutions, and have a consultative role in the Committee of the Regions (see Sec. 2.1.4).

The absence until recently of a direct regional input to the Community decision-making processes has given rise to certain difficulties. National governments are remote from 'grass-roots' policy-making in areas that are primarily the responsibility of regional administrations—and this is liable to detract from the quality of their input to the Community legislative process. Moreover, action to implement eventual Community legislation in these areas is a matter for the regional government, and difficulties have arisen in ensuring consistent application of legislative provisions which were never subject to the formal approval of the regional adminstration. For example, in Germany there are differences in policy instruments between the Länder, so that it is difficult to determine the consistency of legislation; while in Belgium the regional administrations (particularly in Wallonia) have delayed the enactment of measures necessary to implement Community legislation in areas where central government lacks legislative powers (European Commission 1991: 209–10).

Community intervention can also give rise to constitutional problems: it may have a 'side-effect' on the distribution of power in member states between national and regional administrations. The national government has responsibility both for representation in the Council and for ensuring that Community legislation is implemented. This can lead to problems when the Community seeks to legislate in areas which under national constitutions are primarily (or exclusively) a matter for regional administrations. For example, prior to the EU Treaty the German Länder opposed Community legislation on education and cultural matters, on the grounds that the German federal government has no right to conclude agreements in these areas, which under the constitution are the responsibility of the Länder (Wilkie and Wallace 1990: 33).

2.2.3   Application of the subsidiarity principle

Practical application of a theoretical concept is usually subject to complications, and the subsidiarity principle is no exception. In reality, policy issues are usually multi-faceted and multi-dimensional; and policy instruments are deployed at different levels (Community, national, regional and local) to attain a variety of objectives, defined with varying degrees of explicitness and precision. Thus, subsidiarity is not, and cannot be, a 'mechanistic' system for allocating exclusive competence over separate, and self-contained, areas of policy. A single objective may come within a number of areas of policy, and its achievement may depend upon policy measures taken at various levels.

Policy interventions   It is therefore not a straightforward matter to define the tasks to be performed by the Community. A Community dimension may arise if there are Treaty provisions relevant to any facet either of the problem, or of potential solutions. This can be illustrated by considering the interrelationships between two areas of policy that figure in the EC Treaty, the single market and environmental policy:

1. The Community is empowered (under Articles 85–102 EC) to take action necessary to facilitate the operation of the single market.
2. There is provision for Community action (under Article 130s EC) in so far as environmental objectives cannot be sufficiently achieved by action at national or local level.

Table 2.3   Possible interactions between Community areas of responsibility

		MARKET IMPACT	
		European Community	*National*
ENVIRONMENTAL IMPACT	European Community	I	II
	National	III	IV

Either, or both, of these sections of the Treaty may provide a basis for Community action in the context of a specific policy issue. Thus, a Community interest can arise in various ways:

- where environmental problems transcend boundaries between member states
- where Community level action is required because national policy measures give rise to barriers between member states
- where, in the absence of co-ordination at Community level, policy measures in member states are not sufficiently effective, or have undesirable side-effects.

The last two points illustrate the interactions (and interdependence) between the Community areas of responsibility with respect to the environment and economic matters. Where policy measures may lead to distortions of trade or competition, there is a basis for Community intervention, even if the environmental problems are confined to a single member state.

The various possibilities are shown (in a simplified representation) in Table 2.3 (It must be emphasized that, for the purposes of this illustration, it is assumed that there is no other basis for Community intervention.) Taking these cases in turn:

I. There is both an economic and an environmental basis for action at Community level—one example is emission standards for vehicles, which are driven, and traded, across national frontiers.
II. There is a Community dimension purely for environmental reasons—as for example in the case of trans-frontier pollution from sources such as power stations.
III. National environmental measures—such as product standards, taxes or subsidies—affect the functioning of the single market through their effect on trade between member states.
IV. There is no direct Community involvement—for example in the implementation of local land use regulations.

In practice, policies have many facets, and it is not feasible to delineate exclusive areas of competence for the Community or national levels. In many instances—such as energy, consumer protection and environmental policies—the Community's role has evolved pragmatically as the common market has developed.

Furthermore, there is considerable interdependence between policies at different levels. For example, measures to combat air pollution from mobile sources, such as motor vehicles, call for co-operation between the Community and various levels of government, each acting within its own area of competence. The Community has responsibility for vehicle emission standards, because motor vehicles are a product traded across national frontiers, and a single market requires common standards for such products (and there are now several Directives which specify these standards). On the other hand, air quality tends to deteriorate as vehicle density increases, so that additional measures—such as urban traffic management and detailed land use planning—are required to safeguard the urban environment; these measures are the responsibility of local authorities.

Hence there is a symbiotic relationship between policy measures at different levels. In aggregate, local requirements have an influence upon decisions with respect to Community standards, while the latter, when established, constitute the background against which decisions are taken at local level.

Subsidiarity and Community policy measures   The Commission has characterized subsidiarity as 'a state of mind' and 'first and foremost a political principle', the function of which is not to distribute powers, but rather to regulate the use of the powers conferred by the Treaties and to justify their use in particular circumstances (COM(93)545, p. 2).

In the light of the subsidiarity requirements of Article 3b of the EC Treaty (see Sec. 2.2.2), the Commission has proposed three questions to be addressed when a policy initiative is under consideration (COM(93)545, p. 1):

1. What is the Community dimension of the problem?
2. What is the most effective solution?
3. What is the added value of common action rather than action by individual member states?

The European Council in 1992 called on the Commission to review existing and proposed Community legislation in the light of the subsidiarity principle. There were, broadly, two motivations: a desire to reassert the role of national governments *vis-à-vis* the Community, and a concern over the levels of expenditure necessary for compliance with Community legislation.

The Commission's subsequent report conceded that there was scope for simplification and consolidation of policy measures, but held out no expectation of wholesale repeal of legislation. In the environmental field, for example, Community legislation needed to focus on essential objectives, while member states could where appropriate add their own supplementary requirements; however, the Commission was adamant that subsidiarity was not a device for lowering standards below the levels specified in existing Community legislation. In other words, the level of decision-making and the level of environmental standards are separate issues; and if the costs of achieving the standards are thought excessive, a case would have to be made for revision, rather than repeal, of Community legislation (COM(93)545, pp. 15–17).

Subsidiarity is applicable in the implementation, as well as the enactment, of legislation. For instance, member states are responsible for measures to achieve the objectives set out in Community Directives (see Sec. 2.6.3). Moreover, detailed administration of Community-funded programmes is usually undertaken by national or local authorities, and not by the Commission.

While the subsidiarity principle defines limits for Community intervention, it should also restrain authorities in member states from seeking to involve the Community in essentially national or local matters. This latter aspect is often overlooked, and its non-observance has led the Commission to complain over 'constant pressure on the Commission to act as arbiter in decisions which are properly taken at national level or below, whether or not European Community funds are involved' (COM(93)67, p. 15).

2.3 COMMUNITY INSTITUTIONS AND THE DECISION-MAKING PROCESS

Changing concepts of the Community's role have been reflected in the relationship between Community institutions. The member states initially devolved substantial elements of sovereignty, in specific areas, to the ECSC High Authority; the EEC Treaty gave more power to member states, through the Council. In the 1960s there was some reassertion of national sovereignty, which tended to reduce the Community's effectiveness in the face of economic recession. This lack of effectiveness—which became characterized as 'Euro-sclerosis'—caused a reaction in favour of new legislative procedures which tended to dilute the power of individual member states and to increase the powers of the European Parliament.

The main Community institutions—the Council, the Commission and the European Parliament—are involved in decision-making procedures under the Treaties, with respect to legislation, the budget and external relations. The Parliament also has supervisory powers over the Commission. The powers of the various institutions are analysed below, from two perspectives:

1. the *formal* powers and responsibilities that are ascribed by the Treaties;
2. the *implicit* balance of power in the inter-institutional bargaining process.

A development of particular significance in this context was the amendment of the EEC Treaty in 1987 (by the Single European Act) with a considerable extension of qualified majority voting in the Council: this meant that in many areas unanimity was no longer essential to enact Community legislation—and so an individual member state would not have a power of veto. In parallel with this change, a new legislative procedure was introduced—the 'Co-operation Procedure'—which tended to enhance the power of the Commission and the Parliament. Subsequently the EU Treaty extended the scope of the Co-operation Procedure and introduced the 'Co-Decision Procedure', under which legislation is enacted jointly by the Parliament and the Council.

2.3.1   Changing relationships between Community institutions

The Community's first Treaty, establishing the Coal and Steel Community in 1951, was concluded against a background of severe economic problems (see Sec. 1.2.3). Amidst the difficulties of post-war reconstruction, the ECSC Treaty gave considerable power to the Commission to direct the coal and steel industries. The Commission is empowered to impose levies on coal and steel production (Article 49), to institute production quotas in times of crisis (Article 58) and to fix maximum and minimum product prices (Article 61). Enactment of legislation under the ECSC Treaty is the responsibility of the Commission (Article 14); in some cases the Council's assent is required, but only in certain specified instances must this assent be unanimous, rather than by majority vote.

Subsequent developments tended to reduce the power of the Commission *vis-à-vis* the Council. The 1957 EEC and Euratom Treaties (Articles 189 and 161 respectively) empower the Council to adopt legislation, albeit normally acting on a Proposal from the Commission. Member states possessed extensive rights of veto, since important decisions were to be taken in the Council by a unanimous vote. Although there was provision for a staged extension of majority voting, this was effectively nullified at the insistence of France, which boycotted the Council for several months in 1965. The French position was accommodated in the 'Luxembourg compromise' in 1966, which committed the Council to strive for unanimity in any case where 'very important interests' of any member state were at stake.

The effect was to swing the balance of power towards national governments, represented in the Council. Nevertheless, the development of the Community as a supranational institution continued to be influenced by economic forces: the recession of the mid-1970s, like the pressures of postwar reconstruction (see Sec. 1.2.1), highlighted the need for economic co-operation.

The unanimity requirement impeded the Community's response to economic crisis, since the collective interest of the Community did not necessarily amount to the sum of (narrowly defined) national interests. Moreover, the Community was still a long way from achieving its original Treaty objectives. Considerable impediments remained to the 'four freedoms' of movement, for people, goods, services and capital; although tariff barriers were being removed, there had been little success in eliminating other barriers within the Community. Urgent action was also required in other areas, such as budgetary policy, and reform of the Common Agricultural Policy.

A growing disparity occurred between the need for Community action and what could actually be achieved. This placed increasing pressure on the Community's decision-making processes, as is illustrated by Table 2.4. The number of Commission Proposals brought forward in 1986 was close to twice the number 12 years earlier. The number of Proposals pending grew almost three-fold over the same period, despite an increase in the rate at which the Council enacted legislation (as measured by the percentage of Proposals adopted within 22 months).

Table 2.4 Commission legislative proposals, percentage adopted, 1975–1986

	No. of proposals	% adopted within 22 months	No. of proposals pending
1975	329	75	45
1979	456	77	68
1981	474	80	92
1984	522	84	112
1986	617	87	120

Source: Sloot and Verschuren (1990: 83).

The result of this pressure was to place majority voting and relations between Community institutions back on the agenda: and this led to the Single European Act, which in 1987 amended the Treaties in three significant respects:

1. extension of qualified majority voting in the Council;
2. increased powers for the European Parliament and the Commission through the 'Co-operation Procedure' (see Sec. 2.3.2);
3. extension of the Community's competence into areas such as regional policy, research and technology and environmental policy.

The Single European Act provided a framework within which the Community could make faster progress towards its original goal of a common market; and the treaty amendments set a target date of 1992 for completion of the Community's single market (see Sec. 3.1.2).

The EU (Maastricht) Treaty, which came into force in 1993,

1. further extended the scope of qualified majority voting and the Co-operation Procedure;
2. further increased the powers of the Parliament through the 'Co-Decision Procedure' (see Sec. 2.3.2);
3. further extended the Community's role, marking out a new policy agenda, which is discussed in Chapters 5 and 6.

2.3.2   The Community's legislative procedures

Much of the work of the Community's institutions is concerned with the legislative processes. The Community—uniquely among international organizations—has power to legislate, and its laws assign rights and responsibilities to member states and to their citizens. The Community's legal system is discussed in Sec. 2.6. The various forms of Community legislation are summarized in Table 2.7 below.

Legislation under the ECSC Treaty is enacted by the Commission: depending on the specific Article on which the legislation is based, the Commission may be required to obtain the assent of the Council and the Opinion of the Consultative Committee established under the Treaty. The most important items of legislation require the unanimous assent of the Council.

Major legislation under the EC Treaty and the Euratom Treaty is enacted by the Council (or, when the Co-Decision Procedure applies, jointly by the Council and the Parliament) acting on a Proposal from the Commission. Depending on the specific Treaty provisions under which legislation is adopted, the Council may act by a qualified majority vote, or only by unanimity. Where the Council acts on a Proposal from the Commission, it may amend the Proposal only by a unanimous vote (Article 189a EC), except where legislation is enacted following agreement in a Conciliation Committee (see p. 68). The Commission is empowered to enact legislation on competition rules for public undertakings (Article 90 EC), and to enact subordinate legislation when this is provided for in legislation enacted by the Council. The European Central Bank (which is to be established following monetary union—see Box 5.4) will also be empowered to enact Regulations and Decisions, in accordance with its Statute and Treaty provisions (Article 108a EC).

There are various legislative procedures, depending on the Article of the Treaty on which the legislation is based and enacted (this is known as the *legal base* of legislation). The Appendix to this chapter lists the Articles of the EC Treaty which provide a legal base for legislation, classified according to the legislative procedures and consultation requirements (if any) that are applicable.

Almost all legislation begins with a Commission Proposal; depending on the legal base, consultation may be required with the Economic and Social Committee and (where there is a significant regional dimension) the Committee of the Regions. Where appropriate, Community legislation is enacted 'having regard' to the Committees' 'Opinions', which are purely advisory.

The legislative role of the Parliament also depends upon the legal base. There are a few Treaty provisions under which the Council decides on a Commission Proposal, but enactment requires the assent of the Parliament; there are also instances in which the Council can enact legislation without being required to consult the Parliament at all. Otherwise there are three alternative legislative procedures involving the Parliament under the EC Treaty: the Consultation Procedure, the Co-operation Procedure and the Co-Decision Procedure. These procedures are summarized in Figs. 2.1, 2.2 and 2.3, which show how Community legislation progresses from a Proposal drawn up by the Commission, via deliberations by the Parliament and advice from the Economic and Social Committee, to enactment by the Council (or by the Parliament and the Council jointly, where the Co-Decision Procedure applies).

Under the *Consultation Procedure*, the Parliament's function is advisory. It gives Opinions on Commission Proposals, to which the Council must 'have regard'. This is the original procedure of the EEC Treaty, and it remains applicable in many areas of legislation.

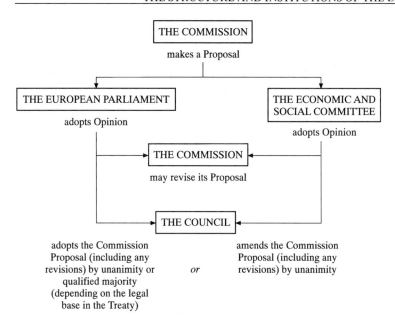

Figure 2.1   Community legislation: the Consultation Procedure

The *Co-operation Procedure* gives the European Parliament influence over legislation, while leaving the final decision with the Council. The procedure (set out in Article 189c EC), was introduced by the Single European Act in 1987, and its use was extended in 1993 by the EU Treaty. Under this procedure, Commission legislative Proposals go to the Parliament for a *first reading*. The Council then adopts a *common position*, by a qualified majority, after obtaining the Parliament's Opinion, and the Commission takes a position on the Parliament's Opinion. The Council and the Commission are required to explain their positions to the Parliament. The Parliament may then have a *second reading*; in which, by a vote of the majority of its members, it may propose amendments to, or reject, the common position of the Council. (If the Parliament does nothing at this stage, the Council's common position is then enacted into legislation.) In the event of rejection, the Council can act upon the Commission Proposal only by unanimity. If the Parliament proposes amendments, the Commission then re-examines its Proposal, and sends a revised Proposal to the Council, together with its opinion on any amendments which it has not incorporated into the revised Proposal. The Council can then act by a qualified majority, but only to adopt the revised Proposal—any other action (including adoption of Parliamentary amendments *not* accepted by the Commission) requires a unanimous vote.

Where the *Co-Decision Procedure* applies, the Parliament enacts legislation jointly with the Council. The Procedure, set out in Article 189b EC, was introduced in 1993 by the EU Treaty. Under this procedure Commission legislative Proposals are submitted to the Council and to the Parliament. The Parliament gives a *first reading*, and the Council then adopts a *common position*, by a qualified majority, after obtaining the Parliament's Opinion. The Council and the Commission are required to explain their positions to the Parliament. The Parliament may then have a *second reading*, in which, by a vote of the majority of its members, it may propose amendments to, or indicate its intention to reject, the common position of the Council. (If the Parliament does nothing at this stage, the Council's common position is then enacted into

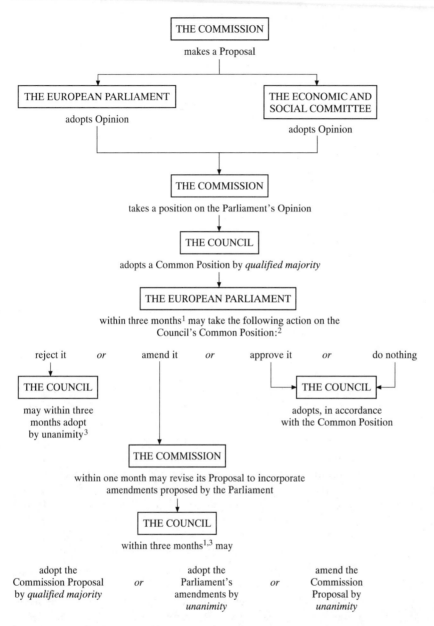

reject it   *or*   amend it   *or*   approve it   *or*   do nothing

THE COUNCIL

may within three
months adopt
by unanimity[3]

THE COUNCIL

adopts, in accordance
with the Common Position

THE COMMISSION

within one month may revise its Proposal to incorporate
amendments proposed by the Parliament

THE COUNCIL

within three months[1,3] may

adopt the
Commission Proposal   *or*
by *qualified majority*

adopt the
Parliament's   *or*
amendments by
unanimity

amend the
Commission
Proposal by
unanimity

[1] This period may be extended by one month by agreement between the Council and the Parliament.
[2] The Parliament acts by a vote of the majority of its members.
[3] If the council fails to act, the Proposal is deemed not to have been adopted.

Figure 2.2   Community legislation: the Co-operation Procedure

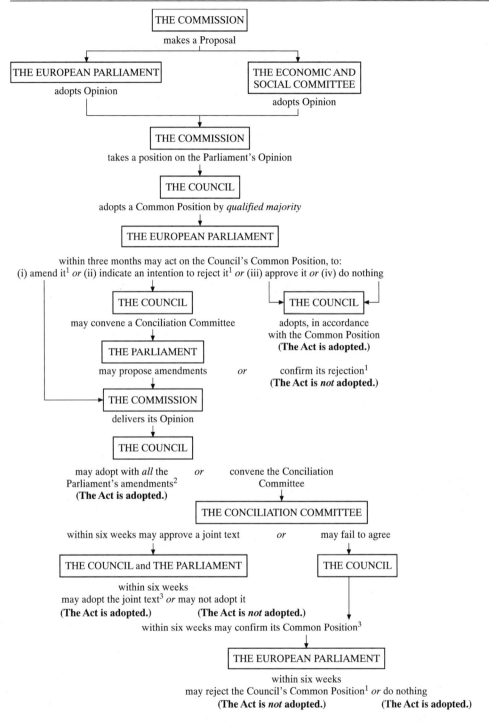

Figure 2.3   Community legislation: the Co-Decision Procedure

[1] The Parliament acts by a vote of the majority of its members.

[2] The Council acts by qualified majority, except that amendments on which the Commission has delivered a negative Opinion can be accepted only by unanimity.

[3] The Council acts by qualified majority.

legislation.) If the Parliament indicates that it will reject the common position, the matter is referred to a *Conciliation Committee* of representatives of the Parliament, the Council and the Commission; following discussion in the Conciliation Committee, the Parliament may either confirm its rejection (in which case the proposed legislation is not enacted), or propose amendments to the common position. If the Council agrees the Parliament's proposed amendments, the legislation is enacted. (The Council must be unanimous in accepting amendments not agreed by the Commission; where the Commission is in agreement, only a qualified majority is required.) If disagreement persists between the Council *and* the Parliament, the Conciliation Committee may approve a text which will be enacted into legislation provided that it is agreed by a qualified majority in the Council *and* by a majority of the votes cast in the Parliament; otherwise, the legislation is not adopted.

The introduction of the Co-operation Procedure, and subsequently the Co-Decision Procedure, tended to change the balance of power between Community institutions. The procedures may appear complex, but their effect is quite simple—to enhance the power of the European Parliament and the Commission *vis-à-vis* the Council, and to diminish the possibilities for a member state to block legislative proposals.

The legislative procedure in any particular instance depends on the *legal base* of the proposed legislation—the specific Treaty provision(s) under which the Proposal is drawn up. In 'border-line' cases where there may be some choice in the matter, it is sometimes to the advantage of the Commission to present Proposals under Treaty Articles which permit Council decisions by qualified majority. Conversely, a member state that fears isolation in the Council would favour a legal base requiring that the decision be unanimous. The European Parliament naturally prefers the Co-Decision Procedure and, after that, the Co-operation Procedure to the Consultation Procedure; and consultation is preferable to having no role. In the event of a challenge to the legal base on which legislation is adopted, the Court of Justice (see Sec. 2.6.1) is the final arbiter, and will decide the question with reference to the subject matter of the legislation and of any relevant Treaty provisions.

The Parliament has on occasion challenged legislation on the grounds that its legal base was incorrect. The objective of the Parliament was to enhance its influence, by bringing the measure in question within the scope of the Co-operation Procedure, rather than procedures that—at best—required only that the Parliament be consulted. For example, Regulation (Euratom) 3954/87, concerning radioactivity standards for foodstuffs and animal feed, was adopted under the health protection provisions of the Euratom Treaty (Article 31); the Parliament contended—unsuccessfully—that it was a measure concerning the single market, which should have been based on Article 100a EEC and thus subject to the Co-operation Procedure (Case C-70/88). The Parliament did secure the annulment of a Directive on students' right of residence in member states which was based on the 'miscellaneous' provisions of Article 235 EEC,[1] and enacted under the Consultation Procedure; the Court ruled (Case C-295/90) that the proper base was Article 7, dealing with discrimination on grounds of nationality, to which the Co-operation Procedure was applicable, and a new Directive was subsequently enacted (Directive 93/96).

The legal base of legislation enacted by the Council, or by the Council and Parliament jointly, need not necessarily be the same as that cited in the Commission's Proposal. Here again, the Parliament has taken legal action—with mixed success—to bring measures within the Co-operation Procedure. One major instance was legislation on wastes, enacted by the Council under the environmental provisions of the EEC Treaty (Article 130s),[2] when the original Commission Proposals were presented as measures relating to the single market (under Article 100a EEC); this change in legal base curtailed the role of the Parliament (and of the

Commission), by substituting the Consultation Procedure (under Article 130s) for the Co-operation Procedure (under Article 100a). The Parliament secured annulment of a Directive on waste from the titanium dioxide industry (Case C-300/89), establishing that this area of legislation was subject to the Co-operation Procedure based on Article 100a. Similar challenges to Directive 91/156 on waste (Case C-155/91), and to Regulation 259/93 on shipments of waste (Case C-187/93) were unsuccessful.

The legislative procedures therefore establish a framework for the interaction of the various Community institutions. Within this framework, each institution has its role to play. The following sections show how the Commission, the Parliament and the Council function in the legislative process.

The Commission as initiator of legislation   The Commission is given responsibility under the Treaties for the preparation of Proposals for Community legislation. These Proposals are normally the outcome of processes—of varying degree of formality—which include policy studies, lobbying by interest groups, consultation with national governments, meetings of national experts. Preliminary drafts for Proposals are prepared by officials of the appropriate Commission services, usually after wide-ranging consultation; they are then circulated for comment within the Commission services. The draft Proposal is then revised in the light of these comments, and sent to the Cabinets of members of the Commission. Following discussion by *Chefs de cabinet*, the Proposal may be adopted by the Commission, either with written approval by the Commissioners or (if the issue is sufficiently important or controversial) following discussion at a meeting of the Commission.

The Commission also has powers to enact legislation, in the forms summarized in Table 2.7 below. This is a general power under the ECSC Treaty (although in all important matters subject to the unanimous assent of the Council). The Commission may also address Directives and Decisions to member states concerning the application of competition rules to public undertakings (Article 90(3) EC). Furthermore, Community legislation in many instances requires the Commission to promulgate Regulations and Decisions concerning the detailed application of the legislation.

Although the Commission is a collegiate body with collective responsibility, its members are not bound by any common political or ideological position. In this respect there is a strong contrast with the model of a parliamentary democracy, in which a government is formed by elected politicians, either from a single party or in coalition, who then introduce a legislative programme based upon proposals presented at the election.

This absence of ideological perspective has certain advantages in the particular context of Community policies. In many areas member states have developed their own policies, which reflect both national priorities and pressures and the political complexions of governments. The problem, from a Community viewpoint, is that policies adopted in member states may be inconsistent and incompatible to a degree which obstructs the functioning of the common market. In such circumstances the solution lies in harmonization, or approximation, taking national measures as a starting point and seeking an accommodation which is broadly acceptable and does not compromise vital national interests.

The Council: responsibility for enactment   When the Council receives from the Commission a Proposal for legislation, it is normally referred to the appropriate working group for expert consideration. The Proposal is then sent via COREPER to the Council. The Commission may amend the Proposal in the light of discussion at any stage. The Council may accept the Proposal (with Commission amendments, if any) by unanimity, by a qualified majority or (occasionally) by a simple majority, depending on the Treaty provision under which the legislation is to be enacted. However, amendment of a Commission Proposal requires a unanimous decision by the Council: and the general effect of this restriction is to favour adoption of legislation in the form proposed by the Commission. If the Council does not accept the Proposal, it is not enacted into legislation; the Council also has the option of remitting the Proposal to COREPER and working groups for further consideration.

The Council's voting procedures are specified in the Treaties: decisions may be taken by unanimity, by a qualified majority, or—in a few instances—by a simple majority of the member states. In the case of a qualified majority vote, member states cast votes as shown in Table 2.5. The votes of the member states are weighted in relation to their populations, but with the smaller countries having proportionately more votes. Numbers of votes range from 2 (for Luxembourg) to 10 (for France, Italy, Germany and the United Kingdom). There are 87 votes in total, and the Treaties specify that a qualified majority requires at least 62 votes. This implies that an alliance of the five biggest countries cannot ensure the acceptance of a Proposal—they command only 48 votes, 14 short of the required number. Conversely, 26 votes are sufficient to block acceptance of a Proposal. There are numerous combinations that would add up to 26 votes: but it should be noted that one, or even two, large countries would be unable to block a Proposal that is favoured by all other member states.

Table 2.5 Council of Ministers: distribution of votes by member state, when voting by qualified majority

	No. of votes	*% of total votes*	*Votes per 1m population*
Austria	4	4.6	0.51
Belgium	5	6.6	0.50
Denmark	3	3.9	0.58
Finland	3	3.4	0.59
France	10	13.2	0.18
Germany	10	13.2	0.13
Greece	5	6.6	0.50
Ireland	3	3.9	0.85
Italy	10	13.2	0.17
Luxembourg	2	2.6	5.28
Netherlands	5	6.6	0.34
Portugal	5	6.6	0.48
Spain	8	10.5	0.20
Sweden	4	4.6	0.46
United Kingdom	10	13.2	0.17
European Union	87	100	0.24

Source: derived from the EC Treaty, Article 148 (2).

Public access to the Council's deliberations is severely restricted, notwithstanding a Declaration attached to the EU Treaty which states that 'transparency of the decision-making process strengthens the democratic nature of the institutions and the public's confidence in the administration'. The Council and its subordinate bodies usually meet in private, except on the occasion of the Council's twice yearly policy debates, and (rare) instances when by unanimous agreement meetings are 'subject to retransmission by audio visual means'—i.e. televised (Decision of 6 December 1993). The Council has decided that access to its documents may be refused 'in order to protect the confidentiality of its proceedings' (Decision 93/731; this Decision has been subject to a legal challenge—Case C-58/94). Confidentiality has been cited to refuse public access to minutes and attendance and voting records of Council meetings. (This also has been subject to a legal challenge—Case T-194/94.)

The Council is thus in the unusual position of a legislative body which meets behind closed doors and does not publish a full record of its proceedings. This is normal practice for negotiations between sovereign states, where any eventual agreements are subject to ratification by the legislatures of the parties involved. However, the Community (in contrast with the intergovernmental components of the EU Treaty) is more than a forum for negotiation between the member states: national representatives are enacting legislation, rather than intergovernmental agreements. (In terms of the models described above, the Community is federalist, rather than pluralist.) In these circumstances, the democratic legitimacy of confidential deliberations is open to question.

Ministers (and Commissioners) do of course comment at length *outside* the Council meetings, expounding their own positions, and presenting eventual Council decisions in a light which is favourable to them. Such pronouncements for public consumption naturally tend to understate the degree of flexibility that emerges in the course of discussion in the Council (and in private deliberations). The outcome of a successful Council meeting is usually a compromise, which participants then must 'sell' to the parties that are affected. The process is illustrated by the following quotation from the then Commission President (Delors 1993):

the debate in the Council of Ministers of Economic and Financial Affairs was positive. However when these gentlemen emerged again, they all had to think of their political life on the domestic front, so they had to find a scapegoat, a whipping boy: and that was the Commission report.

The European Parliament's role in legislation   The role of the European Parliament in the legislative process depends upon the Treaty provision on which the legislation is based. Prior to 1987, the Consultation Procedure was the only basis on which the Parliament could influence legislation; and it remains applicable except in those instances where it has been superseded by the Co-operation Procedure or the Co-Decision Procedure.

The key to the Parliament's power under the Co-operation Procedure lies in the distinction between unanimity and qualified majority voting in the Council. The Parliament—in agreement with the Commission—can determine what the Council is able to enact by qualified majority. The Parliament has the right to propose amendments, which if accepted by the Commission are included in a revised Proposal, which is then sent to the Council. The Council can accept this Proposal by a qualified majority; but a modified version of the Proposal can be adopted only by a unanimous vote.

One measure of the Parliament's influence is its 'success rate' in terms of acceptance of its amendments to legislative proposals. This is illustrated by Table 2.6, which records the number and percentage of proposed amendments that were accepted by the Commission and by the Council, on first and second readings, following the introduction of the Co-operation Procedure.

Table 2.6   Amendments proposed by the European Parliament: acceptance by the Commission and the Council, July 1987–September 1991

	First reading	Second reading
Total amendments proposed by the Parliament	2734	716
Amendments accepted by the Commission	1626 (60%)	366 (48%)
Amendments accepted by the Council	1216 (45%)	194 (27%)

Note: Covers 208 procedures. Figures in parenthesis show the percentage of amendments accepted.
Source: Jacobs *et al.* (1992: 187).

The figures in Table 2.6 reflect the Parliament's significant influence on legislation. They are nevertheless a somewhat crude measure: on the one hand they include amendments that are proposed in order to make a political point, with little expectation of their acceptance; but on the other hand they do not take account of the Parliament's use of its enhanced influence in informal consultation with the Commission and the Council, to secure adoption of amendments favoured (but not formally proposed) by the Parliament.

The advantage of the Co-operation Procedure for the Parliament is illustrated by the case of Directive 89/458 on small car emissions (see Box 2.5). In the late 1980s there were essentially three options, of progressive degrees of stringency, for improved emission standards for new cars. The Commission initially proposed a 'medium' standard, which was accepted by the Council in its common position. The Parliament in response proposed a more stringent standard. The Commission then saw the possibility of building a qualified majority in the Council in support of the Parliament's amendment, and the Proposal was revised accordingly. The eventual outcome was a Directive incorporating a stringent emission standard, which was largely a result of pressure exerted by the Parliament.

Where the Co-Decision Procedure applies, both Parliament and Council can ultimately block proposed legislation, and so—conversely—neither can prevail over the other. The Parliament's initial role is reactive: it gives an Opinion on the Commission Proposal, and then responds to the Council common position. For the Parliament to block legislation based on the common position it must vote twice in favour of rejection: first to indicate an intention to reject, and a second vote following discussions in a Conciliation Committee. Each time rejection must be supported by a majority of members (rather than simply a majority of those voting)—so members of the Parliament who abstain are in effect supporting the Council's common position. A similar majority is required to propose amendments to the common position, and thus to place the onus on the Council to agree the amendments or proceed to a Conciliation Committee. In contrast, adoption of a text agreed by the Conciliation Committee requires only the support of a majority of the votes cast.

Assertion of the Parliament's powers depends on the construction of coalitions of like-minded members, notwithstanding the absence of strong party discipline. Opposition in the Parliament must maintain solidarity if it is to succeed in rejecting or amending legislative proposals. Opponents of the common position will be better able to insist on amendments if they can credibly demonstrate that rejection is a real possibility. To counter the threat of rejection, the Council must offer sufficient concessions to opponents in the Parliament to ensure the passage of (amended) legislation.

BOX 2.5
The Co-operation Procedure in action: the case of small car emission standards

In 1987 the Community adopted new procedures, whereby the Council of Ministers, acting 'in cooperation with' the European Parliament, can in some circumstances enact legislation by a qualified majority vote. The practical importance of the Parliament's new powers under the 'Co-operation procedure' was demonstrated in the process of legislating for emission standards for small cars (of less than 1.4 litres engine capacity).

The Commission proposed at the outset a standard of:

30 g/test of carbon monoxide, 8g/test of unburnt hydrocarbons and nitrous oxides

The Council endorsed this Proposal, reaching a 'common position' by qualified majority (with a minority favouring a higher standard).

However the Common position did not find favour in the Parliament, where there was a strong support for a higher standard of:

20 g/test of carbon monoxide, 5g/test of unburnt hydrocarbons and nitrous oxides

The Commission then modified its Proposal in line with the higher (20g/5g) standard. Under the terms of the Co-operation procedure, the Council could insist on the standard in the original proposal only if it enjoyed unanimous support.

The possibilities for the Council were therefore as follows:

1. *unanimous agreement* on the 30g/8g standard;
2. *adoption by qualified majority* of the 20g/5g standard;
3. *no agreement*—retain existing standard.

Since there was no prospect of unanimity, the Council faced a choice between the higher standard and no new Community standard. In these circumstances, the Council finally agreed to the modified Proposal, and adopted a Directive incorporating the higher standard (Directive 89/458).

Changes in the legislative procedures have had a marked effect on the evolving relationship between Community institutions. The Co-operation Procedure, and subsequently the Co-Decision Procedure, have increased the Parliament's political leverage. Nevertheless, for many purposes the Parliament is restricted to a consultative role, and there remain a number of provisions under which the Council may legislate without consulting the Parliament.

The legislative procedures are in some instances combined in a way that retains Council control over the critical stages of the decision-making process. This is illustrated by the provisions for Community support for research and technological development (EC Treaty Title XV). The matters to be decided, and the legislative procedures applicable, are set out in Table 2.7. The Parliament decides the multi-annual framework programme jointly with the Council (under the Co-Decision Procedure); but the vital question of priorities within this framework—which activities are actually to be supported with specific programmes—is a matter for the Council (after consulting the Parliament). The Parliament has more influence over implementation of the programmes (where the Co-operation Procedure applies), but the establishment of organizational structures (including joint ventures) to execute the programmes is decided by the Council under the Co-operation Procedure. A similar procedural relationship applies to environmental policy: the framework programme is decided under the Co-Decision Procedure (Article 130s(3)), and specific action is decided under the Co-operation Procedure (130s(1)), while provisions in 'sensitive' areas, including taxation, land use planning, water management and energy, are decided by the Council under the Consultation Procedure.

Table 2.7 Decision-making procedures under the EC Treaty: research and technological development programmes

Subject	Procedure	EC Treaty Article
Framework programme	Co-Decision	130i(1)
Specific programmes	Consultation	130i(4)
Organizational structures	Consultation	130o(1)
Implementation of programmes	Co-operation	130o(2)

2.3.3 The Community's budgetary procedures

The procedure for adoption of the Community budget is summarized in Figure 2.4. The process begins with the preparation of expenditure estimates for each Community institution by 1 July preceding the beginning of the new financial year on 1 January. The Commission then consolidates the estimates in a draft budget by 1 September.

Expenditure from the Community budget is divided between 'compulsory' and 'non-compulsory' elements. Compulsory expenditure is defined as expenditure necessarily resulting from the Treaties or from Community legislation. Non-compulsory expenditure represents the remainder of the budget; a maximum increase in this expenditure (compared with the previous years) is established by the Commission on the basis of economic criteria—growth in gross national product (GNP), variation in member states' budgets and trends in living costs. This maximum can be exceeded in certain circumstances at the initiative of the Council or the Parliament (Article 203 EC). While in principle the basis for the compulsory/non-compulsory distinction is clear, there are frequently differences between Parliament and Council with respect to the classification of individual items of expenditure. The breakdown of provisions in the 1994 Community budget for Commission expenditure on the development and implementation of policies is shown in Table 2.8: the most striking aspect is that, despite recent efforts to reduce the cost of the Common Agricultural Policy, farm price (EAGGF) guarantees still account for more than half the total expenditure.

The Commission draft is submitted to the European Parliament, and then to the Council. It is then sent back to the Parliament, which may change the provisions only for non-compulsory expenditure. Thus, the Treaties give the Parliament power to decide the allocation of non-compulsory expenditure, while the final decision with respect to compulsory expenditure lies with the Council. The Parliament may adopt amendments relating to the non-compulsory element of the draft Community budget: these require the support of a majority of the Parliament's members. The Parliament can override any subsequent modifications proposed by the Council, by a vote of the majority of members and three-fifths of the votes cast. The Parliament can also propose modifications to the draft budget with respect to compulsory expenditure but their acceptance depends on the Council.

The Parliament nevertheless has the final word, since it has power to reject the entire budget, by a vote of the majority of the Parliament's members *and* two-thirds of the votes cast. If this happens, the entire budgetary process must begin again: the Community's business may continue in the absence of a budget, with monthly expenditure under each budget heading limited to one-twelfth of the previous year's level (Article 204 EC).

THE COMMISSION

prepares draft budget by 1 September

THE COUNCIL

establishes draft budget by 5 October[1]

THE EUROPEAN PARLIAMENT

within 45 days may:
(i) make *amendments* relating to 'non-compulsory' expenditure[2]
and/or
(ii) propose *modifications* which would not increase
'compulsory' expenditure[3]
and/or
(iii) propose *modifications* which would increase 'compulsory'
expenditure[3]
or
(iv) approve the budget, which then stands adopted
or
(v) do nothing (**The budget is deemed adopted.**)

THE COUNCIL

within 15 days may[1]
(i) modify the Parliament's *amendments* relating to
'non-compulsory' expenditure
(ii) reject the Parliament's *modifications* which would not
increase 'compulsory' expenditure (**Otherwise they are deemed
accepted.**)
(iii) accept the Parliament's *modifications* which would increase
'compulsory' expenditure (**Otherwise they are deemed
rejected.***)

THE EUROPEAN PARLIAMENT

within 15 days may amend or reject the Council's *modifications*
relating to non-compulsory expenditure[4]

THE EUROPEAN PARLIAMENT

may then reject the entire budget[5]

---

* If the Council does not modify the *amendments*, and accepts all the *modifications*, the budget is
deemed adopted.
[1] The Council acts by qualified majority.
[2] By a vote of the majority of members of the Parliament.
[3] The Parliament acts by a majority of the votes cast; expenditure is defined separately for each
Community institution.
[4] The Parliament acts by a majority of its members and three-fifths of the votes cast.
[5] The Parliament acts by a majority of its members and two-thirds of the votes cast.

Figure 2.4   The Community budgetary procedure

Table 2.8   European Community budget: expenditure for 1995

Area of expenditure	Amount (bn ECUs)	% of total
Administration	4.01	5.2
EAGGF Guarantee Section	38.42	50.2
Structural operations	23.73	31.0
Training, culture, information	0.63	0.8
Energy, nuclear safeguards, environment	0.19	0.2
Internal market, consumer protection, trans-European networks	0.65	0.8
Research and technological development	2.79	3.6
Development co-operation	4.16	5.4
Common foreign and security policy	0.08	0.1
Guarantees and reserves	1.87	2.4
Total	76.53	100.0*

* Subject to rounding error.
Source: European Parliament final adoption of the general budget of the European Union for the financial year 1995, *Official Journal*, 1994 L369/145.

The budget also sets out the revenue requirements of the Community. The Community's revenue raising powers are established by the Treaties, and by Decision of the Council or the Commission pursuant to the Treaties.

The Community has four main sources of revenue, known as *own resources*:

1. Levies on agricultural imports and on sugar.
2. Customs duties under common external tariffs.
3. Value added tax (VAT) charged on a uniform assessment base.
4. Contributions based on member states' GNPs.

The first two are known as 'traditional' own resources, which are directly linked to common Community policies (agriculture and the customs union).

Total revenue from own resources is subject to maximum limits (expressed as a percentage of the aggregate GNP of member states): this limit was set at 1.15 per cent in 1988, and rose by stages to 1.2 per cent (Decision 88/376/EEC, Euratom).

Over the period 1995–9 the amount and composition of the Community's own resources will change. There is to be a phased reduction of the VAT element, which will be more than offset by an increase in GNP-based contributions. By 1999 the VAT base for each member state will not exceed 50 per cent of its GNP (compared with a maximum of 54 per cent in 1995), and the VAT rate applied to the assessment base will be reduced from 1.32 per cent in 1995 to 1.00 per cent in 1999. Meanwhile the maximum limit for own resources will rise from 1.21 per cent of GNP in 1995 to 1.27 per cent in 1999 (Decision 94/728/EC, Euratom, Articles 2–3).

Revenue from own resources in the 1995 budget amounted to some 76 bn ECUs (which is over 99 per cent of the total revenue of the Community). GNP-based own resources ((4) above) amounted to 0.335 per cent of aggregate GNP, while VAT payments ((3) above) constituted

1.313 per cent of the common assessment base. (This is *not* the same as a levy at this rate on national VAT payments, because the assessment base varies between countries; for example, the UK has zero rating for some products.)

Since 1985, the Community budget has included an adjustment to compensate the UK for an 'excessive budgetary burden in relation to its relative prosperity'; and the European Council has decided that this will continue until 1999. The adjustment is calculated by formulae applied to the VAT and GNP-based own resources, the effect of which is to refund to the UK approximately two-thirds of any 'excess' payment (the 'excess' being measured by the difference between the UK's shares in payments to the Community and expenditure by the Community). Other member states' contributions are increased in proportion, so that the overall amount of own resources is unaffected. The result is a rebate to the UK (and additional payments by others) of 1.87 bn ECUs in 1995, a saving to the UK of 16 per cent of its (unadjusted) contribution, equivalent to 32 ECUs per head of UK population.

Member states' contributions to the various elements of Community own resources are shown in Table 2.9. The table also shows their contributions to the UK's compensation, and the resulting levels of contribution per head of population.

Table 2.9 European Community 1995 budget: revenue from own resources (bn ECUs) and per capita own resources revenue (ECUs)

	Traditional	VAT-based	GNP-based	UK com-pensation	Total	Per capita (ECUs)
Belgium	0.96	1.15	0.68	0.08	2.86	284
Denmark	0.27	0.66	0.43	0.05	1.41	272
Germany	3.98	11.82	6.09	0.41	22.29	276
Greece	0.19	0.56	0.29	0.03	1.07	103
Spain	0.68	2.54	1.42	0.17	4.82	123
France	1.99	7.18	3.94	0.46	13.57	236
Ireland	0.37	0.30	0.14	0.02	0.83	233
Italy	1.19	4.38	2.92	0.34	8.84	155
Luxembourg	0.02	0.10	0.05	0.01	0.17	427
Netherlands	1.47	1.84	0.98	0.11	4.39	288
Austria	0.32	1.08	0.58	0.68	2.05	259
Portugal	0.24	0.57	0.27	0.03	1.11	113
Finland	0.19	0.51	0.30	0.35	1.04	206
Sweden	0.35	0.89	0.57	0.66	1.88	216
UK	2.69	5.82	3.02	−1.87	9.66	167
Total	14.91	39.42	21.68	0.00	76.01	206

Note: Traditional own resources comprise agricultural and sugar levies and customs duties, and are net of member states' 10 per cent deduction for collection costs. GNP-based payments include contributions to reserves.

Source: European Parliament final adoption of the general budget of the European Union for the financial year 1995, *Official Journal*, 1994 L369/145–51.

2.3.4 International agreements

The Parliament and the Council have joint decision-making powers in relation to association agreements with non member countries, and treaties providing for the accession of new member states. Accession treaties are subject to the unanimous agreement of the Council, after consultation with the Commission; association agreements are concluded by the Council acting in unanimity. In both cases, the assent of the Parliament is required, by an absolute majority of its members.

Other agreements with non member countries, or with other international organizations, are negotiated by the Commission, and concluded by the Council; the Parliament is consulted where this is required by the Treaties.

2.3.5 Supervisory powers

The Parliament has the right to dismiss the entire Commission (but *not* individual Commissioners), by a vote of censure carried by a two-thirds majority of the votes cast, representing a majority of members. This is a drastic power which has never been used. The Parliament also has the right to put oral and written questions to the Commission and to the Council.

The Court of Auditors   This is the Community's 'financial watchdog', established in 1977 under the terms of amendments made to the Treaties in 1975. It has 15 members, appointed by unanimous decision of the Council following consultation with the European Parliament. Members should have belonged to external audit bodies or be otherwise well qualified for their tasks.

The Court is responsible for auditing the accounts of the Community and all Community bodies, to determine whether revenue and expenditure have been properly and lawfully handled, and to verify that financial management has been sound. The Court of Auditors can undertake its work 'on the spot' in Community institutions and in member states, in conjunction with appropriate national bodies. The Court's annual report on its activities is published in the *Official Journal of the European Communities*.

2.4 POLITICAL POWER IN THE EUROPEAN COMMUNITY

The Community Treaties, like other constitutional documents, provide a framework for the exercise of political power, and for the allocation of responsibilities, both between Community institutions, and between the Community and national authorities. In this context, a distinction should be made between the powers exercised by authorities within member states, in accordance with the *subsidiarity principle* (see Sec. 2.2.2) and the power of national governments at Community level.

The member states collectively have the ultimate power, inasmuch as they established the Community by Treaty, and they retain the sole power to amend the Treaties, which are the constitutional framework of the Community and the basis for its legal system. This power was used to modify Community law relating to occupational pensions: a ruling by the Court of Justice (Case C-262/88) applying the principle of equal pay for equal work (Article 119 EC) was largely deprived of retrospective effect by a Declaration attached to the EU Treaty.

Within the framework of the Treaties, the Community's decision-making processes entail interaction between the various institutions. The formal procedures set out in the Treaties specify the powers and responsibilities of the participants; the most important powers of member states, the Council, the Commission and the Parliament are summarized in Box 2.6.

BOX 2.6
The distribution of power in the European Community

Member states

- *Member states* have the power to amend the Treaties, by unanimous agreement.
- Each *member state* has a veto on those occasions when the Council has to decide by unanimity; in some circumstances:
    —*an alliance of three member states* can block a Proposal;
    —*a qualified majority of member states* can amend Commission implementing measures.
- The *Council Presidency* sets the Council agenda and chairs meetings at all levels.

The Council

- The *budget*; the Council decides the 'compulsory' expenditure element.
- *Legislation*: enactment normally requires Council assent (ECSC Treaty) or Council adoption of a Commission Proposal (EEC and Euratom Treaties).
- *Appointment of the Commissioners*: the president and members of the Commission are appointed for fixed terms.

The Commission

- *Legislation*: the Commission generally has the exclusive right to initiate Proposals for Community legislation, which the Council can amend only by a unanimous vote.
- *Rule-making powers*: the Commission has these where they are provided for in the ECSC Treaty, in the EEC Treaty and in Community legislation.
- *Implementation of legislation*: the Commission can enforce the application of rules in specific cases; it has exclusive powers to authorize waivers of compliance with legislative requirements ('derogations').
- *Administration of Community funds and programmes*: the Commission has responsibility for this collaboration with advisory or management committees representing member states.

The Parliament

- *Legislation*: under the *Co-Decision Procedure*, enactment requires the Parliament's assent (or at least acquiescence); under the *Co-operation Procedure*, the Parliament (if in accord with the Commission) can determine how the Council is able to amend a Proposal—i.e. by a qualified majority or only by unanimity.
- *The budget*: the Parliament has the power to decide 'non-compulsory' expenditure, and to reject the entire budget.
- *International agreements*: accession treaties and association agreements require Parliament's assent.
- *The Commission*: the Parliament must confirm the Council's nomination of the Commission, and has power to dismiss the entire Commission (but *not* individual Commissioners).

However, it should be emphasized that a recital of formal powers does not tell the complete story, for two main reasons:

1. Influence may be exercised even where an institution has no formal powers. The Economic and Social Committee, for example, is able only to deliver Opinions—but the expert knowledge of the Committee's membership can lend weight to its views, so that its proposed amendments are seen to improve Community legislation.
2. A distinction should be made between powers in defined areas, and the effect of these powers on the general strength of an institution's position. For example, a recent vote by the Parliament against a Proposal to liberalize telecommunication regulations was—at least partially—a move to extend the Parliament's influence in the implementation of eventual legislation, rather than an expression of disagreement with the objectives of the Proposal (European Parliament 1994a).

2.4.1   The powers of the Council

In the overall power balance, the Council is the dominant institution. Its strength derives from its composition: the member states, as founders of the Community, ensured a key role for the Council as the Community institution in which their national interests were directly represented. Legislation can be enacted under the EC Treaty only with the approval of the Council, and a unanimous decision of the Council can amend legislative Proposals over the opposition of the Commission and (except when the Co-Decision Procedure applies) the Parliament. The Council also has the right to decide the Community's expenditure—the 'compulsory' element of the budget, relating to expenditure necessarily resulting from the EC Treaty and legislation pursuant to the Treaty.

However, paradoxically, the composition of the Council is also a source of weakness: representatives of national governments, often defending entrenched positions, do not easily reach unanimous agreement. In principle, each member state possesses a veto whenever a decision must be taken by unanimity; on the other hand, the exercise of this veto has its drawbacks, since insistence on an isolated position may invite criticism and retaliation. So there are incentives to seek a consensus; but the consensus often proves to be elusive. Indeed, the Community's lack of progress under a system dominated by unanimous voting led to the extension of qualified majority voting in 1987, with the Single European Act. Moreover, the Community has decisively retreated from its previous emphasis on national interests. The Luxembourg compromise (see Sec. 2.3.1) is now ineffective, as was demonstrated in April 1992, when the UK's attempt to postpone a vote on agricultural prices was overridden by a majority vote in the Council. Following this experience, a UK parliamentary committee concluded that 'invocation of the [Luxembourg] compromise, although a unilateral move, requires the consent of other member states to be effective' (House of Commons 1986: p. xiii, para. 41).

The decision-making procedure within the Council—unanimity or qualified majority voting—makes no difference to the authority of the Council as an institution, but it does affect the position of individual member states. Specifically, qualified majority voting increases the scope for building coalitions to overcome the opposition of a recalcitrant member state.

The Council, and its members, are also able to influence the implementation of legislation through advisory or management committees (for which model terms of reference are set out in Decision 87/373). These committees are normally provided for in legislation, and consist of national representatives with a chairman representing the Commission. Management committees strengthen the power of member states, since their procedure provides for referral to the Council in the event of a disagreement between the Commission and the committee voting by a qualified majority of its members. A Declaration attached to the 1986 Single European Act calls on the Council to opt for the advisory Committee procedure 'in the interests of speed and efficiency of the decision-making process', when legislating for the single European market; nevertheless, in practice the Council often preferred to augment its members' power through the use of management committees (Cockfield 1994: 105).

2.4.2   The powers of the Commission

The Commission's strength lies in its power to develop Proposals for Community legislation. The EC Treaty normally specifies that the Council acts 'on a Proposal from the Commission'— so that the Council can deliberate only on the basis of a Commission Proposal. In practical terms, this means that the Commission sets the initial agenda for discussion.

The hand of the Commission is further strengthened by provisions governing amendments to Proposals made within the framework of the Treaty. The Commission is free to revise its Proposal, to accept amendments of which it approves, prior to submission to the Council. However, the Council can make amendments only by a unanimous vote—even in those instances where it can enact legislation by a qualified majority. (The only exception to this rule is in the final stages of the Co-Decision Procedure, when the Council and Parliament enact legislation in the form of a text agreed in a Conciliation Committee.) So an amendment is more likely (other things being equal) to be enacted in legislation if it is first accepted by the Commission.

2.4.3   The powers of the Parliament

The Parliament must confirm the appointment of, and has the power to dismiss, the entire Commission (but *not* individual Commissioners). Dismissal requires a motion of censure carried by a two-thirds majority of the votes cast, representing a majority of members. This drastic power has never been exercised, although its use has from time to time been threatened (with varying degrees of seriousness). If the Commission were dismissed, its successor would be nominated by the Council, and would then be subject to confirmation by the Parliament.

The Parliament enacts legislation jointly with the Council where the Co-Decision Procedure applies, and in these circumstances its relationship with the Council is analogous to the two houses of a bicameral legislature. Each institution may develop its own version of draft legislation based on the Commission Proposal, and the 'conciliation' process is designed to reconcile the two versions. (This may be compared with a House/Senate conference committee in the United States Congress.)

The Parliament influences legislation indirectly through the Consultation Procedure and— more decisively—in the Co-operation Procedure, if it can persuade the Commission to amend legislative Proposals which it submits to the Council. (The Council often can adopt the Commission Proposal by qualified majority, but can usually amend the Proposal only by unanimity.) The Co-operation Procedure can give the Parliament, in alliance with the Commission, a key role in developing political momentum, and laying the foundation for a position around which a qualified majority can be formed in the Council.

The Parliament, unlike the Council, is not represented in the management/advisory committee system (see Sec. 2.4.1), even where legislation is enacted jointly. The Parliament mounted an unsuccessful legal challenge to this system, on the grounds that it infringed on the

Commission's role as the Community's executive body, and thus indirectly detracted from the Parliament's supervisory powers over the Commission (Case 302/87). More recently, members of the Parliament seeking representation on the committees succeeded in blocking a legislative Proposal (on liberalization of telecommunications regulations) which did not provide for such representation. The Parliament report on the Proposal recommended its rejection, asserting that joint legislative powers (under the Co-Decision Procedure) should imply an equal role for Parliament and Council in implementation, and called on the Commission to submit a new Proposal meeting the requirements of the Parliament (European Parliament 1994a: 6).

The Parliament's role in the budgetary procedure (see Sec. 2.3.3) gives it considerable leverage with both the Commission and the Council. Budgetary allocations for non-compulsory expenditure are important for the Commission in the development of policies in areas not (as yet) covered by the Treaties or legislation. The Parliament can amend those sections of the budget relating to non-compulsory expenditure, by a vote of the majority of its members. The Council can then propose its own amendments, but in this context the Parliament has the final word, since it can modify or reject the Council's amendments, by a vote of the majority of its members and three-fifths of the votes cast.

The Parliament also has the right to reject the entire budget (including compulsory expenditure decided by the Council), by a majority of members and two-thirds of the votes cast. If this happens the budgetary process must begin again, with the Commission preparing a new draft budget; meanwhile the Community can continue only with 'emergency' funding on a monthly basis, limited to one-twelfth of the previous year's allocation. The Parliament has indeed used this power in confrontation with the Council, and has rejected the budgets for 1980, 1982 (supplementary budget) and 1985. Thus, rejection of the budget is a credible threat which the Parliament can use to secure concessions from the Council.

Furthermore, the Commission is ultimately responsible to the Parliament for proper accounting for expenditure. The Parliament, acting on the recommendation of the Council, must 'give a discharge' to the Commission in respect of implementation of the budget.

The Parliament's assent—by an absolute majority of its members—is required for the conclusion of treaties of accession and association agreements. The power to withhold or delay this assent can be used to political effect—as for example in the case of agreements with Israel, Turkey, Syria and Morocco, where objections were raised over human rights policies in those countries.

In addition to its formal powers, the Parliament also has an element of 'moral authority', as the body of elected representatives of the people—in contrast with the Council, meeting behind closed doors, and the unelected Commission. This gives the Parliament a favourable context in which to make full use of its powers to question the Commission and the Council, to discuss the Commission's annual report, and to co-operate with the Court of Auditors in overseeing Community expenditure.

2.5   INSTITUTIONAL REFORM

The development of the single market has led to an enlargement of the Community's policy responsibilities, with a growth in the volume of legislation, and corresponding requirements for implementation and enforcement of policy measures. The subsidiarity principle defines the limits of Community action; but—as a corollary of this principle—where the Community is accorded responsibilities, it must have the appropriate machinery to discharge these responsibilities.

Community institutions and decision-making procedures were originally designed for a group of six member states. As the membership has increased and become less homogeneous, changes have been made, notably extensions of qualified majority voting in the Council and increases in the power of the Parliament. Further institutional reform will be on the agenda of the 1996 intergovernmental conference, and changes can be anticipated in the Treaty provisions with respect to Community institutions. Pressures for change arise mainly from two sources: criticisms of a lack of democratic legitimacy (sometimes characterized as a 'democratic deficit'), and concerns over the viability of the Community's institutions and decision-making procedures, particularly in the event of accessions of further member states.

2.5.1   The 'democratic deficit'

Community legislative procedures now combine decision-making by governments with elements of a supranational political process. The procedures have numerous variants, depending on the role of the Parliament and of the Commission, the voting requirements in the Council, and the provisions for consultation with advisory bodies. (For the details of the procedures in the EC Treaty, see Appendix 2.1.)

Although the European Union is supposedly based on democratic principles, the Community's legislative procedures do not altogether respect these principles. In particular, the Community has been criticized for a lack of openness and accountability in decision-making. The executive body—the Commission—has no electoral mandate, but nevertheless has a key role in policy formulation as the initiator of legislation. The directly elected legislature, the Parliament, has only a limited role; in a number of areas legislation may be enacted by the Council without even consultation with the Parliament.

The question of democratic legitimacy ultimately centres on the role of the member states in the Council. In a system of purely intergovernmental co-operation (the 'pluralist' model—see Sec. 1.1.3) democratic accountability is realized through the ratification process: governments negotiate agreements between themselves, but these agreements come into force only if they are ratified under the constitutional procedures, which normally include approval of the elected legislature. Thus, for example, the EU (Maastricht) Treaty took effect only when ratified by all the member states, through acts of their parliaments and (in some cases) by referendum.

The pluralist model of intergovernmental agreement can be invoked where the Council decides by unanimity; however, there is one crucial difference: decisions of the Council are immediately binding in law, and do not require the approval of national legislatures. Democratic control of governments in these circumstances depends upon consultation with national parliaments prior to, and during, negotiations in the Council (and also on the desire of governments to forestall parliamentary criticism after the negotiations are concluded). The Maastricht intergovernmental conference sought to strengthen this process: a Declaration attached to the 1992 EU Treaty calls for submission of Commission legislative Proposals at an early stage for examination by national parliaments. Nevertheless, accountability will be ineffective if national parliaments have little interest, and expertise, in European affairs.

A more fundamental constraint arises from the negotiating procedure itself. The Council is an unusual legislative body in that most of its deliberations are conducted in private—and this in itself constrains democratic accountability. The bargaining process inevitably entails compromises, which are often arrived at after marathon negotiating sessions. In such a situation negotiators clearly are inhibited in revealing their positions in advance; and even if governments wished to engage in candid discussion with national legislators, they would have difficulty in anticipating the form of any eventual compromise.

In any event, purely intergovernmental decision-making has become less relevant to the

Community (although it is of course applicable to the other 'pillars' of the European Union). Changes to the EC Treaty have increased the scope for Council decision-making by qualified majority, and the introduction of the Co-Decision Procedure has given the Parliament the power to enact legislation under certain Articles of the EC Treaty jointly with the Council. These developments have led the Community towards a bicameral legislative structure, which has some resemblance to national legislatures.

There are now pressures to carry these developments further, in order to increase democratic accountability in the Community's supranational legislative framework. Possible initiatives might include:

- increased public access to Council meetings;
- election of the Commission by the Parliament;
- extension of joint enactment of legislation by Parliament and Council under the Co-Decision Procedure.

The main element is revision of the Treaty to increase the power of the Parliament. Some governments may be reluctant to agree to this, because it will implicitly diminish the supremacy of the Council, and also because they perceive the Parliament as lacking in credibility. At present, parliamentary elections tend to concentrate on national policies towards the European Union, rather than on policy issues at European level, and are often seen as a judgement on the popularity of national governments.

This criticism of the Parliament has an element of circular reasoning. The Parliament's credibility depends on its powers and responsibilities, and if these are increased the Parliament can be expected to receive more attention in its own right. As a result its elections will focus, to a greater extent than hitherto, on the decisions its members will face when elected.

2.5.2 Reform of the institutions and decision-making procedures

In addition to democratic legitimacy, concerns have arisen over the effectiveness and efficiency of the institutional structure. These concerns are likely to be addressed in the 1996 Inter-Governmental Conference. Proponents of reform have identified two key issues:

1. the role, and size, of the Commission;
2. decision-making in the Council.

Reform of the Commission At present there is at least one Commissioner from each member state, and two from the larger countries. This has remained the practice through several rounds of enlargement; so, over the period 1981–95, with accession of six additional member states, the number of Commissioners rose from 13 to 20. Further enlargement would again increase the number, perhaps ultimately to more than 30.

There must be serious doubts as to the viability of a Commission of this size. Indeed, the present membership appears to exceed the number of portfolios that carry substantial responsibilities. This was illustrated in the 1992–94 Commission by a somewhat artificial distinction between international political and economic relations, where a division of responsibilities between two Commissioners had led to a certain amount of confusion in the Community's policies on external relations.

Reduction in the number of Commissioners, or restraint on further increases, will mean an end to the existing practice whereby each national government nominates at least one member of the Commission. This implies self-denial on the part of member states, and there are obvious difficulties in securing their agreement. One possibility might be to have no more than one Commissioner from each member state, and for the smaller countries to form groups for the purpose of nomination (so for example the Benelux countries would collectively make one nomination). Alternatively, the existing procedure might be retained, but with a 'two-tier' Commission, analogous to cabinet members and junior ministers in a national government. A more radical solution (unlikely to be adopted) would be to transfer the main responsibility for selection of Commissioners to an electoral process in the European Parliament.

For most purposes, the Commission has the sole right to propose legislation under the EC Treaty. (There are a few instances where the Council may act without a Proposal—see Appendix 2.1.) Suggestions have been made that the Parliament should also have this right, although such a change might lessen the coherence of the Community's legislative programme. There would presumably need to be some mechanism—perhaps approval by the Commission— to filter out Proposals that are not consistent with Treaty objectives or that would compromise a mass of existing legislation.

The Commission also has the main responsibility for implementation of legislation. Its interventions are sometimes resented by member states, particularly where they cause political difficulties for national governments (although it is also convenient on occasion to blame the Commission for unpopular policies). The Council has sought to circumscribe the Commission's role—for example through the use of management committees (see Sec. 2.4.1)—but a fundamental change in the institutional relationship is unlikely, largely because the smaller member states often regard the Commission as an ally, and a safeguard against the voting strength enjoyed by the larger states in the Council.

Reform of Council decision-making   Since the foundation of the Community, there has been a trend to replace unanimous decision-making in the Council with qualified majority voting. Qualified majority voting tends to accelerate the legislative process, because no single member state can block a legislative Proposal. Governments have a dual interest: they may have reservations over a surrender of veto power in areas in which they perceive 'vital national interests' (as in the 'Luxembourg compromise'—see Sec. 2.3.1), but may welcome changes that ease the passage of legislation that they support.

Relaxations of the unanimity requirement were provided for in the original EEC Treaty, and in the 1986 Single European Act which facilitated enactment of legislation relating to the single market. The EU Treaty gave additional scope for qualified majority voting, notably in environmental policy and in new and expanding policy areas such as infrastructure development, consumer protection and monetary policy.

There have been calls for further extensions of qualified majority voting, particularly in relation to the single market and environmental policy (Articles 100a and 130s EC). Some legislation in these areas remains subject to unanimous decision, including measures relating to taxation, the free movement of people, energy, land use and water resources. The most radical suggestion is that the Council should virtually always decide by qualified majority, with unanimity becoming very much the exception.

The arithmetic of voting has become a further element in the debate. Throughout successive enlargements, a qualified majority has remained approximately two-thirds of the votes in the Council. Consequently the number of votes required to block a Proposal has increased in proportion with the increase in total votes, and individual member states have seen their voting strength diluted. When the 1995 enlargement increased the total number of votes from 76 to 87, the UK sought unsuccessfully to prevent a pro rata increase in the blocking minority from 22 to 26 votes. (Acceptance of the UK's proposal would have meant a qualified majority requirement of 65 rather than 62 votes.) If the blocking minority had been fixed at 22 irrespective of the size of the Community, the advantages of qualified majority voting would have been diminished; and, in the event of further enlargement of the Community, 22 votes would become a smaller percentage of a larger total number of votes.

It was eventually agreed that, when opponents command between 23 and 25 votes, additional efforts are to be made 'to reach within a reasonable time and without prejudicing obligatory time limits . . . a satisfactory solution that could be adopted by at least 65 votes' (Decision of 29 March 1994). This agreement is unlikely to have very significant practical impact: it does not alter the formal legal requirements governing decisions by the Council, and does not ultimately preclude a qualified majority of 62.

Some critics of the present Council voting system have argued that the larger member states are under-represented in relation to their population (see Table 2.5). On the other hand, the function of the Council is to represent the member states, which—at least in principle—have equal sovereign rights, irrespective of their population. The 'representatives of the peoples of the States' are in the European Parliament (Article 137 EC).

2.6   THE COMMUNITY AS A SOURCE OF LAW

The European Community is unique among international organizations inasmuch as it forms a legal order above that of its member states. The Treaties are the primary source of Community law, and are in effect integrated within the constitutional structures of member states. Legislation enacted in the framework of the Treaties constitutes the secondary source of Community law, and overrides any conflicting provisions of national legislation. Community law may be invoked not only in the Community's own courts, but also in national courts in the member states.

2.6.1   Community legal institutions

Just as the Community Treaties established political institutions to enact legislation and implement policy measures, they also established legal institutions to ensure the uniform application of Community law. The institutions established for this purpose are the European Court of Justice and the (subordinate) Court of First Instance.

The European Court of Justice is the European Community's supreme judicial authority, and as such has ultimate responsibility for ensuring that the law is properly observed in the interpretation and application of the Treaties and other Community legislation. The Court is composed of 15 judges, drawn from across the Community (although there are no explicit national 'quotas' for membership of the Court). The judges are appointed for renewable six-year terms, and they select one of their number to be president of the Court for a renewable term of three years. The judges are assisted by six advocates general, who make 'reasoned submissions' on cases brought before the Court. Advocates general are appointed on the same terms as the judges.

The Court has three functions:

1. To rule on cases involving alleged infringements of Community law.
2. To review the legality of actions (and failures to act).
3. To give preliminary rulings on questions of Community law in cases referred by national courts.

A subordinate judicial body, the *Court of First Instance*, was established in 1989; it now has jurisdiction over competition regulations, cases involving import levies to combat 'dumping' (see Sec. 10.2.3) and all types of direct action by private parties against Community institutions (Decision 94/149/ECSC, EC), many of which are cases brought under European Community staff regulations. The Court has 15 judges, but no advocates general. Appeals, on points of law only, may be made to the Court of Justice against decisions of the Court of First Instance.

The European Community Courts should not be confused with the European Court of Human Rights, established under the European Convention on Human Rights: the Court of Human Rights is not a Community institution, although all EU member states (and many other European countries) are parties to the Convention. The EU Treaty (Article F) states that 'the Union shall respect fundamental rights as guaranteed by the European Convention ...', which would suggest that participation in the Convention, and implementation of the judgments of the Court of Human Rights, is a condition for membership of the European Union.

2.6.2   The effect of Community legislation

The Treaties establishing the Community have the force of law in all member states, by virtue of the legislative and constitutional provisions enacted on accession to the Community. Consequently the Treaties have *direct effect*, without the need for any intervening national legislation. Furthermore, Community legislation pursuant to the Treaties prevails over the laws of member states.

The supremacy of Community legislation is a fundamental requirement. The proper functioning of the Community demands that agreements made in the Council of Ministers be implemented uniformly. For example, elimination of trade barriers is essential for achievement of a single market; and to this end, the Community has established harmonized standards for products traded between member states (see Sec. 3.1.2)—but these standards would be ineffective if member states were permitted to maintain product specifications that are incompatible with Community regulations.

The legal systems of all member states acknowledge that Community legislation overrides national provisions; where necessary, member states have amended their constitutions to provide for this. It follows that national courts have a responsibility for enforcement of Community law, and may overrule provisions of national law. This has been made clear by the European Court of Justice, which has ruled that provisions of the Treaty and directly applicable measures ... render automatically inapplicable any conflicting provision of current national law' (Case 106/77, p. 643) and that 'the effect of a [Community] Regulation ... is ... to prevent the implementation of any [national] legislative measure, even if it is enacted subsequently, which is incompatible with its provisions' (Case 43/71, p. 1049). This doctrine has enabled the Court to overrule an act of the UK Parliament (the 1987 Territorial Sea Act) inasmuch as its provisions conflicted with earlier Community legislation (Case C-146/89).

A recent judgment of the Court has emphasized the legal basis of the Community, and makes clear the wide scope of Community law:

The EEC Treaty has created its own legal system, which is integrated into the legal systems of Member States, and which their courts are bound to apply. The subjects of that legal system are not only the Member States but also their nationals. Just as it imposes burdens on individuals, Community law is also intended to give rise to rights ... not only where they are expressly granted by the Treaty, but also by virtue of obligations which the Treaty imposes in a clearly defined manner both on individuals and Member States and the Community institutions.

(Case C-6/90, p. I–5413)

2.6.3   Forms of Community legislation

The Treaties make a distinction between the forms of Community legislation, depending upon the manner in which they are given legal force. The essential differences relate to the nature and extent of binding provisions, and in some instances to the Treaty basis. The various possible types of legislation are summarized in Table 2.10 below.

Table 2.10   Forms of European Community legislation

EC Treaty (Article 189), Euratom Treaty (Article 161)	ECSC Treaty (Article 14)	Binding Force
Regulation	Decision (general)	Of general application: binding in its entirety and directly applicable in all member states
Decision	Decision (individual)	Binding in its entirety on those to whom it is addressed
Directive	Recommendation	Binding as to the result to be achieved on each member state to which it is addressed; but leaves to the national authorities the choice and form of methods
Opinion, Recommendation	Opinion	No binding force

Regulations and *Decisions*, like the Treaties themselves, are immediately applicable with no need for any intervening national legislation, and create legal rights and obligations which can be enforced directly before national courts and tribunals.

In contrast, *Directives* (and *Recommendations*, under the ECSC Treaty) specify objectives, but leave to national authorities the choice and form of methods to achieve the objectives. Enactment of a Directive by the Council of Ministers is followed by implementing legislation in member states. The EC and Euratom Treaties specify that Regulations are 'directly applicable' in all member states; this seems to imply that Directives are not directly applicable, and have no force in the absence of implementing legislation. If so, provisions of Directives could not be pleaded before national courts; where a Directive were not properly implemented, the only remedy would be action against the member state(s) concerned, by the Commission under Article 169 EC, or by other member states under Article 170 (and the latter provision is very seldom invoked). However, decisions of the Court of Justice following the enactment of the Treaties have indicated that in certain circumstances the provisions of Directives can have effect even in the absence of implementing legislation, under the *direct effect* doctrine (see Sec. 2.6.5).

The burden of the legislative process is an important consideration in deciding the form of proposed legislation. Regulations impart certainty with respect to their legal requirements, which are immediately applicable; however, to be enforceable their provisions may have to be very detailed—and discussion of these details can render the legislative procedure (particularly in the Council) extremely protracted. Directives have the advantage of flexibility: the authorities in member states are free to decide the most appropriate means of achieving the specified objective, in the context of their own institutions and legal systems. With this element of flexibility, Directives can be enacted more rapidly than an equivalent Regulation—this has been an advantage, for example, in the case of environmental legislation which is mostly in the form of Directives (see Sec. 7.2). On the other hand, where certainty and uniformity are important—for instance in the administration of agricultural price support—then there is no alternative to legislation in the form of Regulations.

2.6.4   Implementation of Community legislation

The Commission, as the guardian of the Treaties and legislation stemming from them, has a duty to ensure the observance of Community law. Much of the Commission's effort with respect to implementation of Community law is concerned with the transposition of Directives into national law. Where Community legislation does not have direct effect, its impact depends upon member states fulfilling their obligations to ensure that appropriate implementing legislation is enacted.

In fulfilling its responsibilities for implementation of legislation, the Commission is aided by complaints from organizations and individuals in member states: this is indeed a vital source of information in cases where legislation is not properly observed. Such complaints greatly outnumber the instances detected independently by the Commission, as is shown in Table 2.11.

Table 2.11   Suspected infringements of Community law by mode of detection Annual averages 1989–1993

	Number	%
Complaints to the Commission	1150	70
Parliamentary Questions	56	3
Petitions	39	2
Detected by the Commission	339	24
Total	1644	100

Source: Derived from European Commission (1994: Table 1.3, p. 63).

Most complaints are resolved without recourse to formal legal procedures (known as 'infringement proceedings'), as is shown in Table 2.12. Nevertheless, complaints are a very important means of ensuring the observance of Community law.

Infringement proceedings   Where the Commission has reason to believe that legislation may not be properly implemented, it approaches the national authorities concerned. If matters are not settled through informal consultation, the Commission then commences infringement proceedings.

The procedure for infringement proceedings is set out in the EC Treaty (Article 169). The first stage is a *Letter of Formal Notice* from the Commission to the member state concerned. If the situation remains unresolved, the Commission then issues a *Reasoned Opinion*, after giving

Table 2.12 Suspected infringements of Community law, 1989–1991: action taken by the Commission

	1989	*1990*	*1991*
Terminated: no infringement	1102	993	893
Infringement established	1179	542	444
Decision pending	31	57	95
Total	2312	1592	1432

Source: European Commission (1994: Table 1.3, p. 63).

the member state concerned the opportunity to submit its observations. If the member state fails to comply with the requirements of the opinion, the Commission may then take the case to the Court of Justice (Article 169 EC). Most cases of infringement are settled with a letter of formal notice; only very few (generally well under 10 per cent) reach the Court of Justice, and where cases have eventually gone to the Court of Justice, the Commission has usually won. This is illustrated by Table 2.13, which shows the outcome (as of the end of 1993) of infringement proceedings commenced in 1989.

Table 2.13 Infringement proceedings commenced in 1989: stage reached by the end of 1993

Stage of proceedings	*No. of cases*
Terminated by Commission Letter	368
Reasoned Opinion pending	12
Terminated by Reasoned Opinion	190
Court cases	
in preparation	36
withdrawn	41
awaiting judgment	11
judgment for the Commission	31
judgment for the member state	2

Source: European Commission (1994: Table 2.3, p. 66).

Most infringement proceedings brought by the Commission result from failures by member states to notify measures taken to implement Directives. This is clearly shown by Table 2.14: more than half of the proceedings initiated by Commission letters to member states in the period 1989–93 concerned non-notification; most of the remaining cases concerned implementing legislation that did not properly reflect the objectives of Community Directives (Directives 'not properly applied') or legislation that was incomplete (Directives 'not properly incorporated'). Only a small proportion of cases involved alleged violations of the Treaties, Regulations or Decisions (all of which take effect without implementing legislation).

Table 2.14   Infringement of Community law: Commission Letters to member states, by legal basis, 1989–1993

	1989	*1990*	*1991*	*1992*	*1993*
Directives					
Non-notification	354	590	504	934	987
Implementation or application	193	231	198	177	153
Treaties, Regulations, Decisions	144	143	151	105	69
Total	691	964	853	1216	1209

Source: European Commission (1994: Table 2.2, p. 65).

There is some variation between member states' records of compliance with Community law, as is shown in Table 2.15: four countries—Italy, Greece, Portugal and Belgium—account for over half the infringement cases that have gone beyond the 'Commission letter' stage. Where member states have been found not to comply with Community law, they have eventually conformed, albeit in some instances with great reluctance. There are often strong pressures from interest groups opposed to the necessary implementation measures, which governments have been reluctant to confront. (This has been a marked feature of the Common Agricultural Policy.) To combat this, the EC Treaty (Article 171) includes a provision (not hitherto invoked) whereby the Court of Justice can fine member states that fail to meet their legal obligations. Moreover, in some circumstances individuals can claim damages from national authorities where Directives are not properly implemented, by invoking the doctrine of direct effect (see Sec. 2.6.5).

Table 2.15   Member states' infringements of Community law: cases by stage of proceedings Annual averages, 1989–1993

	Commission Letter	*Reasoned Opinion*	*Referral to Court*	*Total*
Belgium	83	30	10	122
Denmark	47	4	1	52
Germany	79	20	4	102
Greece	106	39	7	153
Spain	96	24	4	124
France	83	20	4	107
Ireland	68	19	3	90
Italy	117	57	20	195
Luxembourg	68	23	8	98
Netherlands	66	18	5	89
Portugal	106	33	1	140
UK	68	12	2	81
Total	987	298	69	1354

Source: Derived from European Commission (1994: Table 2.1, p. 64).

2.6.5   The immediate application of Directives: the 'direct effect' doctrine

In its judgments, the Court of Justice has somewhat blurred the distinction between Regulations, Decisions and Directives. The Court has held that a Directive may in certain circumstances have direct effect, without the need for national legislation. This prevents member states from frustrating the objectives of Community legislation, by failing to enact implementing legislation. A member state's act of omission in such circumstances is unlawful and thus—in effect—deemed to be invalid. By the same token, the courts can invoke the direct effect doctrine where national legislation is defective—if for instance it is found to be inconsistent with the Community legislation that is to be implemented.

Directives impose obligations only on member states, and the direct effect doctrine can be invoked only against a body that is part of the machinery of government—the state or an 'emanation' of it (Case 152/84, p. 749). For this purpose the Court has adopted a broad definition of national authorities on which Directives may impose obligations. These include all administrative bodies within member states (Case 103/88), and indeed any body, whatever its legal form, 'made responsible ... by the state for providing a public service under the control of the state ... and with special powers beyond the normal rules applicable in relations between individuals' (Case C-188/89 p. I-3348). This would appear to include licensed utilities, such as water and electricity companies, including those in private ownership.

The Court has also provided means whereby Directives can be invoked in cases other than those brought against 'emanations of the state'. Strictly speaking, the provisions of a Directive cannot be relied upon in disputes between private individuals or non-governmental organizations (Case 102/79, p. 1487; Case 152/84, p. 749), or in proceedings brought by the authorities in a member state against such individuals or organizations (Case 80/86 p. 3986). Nevertheless, the Court has held that, where a member state has not enacted legislation to implement a Directive, national laws should be interpreted *as if* they had been amended by implementing legislation (Case 106/89 p. I-4159). This sidesteps the limitation of the direct effect doctrine to cases brought against national authorities.

In some instances there may be no relevant national legislation. The Court has ruled that in such circumstances member states may be liable to pay damages to individuals and organizations for losses suffered as a result of non-implementation (Case C-6/90 p. I-5414). In practice, compensation can be payable only where the provisions of a Directive attribute rights to identifiable individuals, and where a causal link can be established between the member state's breach of its obligation and damage suffered by an aggrieved person.

These legal innovations may have narrowed the differences between the various forms of Community legislation, but nevertheless the distinctions remain valid. This is due principally to limitations on the direct effect of Community legislation, which are more significant for Directives than for other forms of legislation.

The direct effect doctrine can be applied only to legal provisions that contain unconditional requirements, and that are clearly and unambiguously worded. The Court has recognized that Directives by their nature permit member states a certain amount of discretion, which they may legitimately exercise (Case 38/77, p. 2212); and it has ruled that national regulations may prevail with respect to implementation procedures provided that they are not specifically contrary to the provisions of Directives (Case 45/76, p. 2053). Thus, there are difficulties in applying the direct effect doctrine where Directives commit member states to legislate, but do not specify in detail the form the legislation must take.

The practical scope of the direct effect doctrine also depends upon the possibilities for taking legal action under the provisions of legislation. Individuals who have suffered as a result of improper implementation may take legal action against national authorities. However, where the purpose of legislation is to safeguard the general quality of life, there may be no one with standing to mount a legal challenge. This problem is not uncommon in the case of environmental legislation: effects of pollution on human health may be too diffuse to identify damage to specific individuals, while affected wildlife is not the property of any party. It would be possible to enact legislation that permits environmental organizations to initiate legal action in such circumstances, but this has not—as yet—been done by the Community.

2.6.6   The Enforcement of Community legislation

Community legislation is enforced in various ways, through action by the Commission, by national authorities, and by legal actions brought by individuals and organizations whose interests are at stake. The latter has been greatly assisted by the development of the direct effect doctrine, as was shown in the previous section.

In some instances the Commission may impose financial penalties, subject to review by the Court of Justice: policing in this way by a supranational authority is unique in the world. Legislation pursuant to Article 87 EC (Regulation 17/62) empowers the Commission to impose fines on businesses and individuals for failure to supply information relating to their compliance with Community rules on competition established under the Treaty, or for non-compliance with these rules. The Commission also has powers under the ECSC Treaty (Article 65(5)) to impose fines for anti-competitive practices in the coal and steel industries. However, fines imposed under Community law are actually levied under the procedures of member states, by order of the national authorities (see Articles 192 EC, 92 ECSC).

The development of Community jurisprudence has opened the way to enforcement of Community law through the legal systems of member states, irrespective of the wishes of their governments. Where Community legislation has direct effect, it becomes for practical purposes a part of national law; and so national courts function as courts of Community law. In such circumstances it is not open to member states to legislate non-compliance with Community law—any national provisions inconsistent with Community legislation are simply set aside by national courts. Where appropriate, national courts may refer cases to the European Court of Justice for a preliminary ruling on points of Community law; in the period 1990–3 there were on average 173 references per year (European Commission 1994a: 174). Where governments act unlawfully, there are remedies in national law for those who suffer as a result.

However, the mere existence of legislation does not guarantee that it will have effect. Almost all official action to enforce legislative provisions is undertaken not by Community officials, but by the authorities in member states. Consequently the vigour, and extent, of the enforcement effort may tend to reflect national rather than Community priorities. The resulting practical problems are illustrated by the 1993 Commission report on the monitoring by national authorities of agricultural exports, which is necessary for the implementation of a key aspect of the Common Agricultural Policy: 'some member states indicated that compliance has or will have a negative effect on other customs inspection tasks given that budgetary constraints do not permit an increase in the number of inspectors' (COM(93)13, p. 8)

The problem was highlighted in a case in which the Greek authorities did take not adequate measures to combat fraud by government officials involving the evasion of Community import levies. The Court of Justice warned that member states should accord the enforcement of Community law a priority equal to that of national law. Thus:

[Member States] must ensure that infringements of European Community law are penalised under conditions ... which are analogous to those applicable to infringements of national law of a similar nature and importance and which in any event make the penalty effective, proportionate and dissuasive. Moreover the national authorities must proceed with respect to infringements of European Community law with the same diligence as that which they bring to bear in implementing corresponding national laws.

(Case 68/88, p. 2985)

2.7   EUROPEAN COMMUNITY INSTITUTIONS: KEY POINTS AND ISSUES

The European Community (as distinct from the other 'pillars' of the European Union) has a supranational institutional structure which in many ways resembles that of a federal nation state; this includes a legislative system, an executive and a judiciary. Although the subsidiarity doctrine specifies that the Community should intervene only where objectives cannot be 'sufficiently' achieved by the member states, the integration process has nevertheless tended to enlarge the Community's role. The need to streamline decision-making has led to new legislative procedures which have diminished the power of individual member states, and enhanced the role of the Parliament.

The functioning of the single market requires a body of laws that prevail throughout the Community. For this reason, European Community law overrides conflicting provisions of national law. In many instances Community law is directly applicable and can be invoked by organizations and individuals in the member states, even against national governments.

With respect to the development and the future of Community institutions, the following issues can be identified:

1. How have the power and influence of Community institutions changed over time? What changes can be anticipated in the future?
2. How do the Community's legislative processes resemble or differ from those of a nation state? Are changes necessary or desirable to make the Community more democratic or accountable?
3. What are the implications for the Community and member states of the subsidiarity principle?
4. To what extent has the Court of Justice increased the role and influence of the Community?
5. The number of member states has increased since the Community's foundation, and there are prospects for further enlargement, to the east and possibly to the south: what are the implications for Community institutions?

NOTES

[1] 'If action ... should prove necessary to attain ... one of the objectives of the Community ... the Council shall ... after consulting the European Parliament take the appropriate measures' (EC Treaty Article 235).

[2] At that time (prior to the EU Treaty) environmental measures came under the Consultation Procedure, while single market legislation was normally subject to the Co-operation Procedure.

REFERENCES

Cockfield, Lord (1994) *The European Union: Creating the Single Market*, Wiley Chancery Law, Chichester.

Delors J. (1993) Speech to the European Parliament, *Official Journal*, 1993 Annex 3-439/45.

European Commission (1991) 'Monitoring the application by member states of environment Directives', *Official Journal*, 1991 C338/204.

European Commission (1994) 'Eleventh Annual Report to the European Parliament on Commission Monitoring of the Application of Community Law', *Official Journal*, 1994 C154.

European Parliament (1994a) *Report following the Conciliation Procedure on the Proposal for a Directive on the Application of ONP to Voice Telephony*, Document PE209.088 fin, 15 July 1994.

European Parliament (1994b) Final adoption of the general budget of the European Union for the financial year 1995, *Official Journal*, 1994 L369.

House of Commons (1986) *The Single European Act*, Third Report from the Foreign Affairs Select Committee Session 1985–86.

Jacobs, F., Corbett, R. and Shackleton, M. (1992) *The European Parliament*, 2nd edn, Longman, Harlow.

Sloot, T. and Verschuren, P. (1990) 'Decision making speed in the European Community', *Journal of Common Market Studies*, 29(1): 83.

Wilkie, M. and Wallace, H. (1990) *Subsidiarity: Approaches to Power Sharing in the European Community*, Discussion Paper No. 27, Royal Institute of International Affairs, London.

Community legislation

Regulations

Regulation 17/62, *Official Journal*, 1962 204.

Regulation (Euratom) 3954/87, laying down maximum permitted levels of radioactive contamination of foodstuffs and of feedingstuffs, *Official Journal*, 1987 L371/11.

Regulation 259/93, on the supervision and controls of shipments of waste within, into and out of the European Community, *Official Journal*, 1993 L30/1.

Directives

Directive 89/458, on emission standards for cars below 1.4 litres, *Official Journal*, 1989 L226/1.

Directive 91/156, on waste *Official Journal*, 1991 L78/32.

Directive 93/96, on the right of residence for students, *Official Journal*, 1993 L317/59.

Decisions

Decision 87/373, laying down the procedures for the exercise of implementing powers conferred on the Commission, *Official Journal*, 1987 L197/33.

Decision 88/376/EEC, Euratom, on the system of the Community's own resources, *Official Journal*, 1988 L185/24.

Decision of 6 December 1993 adopting the Council's rules of procedure, *Official Journal*, 1993 L304/1.

Decision 93/731, on public access to Council documents, *Official Journal*, 1993 L340/43.

Decision 94/149/ECSC, EC amending Decision 88/591/ECSC, EEC, Euratom establishing a Court of First Instance, *Official Journal*, 1994 L66/29.

Decision of 29 March 1994 concerning the taking of Decision by qualified majority of the Council, *Official Journal*, 1994 C105/1 (as amended by Decision of 1 January 1995, *Official Journal*, 1995 C1/1).

Decision 94/728/EC, Euratom, on the system of the Community's own resources, *Official Journal*, 1994 L293/10.

European Commission documents

COM(93)13, *Report on the Application of Regulation (EEC) No. 386/90 on the Monitoring Carried Out at the Time of Export of Agricultural Products*, 25 January 1993.

COM(93)67, *The Community's Structural Fund Operations 1994–99*, 10 March 1993.

COM(93)545, *Commission Report to the European Council on the Adaptation of Existing Legislation to the Subsidiarity Principle*, 24 November 1993.

Court judgments

Case 43/71, *Politi* [1971] ECR 1039.
Case 45/76, *Comet* [1976] ECR 2043.
Case 38/77, *Enka* [1977] ECR 2203.
Case 106/77, *Simmenthal* [1978] ECR 629.

Case 102/79, *Commission v. Belgium* [1980] ECR 1473.

Case 152/84, *Marshall* [1986] ECR 723.

Case 80/86, *Kolpinghuis Nijmegen* [1987] ECR 3969.

Case 302/87, *European Parliament v. Council* [1988] ECR 5615.

Case 68/88, *Commission v. Greece* [1989] ECR 2965.

Case C-70/88, *European Parliament v. Council* [1991] ECR I-4529.

Case 103/88, *Fratelli Constanzo v. Comune di Milano* [1989] ECR 1861.

Case C-262/88, *Barber v. Guardian Royal Exchange* [1990] ECR I-1889.

Case 106/89, *Marleasing* [1990] ECR I-4135.

Case C-146/89, *Commission v. United Kingdom* [1991] ECR I-3533.

Case C-188/89, *Foster and Others v. British Gas* [1990] ECR I-3313.

Case C-300/89, *Commission v. Council* [1991] ECR I-2895.

Cases C-6/90, C-9/90, *Francovitch and others v. Italian Republic* [1991] ECR I-5357.

Case C-295/90, *European Parliament v. Council* Judgment, 7 July 1993, not yet reported.

Case C-155/91, *Commission (with the European Parliament intervening) v. Council (with Spain intervening)* Judgment 17 March 1993, not yet reported.

Case C-187/93 *European Parliament v. Council* [1994] ECR I-2857.

Legal actions

Case C-58/94, Action brought by the Netherlands against the Council, *Official Journal*, 1994 C90/11.

Case T-194/94, Action brought by J. Carvel and Guardian Newspapers against the Council, *Official Journal*, 1994 C202/13.

EC TREATY PROCEDURES FOR ADOPTION OF LEGISLATION AND INTERNATIONAL AGREEMENTS

Note: The references are to Articles in the 1957 Rome Treaty establishing the European Community, as amended by the 1986 Single European Act and the 1992 Treaty on European Union. The main provisions for legislation and conclusion of international agreements are classified according to the decision-making procedure that is applicable (Consultation, Co-operation or Co-Decision—see Figs. 2.1, 2.2 and 2.3), and the requirements for consultation with other Community institutions. The listing excludes provisions that are obsolescent, the procedure for adoption of the budget (see Fig. 2.4), decisions exclusively concerned with the functioning of Community institutions, and provisions contained in the ECSC and Euratom Treaties and in the intergovernmental 'pillars' of the Maastricht Treaty on European Union.

CO-DECISION PROCEDURE (Art. 189b)

56(2)	Right of establishment: restrictions on grounds of public policy, security or health
57(1)	Right of establishment: mutual recognition of qualifications
57(2)	Right of establishment for the self-employed, not involving amendment of regulations governing professions
130i(1)	Research and technological development framework programmes (requires Council unanimity)

Mandatory consultation with Economic and Social Committee

49	Free movement of workers
54(2)	Right of establishment: measures relating to specific activities
100(a)	Single market, other than fiscal provisions, free movement of persons, rights of employed persons
100(b)	Single market: mutual recognition
129a(2)	Consumer protection (other than single market measures)
130s(3)	Environment programmes

Mandatory consultation with Committee of the Regions

128(5)	Culture: incentive measures, excluding harmonization provisions (requires Council unanimity throughout the procedure)

Mandatory consultation with both Economic and Social Committee and Committee of the Regions

126(4)	Education: incentive measures
129 (4)	Public health: incentive measures
129d	Guidelines on trans-European networks

CO-OPERATION PROCEDURE (Art. 189c)

4b	European Investment Bank statute
6(2)	Prevention of discrimination on grounds of nationality
103(5)	Economic policy: rules for surveillance
104a(2)	Prohibition of privileged access by public bodies to financial institutions
130w	Development co-operation

Mandatory consultation with Economic and Social Committee

75(1)	Transport (apart from the derogation in Art. 75(3))
118a(2)	Health and safety measures
125	European Social Fund implementation measures
127(4)	Training (excluding harmonization measures)
130o(2)	Implementation of research and technological development programmes
130s(1)	Environmental measures (other than fiscal, land use planning, water resource management, and energy policy measures)

Mandatory consultation with both Economic and Social Committee and Committee of the Regions

129d	Trans-European networks: guidelines and interoperability of systems
130e	European Regional Development Fund implementation

Mandatory consultation with European Central Bank (when established)

104b(2)	Prohibitions of credit facilities with ECB
105a(2)	Common currency: technical specifications of coins

PROVISIONS FOR WHICH THE ASSENT OF PARLIAMENT IS REQUIRED

106(5)	Amendment of the Statute of the European System of Central Banks (Council decides by qualified majority on a recommendation from the European Central Bank (ECB) after consulting the Commission, or by unanimity on a Proposal from the Commission after consulting the ECB)
130d	Tasks, objectives, priorities and general rules of the structural funds; establishment of the Cohesion Fund (Council decides by unanimity on a Proposal from the Commission and after consulting the Council of the Regions)
138(3)	Uniform procedure for elections to the European Parliament (Council decides by unanimity on proposals drawn up by the Parliament; Parliament gives assent by majority of its members)

CONSULTATION PROCEDURE

Council may decide by qualified majority

43	Common organization of agricultural markets
87	Competition rules applying to undertakings
94	State aid regulations
100c(3)	Visa requirements for non-EU citizens (from 1996); uniform visa format
109j(3)	Adoption of a single currency
109k(2)	Abrogation of derogations from participation in monetary union

Mandatory consultation with Economic and Social Committee

63	Freedom to provide services
79(3)	Transport: elimination of discrimination between carriers
130i(4)	Research and technological development programmes

Mandatory consultation with European Central Bank

104c(14)	Application of the Protocol on excessive deficit procedure
106(6)	Operations of the ECB

Council must decide by unanimity

8b	Voting rights in municipal and European Parliament elections
8e	Rights of European Community citizens
57(2)	Right of establishment for the self-employed, where regulations governing professions are amended
100c(1)	Visa requirements for non-EU citizens (up to 1996)
104c(14)	Provisions on excessive deficit procedure
109(1)	Agreements on exchange rate system for ECU in relation to non-EU currencies (Council acts on a recommendation from the Commission *or* the ECB)
109f(7)	Tasks of the European Monetary Institute
188b(3)	Appointment of the Court of Auditors
209	Implementation of the budget (Opinion of Court of Auditors required)
235	Action where the Treaty has not provided the necessary powers

Mandatory consultation with Economic and Social Committee

75(3)	Transport regulations liable to have a serious effect on regional living standards and employment and transport operations
99	Harmonization of taxes
100	Single market (where Art. 100a does not apply)
130	Industry policy: measures in support of action by member states
130o(1)	Structures for implementation of research and technological development programmes
130s(2)	Environment: fiscal, land use planning, water resource management and energy policy measures

Mandatory consultation with both Economic and Social Committee and Committee of the Regions

130b	Measures outside the structural funds to promote economic and social cohesion

COUNCIL ACTS ON A PROPOSAL, WITHOUT NEEDING TO CONSULT THE PARLIAMENT

Council may decide by qualified majority

20	Common customs tariff duties
25	Common customs tariff: relief of duty
28	Alteration or suspension of customs duties
55	Exclusion of certain activities from freedom of establishment
59	Extension of freedom of non-Community citizens to provide services
73c(2)	Measures to liberalize movement of capital to or from non-Community countries
73g(2)	Amendment or abolition of national restrictions on movement of capital to or from non-Community countries
92(3)(d)	Categories of state aid which may be compatible with the common market
98	Approval of national import charges and export rebates
101	Elimination of competitive distortions caused by differences between national laws
103(2)	Guidelines for economic policies of member states (Council acts on a Commission recommendation, and informs the Parliament)
103a(2)	Assistance to member states in difficulty as a result of natural disasters (Council must inform the Parliament after the decision is taken)
103(4)	Recommendations to member states on economic policy
104c(6)	Determination of the existence of an excessive deficit in a member state (in the light of observations of the member state concerned)
104c(7–9,11,12)	Implementation of an excessive deficit procedure (Council decision requires a two-thirds majority)
109h	Assistance to member states in balance of payments difficulties (Council acts on a recommendation from the Commission)
112	Harmonization of export assistance measures
113	Measures to implement the common commercial policy
126	Education—recommendations
129	Public health—recommendations
228a	Economic sanctions against non-Community countries

Mandatory consultation with European Central Bank

109(1)	Exchange rate system of the ECU against non-EU currencies (Council acts on a recommendation from the Commission *or* the ECB)
109(2)	Exchange rate policy (Council acts on a recommendation from the Commission *or* the ECB)
109(3)	International monetary agreements
109(4)	International monetary issues: negotiating position
109c(3)	Composition of the Economic and Financial Committee

Council must decide by unanimity

51	Free movement of workers: social security provisions
73c(2)	Measures to restrict movement of capital to or from non-Community countries
103a	Assistance to member states in difficulty (other than as a result of natural disasters)
109(4)	Representation in international monetary negotiations (consultation with ECB required)
128(5)	Culture—recommendations
223	Listing of products to which member states may apply trade restrictions in the interests of national security

INTERNATIONAL AGREEMENTS (Art. 228)

Council may decide by qualified majority

109(3)	Agreements on monetary and foreign exchange matters (Derogation from Art. 228: Council acts by qualified majority on a recommendation from the Commission after consulting the ECB)
113	International trade agreements (consultation with Parliament *not* required)

Mandatory consultation with European Parliament

130m	Implementation of research and technological development programmes
130r(4)	International environmental agreements
130y	Development co-operation agreements

Assent of the European Parliament required

228(3)	Agreements with institutional or budgetary implications, or requiring amendment of legislation adopted under the Conciliation Procedure

Council must decide by unanimity

228(2)	Agreements covering a field in which Community legislation requires unanimous Council decision, and association agreements with international organizations and non-Community countries

COUNCIL MAY ACT WITHOUT A PROPOSAL

Council may decide by qualified majority

84(2)	Application of the common transport policy to sea and air transport
204	Authorization of expenditure in excess of provisional monthly allocations, in the absence of Community budget

Council must decide by unanimity

93(2)	State aid: authorization (Council acts on the application of the Member State concerned)

TWO

POLICIES FOR ECONOMIC INTEGRATION

The central purpose of the European Community is economic integration within a single market, to achieve gains from increased trade and productive efficiency. This implies convergence of the economies of member states and, increasingly, co-ordination of policies at Community level. The process has its difficulties, in terms both of adjustment costs and the necessary political accommodations.

The underlying concept of the Community is a free market economic system, in which the key to increasing prosperity lies in the functioning of competitive markets. Operation of a market system requires a framework with the following essential components:

1. *A legal system*: Ownership, and its transfer, are implicit in markets, so laws of property and contract, and the means to enforce these laws, are essential preconditions.
2. *Standards*: Specifications for products and services are also necessary.
3. *Infrastructure*: The supply of goods and services to the market depends upon information and communication networks, and the availability and quality of factors of production— land, labour and capital.
4. *Policy interventions*: Public authorities seek to influence the functioning of the market for many and varied reasons; examples include measures to alleviate poverty, to improve working conditions, to safeguard the environment and to prevent monopolists' abuse of market power.

Economic integration driven by the single market has extended the scope of the Community's legal system and policy-making procedures. Community policies for the single market initially focused on measures to facilitate movement between member states, to ensure free competition, and to aid less prosperous regions. There is now the prospect that the single market will in due course have a single currency, and hence a common monetary policy.

Economic integration has led to a broadening of the Community policy agenda, because in many instances policy measures at purely national level are no longer viable. In consequence, there are now evolving Community economic and social policies, as well as policies for consumer protection, education, culture and public health.

THREE

THE FOUNDATIONS OF THE EUROPEAN SINGLE MARKET

The single market is the 'nucleus' of the European Community. The central objective of the Treaty establishing the Community (the EC Treaty) is integration of the economies of member states within an economic entity which is greater than the sum of its parts. The purpose is to create the conditions for greater economic efficiency, so that more goods and services can be produced at lower cost, and this is achieved principally through increased productivity and competition; hence the EC Treaty's repeated references to 'an open market economy with free competition'[1] as the basis for Community policies.

Economic integration permits the exploitation of economies of scale: producers have lower costs per unit of output if they are serving a large Community market, rather than individual national markets. A large market also has more scope for competition between producers; for example, France, Germany and Italy each have one or two dominant car manufacturers—but the Community market as a whole is served by numerous competing manufacturers.

The legal foundation of the Community single market is the 'four freedoms'—free movement of goods, services, labour and capital—set out in the EC Treaty. To make a reality of these freedoms, and to enable market forces to operate freely, the Community has developed a framework of rules. These cover (for example) specifications for products and services, public procurement regulations and minimum rates of indirect tax.

In a single market consumers are free to make purchases across national frontiers, and (unless specific prohibitions apply) companies can exercise an 'arbitrage' function, buying goods in one member state for resale in another. These transactions, known as 'parallel imports', are potentially important in combating segmentation of the single market between countries. In general, restrictions on sales across national frontiers are contrary to the Community's rules on competition (see Chapter 4), although sellers sometimes argue that market segmentation is unavoidable, and justified, as long as the single market has multiple currencies with exchange rates that are liable to fluctuate (see Sec. 5.1.2).

Integration of national economies into a single market involves adjustments, which can be painful. Economic restructuring in response to increased competition can lead to unemployment. As part of the single market 'package', the Community has provided financial resources to ease the process of adjustment, and to improve the competitive position of economically disadvantaged regions.

3.1 THE SINGLE MARKET FRAMEWORK

The creation of a common market was from the beginning a prime objective of the European Community; as discussed in Sec. 1.2, it was seen as the key to increased prosperity. The original EEC Treaty in 1957 (Article 8) specified a transitional period of between 12 and 15 years, during which the common market was to be progressively established.

By 1972, at the end of the transitional period, the Community had enjoyed mixed success. Tariff barriers were fully eliminated between member states in 1968, but non-tariff barriers persisted, and proliferated. One observer in the mid-1980s characterized modern trade restrictions as 'an arsenal of measures which lie semi-concealed in the most diverse rules and regulations' (Mattera 1984: 283). This 'arsenal' included technical and trading standards, customs formalities, purchasing requirements, sale and advertising restrictions, financial controls and subsidies, all of which were used to discriminate against imports, or to support exports.

Trade restrictions can to a certain extent be alleviated by *demand-side* measures, to allow purchasers to buy freely from suppliers in other countries. This freedom is ensured in the European Community by the principle of *mutual recognition*, under which products (and services) lawfully marketed in one Community country may normally be sold elsewhere in the Community.

Nevertheless, *supply-side* action was also required to prevent national authorities from restricting the market access of imports from other member states. Discrimination against imports is in practice difficult to combat, since it is often disguised by technical complexities, and the discrimination (although often very effective) is indirect. The governments that instituted these measures usually claimed that they were necessary to protect the well-being and quality of life of the citizens. In these circumstances the Community had to act, to ensure that legitimate protection was maintained, while eliminating the element of trade restriction. This objective was achieved through *harmonization*.

Mutual recognition and harmonization measures are designed essentially to provide a 'level playing field' for competition across the single market. It should be emphasized that the purpose is to eliminate *artificial* restrictions on competition, so that regions of the Community may exploit to the full their natural advantages. Limits on competitiveness arising from different resource endowments will remain, and indeed will be intensified; for example, cultivation of grapevines in northern Europe will remain exposed to competition from southern regions which enjoy the advantage of a warmer climate, and hence lower costs.

Most of the legal framework for the single market was in place by the end of 1992. The response in terms of increasing competitiveness and economic restructuring will unfold in the years to come. Forecasts have predicted that the development of the single market will lead to an acceleration of economic growth, and hence to increased prosperity for the Community's citizens. However, this may not be immediately apparent, in part because the inauguration of the single market coincided with recession and high unemployment, and also because the negative effects of economic restructuring (particularly increased unemployment) appear more rapidly, and are more noticeable, than the ultimate benefit.

3.1.1 The principle of mutual recognition

The European Community can be a single market only if there is freedom to sell goods and services between member states. On the other hand, a totally free and unregulated market system is an impossibility: the provision of goods and services is always subject to regulations, which serve many purposes—for example, to achieve technical standardization, to safeguard property rights, and to protect consumers and the environment. So the Community single market is achieved not by eliminating regulation, but rather by preventing its misuse. The problem then is to ensure that member states pursue legitimate objectives in a way that does not obstruct or distort trade within the Community.

The solution in many instances has been to require that member states recognize each other's regulations—so for example a product accepted as meeting safety standards in one country is deemed to meet the required standards in other member states. This rule is known as the *principle of mutual recognition*, and also as the *country of origin principle*, because member states must recognize the validity of the product standards of the country in which the product originated. Under this system it is clearly not possible for a member state to use safety regulations to restrict imports from elsewhere in the Community, because imported goods need only conform to the requirements of their country of origin. Such mutual recognition does of course imply a need for mutual trust; and where necessary this can be reinforced by the adoption of Community-wide standards.

The basis for the doctrine of mutual recognition is Article 30 EC, which provides that 'quantitative restrictions on imports and all measures having equivalent effect shall ... be prohibited between member states'. This prohibition was given very broad scope by the Court of Justice in the 1974 *Dassonville* judgment, which states that 'all trading rules enacted by member states which are capable of hindering directly or indirectly, actually or potentially, intra Community trade are to be considered as measures having an effect equivalent to quantitative restrictions' (Case 8/74, p. 852).

There is consequently a general presumption that a product lawfully sold in one member state may be marketed throughout the Community. This was affirmed by the Court of Justice in the *Cassis de Dijon* judgment (Case 120/78), in which it held that Germany could not prohibit the sale of a French liqueur merely because the alcoholic strength was below the minimum specified for German liqueurs.

Since mutual recognition derives directly from the Treaty, its effect does not depend on Community or national legislation. It may be invoked in legal cases brought by private parties, even if the Commission takes no action (although as 'guardian' of the Treaties the Commission clearly has an interest in ensuring that the principle is respected).

Mutual recognition, as expressed in the *Cassis de Dijon* doctrine, can be effective in countering the more blatant forms of non-tariff barrier within the Community; but member states may legitimately restrict imports and exports if this is necessary to implement national policies with respect to certain specified objectives. The EC Treaty (Article 36) defines these objectives as: public morality, policy or security; protection of human, animal or plant health; safeguarding of cultural heritage; and protection of industrial or commercial property.

The Court of Justice subsequently added environmental protection to this list, in a ruling which made clear that freedom of movement is balanced against imperative requirements of national policies. Thus, 'the principle of freedom of trade is not to be viewed in absolute terms, but is subject to certain limits justified by the objectives of general interest pursued by the Community' (Case 240/83, p. 549).

However, these 'limits' are not absolute, either: the Treaty stipulates that the exceptions set out in Article 36 must not be used (or *ab*used) 'as a means of arbitrary discrimination or a disguised restriction on trade between member states'. So in each case it is necessary to decide what is the main purpose and effect of the restriction in question: is it genuinely necessary to achieve policy objectives within the exceptions permitted under Community law? or is it actually more concerned with protection of industry from legitimate competition from imports?

This 'proportionality' concept is implicit in the *Cassis de Dijon* judgment, which states that 'a measure restricting imports must have 'a purpose which is in the general interest and such as to take precedence over ... the free movement of goods'; moreover, a restriction must be suitable and necessary to achieve the stated aim, and no more restrictive than is absolutely necessary. In this particular case the Court was evidently not satisfied with the purported justification—as a consumer protection measure—of the German regulation that restricted the sale of *Cassis de Dijon*. (The German authorities had argued that, if low strength liqueurs were permitted this would induce a tolerance for alcohol, and—somewhat inconsistently—that it would unleash competitive pressures on the producers leading to a reduction in the alcoholic strength of beverages.)

In other instances, the Court has upheld national restrictions on imports from other member states. A notable example is the so-called 'Danish Bottles' case (Case 302/86), in which the Danish authorities required, for environmental reasons, that beverages (including imports) be sold in specified returnable containers. In this case the Court accepted that the Danish regulation was for the most part a bona fide environmental protection measure, and that its effect on freedom of trade was not inherently disproportionate.

The balance between free trade and legitimate restrictions has given rise to extensive case law. Two similar cases involving imports of poultry demonstrate the conditions under which import restrictions are and are not permissible: import licensing in Ireland was held to be lawful (Case 74/82) because it involved only measures genuinely necessary for health protection, while a total ban on imports into the UK was ruled unlawful (Case 40/82) because it went beyond the requirements of health policy, and was thus a quantitative restriction on imports prohibited by Article 30 EC.

Moreover, the 'public policy' invoked to restrict imports must be applied in a way that does not discriminate against imports from other member states. For example, the United Kingdom was held to have acted unlawfully in applying dual standards of 'public morality' protection, whereby imports from other member states were restricted more severely than goods produced in the UK (Case 121/85). Conversely, *non-discriminatory* restrictions on trade are permissible, as was demonstrated when the Court upheld national regulations in the UK and France which respectively limit retailers' freedom to operate on Sundays (Case C-169/91) and to resell goods at a loss (Cases C-267 and 268/91). In these cases the regulations in question applied equally to sales of imported and non-imported goods, and had no significant indirect discriminatory effects. So in terms of the *Dassonville* case, 'hindrance to intra Community trade' may be tolerated if it is incidental to the achievement of legitimate national policy objectives.

3.1.2   Harmonization: the single market programme

In the decades following the EEC Treaty, it became increasingly evident that the realization of the single market depended upon positive action to combat restrictions on freedom of movement between member states. Mutual recognition is not sufficient where 'vital' interests are concerned: member states may justify trade restrictions (under Article 36 EC) on grounds such as morality, security, health or environmental protection (see Sec. 3.1.1). Moreover, progress towards a single market has been impeded by a proliferation of national administrative formalities, technical specifications and purchasing restrictions, together with the distorting effects of differing tax regimes.

Where mutual recognition or deregulation is not sufficient, action at Community level is necessary to permit freedom of movement. This may take the form of legislation, or objectives may be achievable by mutual agreement between the parties involved. In general the process initially entails a harmonization of national provisions. Reconciliation of systems that are often very different is naturally not without problems, and the development of the necessary measures frequently entails substantial expert studies and wide-ranging consultations; and in the process misunderstandings can arise, occasionally leading to bizarre reports in the press. (For illustrations of the genre see FCO, 1993, the cover of which depicts the renaming of London's Metropolitan Police headquarters as 'Scotland Metre'.)

When harmonization is achieved through Community legislation, the Community acquires a role in—and sometimes exclusive responsibility for—development of policies in the area concerned. This is usually because the necessary policy instruments can operate only at Community level; for example, the single market has required the harmonization of environmental and safety standards for vehicles, and so any future modifications to these standards will be bought about by revision of the relevant Community legislation. For this reason, the single market has been a powerful force in extending the policy responsibilities of the Community.

The effect of Community legislation is illustrated by a decision of the Court of Justice, which overruled Belgian restrictions on imports of *toxic* waste but allowed restrictions on *non-toxic* waste (Case 2/90); the apparent anomaly arises because movement of toxic waste is governed by Community legislation, which was in this case held to supersede national provisions; the position with non-toxic waste is quite different, inasmuch as there is no Community legislation, and so member states are permitted to restrict imports.

Development of the single market was greatly facilitated by the Single European Act, which came into force in 1987. This Act made a number of amendments to the EEC Treaty, which are outlined in Sec. 2.3.1. The Community's legislative processes were accelerated with the extension of qualified majority voting in the Council. Article 100a of the revised Treaty extended the Co-operation Procedure (with qualified majority voting in the Council) to legislation necessary for the establishment and functioning of the internal market, so that one or two countries could not block legislative Proposals which enjoy substantial support among member states and in the European Parliament. (Following the EU Treaty, legislation under Article 100a is now enacted under the Co-Decision Procedure, except that measures relating to fiscal provisions, free movement of persons and the rights of employees have remained subject to unanimous decision in the Council, under the Consultation Procedure.)

The Single Act set a target date—the end of 1992—for adoption of measures necessary to establish a single internal market, which is defined as 'an area without internal frontiers in which the free movement of goods, persons, services and capital is ensured in accordance with the provisions of this Treaty' (Article 7a EC (formerly 8a EEC)). This deadline was generally very successful in ensuring that the Council enacted the legislation needed to operate the single market.

There is a possibility for tension between the single market and national measures under Article 36 EC, as for instance in the 'Danish bottles' case (see Sec. 3.1.1), in which trade restrictions were permitted on environmental grounds. The solution in the EC Treaty is to require that Commission Proposals for legislation should 'take as a base a high level of protection' with respect to health, safety and environmental and consumer protection. Moreover, the Commission formulates its Proposals knowing that Council amendments to adopt lower standards require the unanimous approval of member states (under Article 189a EC), and that member states may legitimately maintain higher standards provided that this does not involve 'arbitrary discrimination or a disguised restriction on trade between Member States' (Article 100a(4) EC). The effect of these provisions is a bias in favour of high standards in Community legislation.

Most of the Community's single market legislation originated with the programme set out in the 1985 White Paper on the internal market (European Commission 1985), which constituted a framework for legislative Proposals necessary for completion of the internal market. This was designed to give a new impetus for achievement of a common market—the objective to which the Community had ostensibly been committed since 1957.

The White Paper identified three types of barrier—physical, technical and fiscal—the removal of which was a precondition for achievement of a single market, and it outlined the action required as a prelude to the lifting of these barriers.

Physical barriers   As the White Paper observed, 'the customs posts, the immigration controls, the passports, the occasional search of personal baggage . . . to the ordinary citizen are the most obvious manifestation of the continued division of the Community'. Frontier controls also imposed 'an unnecessary burden on industry, flowing from the delays, formalities . . . and handling charges . . . adding to costs and damaging competitiveness' (European Commission 1985: 9).

Up to 1992, frontier controls between member states essentially served two purposes: tax collection, and a 'policing' function to enforce regulations controlling movements of people, goods and money. The specific functions of customs controls included the:

- application of national import restrictions;
- enforcement of national import quotas for products originating in non-EC countries;
- collection (and reimbursement) of taxes and agricultural levies;
- checking of road transport licences and of compliance with regulations governing transport of dangerous substances;
- collection of trade statistics.

Systematic customs controls at frontiers within the Community were discontinued at the end of 1992, in accordance with the deadline for achievement of 'an area without internal frontiers' (Article 7a EC). The tasks listed above are not now performed at frontiers, and their objectives are now achieved by other means.

As a result of legislation to bring about harmonization, and the mutual recognition of product standards, there are now few restrictions on imports of goods lawfully purchased in, or imported into, another member state. Movements of goods, and of 'bads' that are restricted throughout the Community (e.g. illicit drugs, stolen property and hazardous substances) are policed by co-operation between law enforcement bodies in the member states. (This co-operation is provided for in the EU Treaty, Article K1.)

The Commission strongly emphasized the importance of complete removal (rather than merely lightening or simplification) of physical controls at frontiers. This was to some extent a matter of symbolism: according to the White Paper, the removal of frontier posts was 'the clearest sign of the integration of the Community into a single market'. More fundamentally, it was seen as a guarantee of the integrity of the single market: the White Paper noted that 'the maintenance of any internal frontier controls [would] perpetuate the costs and disadvantages of a divided market' (European Commission 1985: 9).

Abolition of customs controls has led to a major shift of responsibilities—and powers—to the Community level. Member states had used frontier controls as a mechanism for implementing a wide range of national policies; and in many instances these policies became non-viable at national level when the controls were removed. For example inspections were previously undertaken at frontiers to ensure that meat conformed to *national* standards; following the removal of frontier controls, inspections are made at the abattoirs where the meat originates, in order to certify that it complies with a *Community* standard; and this certification is recognized in all member states.

Technical barriers Achievement of a single market was heavily dependent on the reconciliation of differing national regulations, standards and specifications. One consequence of these differences was segmentation of markets, which tended to deprive consumers of the benefits of competition between producers and to increase the costs of manufacturers and suppliers of services. Technical barriers also impeded mobility of labour and capital: workers found that qualifications obtained in their own country were not recognized elsewhere, while the movement of capital was constrained by national regulations governing financial markets and foreign exchange transactions.

Technical barriers essentially had three sources:

1. *Legislation* In some instances standards for products and services have legal force; for example, all cars must by law be equipped with seat belts.
2. *Standardization* Standards are developed by non-governmental organizations established for this purpose such as the BSI (in the UK), AFNOR (France) and DIN (Germany);[2] these do not have the force of law, but are generally accepted, and may be written into contractual specifications and insurance requirements. For example, companies may require that their suppliers are certified to conform to the international 'quality standard' ISO 9000.
3. *Testing requirements* These are another form of product standard. For example, new chemicals and medicines have to undergo standard tests before they can be released into the market.

Although technical barriers were to some extent eroded by mutual recognition—as in the *Cassis de Dijon* case (see Sec. 3.1.1) differences between national technical specifications nevertheless hampered freedom of movement within the Community.

Furthermore, member states maintained trade restrictions on grounds such as safety, health or environmental protection. Such restrictions are of course difficult to sustain in the single market, because in the absence of frontier controls it is not possible to keep out imports from other member states that do not necessarily conform to the national standards.

The solution in such circumstances was harmonization. Typically, this involved the formulation of standards which would be valid throughout the Community. This procedure differs from mutual recognition inasmuch as it involves acceptance of an agreed Community standard rather than standards adopted independently by member states.

Harmonization may if necessary be implemented through Community legislation. The EC Treaty provides for 'directives for the approximation of such provisions . . . in Member States as directly affect the establishment or functioning of the common market' (Article 100 EC). Prior to the Single Market Programme, the Commission tended to advance Proposals for detailed legislation: enactment of this legislation, which required unanimous approval by the Council, proceeded very slowly.

In order to accelerate progress, and to meet the 1992 deadline for achievement of the single market, the Commission introduced a new approach, which is summarised in Box 3.1. Harmonization is based as far as possible on co-operation between national standards bodies (which are non-governmental organizations), avoiding detailed legal provisions. Legislation is confined to essential requirements for the protection of health and safety, consumers and the environment; standardization bodies then define the detailed technical specifications for conformity with these requirements.

Technical standards are co-ordinated by two European bodies, CEN (the Comité Européen

---

BOX 3.1
Principles of standardization in the European Community

- Member states should maintain a constant check on technical regulations and abolish any that are obsolete or unnecessary.
- Member states should ensure mutual recognition of tests and harmonized rules for certification bodies.
- There should be early European Community consultation at an appropriate level where national regulatory initiatives or procedures might affect the internal market.
- Technical standards should be extended, preferably at Community level, for health and safety.
- There should be a general commitment to Community-level standards, especially for new technologies, in conjunction with European standardization bodies.

Source: Council Resolution of 7 May 1985 on a new approach to technical harmonization and standards, *Official Journal*, 1985 C136/1.

---

de Normalisation) and CENELEC (the Comité Européen de Normalisation Électrotechnique, which is responsible for electrical standards). National standardization bodies are required to inform CEN or CENELEC of technical standards in preparation, and to delay implementation of standards while European standards, or relevant Community legislative measures, are being drawn up (Directive 83/189, Articles 7–9). European standards are developed by consensus, following discussion where necessary in an expert technical committee, and in collaboration with the ISO (International Organization for Standardization).

Public procurement   Community law prohibits discrimination against undertakings in other member states in the award of public procurement contracts. Relevant provisions of the EC Treaty include Articles 7(1) (prohibiting discrimination on grounds of nationality); 30 (prohibiting trade restrictions); 52 (on freedom of establishment); 57 (on freedom to provide services).

Public purchasing has historically been subject to national protectionist rules, instituted for a variety of reasons, including the safeguarding of employment, support for emerging high-technology industries and implementation of industrial strategies. Notwithstanding the provisions of the EC Treaty, barriers to transfrontier procurement have persisted. Difficulties arise in obtaining information on tenders, in overcoming covert discrimination and in securing redress when unlawful discrimination does occur. Procedures for awarding of contracts can sometimes be obscure, rendering discriminatory practices difficult to detect.

Furthermore, biases can be institutionalized in the form of unnecessarily restrictive specifications. This phenomenon is illustrated by the Dundalk Water Supply case. Potential contractors were required to be certified to comply with Irish standards; the Court of Justice ruled that this requirement was a measure hindering intra-Community trade—and so contrary to Article 30 EC—because compliance was excessively onerous for non-Irish undertakings (Case 45/87).

Procedures for the award of public procurement contracts are governed by Directives concerning public services, supply and public works (Directives 92/50, 93/36 and 93/37), which require publication of tender notices in the *Official Journal*, and specify criteria for adopting procedures and awarding contracts. Contracts relating to infrastructure areas—water, energy, transport and telecommunications—are covered by a separate legislation (Directive 90/531) which allows somewhat more flexibility.

Fiscal barriers   All Community member states levy excise taxes and value added tax (VAT). Excises are charged on the sales of specific products, while VAT is a general tax on the sale of

> **BOX 3.2**
> **Value added tax: an example**
>
> Assume that the VAT rate is 10 per cent, and all transactions are within a single country. Then a company selling 100 ECUs worth of goods must add 10 ECUs tax on to the amount it charges its customer. But if the company pays 60 ECUs (plus 6 ECUs VAT) to its own suppliers, it may reclaim the 6 ECUs VAT. So the company pays 10 ECUs to the tax authorities, and is repaid 6 ECUs, and its net tax payment amounts to 4 ECUs. In other words, its value added is $100-60=40$ ECUs, on which it pays tax (at a rate of 10 per cent) of 4 ECUs.
>
> Different rules apply if the company and its suppliers are not located in the same country. The company would pay 10 ECUs VAT to the authorities in its own country. The refund of 6 ECUs would be paid *to the suppliers* by the authorities in their country.

goods and services. The adoption and implementation of VAT is governed by a series of Directives dating back to 1967, pursuant to Article 99 EC, which provides for the approximation of indirect taxes to the extent necessary for the functioning of the single market.

VAT is a tax levied on the sale of goods and services. Where transactions are confined to a single country, sellers (other than those who are exempt) pay the tax, but are able to reclaim VAT paid to their own suppliers. However, in the case of cross-border transactions the supplier reclaims any VAT paid in the exporting country, and the purchaser must pay the tax in the importing country. This is known as the 'destination principle' because tax liability is incurred only in the country of destination. The system is explained in Box 3.2; it should be emphasized that the example is highly simplified, and takes no account of complications arising from multiple tax rates and differences in rates between member states.

The main excise taxes are those levied on alcoholic beverages, tobacco and mineral oils. Commercial trade in these products is taxed on the destination principle: exports are exempt from tax in the exporting country, and subject to the full excise tax of the importing country when sold to the final consumer. Products obtained for personal use (and not for resale) are taxed in the country of purchase.

Before 1993, administration of both excise taxes and VAT depended on frontier controls: exports and imports were declared to Customs at the frontier so that tax could be levied and refunded as appropriate. Goods subject to excise duties were taxed, or registered for taxation on sale to the public in the importing country. VAT was refunded on exports, and levied on imports.

In 1993, following the removal of frontier controls, a 'transitional regime' was introduced for VAT. The transitional period lasts until the end of 1996, and the system may subsequently be modified. The destination principle is retained, so that tax continues to be refunded on exports. A company submits to the VAT authorities in its own country a declaration in which tax is reclaimed on exports to other member states; to obtain the refund the declaration must give details of VAT registration of the purchaser. Similarly, an importer must account for VAT in the country to which the export is destined—so for each export refund in the country of origin there should (in principle) be a corresponding payment on import into the country of destination (Directive 91/680, Articles 28l, 28h).

The Commission originally proposed that VAT in the single market should be levied on the 'origin' principle. This would mean a Community-wide system treating sales and purchases across borders in the same way as those within member states, with VAT refunded to the purchaser, irrespective of the member state in which it had been charged; VAT collected in the exporting country would be credited to the importing country through a 'clearing house'. This would be a simpler system, but it is difficult to operate if member states continue to charge VAT at different rates. For example, if the exporting country has a VAT rate of 15 per cent, while the rate in the importing country is 20 per cent, there would be a 5 per cent shortfall when payment is made through the clearing system). Alternatively, the system could operate without the clearing house, although this might be seen as inequitable (especially as the authorities in low taxing countries would have to pay refunds against tax paid in high tax countries). The alignment of VAT rates across the Community would go a long way to resolving this.

In the single market there are no limits on tax paid imports for personal use. Up to 1993 personal imports from other Community member states goods in excess of specified allowances were subject to tax levied by Customs at the frontier, irrespective of whether tax had already been paid in the country of origin. Variations in rates of tax created incentives for cross-border purchases in countries with lower tax rates. Frontier controls were necessary to counter this, and thus to prevent loss of tax revenue in high-tax countries.

Anticipating the removal of frontier controls, the Community enacted legislation specifying *minimum* rates of VAT and excises. Directive 92/77 requires member states to levy VAT at a 'standard' rate which must be at least 15 per cent; certain categories of product may be taxed at 'reduced' rates, which are not less than 5 per cent. (Member states may have no more than two reduced rates.) The Directive provides for transitional exceptions, and permits member states to maintain zero rates which were in force prior to the legislation. (The United Kingdom was the main beneficiary of the latter provision, although its significance has been reduced by the introduction of VAT on domestic fuel in the UK by the Finance Act 1993, Section 42.)

Further Directives specify minimum rates of excise duties on tobacco, alcoholic beverages and mineral oils (Directives 92/79, 92/84, and 92/82). These are the only instances in which taxes on specific products are the subject of Community legislation. Member states may levy excise taxes on other products, *provided that* they are compatible with Community law; in the context of the single market, this means that the tax must not give rise to distortions of trade, and also that there can be no recourse to frontier controls in the enforcement of the tax.

These conditions limit the effectiveness of national taxes. Taxation tends to reduce demand for the product that is taxed, and the resulting effects on consumption are liable to be perceived as market distortions, contrary to the EC Treaty (Article 30). Moreover, in the absence of frontier controls a national tax can be avoided by importation of untaxed products from neighbouring countries. This tends to restrict the scope of fiscal mechanisms as instruments of national policy, and to constrain any major restructuring of national tax systems. For example, product taxes are used to deter consumption of environmentally damaging products and to encourage recycling, but Community member states have not thus far given such taxes a major role—notwithstanding instances such as the plastic bag tax in Italy, and taxes on pesticides and disposable beverage containers in Denmark (OECD 1993: 43–4).

The Commission originally envisaged approximation of VAT and excise tax rates so that they were 'sufficiently close [to avoid] distortions of trade, diversions of trade and effects on competition'. The Commission estimated, referring to experience in the United States, that rates of indirect tax could differ by up to 5 per cent between neighbouring member states without giving rise to very significant cross-border shopping and loss of tax revenue in the country with a higher tax rate (European Commission 1985: 46). With one exception (between Germany and Denmark), differences between standard VAT rates in adjoining Community member states were within this range by 1992 (European Commission 1992a), leading the Commission to conclude that there is on the whole a 'sufficient' degree of VAT convergence (COM(94)584, p. 9).

There is much greater variation in excise taxes, particularly on alcoholic beverages, which historically have been taxed more heavily in northern Europe than in the south. Cross-border shopping, particularly for wine and beer, has increased dramatically with the advent of the single market. For instance, there has been a massive growth in personal imports into the UK from France, stimulated by differences in excise duties (the duty on beer in the UK is approximately seven times the level in France): the loss of business to UK retailers has been estimated at £700 m in 1993, and the loss of tax revenue to the UK government may be up to £350 m (*Financial Times*, 23 December 1993).

3.2   THE SINGLE MARKET: UNFINISHED BUSINESS

The programme of Community legislation set out in the Internal Market White Paper was largely completed on schedule by the end of 1992. This does not of course mean that the single market has now been achieved: it merely marks the completion of an essential precondition, which must be followed by changes in administrative practices and—crucially—in attitudes. The single market will ultimately become a reality when people show by their behaviour that they believe it to be so.

The legislative programme had an essentially 'catalytic' function, providing a framework for far-reaching economic and political changes over a period of years: the effects of the single market will become apparent only gradually, and may well be more obvious with hindsight than to contemporary observers.

3.2.1   Progress of legislation

The Commission brought forward 282 Proposals based on the internal market White Paper (European Commission (1985)), 265 (95 per cent) of which were enacted into Community legislation by the end of 1993. Of the 282 Proposals, 222 required transposition into national law through implementing legislation in member states: 87 per cent of this legislation had been completed by the end of 1993 (COM(94)55, p. C).

However, only half of the measures were fully transposed in all member states, and particularly in the areas of public procurement, company law, and intellectual property there was still some way to go (see Box 3.3).

At the end of 1993, 17 White Paper Proposals had yet to be enacted as Community legislation. These were mainly in the areas of company law (notably, the Proposal for a European company statute) and taxation (including a special VAT regime for small firms and measures to eliminate double taxation). In addition, some supplementary Commission Proposals were awaiting adoption by the Council: these included provisions for the protection of investors and of intellectual property, and various technical harmonization measures.

In general, fiscal legislation has made slow progress. Legislation to harmonize VAT was adopted only a few months before the 1992 deadline. Measures relating to direct taxation have fared even worse: the first provisions to eliminate double taxation (Directives 90/434 and 90/435) were enacted some twenty years after the original Commission Proposal. Fiscal provisions remain subject to unanimous decision-making in the Council (Article 100a(2) EC); and, given the sensitivities of national governments and the consequent difficulties of securing unanimous agreement, taxation is likely to continue as an area of unfinished business for some time to come.

With the single market programme largely completed, the focus of attention is moving from enactment to enforcement of legislation. The reason for this was succinctly expressed in a Commission report which observed that 'it is not enough to pass laws and simply hope that

BOX 3.3
Directives requiring implementing legislation: progress of transposition into national law, 1993

Percentage fully and partially transposed by 1993

Fully transposed	50%
Transposed in 10 member states	75%

Percentage of transposition completed by area, 1993

Area	Percentage completed
Public procurement	59%
Company law	60%
Intellectual property	61%
Insurance	73%

Source: European Commission (1994), *The Community Internal Market—1993 Report*, COM(94)55, 14 March 1994, p. C.

they will be applied evenly in all member states: the need is for a more effective and clearly expressed dialogue between Community institutions and European citizens and business' (Sutherland *et al.* 1992: 3). Enforcement is primarily a matter for the authorities in member states (see Sec. 2.6.6); the Commission has direct powers only in a few specific areas such as competition policy and industries covered by the ECSC Treaty. National authorities have a general duty to secure the enforcement of Community legislation, and to provide for appropriate penalties for breaches of the law. However, there are few *specific* obligations in this respect: little has been done to harmonize enforcement priorities, or penalties for wrongdoing.

3.2.2 The VAT system

One of the main functions of customs posts at frontiers was to administer value added tax, and to collect statistical information on imports and exports based on VAT declarations. The VAT system, although no longer reliant on physical frontier controls, nevertheless retains the concept of a 'fiscal frontier', whereby tax is charged on imports and rebated on exports (the 'origin' principle). Movement across the frontiers is now monitored, for taxation and statistical purposes, through accounting procedures. The Commission has established a system—known as Intrastat—to collect statistics for intra-Community trade based on information generated by VAT returns.

The system has been beset by complexities: exporters are obliged to supply information on the fiscal status of their customers in other member states, and businesses require agents for VAT purposes in all the countries where they trade. There have been delays in submission of returns, and the information appears to be somewhat unreliable. If it appears that these difficulties are inherent in the system, there is likely to be renewed pressure when the system is reviewed in 1996 for a change to the destination principle and for harmonization of VAT rates, on the lines originally envisaged by the Commission.

3.2.3 Company law and taxation

There is no unified legal framework for a company operating across the single market. The Commission has advanced Proposals for a 'European company statute', which would avoid the legal and practical constraints arising from differences between national systems. To operate under the proposed statute, a company would require a capitalization of at least 100 000 ECUs (COM(89)268). As of 1995 (seven years after the original Commission Proposal), no legislation has been adopted.

In a number of member states there are severe limits on transfrontier investment by pension funds. These restrictions may not be consistent with Community law, although there are prudential arguments for maintaining assets that are denominated in a 'matching' currency, in which the fund's eventual liabilities are also denominated. (This of course will no longer be a consideration after the single market adopts a single currency—see Chapter 5.) The Commission has made a Proposal for legislation to liberalize transfrontier investment: this would allow up to 40 per cent of a fund's assets to be held in 'non-matching' currencies, and would define the ECU as a matching currency for this purpose (European Commission 1991: Article 4). This Proposal has not been adopted.

In a single market with mobility of capital, differences in direct taxation can give rise to economic distortions manifested in effects on competition or locational decisions. Ideally, the tax system would be neutral in its influence on economic decisions; and this would imply harmonization of tax structures and rates. Corporate tax rates remain a purely national responsibility, and there is variation between member states. (In 1991 the average rate of tax was 40.1 per cent, with a standard deviation between member states of 6.7: European Commission 1992b: 173.) The Commission has had limited success in harmonization of tax structures: legislation has been enacted on arrangements for capital gains tax, and to prevent double taxation of profits remitted by a subsidiary to its parent company in another member state (Directives 90/434 and 90/435). Taxation of joint operations across national frontiers is the subject of a 1990 Convention (90/436/EEC) between member states, providing for arbitration in the event of disagreement; this Convention awaits ratification. However, little progress has been made with Proposals to extend legislation to cover double taxation of interest and royalty payments, and to allow tax relief for losses incurred by a subsidiary in another member state.

3.2.4 Frontier controls

The EC Treaty provision for 'free movement of goods, persons, services and capital' (Article 7a) led to the removal of customs controls at frontiers; and logically it should do the same for immigration controls. The economic arguments for removal of customs posts at frontiers apply also to immigration controls. There are potential economic benefits from time savings and redeployment of officials manning frontier posts. There will be less duplication of effort in issuing visas to non-European Union citizens, and benefits to business and tourism from free circulation of people—as well as goods—within the Community.

The final removal of frontier controls between member states has been impeded by slow progress in securing agreement on common policies with respect to policing and immigration control (including visas and asylum). Free movement was established between eight member states under the intergovernmental Schengen Agreement which came into effect in March 1995. The 'Schengen area' initially comprised the Benelux countries, Germany, France, Spain and Portugal, with provision for eventual inclusion of Austria, Italy and Greece. Denmark, Sweden and Finland (together with Norway) are members of the Scandinavian passport area, while the UK and Ireland comprise a common travel area (but without mutual recognition of visas).

Meanwhile, the legality of the remaining frontier controls is open to question, and the European Parliament has brought an action to require the Commission to seek their removal (Case C-445/93). Some governments (notably that of the UK) do not accept that frontier controls are necessarily inconsistent with the EC Treaty: their argument appears to be based on a restrictive interpretation of Article 7a EC (which provides for freedom of movement 'in accordance with the provisions of this Treaty'), and the 1986 Declaration permitting member states 'to take such measures as they consider necessary for the purpose of controlling immigration from third countries, and to combat terrorism' (General Declaration on Articles 13–19 of the Single European Act).

On the other hand, it can be plausibly argued that immigration policies come within the scope of the EC Treaty. The Treaty's Chapter on the internal market covers provisions that 'directly affect the establishment or functioning of the common market' (Article 100), and also provides a basis for Community legislation on visas. There is provision for Community legislation specifying the countries whose citizens must be in possession of a visa when crossing the external borders of the member states (Article 100c(1)) and establishing a uniform format for visas (Article 100c(5)), and the Commission has formulated Proposals accordingly (COM(93)684). Furthermore, the provisions for intergovernmental co-operation in immigration matters under the EU Treaty are 'without prejudice to the powers of the European Community' (EU Treaty Article K1).

3.3   THE ECONOMIC IMPACT OF THE SINGLE MARKET

The single market has set in train a process of economic restructuring, as producers and consumers respond to new opportunities. On balance, substantial long-term economic gains can be anticipated, from acceleration in economic growth and the dissemination of new technologies. However, the process of adjustment is not uniformly smooth, and in some instances economic security is liable to be threatened by intensified competitive pressures.

3.3.1   Industrial sectors

The advent of the single market particularly affects economic activities that previously were protected from cross-border competition, and require a regulatory framework in order to function satisfactorily. Some of the key areas in which the single market programme has had an impact are set out in Box 3.4, together with the policy instruments that have been applied to bring about the single market.

The single market represents both challenges and opportunities for industry. The most immediate effects are liable to be felt by industries that have enjoyed a measure of protection, and that suffer from excess capacity, such as steel, cars and textiles. Diminution of non-tariff barriers to trade reduces the costs of market segmentation, and stimulates cross-border competition: notable examples are in the transport and financial services sectors.

In the longer term, industrial development is geared to the requirements of a large single market. Comparative advantages change, as resources (especially capital and technology) exploit their mobility. Sectors most affected are those that are changing most rapidly, such as telecommunications, electronics and data processing.

BOX 3.4
Single market policy instruments in key areas

Area	Policy instruments
Financial services	Home country control, Mutual recognition
Technology	Harmonized standards, Market access
Transport	Harmonized regulation, Liberalization
Public procurement	Information
Plant and animal health	Mutual recognition of controls at the point of origin

3.3.2   Projected benefits of the single market

The removal of barriers between member states set in motion a process of far-reaching economic—and political—change within the Community. A weakening of segmentation between national markets stimulates the process of integration, and thereby leads to a restructuring of economic activity. In a large single market, the consumer benefits from increased competition between sellers, and from the realization of economies of scale through the locational concentration of productive activities. Some producers will benefit from increased competitiveness; others will suffer.

Among the regions of the Community, those with uncompetitive industries will undergo the greatest restructuring, but will also have the most to gain in the longer term. The less prosperous member states in particular require Community assistance to compete in the single market, and are receiving aid from the structural and cohesion funds (see below). By the same token, countries that are at present disadvantaged by poor infrastructure and uncompetitive industries have the most to gain when these obstacles are removed; this is illustrated in Table 3.1, which presents Commission forecasts showing such countries—Portugal, Greece, Spain and Ireland—as set to enjoy some of the highest rates of economic growth up to the year 2005.

The economic benefits of the single market were assessed in a substantial research project undertaken for the Commission (popularly known as the Cecchini Study, named after the Commission official who directed the project). This concluded that resources would be made more productive, with increases in consumption and investment, mainly through the following effects (European Commission 1988: 17):

1. Cost reductions resulting from an exploitation of economies of scale.
2. Increased competition, leading to enhanced economic efficiency.
3. Cost reductions arising from industrial restructuring to exploit the comparative advantages of member states.
4. A flow of innovations, new processes and products, stimulated by the single market.

The report of the Cecchini Study predicted an acceleration in economic growth resulting from the elimination of barriers between member states. This is projected to raise Community GDP by between 4.5 and 7 per cent, depending on the priorities of accompanying macroeconomic policies: if the emphasis is given to containment of inflation, the GDP increase will be at the lower end of the range.

Accelerated economic growth in the single market is due mainly to a realization of economies of scale, with liberalization and deregulation of trade within the Community. With the removal

Table 3.1   European Union member states: projected economic growth, 1990–2005

	% increase in GDP
Portugal	76.7
Spain	53.5
Luxembourg	51.9
Ireland	47.8
Greece	46.2
Italy	44.1
Belgium	39.4
Denmark	39.3
France	39.0
European Community*	38.6
Germany*	37.9
Netherlands	37.5
UK	25.4

* Excluding the eastern Länder of Germany.
Source: European Commission (1992c).

of barriers to trade between member states, there will be a tendency to concentrate productive activities where unit production costs are lowest—and this is of course facilitated by greater mobility of investment in the internal market.

The Cecchini estimates relate to a once-and-for-all stimulus to economic activity: this can be characterized as the static effect (although its full extent will be realized over a period of years). However, there will also be longer-term dynamic impacts, leading to additional economic growth, as the process of industrial restructuring and relocation proceeds. The key factor is an increase in productivity: the existence of a large barrier-free market stimulates the development and introduction of new technologies and their dissemination within the Community; harmonization of regulations and standards will also reduce the costs of developing new products and processes (see Baldwin 1989). The Commission identified information technology as a leading example of the phenomenon, since achievement of its full potential requires a large market with common standards (European Commission 1985: 30).

The magnitude of the medium and long-term effects, in terms of increases in the rate of economic growth, is subject to considerable uncertainties. It should however be recognized that even a small increase in economic growth, if sustained over a long period, may eventually lead to considerably higher levels of GDP, thus overshadowing the transient impact of the short-term static effects.

3.3.3   The need for economic and social cohesion

Member states differ widely in levels of prosperity, and in the capacity of their economies to compete in the single market. The Community has instituted expenditure programmes to assist member states (particularly the less prosperous) in developing the necessary foundations for economic competitiveness. The objective, as defined in the EC Treaty, is to promote 'cohesion' by reducing economic disparities between member states; this was seen as an essential complement to the single market, particularly to safeguard the position of countries that might initially be at a competitive disadvantage.

The removal of barriers between member states, and the opening of markets, exposes many types of economic activity to the 'chill winds' of increased competition. This in turn leads to restructuring, as some industries in some countries succumb to competitive pressures, while others prosper and expand. The gains from the single market depend in the longer term upon shifts in economic activity to locations in which they are most competitive, and on the concentration of production to realize economies of scale.

The impact of economic restructuring is liable to be most acute in those member states that have hitherto been insulated from foreign competition. Without the stimulus of competition from imports, industry tends to be less efficient than would be the case if the economy were open to foreign competition. Furthermore, the economy forgoes potential gains—from specialization and, in some instances, from economies of scale.

Table 3.2 shows how certain member states are particularly exposed to structural change because their economies have been less open to competition. The measure of 'openness' is foreign trade in proportion to GDP, which provides a comparison of exposure to international competition for economies of approximately similar size. (In a large economy this proportion tends to be lower because there is relatively more trade *within* the economy; so to avoid misleading comparisons the table excludes Germany, France, Italy and the United Kingdom, the four largest member states.)

The countries shown in Table 3.2 as having a low degree of 'openness' are (with the exception of Denmark) among the less prosperous member states, while (apart from Ireland) all of the more 'open' economies enjoy living standards (as measured by GDP per capita) above the Community average.

This suggests that in general it is the weaker economies that face intensified competitive pressures. Economic restructuring in response to these pressures entails redeployment of resources, with increased specialization in areas where they possess a competitive advantage. This in turn calls for development of the necessary infrastructures, both in physical terms and also in the form of human resources.

Table 3.2 Smaller economies: degree of openness

Openness of the economy	
High	*Low*
Belgium	Denmark
Luxembourg	Greece
Ireland	Spain
Netherlands	Portugal

Notes: A 'small' economy is defined as one with GDP less than 500 bn ECUs per year.
'Openness' was measured by the average of exports and imports in proportion to GDP: the 'low' category is defined by a proportion up to 40 per cent; the 'high' category is above 40 per cent.
Source: calculated from Eurostat (1993: Table 6.1).

The problem for the weaker economies is to modernize their infrastructure in order to be competitive, and to manage the process of transition, especially the structural unemployment associated with the redeployment of labour. On the other hand, countries in this position will eventually gain substantially from economic integration. The prospect of removing disadvantages of small size and isolation represents an opportunity to raise living standards towards the levels already enjoyed by countries that have not suffered from these disadvantages. (This is the main reason why some of the poorest countries have the highest projected economic growth rates—see Table 3.2 above.) So it is very likely that those with most to lose in the short term also have most to gain in the long term: the immediate problem is of course to minimize the intensity and duration of the pain of adjustment.

3.4   THE STRUCTURAL FUNDS: AN INSURANCE POLICY

The Community's main policy instrument to ease the path of structural adjustment is expenditure on physical and human resources. This is mainly channelled through three structural funds: the European Regional Development Fund, the European Social Fund, and the Guidance Section of the European Agricultural Guidance and Guarantee Fund, which together account for approximately one-third of the total Community budget. These are supplemented by the Cohesion Fund, the fisheries guidance financial instrument, and by loans and loan guarantees provided by the Community and the European Investment Bank.

The present system of structural funds was introduced in 1988, in conjunction with the single market programme. The funds are specifically geared to easing the process of economic integration, and their resources are concentrated on the less developed and declining industrial regions. The role of the funds has been characterized as an 'insurance policy' for regions that suffer during the process of economic restructuring (European Commission 1988: 21).

The Structural Funds are a means towards the achievement of a policy objective of the Community—namely, economic and social cohesion. It is therefore appropriate that their expenditure should reflect the priorities of the Community, rather than of the member states or of regional administrations within the member states. Thus for example support for highway projects should be given on the basis their contribution to a Community-wide network; and training activities should facilitate mobility of workers within the single market, and the competitiveness of the Community in world trade.

The funds are nevertheless administered through, and by, the authorities in member states. This is unavoidable, given the very limited size of the Commission's staff, but it can give rise to difficulties in ensuring the effectiveness of the funds in achieving the objectives set by the Community.

3.4.1   Additionality

Prior to their reform in 1988, Community funds were often used as a substitute, rather than a supplement, for national expenditure. A member state might for example draw up a programme of investment in sewage works, without reference to any Community priorities, and then nominate a proportion of the necessary expenditure for support from Community funds; so the Community financing does not represent an addition to the amount that would in any case be spent on sewage treatment. This clearly defeated the purpose of Community funding as a policy instrument, since the Community's role was simply as a mechanism for distribution of finance between member states.

The 1988 reform sought to ensure that Community funding was in accordance with Community priorities, and represented expenditure that would not otherwise be undertaken. (This is referred to as *additionality*, because the Community expenditure is an addition to, rather than a replacement for, funding from other sources.) Thus, increases in expenditure should have 'a genuine economic impact' with—at least—an equivalent increase in the total volume of public expenditure for infrastructure (Regulation 2052/88, Article 9).

The Commission has encountered problems in its efforts to ensure the observance of this requirement: its 1993 review of structural funds called for a more rigorous application of this principle, observing that 'some Member States are unable or indeed reluctant to supply the information which would allow additionality to be verified' (COM(93)67, p. 21)

The commitment to additionality was strengthened in 1993: implementing legislation for the structural funds decreed that structural fund expenditure 'may not replace public expenditure ... by Member States', and that member states should maintain 'public structural expenditure' at least at its previous level (Regulation 2082/93, Article 9).

In practice, additionality is difficult to ensure because it depends upon a comparison of the amounts that would be spent *in the same period* with and without Community funding. A direct comparison is of course not possible: instead, additionality is assessed with reference to changes in expenditure over time—so that member states are to refrain from using Community funding as a device for reducing their own expenditure below its previous level. The problem then is that circumstances change—and this is acknowledged in the implementing legislation, under which exceptions to additionality may be permitted if the general economic situation changes, if privatizations occur, or if previous expenditure was 'unusually high' (Regulation 2082/93, Article 9(2)).

3.4.2   Objectives of the structural funds

Structural fund expenditures are focused on six specific priority areas (Regulation 2081/93, Article 1):

Objective 1: *Less prosperous regions* the development and structural adjustment of regions whose development is lagging behind.

Objective 2: *Declining industrial regions* converting regions ... or parts of regions seriously affected by industrial decline.

Objective 3: *Employment* combating long-term unemployment and facilitating the integration into working life of young people and persons exposed to exclusion from the labour market.

Objective 4: *Training* facilitating the adaptation of workers of either sex to industrial changes and to changes in production systems.

Objective 5: *Rural development*:
    (a) speeding up the adjustment of agricultural structures.
    (b) facilitating the development and structural adjustment of rural areas.

Objective 6: *Thinly populated regions* the development and structural adjustment of regions (in Finland and Sweden) with a population density of 8 persons per square km or less.

The expenditures of the three structural funds with respect to these objectives are summarized in Box 3.5

BOX 3.5
Structural funds: objectives and areas of expenditure

Fund	Objective	Areas of expenditure
Regional development	1, 6	Education and health } Job creation, infrastructure, local development initiatives small and medium enterprises
	2	
	5(b)	Infrastructure to support rural diversification
Social	1, 6	Education and training systems } Vocational and research training; guidance and counselling, especially for those in small and medium enterprises and for the unemployed
	2	
	3	Training, temporary employment aids, training structures, guidance and counselling
	4	Training, training systems, guidance
	5(b)	Vocational and research training guidance and counselling, especially for those in small and medium enterprises and for the unemployed
Agricultural guidance	1, 6	Infrastructure, diversification, conservation
	5(a)	Farm income support, improvement in productive efficiency and marketing
	5(b)	Infrastructure, diversification, conservation

3.4.3 Structural fund expenditure programmes

Expenditure allocated for the three structural funds and other structural operations amounts to some 23.7 bn ECUs in 1995. Of this expenditure, approximately 12 bn ECUs (more than half the total) is to be spent from the three structural funds on 'Objective 1' regions, which have levels of GDP per capita up to three-quarters of the Community average. Planned expenditure for the period 1994–9 totals 141 ½ bn ECUs (1992 prices), of which 96 bn is for Objective 1 (Regulation 2081/93, Annex II).

The Commission has a central responsibility for the co-ordination of assistance to facilitate structural adjustment from the following sources:

1. Expenditure from the three structural funds and the Financial Instrument for Fisheries Guidance, and the Cohesion Fund.
2. Grants and loans under the ECSC Treaty and the Euratom Treaty.
3. Loans and loan guarantees from the European Community budget under the 'New Community Instrument' (see Decision 87/182) and from the European Investment Bank. (These use the Community's high credit rating to make loans at favourable rates of interest.)

Structural fund operations are designed to complement or contribute to corresponding initiatives at national level, and are conducted through 'partnerships', which comprise the Commission, national authorities and an appropriate 'economic and social partner'.

Expenditure from the structural funds is planned in a three-stage process:

1. *Plans* indicating expenditure proposals and financing requirements for three or six-year periods are drawn up by authorities at the appropriate national, regional or local level, and are submitted by member states to the Commission.
2. *Community support frameworks* covering three or six years are prepared by the Commission, in consultation with member states: the frameworks identify priorities and specific objectives, set out the financing and procedures for monitoring and evaluation, including the verification of additionality.
3. *Programmes* are subject to approval by the Commission, but are implemented through 'partnerships', which comprise the Commission, national authorities, and an appropriate 'economic and social partner' (Regulation 2081/93, Article 4).

Programmes outline objectives and proposed measures, and identify indicators—physical, financial, and socioeconomic—to be used in assessing performance and impact of expenditures.

The Commission has sought to simplify and accelerate these procedures, urging member states to avoid excessive detail and to present programmes in preliminary draft form at an early stage, along with their plans (COM(93)282, p. 18).

Programme management and selection of projects is primarily a matter for the authorities in member states, in partnership with appropriate organizations. Applications for assistance with specific projects are submitted to the Commission by governments of member states or by bodies which they designate; in general, projects are eligible for assistance only if they are in accordance with Community objectives and priorities as set out in the relevant Community support framework. Projects are financed jointly by the Community and organizations in member states: in Objective 1 regions Community contributions are limited to maxima of 50 per cent of public expenditure and 75 per cent of total project cost. (In exceptional cases the latter may be raised to 80 per cent in member states covered by the Cohesion Fund, and to 85 per cent in remote regions.) In the rest of the Community these maxima are respectively 50 and 25 per cent. In deciding the rate of Community contribution for specific projects, the following criteria apply (Regulation 2081/93, Article 13):

- the gravity of regional or social problems
- importance for the Community, and—at national and regional level—for the member state
- relevant specific characteristics of the project.

Community initiatives   In 1994 and 1995, 9 per cent of structural fund expenditure was available for *Community initiatives*, which are proposed by the Commission rather than by member states. (The procedure actually requires that the Commission 'decide to propose to member states that they submit applications for assistance in respect of measures of significant interest to the Community'—Regulation 2082/93, Article 11(1).) The purpose is to enable the Community to act when its interests and priorities diverge from those of member states: this is achieved through Community support for measures which, although not included in the plans submitted by member states, are nevertheless of significant interest to the Community. Community initiatives have been used to promote activities across national frontiers, to develop border regions and to support innovative activities which may subsequently be absorbed into the mainstream of structural fund expenditure. Since 1988 a number of programmes of Community initiatives have been undertaken: these are outlined in Box 3.6.

BOX 3.6
Community initiatives under the structural funds

Programme	Fund(s)	Budget	Purpose
STRIDE*	ERDF and ESF	460 m ECUs[2]	To strengthen the capacity for technological development
TELEMATIQUE*	ERDF	233 m ECUs[3]	To promote the use of advanced telecommunications services
PRISMA*	ERDF	114 m ECUs[3]	To improve business services for small and medium enterprises
ENVIREG	ERDF, ESF, EAGGF	580 m ECUs[2]	To improve and protect the environment in coastal areas, especially in Objective 1 regions
REGIS	ERDF, ESF, EAGGF	234 m ECUs[2]	To promote the socioeconomic integration of overseas territories
INTERREG	ERDF, ESF, EAGGF	1014 m ECUs[2]	To assist cross-border economic co-operation
REGEN	ERDF	347 m ECUS[2]	To further the development of energy transmission networks
RECHAR[†]	ERDF and ESF	369 m ECUs[1]	To assist the conversion of coal mining regions
RETEX	ERDF and ESF	100 m ECUs[4]	To assist the conversion of areas dependent on the textile industry
KONVER	ERDF and ESF	130 m ECUs[4]	To aid the conversion of areas dependent on defence industries
LEADER	ERDF, ESF, EAGGF	450 m ECUs[3]	To promote rural economic development
EUROFORM	ERDF and ESF	302 m ECUs[2]	To promote vocational training
NOW	ERDF and ESF	153 m ECUs[2]	To work for equal opportunities in vocational training
HORIZON	ERDF and ESF	305 m ECUs[2]	To further the social and economic integration of the disabled and disadvantaged

* In Objective 1 regions only   [†] Plus expenditure from ECSC funds.
[1] 1989–93.   [2] 1990–3.   [3] 1991–3.   [4] 1993.
Source: European Commission (1993), *The Future of Community Initiatives under the Structural Funds*, COM (93) 282, 16 June, pp. 26–32

3.5   THE COHESION FUND: ASSISTANCE FOR THE LEAST PROSPEROUS MEMBER STATES

The Cohesion Fund is designed to facilitate economic integration of the least prosperous member states, defined as those with per capita GDP in 1993 below 90 per cent of the Community average. Up to 1999, the scope of the Fund is limited to the four countries within this category when the Fund was inaugurated: Greece, Spain, Ireland and Portugal. The Fund will be reviewed in 1996, and if any of these countries' GDP is above 90 per cent of the Community average at that time, eligibility will be lost.

The Cohesion Fund is in addition to, and separate from, the structural funds, although both types of fund are involved in financing infrastructure expenditures. The purpose of the Cohesion Fund is to provide financial assistance for environmental projects contributing to the objectives set out in the EC Treaty (Article 130r), and to transport infrastructure projects defined as being of 'common interest' (under Article 129c EC). Allocations of finance to eligible member states is show in Table 3.3.

Table 3.3   The Cohesion Fund: allocations to eligible countries, 1993–1999
Total and per capita allocations in 1992 prices

	Percentage shares	Allocation (bn ECUs)	Allocation per capita (ECUs)	GDP per capita 1991 (EC12 = 100)
Greece	16–20	2.4–3.0	231–289	48
Spain	52–58	7.9–8.8	202–225	77
Ireland	7–10	1.1–1.5	300–428	70
Portugal	16–20	2.4–3.0	246–308	59
Total	100	15.15	240	100

Source: derived from Regulation 1164/94 establishing a Cohesion Fund, *Official Journal*, 1994 L130/1, Article 4 and Annex 1.

To put these figures in perspective, the 1993 Cohesion Fund expenditure is of the order of 0.5 per cent of GDP in Greece and Portugal, and somewhat less in Ireland and Spain. Planned expenditure up to 1999 amounts to approximately 240 ECUs per capita, equivalent to 35 ECUs per year.

3.6   ACHIEVING ECONOMIC AND SOCIAL COHESION

Planned expenditure from Community funds for structural purposes in the period 1993–9 is shown in Table 3.4. Expenditure figures tend to understate the impact of Community funds, because money spent by the Community is used by the recipients to finance their own purchases (the so-called *multiplier effect*). However, the benefit to poorer regions is reduced by 'leakage' of expenditure: if for example a contract for an infrastructure project in Portugal is given to a company in Germany, then much of the multiplier effect would accrue in Germany. With public procurement open to Community-wide competition, the *more* prosperous regions may gain significantly from structural and cohesion fund expenditure.

Table 3.4   Expenditure on structural funds and financial instrument for fisheries guidance, and Cohesion Fund, 1993–1999

	bn ECUs[†]
Total structural funds and FIFG[*]	162.10
of which Objective 1 regions	106.55
Cohesion Fund	15.15

[*] *Financial Instrument for Fisheries Guidance.*
[†] 1992 prices.
Note: These are appropriations for expenditure commitments.
Sources: Structural funds and FIFG 1993: European Parliament final adoption of the general budget of the European Union for the financial year 1994, *Official Journal*, 1994, L34; 1994–9: Regulation 1081/93, *Official Journal*, 1993 L193/19. Cohesion Fund: Regulation 12164/95 establishing a Cohesion Fund, *Official Journal*, 1994 L130/1.

The amounts in Table 3.4 are substantial, totalling over a hundred billion ECUs, and will account for an appreciable share of the Community budget. On the other hand, they are only a small proportion of GDP, even in the poorest member states, and the net amounts transferred from the richer to the poorer countries is smaller still. This is unavoidable given the size of the Community budget, which is less than 1.5 per cent of GDP; there is a marked contrast with the United States, where the federal budget is more than one-fifth of total GDP, and poorer states benefit from concentrations of federal expenditure, particularly in the defence field.

If the structural funds are to make substantial inroads on interregional disparities, their effect must be primarily catalytic. This is indeed the purpose of infrastructure investment: to relieve bottlenecks—such as poor communications—which constrain economic development. The degree of success in increasing the cohesion of the Community remains to be seen; but the evidence thus far is not encouraging, as is illustrated by Table 3.5, which shows an index of variance in GDP per capita. Over the period 1982–91 there has been no sustained tendency for disparities to narrow. This may be because the benefits of structural fund expenditure take time to accrue. Investment in infrastructure and training does not in itself dramatically improve the position of the less prosperous regions. Its role is rather to facilitate economic restructuring, so that new investment is attracted by a high-quality infrastructure and a well qualified workforce.

Cohesion measures have to be balanced against other policy concerns, which are considered in subsequent chapters. One of these is the competitiveness of the Community as a whole: an important objective of the single market is to enable Community industry to concentrate economic activity where it is most competitive on a global scale; and this may tend to increase economic disparities within the Community.

A further significant consideration is the impact of economic development on the quality of life. While the less prosperous regions may be lacking in infrastructure, they frequently offer the attraction of a high-quality environment. The Community has procedures for assessing the environmental impacts of specific projects, but less attention has been paid to the long-term effects of programmes and the economic growth that is stimulated. It can be counter-productive to remedy deficiencies at the expense of advantages. Nevertheless, subject to the various constraints described above, the Community mechanisms for economic cohesion will have a

Table 3.5   Cohesion Index, European Community, 1982–1991

	1982 = 100
1982	100
1983	100
1984	103
1985	102
1986	102
1987	99
1988	105
1989	103
1990	103
1991	102

Note: This index is calculated from weighted variance of GDP per capita in the 12 states that constituted the European Community from 1986: GDP per capita is measured in terms of purchasing power, in order to remove the effect of short-term exchange rate fluctuations.

crucial role if all member states are to participate in economic and monetary union, which is the subject of Chapter 5.

3.7   FOUNDATIONS OF THE SINGLE MARKET: KEY POINTS AND ISSUES

The single market has taken integration within the European Community to a level that is unique and unprecedented in the history of economic co-operation between nation states. The ultimate purpose is to realize the benefits of increased specialization and competition, and of accelerated technological change. The development of the single market has required a massive effort to eliminate barriers between member states. This has had several facets, including legal action to secure mutual recognition of national standards, legislation to establish Community-wide standards, and measures to harmonize taxation.

The development of the single market involves considerable economic restructuring, particularly in the less prosperous and peripheral member states. Hitherto protected industries are being exposed to intensified competition; some will decline while others will prosper from exploiting new competitive opportunities. In any event, this process will lead to a massive shift in resources which, although ultimately beneficial, is liable to be painful in the short term. The Community has sought to ease the process primarily through expenditure on infrastructure and training, concentrated in the less prosperous regions.

The achievement of a single market gives rise to a number of important issues, which may be identified as follows.

- There is a general presumption that national regulations and standards should be subject to mutual recognition in the single market: what are—or should be—the limits of mutual recognition?
- Where mutual recognition is not appropriate, harmonization measures may be instituted,

through legislation or on a voluntary basis: what influences the extent and scope of harmonization?

- Community legislation specifies minimum rates of excise and value added taxes, and requires taxes to be levied on a 'destination' basis: what changes might be made in Community tax legislation?
- The development of the single market is predicted to accelerate economic growth and lead to structural change: how will this happen? What is the evidence of these effects?
- There are significant economic disparities between the regions of the Community, and the main policy response has been financial assistance for infrastructure development and training: how effective is this?
- Under the principle of additionality, Community expenditure should be geared to Community priorities, and should not merely replace national expenditures; under the principle of subsidiarity, expenditure programmes should as far as possible be implemented by the authorities in member states: how are these principles reconciled in practice?

NOTES

1 The phrase 'in accordance with the principle of an open market economy with free competition' occurs three times in the EC Treaty, in Article 3a (twice) and in Article 102a, and also in the Protocol on the statute of the European Monetary Institute, Article 4.4.2.
2 Respectively, the British Standards Institution, the Association française de normalisation and the Deutsches Institut für Normung; standards institutions in the European Community are listed in the Annex to Directive 89/189.

REFERENCES

Baldwin, R. (1989) 'The growth effects of 1992', *Economic Policy*, No. 9.

European Commission (1985) *Completing the Internal Market: White Paper from the Commission to the European Council*, Office for Official Publications, Luxembourg.

European Commission (1988) 'The economics of 1992', *European Economy*, No. 35.

European Commission (1991) 'Proposal for a Directive on transfrontier investment by pension funds', *Official Journal*, C312, 3 December, p. 3 (amended Proposal in *Official Journal*, C171, 22 June 1993, p. 13).

European Commission (1992a) *Guide to VAT in 1993: The New VAT System in the Frontier-Free Community*, European Commission, Brussels.

European Commission (1992b) *Report of the Committee of Independent Experts on Company Taxation*, Office for Official Publications, Luxembourg.

European Commission (1992c) *Energy in Europe: a View to the Future*, Office of Official Publications, Luxembourg.

Eurostat (1993) *Basic Statistics of the Community*, 30th edn, Office of Official Publications, Luxembourg.

FCO (1993) *The European Community: Facts and Fairytales*, Foreign and Commonwealth Office, London.

Mattera, A. (1984) 'Protectionism inside the EC: decisions of the European Court', *Journal of World Trade Law*, 18(4).

OECD (1993) *Taxation and the Environment: Complementary Policies*, Organisation for Economic Co-operation and Development, Paris.

Sutherland, P. *et al.* (1992) *The Internal Market after 1992: Meeting the Challenge*, Report to the European Commission by the High Level Group on the Operation of the Internal Market.

European Community legislation

Regulations and Decisions

Regulation 2052/88, on the tasks of the structural funds and their effectiveness and on co-ordination of their activities between themselves and with the operations of the European Investment Bank and the other existing financial instruments, *Official Journal*, 1988 L185/9.

Regulation 2081/93, amending Regulation (EEC) 2052/88, *Official Journal*, 1993 L193/5 (as amended by Protocol No. 6 to the 1995 Act of Accession, *Official Journal*, 1995 L1/11).

Regulation 2082/93, as regards co-ordination of the activities of the different structural funds between themselves and with the operations of the European Investment Bank and the other existing financial instruments, *Official Journal*, 1993 L193/20.

Regulation 1164/95, establishing a Cohesion Fund, *Official Journal*, 1994 L130/1.

Decision 87/182, empowering the Community to borrow under the New Community Instrument, *Official Journal*, 1987 L71/34.

Directives

Directive 83/189, laying down a procedure for the provision of information in the field of technical standards and regulations, *Official Journal*, 1983 L109/8, as amended by Directive 88/182, *Official Journal*, 1988 L81/81, and Commission Decision 90/230/EEC, *Official Journal*, 1990 L128/16.

Directive 90/434, on the common system of taxation applicable to mergers, divisions, transfers of assets and exchanges of shares, *Official Journal*, 1990 L225/1.

Directive 90/435, on the common system of taxation applicable in the case of parent companies and subsidiaries, *Official Journal*, 1990 L225/6.

Directive 90/531, on the procurement procedures of entities operating in the water, energy, transport and telecommunications sectors, *Official Journal*, 1990 L297/1.

Directive 91/680, supplementing the common system of value added tax with a view to the abolition of fiscal frontiers, *Official Journal*, 1991 L376/1.

Directive 92/50, relating to the co-ordination of procedures for the award of public service contracts, *Official Journal*, 1992 L209/1.

Directive 92/77, supplementing the common system of value added tax (approximation of VAT rates), *Official Journal*, 1992 L316/1.

Directive 92/79, on the approximation of taxes on cigarettes, *Official Journal*, 1992 L316/8.

Directive 92/82, on the approximation of the rates of excise duties on mineral oils, *Official Journal*, 1992 L316/19.

Directive 92/84, on the approximation of the rates of excise duties on alcohol and alcoholic beverages, *Official Journal*, 1992 L316/29.

Directive 93/36, co-ordinating procedures for the award of public supply contracts, *Official Journal*, 1993 L199/1.

Directive 93/37, concerning the co-ordination of procedures for the award of public works contracts, *Official Journal*, 1993 L199/54.

Intergovernmental Convention

Convention 90/436/EEC, on the elimination of double taxation in connection with the adjustment of profits of associated enterprises, *Official Journal*, 1990 L225/10.

European Commission documents

COM(89)268, *Proposal for a Council Regulation on the Statute for a European Company*, 25 August 1989 (as amended by COM(91)174-2, 22 May 1991).

COM(93)67, *The Community's Structural Fund Operations 1994–99*, 10 March 1993.

COM(93)282, *The Future of Community initiatives under the Structural Funds*, 16 June 1993.

COM(93)684, *Proposals for a Common Visa List under Article 100c*, 10 December 1993.

COM(94)55, *The Community Internal Market—1993 Report*, 14 March 1994.

COM(94)584, *Harmonization of the Laws of Member States relating to Turnover Taxes*, 13 December 1994.

Court judgments

Case 8/74, *Procureur du Roi v. Dassonville* [1974] ECR 837.

Case 120/78, *Rewe Zentrale Bundesmonopolverwaltung für Branntwein* [1979] ECR 649.

Case 40/82, *Commission v. United Kingdom* [1982] ECR 2793.

Case 74/82, *Commission v. Ireland* [1984] ECR 317.

Case 240/83, *Procureur de la République v. Association de défense des brûleurs d'huiles usagées* [1985] ECR 531.

Case 121/85, *Conegate v. H.M. Customs and Excise* [1986] ECR 1007.

Case 302/86, *Commission v. Denmark* [1988] ECR 4607.
Case 45/87, *Commission v. Ireland* [1988] ECR 4929.
Case 2/90, *Commission v. Belgium*, Judgment 9 July 1992, not yet reported.
Case C-169/91, *Stoke on Trent and Norwich City Councils v. B&Q*, Judgment 16 December 1992, not yet reported.
Cases C-267 and 268/91, *Bernard Keck* and *Daniel Mithouard*, Judgment 24 November 1993, not yet reported.

Legal actions

Case C-445/93, European Parliament v. Commission, *Official Journal*, 1994, C1/12.

FOUR
COMPETITION POLICY

The previous chapter shows how opportunities arise from economic integration in the single market. Elimination of regulatory restrictions on cross-border trade should increase competition and consumer choice. It is necessary to ensure that this purpose is not frustrated by anti-competitive practices which distort the operation of markets, or which effectively perpetuate the segmentation of markets between member states.

Enterprises are rewarded when they take advantage of the single market; but there is a danger that in some instances the rewards stem from monopolistic domination of markets and anti-competitive practices rather than from economic efficiency. If the Community is to benefit to the fullest extent from economic integration, and realize the benefit of the single market, a balance has to be struck between promotion of competition and preventing the abuse of competitive strength.

To ensure a proper balance, the Community has 'a system ensuring that competition in the internal market is not distorted' (Article 3g EC). The objective is to promote efficient operation of market forces, by restraining both the dominance of large corporations and interventions by governments. Thus, the original ECSC and EEC Treaties included provisions to counter anti-competitive practices and to restrict subsidization of enterprises by national authorities. There is now a substantial body of competition legislation and case law based upon the Treaties.

4.1 THE FRAMEWORK FOR COMPETITION BETWEEN ENTERPRISES

The Community has a regulatory framework designed to realize the economic benefits of competition between enterprises, and hence to combat monopolistic exploitation of markets. The basis for competition policy is set out in the Treaties, and supplemented by legislation on mergers.

4.1.1 Competition rules applying to firms: the economic rationale

The economic argument for competition and against monopoly is essentially that, compared with a competitive market, monopolists charge higher prices for less output. So the monopolist profits at the expense of the consumer, and the amount of consumption is restricted by higher prices. Under certain assumptions, it can be shown that economic efficiency is improved by breaking up a monopoly or by forcing the monopolist to behave like a competitive firm.

This is the essence of the theory. Its practical application is subject to numerous qualifications and complications. The most important of these (in terms of policy relevance) are as follows.

- *Economies of scale* such that large firms have lower costs per unit of production. In these circumstances a competitive market structure might have higher prices and lower output than would be the case with a monopoly.
- *Oligopoly*   In many industries a small number of firms account for a large proportion of total output; such industries are highly *concentrated*, but they are not monopolies. Some of the most important industries (particularly those in which multinational corporations are a significant presence) are structured in this way. In such industries there is no clear-cut relationship between structure and conduct. There may be strong rivalry, as firms battle with one another for market share; or on the other hand the firms may attempt to collude so that they collectively enjoy monopolistic dominance of the market.
- *Possibilities for market entry (and exit)*   A firm in a monopolistic market may be constrained by potential competition, if high profits (and high prices) render the market attractive to new entrants who can erode the monopolist's dominant position. The practical importance of this effect depends upon the ease with which firms are able to enter the market, and also to leave the market if prices fall. (Where barriers to entry and exit are low, there is said to be a *contestable market*.)
- *Progressiveness*   The interests of the consumer are served not only by low prices at a single point in time: perhaps more significant is investment and technological development leading over time to reduced prices and product improvements. Firm size and market dominance may reflect competitive success in these important respects, benefiting rather than exploiting the consumer.

All these considerations imply that competitiveness is not synonymous with the number of buyers or sellers in the market. There is in practice a complex relationship between market structure and the conduct and performance of firms.

- *Market structure* is a combination of two necessary conditions for market dominance: concentration and barriers to entry and exit. These barriers are in turn influenced by factors such as firms' control over stages of the production process (vertical integration), the uniqueness of their products (product differentiation), the volume and nature of investment required and diversification between markets.
- *Conduct* of firms has numerous aspects, including pricing and output strategies, and inter-firm collaboration which may or may not be benign. Possibilities for anti-competitive conduct depend upon structural conditions—market dominance is unlikely if there are numerous competitors, both actual and potential.
- *Performance* is the basis on which the scope of policy interventions should be decided. In economic terms, performance is assessed with reference to issues such as the source of profitability (competitive prowess or market dominance?) and benefits to consumers and to the community as a whole, for example as a result of technological progress.

There is no straightforward causal relationship between structure, conduct and performance, because today's structure is a reflection of past performance and conduct, which has brought some firms to prominence (and led others to oblivion).

4.1.2   Competition rules applying to firms: the legal basis

Community competition policy towards commercial enterprises is based on Articles 85 and 86 of the EC Treaty and Council Regulation 4064/89 concerning mergers (and corresponding provisions in the ECSC Treaty): the fundamentals are highlighted in Box 4.1. The competition

BOX 4.1
Competition: the legal framework

Anti-competitive practices

EC Treaty Article 85   Prohibits 'agreements ... decisions ... and concerted practices which may affect trade between Member States and which have as their object or effect the prevention, restriction or distortion of competition within the common market'. Exceptions may be made for arrangements that contribute to improving the production or distribution of goods, or to promoting technical or economic progress, while allowing consumers a fair share of the resulting benefit.

ECSC Treaty Article 65   Prohibits 'agreements ... decisions ... and concerted practices tending ... to prevent, restrict or distort normal competition within the common market'. Exceptions may be made for arrangements that contribute to improving the production or distribution of products, where these do not give producers power over the market.

Market dominance

EC Treaty Article 86   Prohibits 'abuse of a dominant position within the common market or a substantial part of it ... insofar as it may affect trade between Member States'.

ECSC Treaty Article 66(7)   Empowers the Commission to determine prices and conditions of sale, or to draw up production and delivery programmes, where undertakings 'hold or acquire ... a dominant position ... in a substantial part of the common market' which is being used 'for purposes contrary to the objectives of [the] Treaty'.

Mergers

Regulation 4064/89   Prohibits any concentration 'which creates or strengthens a dominant position as a result of which effective competition would be significantly impeded in the common market or a substantial part of it' (Article 2.3).

ECSC Treaty Article 66(1–2)   Mergers which bring about a concentration require prior authorization by the Commission, which will be granted if it does not confer market power on the merged undertaking.

rules under the two Treaties are broadly similar, although the ECSC Treaty provides for a more interventionist role on the part of the Commission (compare Article 66(7) with EC Treaty Article 86), and gives wider scope for exceptions. (This is implicit in the reference to 'normal competition' in Article 65; in recent years conditions in the steel industry have usually been abnormal—see Box 6.2.)

It is also noteworthy that the EC Treaty has no provision corresponding to ECSC Treaty Article 66(1–2) on mergers between undertakings; and until Regulation 4064/89 came into force there were no rules under the EC Treaty relating specifically to mergers (although some case law had developed).

The EC Treaty provisions relate primarily to conduct, rather than structure. Article 85 is concerned solely with conduct, and specifically with arrangements between undertakings that restrict or distort competition, or that may have this effect. Article 86 relates to conduct that arises from market structure: 'abuse' of a dominant position is prohibited, although the dominant position itself is not an offence. (This contrasts with the US Sherman Act Section 2, under which monopolization is an offence.) In a sense, Articles 85 and 86 may be seen as analogous to the rules on governmental restrictions on trade between member states (Articles 30–36). The objective in both cases is to prevent the distortion of trade within the Community, whether by governments or by commercial undertakings.

The Community has limited powers over industry structure, under Regulation 4064/89 on the control of concentrations. This Regulation is concerned with *changes* in structure: it restricts the creation, or strengthening, of dominance by means of a merger between enterprises—although the *existence* of a dominant position is not in itself unlawful.

4.2 COMPETITION BETWEEN ENTERPRISES: EC TREATY PROVISIONS

The primary purpose of the EC Treaty provisions relating to competition is to facilitate free movement of goods within the single market. Thus, Articles 85 and 86 concern practices 'which may affect trade between member states'. This phrase has been clarified by the European Court as follows:

> An agreement, decision or practice will affect trade between Member States if it is capable of constituting a threat, either direct or indirect, actual or potential, to the freedom of trade between Member States in a manner which might harm the attainment of the objective of a single market between states.
>
> (Joined Cases 56 and 58/64, p. 341)

It is not necessary to establish actual harm: it is sufficient that the agreement be *likely to* prevent restrict or distort competition to a sufficient degree (see Case 5/65).

Furthermore, trade between member states may be affected even by practices confined to a single country: this was determined in Case 8/72, involving a cartel agreement between cement producers in the Netherlands, which was found to have a distorting effect on trade in cement between member states. So the division between national and Community responsibilities depends upon a pragmatic application of the subsidiarity principle.

Community competition regulation coexists with national measures: Articles 85 and 86 do not claim exclusive jurisdiction, or preclude member states from conducting their own competition policies. In contrast, the Regulation on mergers gives the Commission sole jurisdiction over mergers 'with a Community dimension' (Regulation 4064/89, Article 21), thus avoiding a risk of double jeopardy from application of Community and national regulations in the same case.

There are similarities between the wording of Articles 85 and 86, in terms of specific anti-competitive behaviour (both refer to discrimination and supplementary obligations); and both Articles may be invoked, if there is an anti-competitive arrangement *and* abuse of a dominant position. This happened where a formal agreement between undertakings was a cover for abuse of a dominant position (Case 66/88, which concerned price fixing in air transport, and the blocking of parallel imports of air tickets into Germany).

4.2.1 Anti-competitive arrangements

Anti-competitive arrangements are subject to Article 85 EC, the provisions of which are summarized in Box 4.2. This Article refers to *agreements*, *decisions by associations of under-takings* and *concerted practices*, and these terms have been broadly defined by the Court of Justice to include arrangements that are not necessarily explicitly binding on the parties involved.

BOX 4.2
Competition: rules on collaboration between undertakings

Article 85 EC prohibits, subject to certain exceptions, 'agreements between undertakings, decisions by associations of undertakings, and concerted practices ... which have as their object or effect the prevention, restriction or distortion of competition within the common market'.

Prohibited: agreements, etc., that:

- fix prices
- limit output, technical development or investment
- share out markets or sources of supply
- discriminate between parties in equivalent transactions
- subject transactions to unconnected supplementary obligations

Permissible exceptions: agreements, etc., that do not eliminate substantial competition, and that make an essential contribution to:

- improving production or distribution, *or*
- promoting technical progress

while allowing consumers a fair share of the resulting benefit.

Agreements between undertakings   Agreements can include informal 'understandings', whether written or oral (Case 45/69); agreements may be 'horizontal', between competitors (or potential competitors), or 'vertical', between suppliers and their customers.

Decisions by associations of undertakings   These 'decisions' include the rules of trade associations, and decisions and recommendations by these associations even if not binding on their members (see for example Case 8/72).

Concerted practices   Arrangements may be held to be anti-competitive even in the absence of any evidence of explicit agreements. It is sufficient that the behaviour of organizations exhibits a conscious parallelism. The Court of Justice has defined 'concerted practices' within the meaning of Article 85 as 'a form of coordination between enterprises that ... consciously substitutes practical cooperation for the risks of competition' (Joined Cases 48, 49, 51–57/69, p. 655). 'Cooperation' for this purpose requires contact (formal or informal) between the parties (see for example Case 40/73, involving alleged anti-competitive behaviour by a cartel of sugar producers in the Netherlands); in one recent case (involving an alleged woodpulp cartel), concerted practice was defined as 'reciprocation of communications between competitors with the aim of giving each other assurances as to their conduct on the market' (Joined Cases 89, 104, 114, 116, 117, 125–29/85, Opinion of Advocate General Darmon).

Direct evidence of contact is often circumstantial and less than conclusive, and so the Commission has sought to infer the existence of concerted practices from market conditions. To avoid a finding of anti-competitive conduct, the parties involved were required to offer alternative explanations of the observed conditions. However, this approach has recently been heavily circumscribed by the Court, in a judgment that suggests that the onus of proof lies with the Commission to establish that parallel conduct is actually a manifestation of concerted practices, and is not capable of innocent explanation (Joined Cases 89, 104, 114, 116, 117, 125–29/85).

Extra territorial jurisdiction   The Community rules on competition are concerned primarily with effects on markets within the Community, irrespective of the origin of these effects. Consequently the jurisdiction of Community law extends to enterprises that are based in non-member countries, if the conduct of such enterprises is found to be prejudicial to competition in Community markets.

For instance, in 1972 (before the UK joined the Community) the British company ICI was found to have contravened Article 85 by participating in collusive practices (Joined Cases 48, 49, 51–57/69). More recently, concerted action by woodpulp producers in non-member countries (including the USA and Canada) was held to breach Article 85 EC because it had the effect of restricting competition within the Community single market (Joined Cases 89, 104, 114, 116, 117, 125–29/85). The crucial consideration is that the understanding between the companies involved was *implemented* within the Community.

Extra-territorial jurisdiction raises a possibility of conflict between legal systems (although in the case mentioned above this did not arise because no country *compelled* its producers to participate in the cartel arrangement). The guiding principle in such cases is 'territoriality', whereby jurisdiction depends on the location of the markets that are affected by anti-competitive practices. To implement this principle the Community has concluded agreements with competition authorities in other jurisdictions (of which the most significant is the agreement with the United States).

Arrangements that are exempt   The general prohibition in Article 85(1) EC of arrangements that are liable to be anti-competitive is qualified by Article 85(3), which provides for exemption of arrangements that 'contribute to improving the production or distribution of goods or to promoting technical or economic progress, while allowing consumers a fair share of the resulting benefit'—provided that restrictions on undertakings are indispensable and do not give rise to a possibility that competition will be eliminated in respect of a substantial part of the products in question.

Assessment of claims for exemption on an individual basis would impose a heavy administrative burden on the Commission. To avoid this, an exemption is made for agreements of minor importance, where products (including close substitutes) supplied by the undertakings concerned do not represent more than 5 per cent of the total market, and the aggregate turnover of the participating undertakings does not exceed 200 m ECUs (Commission Notice on agreements of minor importance, Paragraph 7).

Furthermore, the Commission has given a number of *block exemptions* for specified categories of agreement. As early as 1965, the Commission was empowered by to grant exemptions to exclusive sale and/or purchase agreements involving two undertakings (Regulation 19/65, Article 1(1)). Other examples of block exemptions include:

- *Motor vehicle distribution and servicing*   Because 'motor vehicles are consumer durables which require expert maintenance and repair, not always in the same place' (Commission Regulation 123/85, Preamble 4th recital), although the Commission has stipulated that freedom to purchase in another Member State must not be unreasonably hindered, and that prices may differ between member states by a maximum of 12 per cent, unless tax and charges amount to more than the net price of the motor vehicle (Notice concerning regulation 123/85).
- *Specialization agreements*   Because 'agreements on specialization in production generally contribute to improving the production or distribution of goods, because the undertakings concerned can operate more efficiently and supply the products more cheaply' (Commission

Regulation 417/85, Preamble 3rd recital); parties to the agreements may not in aggregate have more than 20 per cent of the relevant market, or turnover exceeding 500 m ECUs.

- *Research and development agreements* In the interests of 'increasing dissemination, avoiding duplication, rationalising products and processes' (Commission Regulation 418/ 85, Preamble 4th recital), agreements may cover research and development up to the stage of industrial application.
- *Franchise agreements* These may 'assist the entry of new competitors ... increasing interbrand competition; allow independent traders the possibility of competing more efficiently with large distribution undertakings; allow consumers ... a fair share of the resulting benefit as ... cooperation between franchisor and franchisee ensures a constant quality' (Commission Regulation 4087/88, preamble 7th recital).

4.2.2 Abuse of a dominant position

Abuse of a dominant position is prohibited by Article 86 EC which is summarized in Box 4.3. It should be emphasized that the practices cited are examples, rather than an exhaustive listing; the courts are free to determine that other practices can constitute abuse, and have indeed extended the concept, most notably with reference to mergers.

Definition of a dominant position   The precondition for abusive conduct is a market structure in which one or more undertakings has a dominant position. While 'dominance' is not defined in the Treaty, the Court of Justice has stated that a dominant position is one in which an undertaking can 'behave to an appreciable extent independently of its competitors and customers and ultimately of its consumers' (Case 27/76, p. 277).

In practice, a dominant position is described with reference to a specified market. The Court has defined a relevant market as a group of products with a high degree of substitutability in consumption or use (Case 85/76). A product without close substitutes constitutes a market in itself—in one case a scheduled airline flight on a particular route was held to be in this category (Case 66/88).

Markets may be defined with increasing degrees of precision (for example food/fruit/bananas), and the market share of an individual enterprise can be expected to be higher the more closely the market is defined—so that a company with a large share of the market for bananas has a more modest share of the overall market for fruit. The Court has ruled that a company with approximately 45 per cent of the market for bananas (and twice the share of its nearest rival) enjoyed a dominant position: in this instance the relevant market was defined as bananas rather than fruit, notwithstanding that there is degree of substitutability between fruits (Case 27/76).

BOX 4.3
Competition: abuse of a dominant position

Article 86 EC prohibits 'abuse by one or more undertakings of a dominant position within the common market or a substantial part of it ... in so far as it affects trade between Member states', and in particular:

- unfair prices or trading conditions
- limiting production, markets or technical development
- discrimination between parties in equivalent transactions
- tie-ins which subject transactions to unconnected supplementary obligations

In geographical terms, relevant markets have often been defined as coterminous with the territory of a Member State. Companies tend to define their product distribution arrangements and marketing territories in this way, and it is a logical response to differences in national characteristics and regulations (notwithstanding the single market)—see e.g. Cases 27/76 and 322/81.

Conduct amounting to abuse of a dominant position   For an undertaking to come within the prohibition in Article 86, it must have a dominant position, *and* engage in conduct that abuses that position. Such conduct may take a variety of forms, some examples of which are cited in the Treaty (see Box 4.3). Abuses that have arisen in case law include:

1. Prohibition of resale, refusal to supply, price discrimination between national markets, charging excessive prices—all these occurred in Case 27/76, which involved dominance by United Brands of the market for bananas.
2. Charging low prices in order to deter potential competitors (Case C-62/86).
3. Full line forcing, to require customers to purchase an entire product range thus foreclosing competitors from part of the market (Case 85/76).
4. Tie-ins: for example in Case 322/81, which involved Michelin's use of its dominance of the market for heavy vehicle tyres in order to promote sales of its light vehicle tyres.

4.2.3   Control of concentrations

Although there is no provision in the EC Treaty relating specifically to mergers and concentrations, the Court of Justice has ruled that mergers may constitute 'an abuse of a dominant position', and thus may be subject to Article 86, which prohibits such abuse (Case 6/72). Furthermore, a company that acquires a shareholding in one of its competitors may be entering into an anti-competitive arrangement contrary to Article 85(1) (see e.g. Cases 142 and 156/84).

The main Community legislation on mergers is Regulation 4064/89, which is summarized in Box 4.4. Article 1 defines mergers 'with a Community dimension', over which the Community has exclusive jurisdiction: this 'one stop shopping' procedure avoids conflict between Community and national provisions and the possibility of double jeopardy. A Commission report on the implementation of the Regulation has suggested that, with increased transfrontier economic activity following the inauguration of the single market, there are 'strong economic arguments' for a reduction in the turnover threshold; but the report also acknowledges political difficulties in securing agreement to a reduction (COM(93)385, p. 21).

The division of responsibility between the Community and its member states is subject to three important qualifications:

1. The Commission may refer a case to national authorities, if the latter claim that their member state is a distinct market, and the concentration threatens to create or strengthen a dominant position (Article 9): up to mid-1993 there had been one such referral (COM(93)385, p. 3).
2. The Commission may act at the request of a member state on a merger which falls below the threshold for a Community dimension and which impedes competition within the member state concerned, in so far as there is an effect on trade between member states (Article 22): up to June 1993 there had been only one request, from the Belgian government for an investigation of the British Airways takeover of Dan Air scheduled services (COM(93)385, p. 3).
3. Member states may act to protect 'legitimate interests'. Explicit recognition is given to public

BOX 4.4
Competition: control of mergers

Regulation 4064/89 concerns concentrations 'with a Community dimension'; it:

- applies where the undertakings involved have aggregate turnover exceeding 5 bn ECUs world-wide and 2.5 bn ECUs within the Community *unless* each of the undertakings generates over two-thirds of its aggregate Community wide turnover in one and the same member state (Article 1);
- requires that mergers with a Community dimension are notified to the Commission (Article 4);
- authorizes the Commission to conduct investigations and to require persons and organizations to supply relevant information (Article 13);
- empowers the Commission to block mergers that create or strengthen a dominant position, as a result of which competition would be significantly impeded in the common market or a substantial part of it (Article 8);
- enables the Commission to levy fines and penalty payments respectively up to 50 000 ECUs and 25 000 ECUs per day for procedural irregularities, and up to 10 per cent of aggregate turnover and 100 000 ECUs per day for non-compliance with its decisions (Article 15);
- awards the Commission sole jurisdiction over mergers with a Community dimension, subject to member states' powers to protect 'legitimate interests' in public security, plurality of the media and prudential rules; other areas of 'legitimate interest' are subject to approval by the Commission (Article 21).

security, plurality of the media and prudential rules; other 'legitimate interests' are subject to approval by the Commission (Article 21).

The Regulation empowers the Commission to prohibit mergers that are 'not compatible with the common market'. In determining 'compatibility', the Commission must take account of market structure, actual or potential competition, alternatives for users and suppliers, barriers to market entry and trends in supply and demand. There is no explicit provision for mergers where firms are about to fail: in these circumstances it is necessary to demonstrate that competition will be more effectively maintained with the proposed merger than by allowing the firm to fail. The Regulation does not provide for a merger to be allowed on grounds of employment protection.

Nevertheless, a merger may be allowed if it yields economic benefits, with reference to 'the interests of intermediate and ultimate consumers, and the development of technical or economic progress, provided that it is to consumers' advantage and does not form an obstacle to competition' (Regulation 4064/89, Article 2).

The Commission analysis of a merger begins with a definition of the market, in terms both of products (taking account of substitutability between products) and geographical coverage, to determine whether there is an effect on at least a 'substantial part' of the Community. This is followed by an assessment of the impact of the proposed merger on competition.

The ostensible criteria for assessment of a merger under the Regulation are narrowly defined: there is no 'balancing test' to judge the effects of a merger in the context of the Community's wider strategic objectives. This was a departure from the original Commission Proposal, which would have explicitly allowed mergers if the damage to competition were outweighed by economic benefits such as improved production and distribution, or technical progress (European Commission 1989: Article 2(3)).

In practice, the merger rules have not been applied 'mechanistically'. By the end of 1994 only one proposed merger had been blocked (Commission Decision Case No. IV/M053). Between

September 1990 (when Regulation 4064/89 came into force) and June 1993, 165 mergers were notified, of which 148 (93 per cent) were cleared without further proceedings. (In eight cases this was subject to undertakings given by the parties.) Of the remaining cases, seven were cleared subject to conditions agreed with the Commission and one proposed merger was prohibited (COM(93)385, p. 3).

4.3 STATE AID

In addition to the conduct of enterprises, Community competition policy also regulates government intervention which can distort markets and generate non-tariff barriers to trade. One of the fundamental premisses of the single market is that competition should be on a 'level playing field' and that member states should refrain from subsidizing their industry in order to obtain, or retain, a competitive advantage. A market in which some competitors are subsidized by government is distorted, in the sense that prices do not accurately reflect economic costs of production. Moreover, the taxes required to finance the subsidies may have further distorting effects. As a result, output from the subsidized industry is above the level that would otherwise prevail, whereas in the non-subsidized sectors the opposite is the case.

Not all market distortions are necessarily malign, and in practice a balance must be struck between the ostensible objectives of government financial support and its potential for distortion of competition. Governments give financial support to industry for a variety of purposes, including regional development, employment protection, industrial restructuring, environmental protection and support for innovation. Often these interventions are in effect an alternative to tariff barriers, designed to develop a competitive advantage through support for technological development in strategic sectors, or to improve the economic competitiveness of less prosperous regions and thus combat unemployment and depopulation.

Table 4.1 State aid to manufacturing industry in member states in proportion to value added and employment, 1988–1990

	% of value added	*Aid per employee (ECUs)*
Belgium	4.1	1655
Denmark	2.1	634
Germany	2.5	984
Greece	14.6	1502
Spain	3.6	936
France	3.5	1380
Ireland	4.9	1734
Italy	6.0	2175
Luxembourg	2.6	1270
Netherlands	3.1	1327
Portugal	5.3	758
UK	2.0	582
European Community	3.5	1203

Source: European Commission, *XXIInd Report on Competition Policy*, COM(93)162, 5 May 1993, p. 225.

All member states provide support for industry, which takes a variety of forms including grants, subsidized loans, guarantees, tax relief, reductions in charges and benefits in kind. State aid to manufacturing in member states is shown in Table 4.1, relative to total value added and per person employed in the period 1988–90. In general subsidies are an appreciable, but not a massive, proportion of manufacturing value added; there is a slight tendency for geographically peripheral countries to have higher percentages but—except for Greece—the difference is not great. State aid per employee varies, but not consistently: the figures for Greece are a reflection of low value added per employee. One-fifth of state aid was granted to support specific industrial sectors (and shipbuilding accounted for a quarter of this expenditure); the remainder was split fairly evenly between regional development and 'horizontal' objectives, including research and development, support for small and medium enterprises and trade promotion.

4.3.1   Community regulation of state aid

State aid payments by governments, or through state resources, are subject to regulation (but are not altogether prohibited). The relevant provisions are summarized in Box 4.5; some categories of aid are, and some may be, permitted as 'compatible with the common market'. State aid payments must be reported to the Commission, which, if it finds that the aid is 'not compatible with the common market' or is being misused, can prohibit the aid or require alterations in the terms on which it is paid (Article 93 EC).

The Commission has published a number of documents setting out general criteria for compatibility of state aid with the common market. Some of these cover specific sectors,

---

BOX 4.5
Regulations governing state aid to industry

EC Treaty Article 92

Subsidies paid by national authorities are generally prohibited as 'incompatible with the common market', although exceptions are to be made for aid:

- having a social character, granted to individual consumers
- to make good damage caused by natural disasters
- to compensate for economic disadvantages caused by the division of Germany

Exceptions *may* be made for aid:

- to promote economic development in areas with abnormally low living standards or serious underemployment
- to promote a project of common European interest
- to remedy a serious economic disturbance
- to facilitate development of certain economic areas or activities
- to promote culture and heritage conservation

ECSC Treaty

Article 54 empowers the Commission to prohibit subsidies and aids contrary to the Treaty;
Article 67 permits the Commission to authorize the granting of aids where action by member states is 'liable ... to provoke a serious disequilibrium'.

---

including textiles, motor vehicles, shipbuilding, transport and (under the ECSC Treaty) coal and steel. There are in addition frameworks for state aid that is not restricted to specific sectors ('horizontal' aid): these cover aid to promote regional development, for environmental protection and for research and development. The general theme of the guidance in these documents is that limited aid may be used for restructuring to restore commercial viability and to stimulate innovation prior to commercial application, but that subsidies that give a direct commercial advantage without strong mitigating factors will not be allowed.

There are of course problems in applying these rules amidst strong political pressures and frequently conflicting policy objectives: and the balance between objectives has evolved as the Community's policy interests have broadened. This is illustrated by the Commission's framework for environmental state aid, which initially was seen as an economic distortion to be phased out, but later was recognized as a legitimate instrument of environmental policy. In 1974 the Commission advocated that environment policies should 'make the polluters pay the cost of protecting the environment'; however, 'because we have become aware of the environment only very recently', a transitional period was needed during which financial assistance was permitted for investment required to meet environmental standards; provision of aid was subject to maximum limits expressed as a percentage of expenditure (European Commission 1974: sections II–III). By 1987 the Commission conceded that continuing development and revision of environmental targets 'calls into question the notion of purely transitional state aids' (European Commission (1987: para. 2.4). Subsequent Guidelines issued in 1994 refer to the environmental objectives of the Community (Article 130r EC), and explicitly acknowledge that 'subsidies ... have their place' as instruments of environmental policy (European Commission 1994: para. 1.2): so financial support might be permitted to facilitate adaptation to higher standards, to enable the required standards to be exceeded, or for achievement of agreed levels of performance.

4.3.2   State aid to public enterprises

Particular problems arise in regulating state aid to enterprises substantially or wholly owned by the state. The state, like any investor, may legitimately provide infusions of equity capital to such enterprises; and the investment may or may not achieve an adequate return. However, an 'investment' made with no expectation of a proper return amounts to a disguised subsidy.

To determine whether such transactions involve state aid, the Commission has developed the *market investor principle*, under which state aid is deemed to exist if an investment is publicly financed 'in circumstances that would not be acceptable to an investor operating under normal market economy conditions', or where the financial position 'is such that a normal return ... cannot be expected within a reasonable time'. This does not mean that unprofitable investments automatically constitute state aid: the crucial test is whether an adequate return could reasonably have been anticipated at the time when the investment was made (European Commission 1993: Paras. 2, 16, 28).

The practical implementation of this principle is fraught with difficulty. The Commission requires member states to supply information on their financial dealings with public-sector undertakings (Commission Directive 93/84), but much depends on the interpretation of financial data, which inevitably has an element of judgement. The issue can also be highly political, particularly where expenditure is necessary for the restructuring of large corporations: a notable example is the air transport industry, which is discussed in Sec. 8.1.2.

4.4   COMPETITION RULES: AN ASSESSMENT

When read in isolation, Community competition rules appear—implicitly—to regard competition as a static process. Nevertheless, the degree of concern over a dominant position or apparently anti-competitive arrangements must depend on the likelihood that they will persist—and, if markets are contestable (see Sec. 4.1.1) that any problems may be self-correcting.

In practice, competition regulation must coexist with the Community's other policy interests. Indeed, this is acknowledged in the preamble to Regulation 4064/89 (point 13), which states that appraisal of mergers must be 'within the general framework of the achievement of the fundamental objectives referred to in Article 2 of the Treaty, including ... strengthening the Community's economic and social cohesion'. This might suggest that a merger could be approved because of its contribution to growth in less favoured regions, although no 'test case' has yet arisen.

Similarly, one of the main concerns of economic policy is to ensure the competitiveness of Community industry, not just internally but also on a world stage, and *vis-à-vis* the United States and Japan; and markets apparently subject to anti-competitive arrangements may nevertheless be contestable in global terms. These considerations suggest a pragmatic approach, emphasizing economic efficiency in broad, and dynamic, terms, and concentrating on the contestability of markets.

A further important policy objective is sustainable development. Subsidies can in some circumstances facilitate and accelerate the achievement of environmental objectives, while avoiding economic disruption. So the state aid rules must be applied with proper regard to the multiple policy objectives of the Community.

The present institutional arrangements for competition policy give the Commission wide-ranging powers to investigate, and to act against, enterprises and governments. The Commission also has considerable discretion, particularly in the regulation of state aid, and its decisions are liable on occasion to be controversial, especially where political objectives conflict.

Suggestions have been made to reduce the Commission's role by passing responsibility for policing competition to an independent non-political body; one model for such an organization is the Cartel Office which regulates competition in Germany. Such a body could undertake the necessary economic analysis, but in any eventual decisions a political element is inescapable. This is because the desirability of—for example—a proposed merger or a government subsidy programme can properly be judged only with reference to the broader interests of the Community, as inferred from the various policy objectives set out in the Treaties.

4.5   COMPETITION POLICY: KEY POINTS AND ISSUES

The proper functioning of the single market depends on the avoidance of actions that distort markets for goods and services. Community law includes provisions to deter enterprises from engaging in anti-competitive practices, and to regulate the payment of subsidies by member states. The Commission's policies in this area, particularly with respect to state aid payments, have sometimes been controversial: this reflects the political dilemmas that arise from balancing the promotion of competition against the other objectives of the Community.

- Exemptions may be given from the prohibition of anti-competitive arrangements, provided that there are benefits to consumers: what criteria are appropriate to determine whether a specific exemption is actually beneficial?

- Community law prohibits the abuse (but not the existence) of a dominant position: is this distinction helpful or meaningful in practice?
- The Community's competition rules are concerned primarily with anti-competitive conduct, and mergers have very rarely been prohibited: was the merger Regulation unnecessary? Has it been ineffective?
- Government funding of state-owned enterprises may be an investment or a subsidy: how can the two be distinguished?
- The Commission is responsible for implementation of a wide range of Community policies, and has been criticized for allowing extraneous considerations to influence its decisions on state aid: should the Commission's responsibilities in this area devolve to an independent competition agency?

REFERENCES

European Commission (1974) Letter to Member States SEC(74)4264 6 November 1974, Annex: 'Community approach to state aids in environmental matters'.

European Commission (1987) Letter to Member States SG(87)D/3795 23 March 1987, Annex: 'Community Framework on State Aids in Environmental Matters'.

European Commission (1989) 'Amended Proposal for a Council Regulation on the control of concentrations between undertakings', *Official Journal*, 1989 C22/14.

European Commission (1993) Communication to the Member States on application of Articles 92 and 93 of the EEC Treaty and Article 5 of Council Directive 80/723/EEC to public undertakings in the manufacturing sector, *Official Journal*, 1993 C307/3.

European Commission (1994) Community guidelines on State aid for environmental protection, *Official Journal*, 1994 C72/3.

European Community Legislation

Regulations

Regulation 19/65, *Official Journal*, 1965 36/553.

Commission Regulation 123/85 on certain categories of motor vehicle distribution and servicing agreements, *Official Journal*, 1985 L15/14.

Commission Regulation 417/85, on specialization agreements, *Official Journal*, 1985 L53/1.

Commission Regulation 418/85, on research and development agreements, *Official Journal*, 1985 L53/5.

Commission Regulation 4087/88, on franchising agreements, *Official Journal*, 1988 L359/46.

Regulation 4064/89 on the control of concentrations between undertakings, *Official Journal*, 1989 L395/1.

Directives

Commission Directive 93/84, on the transparency of financial relations between Member States and public enterprises, *Official Journal*, 1993 L254/16.

European Commission Decisions and Notices

Commission Decision Case No. IV/M053, Aérospatiale-Alenia/De Havilland, *Official Journal*, 1991 L334/42.

Notice concerning Regulation 123/85, *Official Journal*, 1985 C17/4.

Notice on agreements of minor importance, *Official Journal*, 1986 C231/2.

European Commission document

COM(93)385, *Report on the Implementation of the Merger Regulation*, 28 July 1993.

Court judgments

Joined Cases 56 and 58/64, *Consten and Grundig v. Commission* [1966] ECR 299.

Case 5/65, *Societé Technique Minière v. Maschinenbau Ulm GmbH* [1966] ECR 235.

Case 45/69, *Boehringer v. Commission* [1970] ECR 769.

Joined cases 48, 49, 51–57/69, *ICI v. Commission* [1972] ECR 619.

Case 6/72, *Continental Can v. Commission* [1972] ECR 157.

Case 8/72, *Cementhandelaren v. Commission* [1972] ECR 977.

Case 40/73, *Vereeiging 'Suiker Unie' v. Commission* [1976] ECR 1663.

Case 27/76, *United Brands v. Commission* [1978] ECR 207.

Case 85/76, *Hoffmann-La Roche v. Commission* [1979] ECR 461.

Case 322/81, *Michelin v. Commission* [1983] ECR 3461.

Case 42/84, *Remia BV v. Commission* [1985] ECR 2545.

Cases 142 and 156/84, *BAT & R.J. Reynolds v. Commission* [1987] ECR 4487.

Joined cases 89,104,114,116,117,125–29/85, *A. Åhlström Osakeyhtio and others v. Commission*, Judgment 31 March 1993, not yet reported.

Case C-62/86, *AKZO Chemie BV v. Commission* [1991] ECR I-3359.

Case 66/88, *Ahmed Saeed v. Zentrale* [1989] ECR 803.

ECONOMIC AND MONETARY UNION

In the late twentieth century economic policy has become increasingly internationalized. Lessons were learned from the disastrous experience of uncoordinated national policies in the 1930s (described in Sec. 1.2.1). Since that time global economic forces, and especially the massive flows of currency through international markets, have in any case reduced governments' scope for independent action. Within the European Community this effect has been intensified by economic integration, and in particular by the development of a single market and moves towards economic and monetary union, with the eventual prospect of a Community currency. As policy-making at national level has been constrained, the Community has taken a more prominent role, not only in co-ordination but also in the formulation of economic policies.

Provisions for economic and monetary union leading to a single currency were introduced into the EC Treaty in 1993. At one level the introduction of a single currency is a technical measure, a logical continuation of the single market programme. At another level, monetary union would greatly increase the Community's role in economic policy, which might give rise to concerns over accountability and the adequacy of Community policy mechanisms, and objections to a perceived diminution of national sovereignty.

The need to exchange currencies is an impediment to trade, capital flows and the movement of people across national frontiers; so the existence of separate national currencies can be seen as a non-tariff barrier which should be removed if the single market is to be complete. In addition to the costs of currency exchange, financial transactions across national frontiers also incur risks of exchange rate fluctuation. In order to mitigate these risks, and thus facilitate international trade and investment, governments have sought to stabilize exchange rates through co-ordination of their economic and monetary policies. This has particular significance in the Community, as national economies become increasingly integrated within the single market: there are well established arrangements for co-operation between member states with respect to interest rates, exchange rates and balance of payments support.

Nevertheless, a single market with a multitude of fluctuating currencies seems anomalous—as the Community implicitly acknowledged when in 1992 it set an objective of a 'single currency',[1] introducing a provision into the EC Treaty that:

The activities of the Member States and the Community ... shall include the irrevocable fixing of exchange rates leading to the introduction of a single currency, the ECU, and the definition of a single monetary policy and exchange rate policy.

(Article 3a EC)

One important consequence would be a transfer of responsibility for monetary policy from national to Community level, taking the process of economic integration well beyond its present state. (The mechanisms for operating a Community monetary policy are discussed in Sec. 5.4.1 below.) As a result, economic and monetary union has become an area of great controversy, and the focus of debate between supporters and opponents of closer integration.

5.1   MULTIPLE CURRENCIES AND THE SINGLE MARKET

Before turning to the issues of monetary policy and economic integration, it is necessary first to consider the technical aspects of a single currency as a logical consequence of the single market. The present situation—a single market with multiple national currencies—may seem paradoxical: currency exchange has costs, which can give rise to barriers within the single market. To mitigate these costs, stable currency exchange rates are desirable and stability requires co-ordination of national economic policies.

5.1.1   Money in the market economy

Money is essential for an efficient market system. Transactions are made by exchanging money for goods and services; budgeting requires an accounting unit; and holding money is a convenient way to provide for future expenditure. Money is whatever is generally accepted as fulfilling these roles, whether it be banknotes, bank deposits, precious metals or exotic shells.

Today money usually takes the form of national currencies. Indeed, a currency is often assumed to be a necessary attribute of a nation state, so that national boundaries define the economy within which an individual currency is used. The authorities in each country issue notes and coins which are defined as legal tender for transactions throughout the national territory. The management and issue of currencies is normally the responsibility of national central banks, which have varying degrees of independence from national governments.

If money were significant only as a means of making transactions, or providing for future transactions, a multiplicity of national currencies would make no sense. Whenever a conversion is made between currencies, there is a cost. Trading could be better served if there were a single world-wide currency, provided that there were general confidence that this currency would retain its value. Before the First World War, gold provided an approximation to such a currency, since under the gold standard major currencies were convertible into gold at a fixed rate. Even today certain currencies (notably the US dollar) are widely used internationally, especially in countries where there is little confidence in the value of the national currency.

Nevertheless, national currencies continue to exist, and even to proliferate. Changes in the exchange rates between currencies provides a mechanism for the adjustment of relative prices. If a country is generally uncompetitive in export markets, its trade balance will be in deficit, and to remedy this situation it must lower the cost of its exports. Devaluation of the currency secures an immediate cost reduction: for example, the devaluation of the pound sterling from DM2.8 to DM2.4 in September 1992 secured a decrease in the DM cost of British exports of some 20 per cent.

Furthermore, money has an important role in national economic policies: governments (or central banks) use monetary policy instruments to regulate the supply of money and its price (which is the rate of interest), in order to influence economic variables, such as the levels of aggregate demand, investment, employment, the rate of inflation and the external exchange rate of the currency. Control over monetary policy is often seen as a key attribute of national sovereignty, without which it is not possible to ensure that economic management reflects the national interest. Such sentiments appear, for example, to have motivated some republics of the former Soviet Union to establish their own currencies to replace the rouble.

5.1.2   National currencies as a non-tariff barrier

In the European Community currencies and monetary policies are at present the responsibility of national authorities.[2] National currencies are traded on the international financial markets, and their rates of exchange fluctuate to varying degrees. The existence of separate national currencies, and exchange rate variability, give rise—both directly and indirectly—to non-tariff barriers to trade within the European Community; and it is arguable that the single market cannot be truly complete until these barriers are removed.

Direct costs   These include transaction costs and other costs (such as additional administrative burdens) associated with the existence of multiple currencies. The changing of money between currencies entails costs which can be a substantial proportion of the value of transactions, particularly for the relatively small amounts exchanged by travellers and small businesses. This was highlighted in a 1988 report by the European Consumers' Bureau, in which a (hypothetical) traveller with BFr40 000 undertakes a tour of all the Community capitals (except Dublin and Luxembourg), starting and finishing in Brussels, and exchanging all his money into national currency banknotes in each country; on his return to Brussels, the cumulative effects of exchange rate margins and bank charges had reduced the money from BFr40 000 to BFr21 300—a cumulative loss of approximately 47 per cent, or 6 per cent on average per exchange (Emerson *et al.* 1992: 66).

A study for the Commission has estimated that the replacement of existing national currencies by a single currency would lead to an overall annual saving in direct costs in the range of 13–19 bn ECUs (1990 prices), about 0.2–0.4 per cent of Community GDP. Table 5.1 gives a breakdown of these cost savings, showing the average of the high and low estimates. Approximately half of the total was accounted for by exchange margins and commission charged on bank transfers used to make payments between firms in different countries; the costs of these payments vary with the amount of money exchanged, the importance of the client and the currencies involved: the effect is to place smaller firms, and smaller countries, at a relative disadvantage. 'In-house' costs, around one-quarter of the total in Table 5.1, include additional

Table 5.1   Transaction cost savings with a single currency

	bn ECUs/yr[*]
Bank transfers	8.5
Banknotes, cheques, credit cards	2.1
In-house costs	4.2
Cross-border payments	1.3
Total	16.1

[*] 1990 prices.
Source: Emerson *et al.* (1992: 267) (by permission of Oxford University Press).

accounting and treasury costs of enterprises, and costs of delays in receipt of payments and of holding cash in multiple currencies. The Commission study found appreciable variation in the burden of foreign exchange transaction costs, ranging from 0.1 to 0.2 per cent of GDP in the larger member states, up to 1 per cent in smaller and less developed countries—the cost burden will tend to be highest in member states in which trade with the rest of the Community is most substantial relative to the size of the economy, and in those member states with the least efficient and competitive banking sectors.

Indirect costs   These arise from distortions in resource allocation resulting from the use of different currencies with risks of exchange rate fluctuations. This tends to inhibit cross-border trade, because suppliers face a risk that their returns will be eroded by currency depreciation in their customers' countries. Currency volatility also causes suppliers to frustrate the objectives of the single market, and of Community competition policy, by seeking to insulate national markets. There is an incentive to perpetuate market segmentation in order to restrict parallel importation of products into countries with appreciating currencies from countries with depreciating currencies. For example, car manufacturers have sought to maintain divisions between national markets by means of exclusive dealership arrangements, in the face of substantial differences in car prices between member states that are due (at least in part) to exchange rate movements.

Furthermore, investments across national frontiers carry an exchange rate risk, inasmuch as the value of an investment made in a foreign currency will be eroded if that currency depreciates against the currency of the investor's home country: if for example a German investor had bought a UK bond for £1000 (DM 2780 at the then exchange rate) on 15 September 1992, the bond would have fallen in value the following day to DM2650 (a loss of approximately 5 per cent) when the exchange rate for the pound sterling fell from DM2.78 to DM2.65 to the pound. A UK investor in Germany would of course have gained, with appreciation in the sterling value of an investment denominated in Deutschmarks; but if the motivation is the underlying value of the investment, possibilities of exchange rate gains or losses represent an unwelcome additional element of risk. So the fear of losses outweighs the attractions of possible gains—in technical terms, investors are *risk-averse*.

Investors who are deterred by currency risks can seek compensation in the form of higher returns (a *transfrontier risk premium*). Alternatively, they can pay others to bear the risks, using financial instruments for forward purchases or sales of currencies (a process known as *hedging*); forward markets generally cover periods up to one year. This is essentially a form of insurance—in the example above the German investing in a UK bond at a rate of DM2.78 to £1 would avoid risks of exchange rate losses by simultaneously purchasing Deutschmarks for pounds a year in advance at the (known) forward exchange rate. Investments made in the investor's own currency are subject only to risks inherent in the investment itself: there is no question of exchange risk premia or hedging. So the additional risk of foreign exchange losses—whether or not it is subject to hedging—gives rise to a bias against transfrontier investment.

Exchange rate risks can be minimized if investment projects are financed by debt issued in the currency of the country in which the investment is made. If for example a company establishes a factory in Greece, financed entirely by borrowing in drachmas, any exchange rate loss on the investment is fully offset by a reduction in the burden of debt. The only exchange rate risk is to profits—after interest payments—which are exchanged into the investor's own currency. Nevertheless, this is unlikely to eliminate the currency barrier: if the investor were borrowing in a single currency to finance projects in several countries, the amount borrowed would be larger, and the terms possibly more advantageous; moreover, rates of interest tend to reflect risk of devaluation. (If in the above example the Greek authorities were to maintain high interest rates to avoid devaluation of the drachma, this would affect the rate of interest paid by the investor borrowing in drachmas.) In any case, this financing technique is suited only to large investment expenditures by enterprises that are sufficiently well established to be able to raise credit in countries other than their own; consequently there is little scope for small and medium enterprises to undertake transfrontier investment on this basis.

In general, the effects of currency barriers are very uneven: they bear most heavily upon small countries, particularly those without highly developed financial markets, and those in which payments to and from other currencies have the greatest economic significance (technically, *open economies*); the costs of dealing in multiple currencies are proportionately higher the smaller the amounts of money involved, so that, for private individuals and for small enterprises, with less access to sophisticated hedging and other financial arrangements, the currency barrier is more severe than for large enterprises.

5.1.3   Measures to mitigate the currency barrier

The previous section shows that existence of multiple currencies involves a cost, and this cost increases with the risks of exchange rate instability. The causes of such instability are highly complex, reflecting the influence of structural differences between economies, policy decisions by the authorities, and the behaviour of those who take economic decisions.

The scope for independent national economic and monetary policies is severely limited in the European single market. In the single market there are no restrictions on exports and imports, or on the transmission of money, between member states. At the same time, it is desirable to avoid exchange rate instability which gives rise to barriers to trade and investment.

Rates of exchange between currencies depend upon the supply of and demand for the various currencies. These are influenced by trade—the value of imports and exports—and by capital movements. In the longer term, exchange rates are influenced mainly by the trade balance (the difference between the total value of exports and imports). If for example the United Kingdom were consistently to have a trade deficit, this would be likely to lead to a decline in the value of the pound, so that UK imports would become more expensive (in terms of pounds) and UK exports cheaper (in terms of foreign currencies). There would then be incentives for the UK to reduce imports, and for other countries to increase their purchases of UK exports, so that the trade deficit is eliminated.

In addition to this long-term effect, there are short-term movements in exchange rates which are driven mainly by capital flows. These are influenced by interest rates and expectations with respect to eventual movements in exchange rates, which are in turn affected by the numerous factors encompassed by the term 'market sentiment'. Market expectations can have an element of self-fulfilling prediction; for example, if a decline is anticipated in the exchange rate of the British pound there will be an outflow of capital from the United Kingdom, which in turn will reduce the demand for pounds, leading to a fall in the pound's exchange rate against other currencies.

In seeking to avoid exchange rate fluctuations, national authorities must set interest rates at levels that attract sufficient (but not excessive) demand for their currencies at the prevailing exchange rate. If interest rates are too low, capital will move elsewhere, the demand for the currency will fall, and so its price (the exchange rate) will decline.

5.2   CO-ORDINATION OF NATIONAL ECONOMIC AND MONETARY POLICIES

The prime objective of monetary policy is to establish credibility: a track record of meeting strict targets, with low levels of inflation, will inspire confidence that the value of the currency will not be eroded by inflation. This reduces the risk that expectations of inflation will themselves generate inflationary pressures in the economy.

Governments conduct their economic policies in the midst of interdependencies, both between economic variables and between internal and external factors. Generally targets (either announced or implicit) are adopted for a limited number of variables: other economic indicators are influenced indirectly by the degree of success in attaining the targets. Policy targets may be set in terms of the inflation rate, growth in money supply, the exchange rate or the balance of payments: their function is to establish criteria for economic performance.

In general, economic indicators should reflect the state of the economy and expectations of its future prospects. However, a variable that is targeted as a policy instrument may not be a reliable indicator, since it is being used by the authorities to influence the future course of the economy. When the views of financial markets and the aspirations of policy-makers pull in different directions, tensions can arise if targets are seen to be inconsistent with economic indicators. One instance was the crisis of 16 September 1992, when the pound sterling exchange rate was seen as no longer credible; notwithstanding a massive rise in interest rates, devaluation, and the UK's exit from the exchange rate mechanism, rapidly ensued.

Since the establishment of the Community, exchange rates have been the most common target variable, or constraining factor—and this implies a heavy degree of interdependence between countries in terms of economic management. Interest rates are the main link between a country's economic management and its currency exchange rate. Aggregate demand is influenced by the quantity of money in the economy, which is in turn affected by the interest rate (which is the price of money). The cost of borrowing, expressed by interest rates, is a determinant of levels of investment and a constraint on government budget deficits. Moreover, growth in government borrowing will tend to raise interest rates, because it increases the demand for funds in the financial markets.

Therefore, if economic management has an exchange rate target, interest rates must be set with a view to maintaining the value of the currency. For many years national monetary policies have been co-ordinated in the European Monetary System (the EMS), within which most member states have pursued exchange rate stability through participation in the Exchange Rate Mechanism (the ERM). Maintenance of exchange rates prescribed by the ERM has required a high degree of co-ordination of national policies, to ensure that the key economic variables in participating countries remain in alignment.

5.2.1   The need for policy co-ordination

Monetary stability depends heavily upon international co-operation, whereby countries follow broadly parallel economic policies. Fundamental misalignments of exchange rates will be avoided if the countries concerned have similar economic performance, in terms of inflation rates and budget deficits, so that their trade balance and interest rates remain consistent with the maintenance of an unchanged exchange rate. In the shorter term, central banks can promote exchange rate stability, through co-ordination of their intervention in foreign exchange markets and the timing and magnitude of interest rate adjustments. Concerted measures have greater credibility, and hence more influence on market expectations, than unilateral action by the authorities in a single country.

The consequences of failure in international economic and monetary co-operation were graphically demonstrated by experience in the 1930s (see Sec. 1.2.1). At that time the industrialized countries sought to gain competitive advantage through devaluation of their currencies and by adoption of protectionist trade measures. The results were disastrous, and it is now generally recognized that policies on these lines lead to inflation and economic recession.

Furthermore, the limits of national discretion in economic policies have become apparent in the years following the Second World War, as economic interdependence has increased, with substantial growth in international trade and capital flows. Against this background, the European Community has recognized the need for a co-ordinated approach to economic policy, as a necessary precondition for the progress of economic integration. So economic and monetary policy has become an area of major Community responsibility because, applying the subsidiarity criterion, 'objectives ... cannot be sufficiently achieved by the Member States' (Article 3b EC).

The Community has from the beginning specified economic policy objectives for its member states: the 1957 EEC Treaty (Article 104) stated that 'each Member State shall pursue the economic policy needed to ensure the equilibrium of its overall balance of payments and to maintain confidence in its currency, while taking care to ensure a high level of employment and a stable level of prices.' The 1957 Treaty (Article 105) also required the co-ordination of national economic and monetary policies to facilitate attainment of Community objectives. In 1992 the EU (Maastricht) Treaty superseded these provisions, so that the EC Treaty now includes a chapter on economic policy which requires that member states must 'regard their economic policies as a matter of common concern' (Article 103), and 'conduct their economic policies with a view to contributing to the objectives of the Community' (Article 102a).

5.2.2 The European Monetary System

Since the establishment of the European Community, there has usually been a framework of some form within which the exchange rates of national currencies have been fixed. Currency arrangements have changed very considerably over the years, and the participation of Community member states has varied. Nevertheless, the desirability of exchange rate stability has been generally recognized, and institutional mechanisms of various forms have been used to fix currency exchange rates.

When the EEC Treaty was signed in 1957, the countries of western Europe participated in the 'fixed rate dollar standard', which developed following the 1945 Bretton Woods agreement. Under this system countries fixed the exchange rates of their currencies against the US dollar, and followed economic and monetary policies designed to ensure the maintenance of the specified exchange rate. Since currencies were fixed against the dollar, they were of course also fixed against one another; exchange rate adjustments could be made if currencies became consistently over (or under)-valued against the dollar, but in practice such adjustments were infrequent.

This system broke down in the early 1970s, approximately 15 years after the formation of the European Economic Community. Since then the Deutschmark, rather than the dollar, has been the key currency at the centre of mechanisms for currency stability in western Europe. Following the collapse of the dollar standard, a system was established centred on the Deutschmark and known as the 'Snake' because it permitted exchange rates to fluctuate within limits; this system of 'fixed but adjustable' rates linked the currencies of the Benelux countries and (more loosely) the French franc and the Italian lira to the Deutschmark.

This somewhat *ad hoc* arrangement was ~~superseded~~ replaced by the European Monetary System (EMS) in 1979. The EMS has three main elements:

1. The European Community currency unit (the ECU).
2. The European Monetary Co-operation Fund.
3. The Exchange Rate Mechanism.

The ECU is defined as the sum of fixed amounts of each of the currencies of the member states; its composition was fixed on 1 November 1993, and will not be revised before the ECU becomes a currency in its own right. (The composition of the ECU in amounts national currencies is shown in Table 5.2.) The relative weights of the national currencies within the ECU depend upon the amount and value of the currency. While the former is fixed, the latter can vary; consequently currencies that decline in relative value will have their weight in the ECU reduced. As a result, the ECU has a bias towards 'hardness'—a tendency to increase the weight given to the stronger currencies.

Table 5.2 Composition of the ECU, 1994

Deutschmark	0.6242
French franc	1.332
UK £	0.08784
Italian lira	151.8
Luxembourg franc	1.130
Spanish peseta	6.885
Danish krone	1.976
Irish £	0.008552
Dutch guilder	0.2198
Belgian franc	3.301
Greek drachma	1.440
Portuguese escudo	1.393

Source: Regulation 3320/94, on the consolidation of the existing legislation on the definition of the ECU, *Official Journal*, 1994 L350/27.

Community institutions use the ECU as an accounting unit for budgetary purposes and to denominate monetary amounts with reference to (for example) agricultural prices and levies, fines for infraction of competition rules and contracts with Community institutions. The actual payments are normally made in national currencies, at the prevailing ECU exchange rate (or in the case of agriculture at the 'green' currency rate—see Sec. 9.4).

In addition, the ECU has some of the attributes of a currency. It is used to denominate loans, for interbank lending, in international trade and transactions between companies, and (to a limited extent) in private financial services. The main use as a currency is for borrowing—by Community institutions, by national governments and in the private sector, both within the Community and in other countries. In this area the ECU has been very successful, becoming one of the major currencies of the international bond market. The attraction of the ECU lies in its stability: as a 'basket' of currencies it is less prone than its constituent currencies to exchange rate instability, since it evens out the fluctuations affecting individual currencies (although the ECU exchange rate against non-Community currencies—such as the dollar and the yen—does of course change as Community currencies fluctuate against other currencies).

2. *The European Monetary Co-operation Fund* was established to provide short and medium-term credits to ease temporary balance of payments difficulties; it has now been taken over by the European Monetary Institute (see Box 5.4 below).

3. *The Exchange Rate Mechanism* (ERM) requires participating countries to maintain the exchange rates of their currencies against the ECU within specified bands. Up to 1993, currencies were normally permitted to fluctuate within bands defined by a margin of 2¼ per cent above or below a central rate. Thus for example, when the central rate of the French franc was Fr6.82 per ECU (the level established in September 1992), the actual rate could vary between Fr6.67 and Fr6.97. Some currencies were permitted wider margins of 6 per cent, pending their accommodation to the standard margin. Provision was made for exchange rate adjustment by agreement within the ERM, when this is necessary to realign national price levels after a currency has become fundamentally overvalued (or undervalued) *vis-à-vis* other ERM currencies.

Although the EMS includes all member states, participation in the ERM has never been Community-wide (see Box 5.1). The United Kingdom did not join the exchange rate mechanism at its inception: the then government's economic policies were geared to money supply, rather than exchange rate, targets. Later on the UK was a 'shadow' participant, targeting an exchange rate while not formally within the ERM; it eventually joined the ERM in October 1990. Greece entered the Community in 1981, and Spain and Portugal in 1986, but Community membership did not automatically entail participation in the ERM: Spain and Portugal did not join the ERM until July 1989 and April 1992 respectively, while Greece has never been a member.

BOX 5.1
The Exchange Rate Mechanism: key developments

Date	Event	EC members not in the ERM
March 1979	Foundation of the EMS[*]	UK
January 1981	Greece joins the EC	UK, Greece
January 1986	Spain and Portugal join the EC	UK, Greece, Spain, Portugal
July 1989	Spain joins the ERM[†]	UK, Greece, Portugal
January 1990	Italy moves to narrow band (±2¼%)	
October 1990	UK joins the ERM[†]	Greece, Portugal
April 1992	Portugal joins the ERM[†]	Greece
September 1992	Italy and UK leave the ERM	Italy, UK, Greece
August 1993	The ERM widens bands to ±15%	
January 1995	Austria joins the EC and the ERM; Sweden and Finland join the EC	Italy, UK, Greece, Sweden, Finland

[*] Italy opted for broad band (±6%); other ERM participants maintain narrow band (±2¼%)
[†] with broad band (±6%)

The record of the Exchange Rate Mechanism   The 1980s was a period of relative stability for currency exchange rates in Europe, after the turbulence that followed the breakdown of the dollar standard. Realignments of exchange rates within the ERM are summarized in Box 5.2. Initially these were frequent, but eventually the system became more stable. In the period between January 1987 and September 1992 there was no realignment, exchange rates of all ERM currencies against the ECU remaining within their prescribed bands. (Although the Italian lira was devalued in 1990, this was merely to accommodate a narrowing of its fluctuation band—see Box 5.1.)

The increasing stability of exchange rates signified an evolution of the ERM into an economic policy instrument, as its members sought economic convergence with low levels of inflation. The exchange rate was increasingly seen as a means of influencing future levels of inflation, rather than as an economic indicator reflecting market expectations of economic prospects.

The Deutschmark assumed a central role, as the currency with the best inflation performance (although formally exchange rates remain linked to the ECU). Other ERM members came to use the fixed exchange rate against the Deutschmark as a means of increasing their own anti-inflationary credibility. Consequently Germany (as the 'anchor' of the ERM) has pursued a monetary policy defined by its independent central bank (the Bundesbank), while monetary policies of other ERM participants followed that of Germany, seeking to limit growth in their money supply so that their rates of inflation are kept in line with the rate in Germany.

BOX 5.2
The Exchange Rate Mechanism: realignments, 1979–1995

Date	Currencies (% change against the ECU)
Sept. 1979	DM(+2), DKr(−4.76)
Dec. 1979	DKr(−4.76)
March 1981	LIT(−6)
Oct. 1981	DM(+5.5), DFL(+5.5), LIT(−3), FFr(−3)
Feb. 1982	BFr(−8.5), DKr(−3)
June 1982	DM(+4.25), DFL(+4.25), LIT(−2.75), FFr(−5.75)
March 1983	DM(+5.5), DFL(+3), DKr(+2.5), BFr(+1.5), LIT(−2.5), FFr(−2.5), IR£(−3.5)
July 1985	BFr(+2), IR£(+2), DM(+2), DFL(+2), FFr(+2), DKr(+2), LIT(−6)
April 1986	DM(+3), DFL(+3), DKr(+1), BFr(+1), FFr(−3)
Aug. 1986	IR£(−8)
Jan. 1987	DM(+3), DFL(+3), BFr(+2)
Jan. 1990	LIT(−3.7)
14 Sept. 1992	DM(+3.5), DFL(+3.5), DKr(+3.5), BFr(+3.5), FFr(+3.5), IR£(+3.5), £(+3.5), PTA(+3.5), ESC(+3.5), LIT(−3.5)
17 Sept. 1992	PTA(−5)
Nov. 1992	PTA(−6), ESC(−6)
Jan. 1993	IR£(−10)
May 1993	PTA(−8), ESC(−6.5)
March 1995	PTA(−7), ESC(−3.5)

Currency-country key: BFr—Belgium; DFL—Netherlands; DKr—Denmark; DM—Germany; ESC—Portugal; FFr—France; IR£—Ireland; LIT—Italy; PTA—Spain; £—UK

The system ran into difficulties in the wake of German unification in 1990. To counter the inflationary pressures that then arose, Germany ran a very restrictive monetary policy, so that the Bundesbank raised interest rates to high levels. This precipitated instability in the exchange rate mechanism, as other ERM participants then had to raise their own interest rates in order to maintain their exchange rates within the prescribed bands.

The instability was seriously compounded by the activities of speculators. Mobility of capital, and the deregulation of capital markets, led to the availability of large amounts of money and the possibility of massive volumes of trading in currency markets. In a volatile market, rumours that a currency is in danger of devaluation can generate heavy selling of that currency, which can lead to excess supply, and lack of demand, for the currency at its existing exchange rate. The authorities can seek to support the currency exchange rate by buying it in the foreign exchange market, and by increasing interest rates. If these measures are overwhelmed by pressure of selling, devaluation is unavoidable.

The tensions in the ERM reached crisis point in September 1992. The UK pound and the Italian lira came under particularly heavy pressure, and the UK and Italy left the ERM on 14 September 1992, unable to maintain their exchange rates within prescribed margins. This episode was marked by a failure to reach a co-operative solution. In the past, realignments had been undertaken by general agreement, and often comprised a mixture of upward revaluation and devaluation.[3] Such an agreed realignment was made two days before the Lira left the ERM, but it was not sufficient to restore stability; it remains a matter of conjecture whether a more extensive and comprehensive realignment might have permitted the UK and Italy to remain in the ERM.

Over the following months, Spain, Portugal and Ireland devalued their currencies, but remained within the ERM. Other currencies, notably the French franc, also came under heavy pressure, but resisted devaluation until a further crisis threatened the ERM in August 1993. On this occasion the permitted margins of fluctuation were widened to ± 15 per cent, although the central rates within the bands remained unchanged. This was widely seen at the time as a severe setback for monetary co-operation, and for eventual monetary union.

The credibility of the system was restored somewhat in 1994: ERM exchange rates were maintained, and most currencies remained fairly close to their ERM central exchange rates. Early in 1995 continuing Spanish budgetary deficits led to pressure on the peseta, which was devalued by 7 per cent in March 1995; there was a further 'knock-on' effect on the Portuguese escudo, which suffered a 3½ per cent devaluation.

The Exchange Rate Mechanism: an assessment   Despite its periodic setbacks, the ERM has shown considerable resilience. Seven of the original eight participants have maintained continuous membership since the foundation of the EMS in 1979, and by 1994 nine of the (then) 12 member states were within the ERM. Early in 1995, following enlargement of the European Union, the ERM covered 10 of the 15 member states, which accounted for approximately two-thirds of the Community's aggregate GDP.

The ERM appears to have had some success in terms of exchange rate stability, with resulting benefits to trade within the single market. In the early 1980s the system was able to adjust to currency misalignments with orderly exchange rate adjustments, but by 1992 the ERM was under great strain following German unification. The September 1992 crisis and subsequent events suggest that the ERM, while a useful stabilizing device, has limited effectiveness as a policy instrument. Thus far, an exchange rate linked to the Deutschmark has proved a credible counter-inflationary weapon for some countries (notably France); for the UK and Italy, it evidently has not done so.

For the future, two lines of strategy can in principle be distinguished:

1. a flexible mechanism, with frequent realignments to accommodate to differences in inflation (so that exchange rates are fixed in real terms, after allowance for inflation);
2. a system of rigidly fixed exchange rates, which constrain national economic policies to bring about a convergence between the rates of inflation of ERM participants (so that fixed nominal exchange rates lead to fixed real exchange rates).

The EC Treaty (as amended by the 1992 EU Treaty) clearly points to the ERM developing in accordance with the second of these strategies. However, even while the EU Treaty was in the process of ratification, the ERM crisis of September 1992 raised doubts about the realism of the Treaty provisions on economic and monetary union.

Indeed, the very concept of a 'fixed' exchange rate may be flawed. Relative values can be fixed if they are no more than an accounting definition; for example, the rate of exchange between dollars and cents is 1:100, because both are issued by the same monetary authority. In contrast, rates of exchange between national currencies are ultimately determined by supply and demand, which are subject to variations beyond the control of governments. Consequently fluctuation in exchange rates must always be a possibility, until the currencies come under the control of a single authority.

So it remains possible that the ERM will develop as a more flexible arrangement on the lines of 1 above. If so, exchange rate stability would reflect, rather than cause, economic convergence. Consequently the onus would be placed on member states to follow policies to establish counter-inflationary credibility, without the aid of an exchange rate 'anchor'. In the meantime, high interest rates may be necessary to maintain the exchange rates of the weaker currencies; exchange controls—which could have been used in the past—are no longer an option, because they would constitute a barrier to movement in the single market.

Thus, the exchange rate mechanism is not a painless route to a single currency, particularly for inflation-prone countries. On the other hand, the importance of exchange rate stability in the single market is such that countries may have little choice in economic and monetary policy, even if they do not envisage eventual participation in a single currency.

5.3 MONETARY UNIFICATION

The philosophy of the single market is that barriers must be removed between member states, and where necessary policy responsibilities transferred from national to Community level. So, inasmuch as multiple currencies are a non-tariff barrier to trade and investment, the logic of the single market points to their replacement by a single currency. However, the corollary—a Community-level monetary policy—has given rise to disquiet over the perceived loss of national sovereignty that would be entailed.

The EC Treaty sets out provisions whereby the Community may progress from the European Monetary System to a single currency which would supersede national currencies. A single currency would have two major benefits:

1. It would eliminate the barriers to trade associated with separate national currencies within the single market.
2. It is—self-evidently—the ultimate solution to problems arising from exchange rate instability between the currencies of member states.

The disadvantages would be a loss of flexibility in economic relations between member states. If differences in inflation rates were not offset by exchange rate realignments, they would have other consequences, which might include chronic unemployment.

Before assessing the single currency provisions, it is necessary to consider whether the European Union or its member states more closely approximate an optimal currency area.

5.3.1 Optimal currency areas

While currency areas are now generally coterminous with nation states, there is no reason why this necessarily has to be the case. Box 5.3 sets out economic criteria (as distinct from any political considerations) defining an area in which a single currency is optimal. Essentially, a single currency is desirable if there is a high degree of interregional movement (trade, and the mobility of labour and capital), and if the benefits of currency stability between regions outweigh the value of flexibility to adjust to interregional economic fluctuations.

As European economic integration has proceeded towards a barrier-free single market, the use of numerous separate currencies may seem anomalous. A single currency has appeared to be a logical progression, in order to eliminate the currency barriers discussed above. To assess the case for and against a Community currency to supersede national currencies, it is necessary first to examine the functions of currencies:

- as a medium for transactions;
- to facilitate economic adjustment;
- as a medium for monetary policy.

BOX 5.3
Criteria for an optimal currency area

Mobility of labour and capital If factors are able easily to move between regions, adjustments can occur by a shift in economic activity, as factors move from regions where their productivity is low into regions with higher productivity. (This process is illustrated by Figure A1.5.) In the absence of factor mobility, changes in exchange rates can provide a substitute adjustment mechanism, provided of course that the regions have different currencies.

Openness of the economy If foreign trade is high relative to the size of the economy, the overall price level is sensitive to changes in the exchange rate, and so a separate national currency is of little assistance in accommodating economic fluctuations. However, in an economy where foreign trade has little importance, exchange rate adjustments have little impact on the price level: their main effect is to switch expenditure between imports and domestic products.

Product diversity A highly specialized economy can benefit from having its own currency, since exchange rate adjustments may be used to maintain the competitiveness of its products. In a diversified economy this is of less significance, since resources can be switched between sectors to maintain the economy's overall competitiveness.

Inflation A currency area is liable to be destabilized if there are consistent differences in inflation rates between its regions. A relatively high price level will make a region economically uncompetitive within the currency area.

Fiscal system A common fiscal system is necessary to provide a mechanism for easing interregional adjustment by fiscal transfers.

These roles are potentially conflicting, inasmuch as they point to fundamentally different conclusions with respect to the desirable number of currencies. The relative weight given to these considerations depends upon the desirability and efficacy of exchange rate adjustments and monetary policies, on which there remain differences of view.

If trade transactions (function 1 above) were the only consideration, the ideal would be a single world currency, in order to avoid the currency barriers outlined above. Failing this, the recommendation would be the fewer currencies the better—so for instance money might be managed by groups of countries in trading blocs, rather than by individual countries.

At the other extreme, the changing of relative costs by exchange rate movements (function 2 above) calls for a multiplicity of currencies. The essential criteria for defining a currency area on this basis are mobility of factors of production (labour and capital), and the importance of external trade, and relative propensity for inflation (see Box 5.3).

The logical extension of this argument is that there may be a case for regions within a country to have their own currencies. If a country has regions of increasing and declining prosperity, economic adjustments might—in principle—be eased by changes in the exchange rates of regional currencies with the ebb and flow of economic fortunes; for example, the less prosperous regions of Italy (the Mezzogiorno) and the UK (the north of England) could have their own lira and pound, and seek to restore economic competitiveness by devaluation against the currencies of the more prosperous regions of those countries.

In practice, the creation of regional currencies is not seriously contemplated.[4] No one suggests that (for example) each region of the USA should have its own dollar in order to ease adjustment to relative economic decline or expansion among the regions. Although the monetary union of Germany in 1990 led to economic difficulties, with high unemployment in the eastern Länder, there was never any serious proposal to reintroduce a separate east German currency as a means of mitigating these problems. So any advantages offered by regional currencies appear to be outweighed by the disadvantages with respect to the role of currencies in trade and economic management (functions 1 and 3 above); and the inference is that Germany as a whole came closer than its regions to the criteria for an optimal currency area.

The predominant concern in the management of the monetary system is with economic policy at the national level (function 3 above). The currency system gives primacy to the requirements of national authorities for monetary policy instruments in the overall framework of economic management, so there is generally one currency per country. (In this context 'country' is defined in economic, rather than political, terms to include territories such as Hong Kong and Taiwan.) In a few instances, such as Ireland up to 1978 and Luxembourg, the currency may for practical purposes be identical with that of a larger neighbouring country, so that autonomy in monetary policy is forgone. The significance of this loss depends of course on the extent to which divergence from the monetary policies of the larger neighbour is possible or advantageous.

5.3.2   A single currency: treaty provisions

Most member states have—at least implicitly—accepted in principle the idea that the European Union approximates to an optimal currency area. The intergovernmental conference at Maastricht in December 1992 agreed on a course for adoption of a Community currency which would supersede national currencies. This would come about through convergence of the economies of member states, building on the progress of the European Monetary System.

BOX 5.4
The European Monetary Institute and the System of Central Banks

The European Monetary Institute (EMI) is composed of the central banks of member states. It is charged with co-ordination of monetary policies, and with preparations for a single monetary policy, a Community currency and the establishment of the European System of Central Banks (ESCB). The EMI administraters short and medium-term credit facilities for member states, and manages foreign exchange reserves.

The ESCB will be established on the inauguration of the ECU as the Community currency, scheduled for 1998. National central banks will be members of the ESCB, together with the European Central Bank (ECB), the successor of the EMI. The main task of the ESCB will be to define and implement monetary policy; and in discharging this responsibility ESCB members will act independently of other Community institutions and national governments. The ESCB will also have the sole right to authorize the issue of ECU banknotes.

The EC Treaty sets out a blueprint for measures that are necessary to achieve, and to operate, a Community currency. Article 3a(2) calls for 'an irrevocable fixing of exchange rates leading to the introduction of a single currency, the ECU, and the definition and conduct of a single monetary policy and exchange rate policy the primary objective of both of which shall be to maintain price stability'. The Treaty also provides for an institutional structure to operate a common monetary policy (see Box 5.4).

The timing of monetary union is specified by a series of deadlines, leading to the adoption of the single currency by the beginning of 1999 (see Box 5.5). This timetable is ambitious and there are serious doubts as to its feasibility, with reference both to the economic preconditions that must be met and to the organizational practicalities. The 1996 intergovernmental conference may well decide that the existing provisions are unviable, and amend the Treaty and its Protocols accordingly.

In practice, it is extremely unlikely that the Community will have a 'single currency' in this century, although a common currency, covering certain member states, is a more realistic possibility. Two member states—the UK and Denmark—have reserved the right to opt out,

---

BOX 5.5
Monetary unification: key deadlines

31 December 1996   Council decision on whether to inaugurate the single currency before 1 January 1999, and if so when (Art. 109j(3)); the European Monetary Institute (EMI) is to specify the regulatory, organizational and logistical framework for the European System of Central Banks (ESCB) (Protocol on the Statute of the EMI, Art. 4.4.2).

1 January 1998   Notification of UK's intention whether or not to participate in the single currency (assuming that the third stage begins on 1 January 1999) (Protocol on certain provisions relating to the UK, Art. 1).

1 July 1998   Establishment of the ESCB and European Central Bank; winding up of the EMI (Art. 109I EC).

1 January 1999   Latest date for adoption of the single currency (Art. 109j(4)EC).

---

and retain their national currencies if they so desire (these opt-outs are specified in Protocols to the EC Treaty): Denmark has already indicated its intention not to participate in the single currency, although it remains committed to the European Monetary System and the Exchange Rate Mechanism (European Council 1992).

Moreover, participation in the 'single currency' will be limited to member states that fulfil the so-called 'convergence criteria' summarized in Box 5.6. Member states must have relatively low inflation and interest rates, stable currency exchange rates, and government debt and deficits below a maximum level expressed as a percentage of GDP. The debt and deficit criteria ensure that budget imbalances, and consequent government borrowing requirements, do not generate inflationary pressures that would compromise the stability of the economy.

There is little chance that *all* member states will fulfil these conditions by 1999. In 1993, in the midst of economic recession and turbulence in the foreign exchange markets, only Luxembourg consistently satisfied all the requirements. European Community monetary arrangements have typically centred on the strong economy of Germany, and depended upon the ability of other member states to maintain a stable link with the German currency.

The record of success has varied: the 'Snake' degenerated into an arrangement involving only Germany and the Benelux countries, while the ERM has survived, albeit with some difficulty. It is likely that the future success of monetary union will depend on the maintenance of economic

---

BOX 5.6
Qualifications for member states to participate in the single currency

1. *Price stability*   The member state must have had an average rate of inflation over the previous year not more than 1 ½ percentage points above that of the three best performing member states in terms of price stability.
2. *Low interest rates*   Average nominal long-term interest rates over the previous year must be not more than two percentage points above that of the three best performing member states in terms of price stability.
3. *Exchange rate stability*   The member state's exchange rate must have remained for at least two years within the normal fluctuation margins of the Exchange Rate Mechanism.
4. *Containment of government budgetary position*   The member state must not be subject to a Council Decision that an excessive budget deficit exists. Criteria relevant to this decision are set out in the Protocol on the Excessive Deficit Procedure, attached to the EC Treaty. These criteria are in the form of 'reference values': if either of these values is exceeded the deficit may be judged excessive. In these circumstances the Council has discretion whether or not to decide that there is an excessive deficit: the requirements implied by the reference values may be waived if a member state shows that it is having success in reducing its deficit.

Criterion	Reference value
Government deficit[*]	3% of GDP[†]
Government debt	60% of GDP[†]

[*] Planned or actual
[†] Gross domestic product at market prices
Note: 'Government' means general government, comprising central government, regional or local government, and social security funds, and excluding commercial operations.

linkage between France and Germany: these two countries, together with the Benelux countries and Austria, could constitute a 'critical mass' with which to inaugurate the Community currency.

The first three criteria in Box 5.6 (price stability, interest rate stability and exchange rate stability) are closely linked: to maintain competitiveness, a country with high inflation will have to depreciate its currency *vis-à-vis* countries with low inflation, and will have to maintain higher interest rates in order to offset the higher risk of currency devaluation. The inflation criterion (point 1) is set in relation to the best performers, and the reference value appears very demanding for those countries that are more prone to inflation. (It is even theoretically possible for one—or indeed two—of the 'top three' inflation performers to fail the test: for example, if the two best performers have rates of 2½ and 3 per cent, the third country will not qualify if its rate exceeds 5 per cent.)

Historically, the inflation records of member states have varied to such an extent that most would not qualify if the reference value were applied to past performance. This is illustrated in Table 5.3: in the period 1980–92 (before the widening of the ERM bands in 1993) all national currencies except the Dutch guilder depreciated significantly against the Deutschmark, and if the EU Treaty criterion were applied to the inflation record, only Germany and the Benelux countries would qualify. If only the more recent years (1987–92) are considered, there is more uniformity: only four countries—Greece, Italy, Portugal and the UK—depreciated significantly against the Deutschmark, and seven would satisfy the inflation criterion: Denmark, France, Germany, Ireland and the Benelux countries. Much now depends on maintenance of the

Table 5.3 Inflation rates and exchange rate movements in European Community member states, 1980–1992 and 1987–1992 (%)

	1980–92			1987–92		
		Exchange rate movement[†]			Exchange rate movement[†]	
	Inflation[*]	ECU	DM	Inflation[*]	ECU	DM
Belgium	4.25	−2.38	−21.75	2.65	3.49	0.99
Denmark	5.28	0.26	−19.64	3.28	0.90	−1.54
Germany	2.80	24.75	0.00	2.83	2.48	0.00
Greece	18.79	−75.80	−80.60	16.56	−36.75	−38.28
Spain	8.74	−24.75	−39.68	6.04	7.31	4.72
France	5.69	−14.18	−31.21	3.04	1.32	−1.13
Ireland	6.92	−11.30	−28.90	3.16	1.84	−0.62
Italy	8.98	−25.45	−40.25	5.87	−6.27	−8.53
Luxembourg	4.26	−2.38	−21.75	2.95	3.49	0.99
Netherlands	2.69	21.59	−2.54	2.42	2.64	0.16
Portugal	15.90	−60.22	−68.11	11.08	−6.94	−9.19
United Kingdom	6.26	−18.97	−35.05	6.33	−4.47	−6.78
EC12	6.24	0.00	−19.84	4.72	0.00	−2.42

[*] Percentage annual increase in the Consumer Price Index
[†] Percentage depreciation (−) or appreciation (+) of currencies against the ECU and the Deutschmark.
Source: calculated from Eurostat (1989, 1993: Tables 2.29 and 2.43).

credibility of the ERM, which in turn requires a high degree of exchange rate stability (notwithstanding the broad bands of permitted fluctuation).

The public finance criteria (point 4 in Box 5.6) relate to economic performance rather than convergence, since the reference values are specified in a way that does not depend on relative performance. Table 5.4 shows member states' performance with respect to budget deficits (shown in the table as negative general government financial balances) and debt (aggregate gross general government debt). The reference values set out in the EU Treaty (see Box 5.6) are 3 per cent of GDP for the budget deficit, and 60 per cent of GDP for debt. It is evident that most member states are a long way from meeting these conditions. In 1992 only Germany and Luxembourg were within both reference values; according to OECD projections for 1996, most member states will make significant reduction in their budget deficits, but the burden of debt will remain substantial. The reference criteria will have to be applied with great latitude if monetary union is to extend to countries such as Italy and Belgium, in which aggregate debt exceeds annual GDP.

Table 5.4 General government financial balances and gross debt, 1992 (actual) and 1996 (projected)
Percentage of nominal GDP

	Financial balances		*Gross debt*	
	1992	*1996*	*1992*	*1996*
Belgium	−6.7	−4.1	133.8	134.0
Denmark	−2.6	−2.2	68.8	83.1
France	−3.9	−4.0	39.6	53.8
Germany	−2.9	−1.8	44.1	58.3
Greece	−11.8	−10.1	92.3	119.4
Ireland	−2.2	−2.0	93.4	83.1
Italy	−9.5	−7.8	108.4	125.3
Luxembourg	−0.3	n/a	6.1	n/a
Netherlands	−3.8	−2.9	79.9	81.4
Portugal	−3.8	−5.5	70.4	83.0
Spain	−4.2	−5.2	48.3	69.7
United Kingdom	−6.2	−3.2	41.8	55.3

Source: © OECD (1994): *Economic Outlook*, Table 9, p. 17. Reproduced by permission of the OECD.

For countries closer to the reference values, the main determinant of success in avoiding 'excessive' deficits will be speed and durability of recovery from recession. This is because government finances are sensitive to the economic cycle: in a recession, tax revenues decline and public expenditures tend to increase in proportion to GDP, leading to budget deficits and increasing government debt.

5.3.3 The prospects for economic and monetary union

Monetary co-operation in the European Community has experienced phases of stability and phases of turbulence. The energy crises of the 1970s built up pressures that led to the decline of the 'Snake', and more recently, the consequences of German reunification caused instability within the ERM. At other times the currency system has been more manageable, and for many years the ERM functioned in an orderly manner, with realignments becoming less frequent.

Attitudes to the single currency, and the feasibility of the timetable set out in the EC Treaty, have also varied. The crises of September 1992 and August 1993 caused severe loss of confidence; but some of the former optimism returned as the ERM survived, and as most currencies remained reasonably close to their ERM central rates, albeit with wider margins of fluctuation.

Economic convergence remains the fundamental precondition for a single currency. If inflation, interest rates and budgets are in alignment, it will be possible to move towards a single currency irrespective of short-term fluctuations in exchange rates. Movements in exchange rates can be irresistible when driven by massive amounts of money in the global market, but there is no reason to suppose that the system cannot recover provided that the fundamental economic conditions are right. So exchange rates should be regarded only as an indicator, and a not very reliable one.

There remain serious questions over the fate of the weaker economies, whether or not they eventually participate in the single currency. If they do not, they face the prospect of maintaining interest rates above the level of the participating countries for a long period until their counter-inflationary credibility is established, while their industry is subject to the non-tariff barrier of a separate currency and at a disadvantage *vis-à-vis* competitors in a large common currency area.

On the other hand, participation in the single currency is not without risks. The exchange rate can no longer adjust to offset domestic inflationary pressures or fluctuations in export demand, and there is a danger that industry will be rendered uncompetitive. In this respect, comparison and contrast with the United States may be instructive. The regions of the USA exist within a single currency area, notwithstanding differences in economic structure, and fluctuations in their relative prosperity. The main focus of adjustment appears to be a high degree of inter-regional labour mobility: a recent study found that, of every 100 workers who become unemployed, on average 65 migrate to other states within one year (Blanchard and Katz 1992: 34). It is doubtful that Europe could approach this degree of mobility, since (notwithstanding the formal rights of Community citizens) the possibilities for migration are constrained by a variety of economic, social and cultural factors.

Economic adjustments can also be eased by fiscal transfers. In the United States the federal budget makes a substantial contribution to this process. As a region suffers economic decline, its tax payments are reduced and its receipts through the social security system increase; in addition, expenditure on public works—such as defence installations—can be channelled to disadvantaged regions. The Community has no comparable redistributive fiscal mechanism: almost all public expenditure in the Community is undertaken, and financed, by the authorities in member states. The structural and cohesion funds contribute to economic regeneration, but their resources would not be adequate to provide a cushion against a significant decline in a region's fortunes.

In the absence of high labour mobility or substantial fiscal transfers, a country that becomes uncompetitive would have to depend for a revival of its fortunes on downward flexibility of wage rates (in effect, replicating the cost reductions that would have been achieved with a devaluation of the national currency). Wage reductions in a low-inflation economy would have to be achieved by decreases in nominal wage rates—which are liable to be resisted, and are certainly more difficult to implement than a currency devaluation. Otherwise, the adjustment process threatens to be 'painful and protracted' (Blanchard and Katz 1992: 56).

Economic management in the single currency area would thus face formidable challenges to accommodate the necessary adjustments while maintaining low rates of inflation. In the absence of an exchange rate 'safety valve', it is conceivable that serious tensions would arise between the interests of more and less prosperous regions. These problems would of course be more manageable if the single currency area were to be restricted to a homogeneous 'core' of a small number of member states centred on Germany; but on the other hand, this would detract from the purpose of monetary unification in furthering the integration of the single market.

5.4   EUROPEAN COMMUNITY ECONOMIC AND MONETARY POLICY

Whatever the eventual fate of the single (or common) currency, the Community will continue to play a key role in economic and monetary policy: the development of the Community's responsibilities in this area are demonstrated by successive changes in the EC Treaty. The original 1957 EEC Treaty called for 'co-ordination' of economic and monetary policies, particularly to maintain balance of payments equilibrium; and in 1987 the Treaty was amended to specify the objective of policy 'convergence'. The current version (Article 103 EC) goes beyond these provisions, stating that economic policies are 'a matter of common concern' which must conform to Community guidelines. The Council monitors the consistency of economic policies with these guidelines, and may recommend any measures it deems necessary.

5.4.1   The policy framework

Following the 1992 EU (Maastricht) Treaty, a framework was established for a Community economic policy 'based on the close coordination of Member States' economic policies, on the internal market and on the definition of common objectives, and conducted in accordance with the principle of an open market economy with free competition' (Article 3a(1)). Both the Community and member states are to comply with the following guiding principles: stable prices, sound public finances and monetary conditions, and a sustainable balance of payments (Article 3a(3)).

The Community policy framework reflects two main influences: current economic thinking, and the German model of monetary policy. The *economic influence* is manifested in an emphasis on controlling inflation: the primary objectives of Community monetary and exchange rate policies is 'to maintain price stability' (Article 3a EC). The term 'stability' is not explicitly defined, although according to Council policy guidelines an inflation rate of 2–3 per cent constitutes a 'step towards price stability' (Recommendation 94/7, p. 10); if the objective is literally a zero inflation rate, many prices would have to decrease over time—and if there is asymmetry between increases and decreases, in terms of the ease of adjustment, markets may be liable to distortion.

References to 'sound public finances' and the discouragement of 'excessive' budgetary deficits in member states appear to deny possibilities for demand management through fiscal measures. The key underlying proposition (reflecting current economic orthodoxy) is that there is no choice in the long term between combinations of inflation and unemployment, so that the pursuit of price stability has no implications for employment. Community policies to achieve 'a high level of employment' (Article 2 EC) are to be pursued at a micro economic level, with measures to promote investment and to train workers (see Sec. 6.2.1).

In the absence of political choices, *monetary policy* becomes essentially a technical matter, to be managed by experts working within broad guidelines, and insulated from political intervention. This requires an institutional structure in which the monetary authorities (the central banks) are independent and are not subject to governmental direction (although they are of course constrained to operate within a legal framework, and are accountable for their actions within that framework). This has long been the system in Germany, where the Bundesbank as the independent central bank has maintained a counter-inflationary monetary policy, even in the difficult period following unification. Germany has consistently had one of the lowest inflation rates in the Community, and the Deutschmark has constituted the strong currency 'anchor' of the Exchange Rate Mechanism.

The Community's monetary policy institutions are closely modelled on the German system. Member states are required to move towards independence for their central banks, which must be established before participation in the single currency (Articles 109e, 109j). Monetary policy with respect to the single currency will be managed by a European System of Central Banks (ESCB), comprising national central banks and a European Central Bank (ECB). The Statute of the ESCB and ECB (set out in a Protocol to the EC Treaty) specifies their independence of governments and Community institutions (Article 7). This is reinforced by the conditions of employment of the ECB Executive Board: its members are appointed by the European Council for a non-renewable eight-year term, and can be dismissed only by order of the Court of Justice (Article 11).

The practical effect of the ESCB's independence is to insulate it from political pressures. So, for example, the Council or the Commission could not instruct the ESCB to reduce interest rates in order to stimulate the economy. The ultimate purpose is to minimize the influence of inflationary expectations on economic decisions: so for example wage bargaining will not anticipate inflation; nor will it generate inflationary pressures, because the bargainers will realize that 'excessive' increases lead to unemployment, and that their political representatives are powerless to adjust monetary policy to allow more inflation.

This at least is the concept. There remain questions concerning the ability of the system to adjust to interregional differences in inflationary pressures or to economic 'shocks' which alter a country's terms of trade—for example if there is a fall in demand for products in which it specializes. With a national currency these effects can be accommodated by exchange rate movements; but a country that is part of common currency area does not have this possibility. Instead the adjustment depends heavily on a reduction in nominal wages, emigration of workers and resource transfers: and all three present difficulties (see Sec. 5.3.3).

A member state that encounters difficulty in financing social expenditure resulting from increased unemployment runs the risk of sanctions under the 'excessive deficit' procedure (Article 104c EC). If the Council determines that a member state has an excessive budget deficit, it can make recommendations for remedial action, backed by possible sanctions; these may include:

- warnings to purchasers of bonds and securities issued by the government concerned
- reconsideration of European Investment Bank lending to the member state in question
- a requirement to make a non-interest-bearing deposit with the Community
- fines.

The 'excess deficit' provision reflects the continuing preoccupation of governments in the early 1990s. There were concerns with both economic recession and inflation: as the recession tended to increase budgetary deficits, there was a danger that these deficits would generate inflationary pressures. There is no procedure for 'excess surpluses', presumably because this would have been thought unnecessary, or even perverse. Nevertheless, the main objective is to maintain economic convergence and cohesion, which is a relative concept, expressed in terms of disparities between member states; and this implies that budgetary balances, whether negative or positive, should be approximately aligned.

> **BOX 5.7**
> **Trans-European communication networks: expenditure and financing**
>
> According to Commission estimates, expenditure requirements for communications infrastructure up to the end of the century amount to 250 bn ECUs for transport and energy, and 150 bn ECUs for telecommunications (COM(93)700, pp. 82–95).
>
> The Commission 1993 White Paper raised the possibility of introducing two new forms of financing in order to fund expenditure on infrastructure projects. 'Union bonds' would be instruments of long maturity issued by the Community to provide finance to project promoters: the Commission envisaged that the bonds could support annual expenditures of the order of 7 bn ECUs. 'Convertible' bonds would give entitlement to subscribe to shares, or to a share of profits; they would be issued directly by project promoters, and guaranteed by the Community (COM(93)700, p, 36).

Apart for the limitation of budget deficits, the Community's role in fiscal policy is very limited. The Community's own budget is very small compared with those of national governments, and is essentially constrained to balance, so that there is no question of using a Community budget deficit as a reflationary measure. The Commission has advanced a proposal for a Community borrowing mechanism (known as 'union bonds') to finance infrastructure investment and aid recovery from economic recession (see Box 5.7), but this proposal has not found favour with the Council.

With respect to fiscal policies at national level, the EC Treaty provisions do not acknowledge that budgetary balances tend to vary over the economic cycle: in a recession tax receipts decline and social expenditure increases, while in a recovery the opposite is the case. The Community nevertheless determines an 'excessive' deficit with reference to a constant figure—3 per cent—for the budget deficit in proportion to GDP (Protocol on the Excessive Deficit Procedure, Article 1); there is no provision for variation in this figure over the economic cycle. (And there is a contrast with other convergence criteria; for example, inflation targets are defined in relative terms, with reference to the inflation rates achieved by the 'best performers'—which will of course vary over time.)

5.4.2   Economic policy guidelines

Community economic policy under the EC Treaty was inaugurated in 1994, with adoption by the Council of broad guidelines for member states and the Community (Recommendation 94/7). Against a background of economic recession, with government budgets generally in substantial deficits, the guidelines reiterated the objective of a 'return to sustainable and non-inflationary economic growth', to reduce unemployment 'significantly'. Two requirements were identified: a 'stable and coherent' macroeconomic framework, and removal of obstacles to growth. The guidelines stressed the importance of credibility in the pursuit of price stability: a lowering of inflationary expectations would permit reductions in interest rates, which in turn would stimulate the economy.

The key policy recommendations in the Guidelines are summarized in Box 5.8. The emphasis is on a lowering of interest rates and budget deficits (having regard to the convergence criteria). Policies to increase competitiveness and employment are essentially 'catalytic': market liberalization, training, reduction of tax disincentives. The guidelines also emphasize provision of infrastructure—the so-called trans-European networks—necessary for achievement of the economic benefits of the single market.

BOX 5.8
Broad guidelines of the economic policies of the member states and the Community

Price and exchange rate stability   This is the crucial objective, with which all policies and behaviour should be consistent. Most member states should have inflation rates of under 3 per cent by 1996; others should take 'determined action' to provide a basis for lower interest rates. The Community 'will intensify its efforts at achieving economic convergence' as a prelude to economic and monetary union.

Sound public finances   Most member states are able to reduce government deficits to 3 per cent of GDP by 1996 and towards zero by 2000, aided by economic growth. Recommended measures include reorientation of expenditure towards productive uses, and action to combat tax evasion. Limits on the Community budget will be respected.

Creating more employment   This is to be achieved primarily through improved competitiveness.

Pay, investment and employment   Economic growth will be stimulated by increased investment; governments, employers and unions should co-operate to avoid short-term increases, and if necessary should permit reductions, in real wages. Public-sector pay moderation is desirable to ease budgetary problems and set an example to the private sector. There may be 'appropriate differentiation' in pay movements, between member states and between economic sectors, to reflect qualifications and work experience.

Reducing the indirect cost of labour   Member states should examine the financing of social protection schemes, and possibilities for substituting new sources of finance.

Employment policies   Employment policies should include training, integration of the long-term unemployed, liberalization of labour markets and the encouragement of labour mobility.

The single market   Member states should commit themselves to measures to enforce legislation, to increase the efficiency of capital markets and to promote infrastructure development (particularly trans-European networks).

Source: Council Recommendation 94/7/EC, on the broad guidelines of the economic policies of the member states and of the Community, *Official Journal*, 1994 L7/9.

5.5   ECONOMIC AND MONETARY UNION: KEY POINTS AND ISSUES

Monetary union represents in one sense a logical consequence of the original (1957) agenda of the European Economic Community, and as such may be seen as a component (albeit an optional extra) of the single market 'package' described in Chapter 3.

As the next major step in the 'deepening' of economic integration, monetary union will involve an appreciable extension of the Community's formal role in economic policy. This prospect has generated political controversy, with differing views on the desirability, and the operation, of a single currency system. At the same time, it appears unlikely in practice that many member states will satisfy the criteria for participation in the single currency which were established by the EU (Maastricht) Treaty. For these reasons it can be expected that monetary union will figure in the 1996 intergovernmental conference, with pressure to review the criteria for participation in a single currency and the schedule for its introduction.

In economic (as distinct from political) terms, the single currency may be seen more as a consequence than a cause of economic integration. The single market generates economic convergence, and requires stable currency exchange rates. (A single currency is of course the ultimate in stability.) So member states' freedom of action in economic policy is in any case circumscribed, and in practice there is already a high degree of co-operation in economic policy.

Whether or not they participate in the single currency, the weaker economies face difficulties. Participation would remove their ability to restore competitiveness through exchange rate adjustment; but the value of this instrument is limited in a single market, particularly if interest rates in non participating countries have to be maintained at levels well above those of the single currency 'bloc'. Ultimately the problem can be diminished only by increased economic cohesion, to reduce the gap between the stronger and weaker economies. The Community has an important role in promoting development of infrastructure to improve the competitive position of the less prosperous regions; the outcome, in terms of economic convergence, is likely to be a significant factor in the success of monetary unification.

In the context of economic and monetary union, the following key issues can be identified:

- The economic benefit of a single currency depends on the extent to which national currencies are an impediment to freedom of movement: how significant is the currency barrier within the single market?
- In economic terms, an optimal currency area is defined by the extent of trade and factor mobility: how far does the European Community approximate to such an area?
- Monetary union will preclude variations in the exchange rates of member states' currencies, and so member states will be unable to devalue their national currency to offset a loss of economic competitiveness: what alternative economic adjustment mechanisms are available? How effective are they likely to be?
- The weaker economies will face competitive pressures within a single currency area, while they risk marginalization, with permanently higher interest rates, if they remain outside: where does their overall advantage lie?
- In order to increase its economic cohesion, the Community has channelled resources to less prosperous regions: are existing fiscal transfers sufficient to accommodate to the pressures of a single currency area?
- Economic convergence and a common currency call for close alignment of economic policies: what problems stand in the way of achieving this? How can they be overcome?

NOTES

1. If, as appears likely, some member states retain their own currencies, there would not be a Community single currency, although it would be the single currency in participating member states, supplanting their national currencies.
2. Luxembourg is in a monetary union with Belgium, with a common currency (albeit with differently designed banknotes); the Luxembourg monetary authority (the Institut monétaire luxembourgois) has a limited central bank function, with little control over monetary policy.
3. For example, in 1982 the exchange rate movements ranged from $+4\frac{1}{4}$ per cent (the Deutschmark and the guilder) to $-5\frac{3}{4}$ per cent (the French franc), and in 1985 a 6 per cent devaluation of the lira was accompanied by a 2 per cent upward revaluation of other ERM currencies—so the devaluation of the lira within the ERM was effectively 8 per cent.
4. In some countries (such as Germany and the USA) regional central banks participate in the management of the national currency, but they do not issue separate currencies.

REFERENCES

Blanchard, O. and Katz, L. (1992) 'Regional evolutions', *Brookings Papers on Economic Activity*, pp. 1–75.
Emerson, M. *et al.* (1992) *One Market, One Money: An Evaluation of the Potential Benefits and Costs of Forming an Economic and Monetary Union*, Oxford University Press.
European Council (1992) *Conclusions of the Edinburgh meeting 11/12 December 1992*, Annex 1.
Eurostat (1989, 1993) *Basic Statistics of the Community*, 26th and 30th edns, Office of Official Publications, Luxembourg.
OECD (1994) *Economic Outlook* 56, OECD, Paris.

European Community legislation

Regulation 3320/94, on the consolidation of the existing legislation on the definition of the ECU, *Official Journal*, 1994 L350/27.
Recommendation 94/7, on the broad guidelines of the economic policies of the member states and of the Community, *Official Journal*, 1994 L7/9.

European Community documents

COM(93)700, *Growth, Competitiveness, Employment: The Challenges and Ways Forward into the 21st Century*, 5 December 1993.

SIX

WIDENING POLICY RESPONSIBILITIES

The European Community has reached the beginning of a new phase in its evolution. The programme of legislation for the single market has been completed, and the 1992 deadline has come and gone. New policy concerns are emerging—and economic integration has greatly enhanced the role of the Community in the response to these concerns.

In the years since its foundation, the Community's progress has always been strongly influenced by prevailing economic and political pressures. Economic growth and institutional crises in the 1960s gave way to economic recession and stagnation of the Community ('Eurosclerosis') in the 1970s. The 1980s saw economic revival, and a renewed determination to complete the single market, with the '1992' programme. Nevertheless, throughout these fluctuations the central preoccupation of the Community was essentially unchanged, focusing on the attainment of the objectives specified in its founding treaties: the achievement of a common market, and the development of harmonized and common policies linked to this goal. The single market programme has to a large extent realized this original purpose, in the sense that the measures necessary for economic integration are now in place.

One of the most notable consequences of the single market has been a widening of the European Community policy agenda, because in many instances it has rendered Community action more effective than national measures. This is an important motivation for Community involvement in economic policies to promote competitiveness and technological development. The single market has also tended to limit the scope for purely national initiatives, because many policy instruments are now viable only at a Community level. For example, the stimulus to mobility of people within the European Union, following removal of frontiers, provisions for citizenship of the European Union and measures to facilitate mobility of labour (Articles 7a, 8, and 48 EC), have heightened the Community role in assuring minimum standards in social policy, consumer protection, health and education.

6.1 THE EXTENSION OF COMMUNITY POLICY-MAKING

The interests of the European Community have from its beginning extended beyond narrowly defined economic objectives to encompass concerns with broader aspects of welfare which contribute to the quality of life. Thus, the preamble to the original (1957) EEC Treaty defined as an essential objective 'the constant improvement of ... living and working conditions'.

Moreover, in the years since the Community came into existence, there has been a growing recognition that it cannot function effectively—still less expand—without attention to cohesion in a broad sense. This has been acknowledged at the highest level; for example, in 1972 Community heads of state or government issued a declaration stating that economic development must be translated into improvement in the quality of life. Hence the Community's market system can operate satisfactorily only within a framework which incorporates protection for consumers, the cultural heritage and the environment. The Community has to address concerns such as these, in order to ensure that the single market functions in a way that is actually beneficial to its citizens.

6.1.1   New policy areas

These considerations have led to the extension of Community policy-making into areas such as environmental, consumer and health protection, which were not explicitly mentioned in the original Treaties. Initially legislation was enacted under the 'catch-all' provision of Article 235 EC, which permits the Community to act by unanimous Council decision even in the absence of a specific Treaty basis.

The Single Market programme subsequently gave a powerful impetus to 'quality of life' measures, particularly where it was necessary to harmonize national provisions. Where these provisions involve health, safety and environmental and consumer protection, the Commission's legislative Proposals must 'take as a base a high level of protection' (Article 100a EC). This provision was added to the EC Treaty by the 1986 Single European Act, which also gave an explicit legal basis for Community environment policy (Articles 130r–t EC). The Treaty was further amended by the 1992 EU (Maastricht) Treaty, which added provisions calling for the Community to contribute to the flowering of culture (Article 128 EC), to the development of quality education (Article 126 EC) and to the achievement of high levels of health protection (Article 129 EC) and of consumer protection (Article 129a EC).

Although, as has been pointed out, Community involvement in the areas mentioned above predates their inclusion in the Treaty, the new provisions are nevertheless important for three reasons:

1. They provide an explicit basis for Community action.
2. They oblige, rather than merely permit, the Community to take appropriate action.
3. They bring legislation in these areas within the Co-Decision or Co-operation Procedures, thus facilitating Community action, with an enhanced role for the Parliament.

The legislative procedures in the policy areas that were added subsequent to the original (1957) EEC Treaty are summarized in Table 6.1. The Co-Decision Procedure—enactment jointly by Council and Parliament—is used for legislation under the Treaty provisions relating to education, culture, public health and consumer protection. The Parliament also has a strong influence—through the Co-operation Procedure—on legislation concerned with training, the environment and development co-operation.

6.1.2   Policy integration

The provisions for specific policy areas also give a basis for general influence across the range of action undertaken by the Community. This is potentially of great importance, because it means that, as a general rule, all policy initiatives must be considered with reference to wider concerns. The relevant Treaty provisions are set out in Box 6.1; particularly for culture, health and environmental protection, the requirements are wide-ranging, so that all Community policies should, in principle, take account of these aspects.

Table 6.1 Developing policy areas: legislative procedures

Policy area (EC Treaty articles)	Procedure	Types of measure
Education, Culture, Public health (126–9)	Co-Decision Non-consultation*	Incentive measures (excluding harmonization) Adoption of recommendations
Consumer protection (129a)	Co-Decision	Specific action
Trans-European networks (129b)	Co-Decision Co-operation	Guidelines Specific Measures
Research and techno-logical development (130f–130p)	Co-Decision Co-operation Consultation	Framework programmes Implementing measures Specific programmes, institutional structures
Environment (130s)	Co-Decision Co-operation Consultation	Framework programmes Specific action not subject to the Consultation Procedure Water resource management, energy supply, land use planning and fiscal measures
Training (127)	Co-operation	Measures excluding harmonization
Economic and Social cohesion (130a–130e)	Co-operation Consultation	ERDF implementation Actions outside the structural funds
Development co-operation (130u–130y)	Co-operation	Policy measures
Industry (130)	Consultation	Specific measures

* The Council may adopt recommendations on a Proposal from the Commission (without consulting the Parliament).

There are of course difficulties in making this approach operational. One is the organization of the Commission Directorates General, with 'vertical' divisions between functional responsibilities. Although in principle the Commission as a whole and its services are responsible for implementation of the Treaties in their entirety, in practice policy initiatives are often developed to an advanced stage within a Directorate General, so that it then becomes difficult to bring wider considerations to bear, except in a superficial 'cosmetic' form.

Furthermore, the notion of an integrated approach to policy (as set out in Box 6.1) is difficult to reconcile with the requirement that legislation must be based on specific Treaty Articles. In practice, an item of legislation with a single legal base may cover a variety of objectives; for instance, in case C-300/89, involving harmonization of waste regulations, the Court of Justice ruled that environmental objectives (set out in Article 130r) may be effectively pursued by single market measures (based on Article 100a). If integration is to be meaningful, logic might suggest that legal bases should be defined more broadly, so that (for instance) the base of most Community legislation would include, among other provisions, Articles 130 (on industry) and 130r (on environmental protection). There would have to be a 'principal' legal base, in order to

> **BOX 6.1**
> **Policy integration: provisions in the EC Treaty**
>
> *The Single Market* 'The Commission in its proposals ... concerning health, safety, environmental protection and consumer protection shall take as a base a high level of protection' (Article 100a(3)).
>
> *Culture* 'The Community shall take cultural aspects into account in its action under other provisions of this Treaty' (Article 128(4)).
>
> *Public health* 'Health protection requirements shall form a constituent part of the Community's other policies' (Article 129(1)).
>
> *Consumer protection* 'The Community shall contribute to the attainment of a high level of consumer protection through measures adopted pursuant to Article 100a in the context of the completion of the internal market' (Aricle 129a(1)).
>
> *Industry* 'The Community shall contribute to the achievement of [conditions necessary for the competitiveness of Community industry] ... through the policies and activities it promotes under other provisions of this Treaty' (Article 130(3)).
>
> *Environment* 'Environmental protection requirements must be integrated into the definition and implementation of other Community policies' (Article 130r(2)).

specify the legislative procedure—Consultation, Co-operation or Co-Decision—but the integration of multiple objectives would be explicit.

6.2   INDUSTRY AND TECHNOLOGY POLICIES

In the late twentieth century economic policy has become increasingly internationalized. Lessons were learned from the disastrous experience of unco-ordinated national policies in the 1930s (see Sec. 1.2.1). Since that time global economic forces, and especially the massive flows of currency through international markets, have in any case reduced governments' scope for independent action.

Within the European Community economic integration has intensified this effect, through the development of a single market and economic and monetary union, with the eventual prospect of a Community currency. With policy-making at national level increasingly constrained, the Community has come to the fore, as the focus not only of policy co-ordination but also of policy formulation.

The EC Treaty provides a basis for Community economic policies, which were inaugurated with Council Recommendation 94/7, which set out broad guidelines for member states and the Community. The Treaty framework covers policies with respect to interest rates, price stability and government budgets (*macroeconomic policy*), discussed in Sec. 5.4; it also gives a basis for Community involvement in measures concerned with the functioning of markets and promotion of international competitiveness (*microeconomic policy*).

The success of the Community's economic strategy depends to a great extent on measures to improve the functioning of markets, and to ensure that decision-makers have the proper incentives. For example, high social protection charges may discourage participation in the labour force, and the Guidelines suggest that the financial burden could be switched to environmental taxes, which give (benign) incentives to limit pollution. Similarly, the development of infrastructure such as highways and telecommunications promotes efficiency, through increased competition and accessibility of markets.

6.2.1   Industry policies

Economic integration has led to Community initiatives in a variety of areas, which can be broadly categorized as 'industry policy'. Measures directly related to the single market (see Chapter 3) form a major component of this policy package; indeed, the Commission has characterized the single market as 'industrial policy par excellence' (COM(90)556, p. 11).

Direct intervention in industry, for example to invest in 'national champions', is less common than in the past, and Community industry policy reflects this trend. The ECSC Treaty gives the Commission explicit and extensive powers to intervene, when necessary, in the operation of the coal and steel industries; these powers were invoked in the late 1970s, but despite renewed crisis in the steel industry the Commission is now reluctant to intervene directly (see Box 6.2).

The EC Treaty provisions on industry policy (dating from 1992) call for the Community and member states to establish conditions necessary for competitiveness (Article 130(1)), favouring enterprise, innovation and rapid structural adjustment. The main instruments of Community industry policy are summarized in Box 6.3. A distinction may be drawn between measures that influence industry priorities ('positive' measures), and those concerned mainly with the prevention or removal of obstacles to the functioning of the market ('facilitative' measures). It should be emphasized that there are many other areas of policy that *affect* industry—notably consumer protection, transport, energy, and environmental policy—and the policies categorized in Box 6.3 also have effects in these areas.

BOX 6.2
Industry policy: the case of the steel industry

In the 1970s the steel industry was hard hit by recession and competition from more efficient Japanese producers. Companies were operating well below full capacity, and incurring massive losses. The Commision secured voluntary agreements to restrict output and thus maintain prices (the 1976 'Simonet plan'). This was followed by the 'Davignon plan', which ran from 1977 to 1988, in which the Commission invoked its powers to act in a 'period of manifest crisis'. The Commission effectively became a monopoly supplier of steel, first fixing the prices of certain products, under Article 61 of the ECSC Treaty, and later in 1980 establishing production quotas under Article 58. The plan also included import restrictions and state aid programmes. By 1988 the industry's annual production capacity had fallen by approximately 30 mte (15 per cent of the 1980 capacity), and its labour force had been reduced by approximately 150 000.

A brief period of prosperity then ensued, but by 1992 the industry was again in crisis. Excess capacity was estimated at 20–30 mte (10–15 per cent of the total), while 50 000 of the 370 000 employees were redundant. The difficulties were compounded by the political sensitivity of the industry, with loss-making plants in economically depressed regions such as the Basque country, southern Italy and eastern Germany; state-owned plant in these regions was subsidized to avoid serious disturbance in the local economies.

The Commission resisted pressures again to invoke its powers to declare a manifest crisis, apparently taking the view that steel no longer was of sufficient importance as a 'strategic' sector to justify the exceptional powers contained in the ECSC Treaty. Indeed, in the early 1990s, serious consideration was given to abrogation of this Treaty (which in any case expires in 2001), so that Community policies towards the coal and steel industries would be subsumed within the EC Treaty.

The Commission sought instead to secure voluntary agreement among steel producers to reduce output. However, the Commission's proposals met with resistance on the part of private-sector non-subsidized producers, who argued that the less efficient loss-making plants should be closed.

BOX 6.3
Community industry policy instruments

Positive	Facilitative
Harmonization of standards	Removal of barriers in the internal market
Programmes to promote industry	Competition regulation
Infrastructure spending	Regulation of subsidies

Community industry policy has consistently emphasized competitiveness as the key to prosperity. A 1990 Commission paper noted 'a return to non inflationary growth, far reaching structural adjustment and ... industrial recovery', but cautioned against complacency in the face of increasing global competition (COM(90)556, pp. 2–3). This caution was well taken: by 1993 the economy was deep in recession, and the Commission was expressing alarm at a deterioration in the Community's competitive position *vis-à-vis* the USA and Japan, linking this to declining investment and economic growth, and—especially—the severity of unemployment (COM(93)700, p. 2).

The 1993 Commission White Paper (COM(93)700) on economic growth, competitiveness and employment noted the absence of 'miracle cures' for unemployment. Several possible measures were dismissed as misconceived, including import restrictions, increased government spending, general reductions in working hours and reductions in wages and social protection (p. 1). The White Paper instead emphasized that unemployment reflects a failure of adjustment to structural and technological change, pointing out that, even in the economic recovery of the 1980s, there were 12 million unemployed, compared with 17 million in 1993 (p. 4).

The Commission strategy is essentially to promote technological innovation, training and the proper functioning of markets. There are various policy instruments (including those listed in Box 6.3) available to support this approach. The Community dimension is especially significant in the context of:

1. Regulations and structures that are related to the single market, including, for example, European economic interest groupings (see Box 6.4) which assist small and medium enterprises in particular.
2. Trade policy (see Sec. 10.2.3): the Community's commitment to free trade in principle coexists with import restrictions in specific sectors, such as agriculture, cars and textiles.
3. Competition policy (see Chapter 4): with respect to agreements between firms, restructuring (up to 1994 the Commission had prohibited only one proposed merger—see Sec. 4.2.3), and state aid regulation.
4. Training: the Community supports training (and retraining) through the structural funds (primarily the European Social Fund) and various special programmes.
5. Infrastructure: the Community spends substantial amounts through the structural funds and the Cohesion Fund (see Secs 3.4 and 3.5).

The way in which the Community deploys various policy instruments is illustrated by the case of the automobile industry. (See Box 6.5, which draws upon the Commission strategy paper COM(94)49.) This is a key sector, accounting for almost 2 per cent of Community GDP, which has suffered from declining demand and employment. There is consequently a need for extensive rationalization, as has been highlighted by the recent BMW takeover of Rover, and the abortive proposed merger between Renault and Volvo.

BOX 6.4
What is a European economic interest grouping?

A European Economic interest grouping is a legal entity, recognized in all EC member states, whereby partners from more than one country are able to co-operate on projects, using *ad hoc* legal structures. Co-operation can cover (for example) the sharing of computer services, submission of joint tenders, the pooling of marketing resources and joint research teams.

BOX 6.5
Industry policy: the case of the automobile industry

European Community policies seek to provide a business environment conducive to the adjustments necessary to develop improved and environmentally sound production techniques, to increase export market penetration and to balance transport needs and environmental impacts. Policies operate through various channels, which include:

- *Single market measures*   Technical specifications—including safety, emission and noise standards—are governed by Community legislation (and extended to the European Economic Area); VAT Directives have reduced divergences in tax rates, and the Commission envisages Proposals to harmonize taxes on vehicle use. These measures give the manufacturers the benefit of a large unified market.
- *Competition policy*   The Commission has allowed the industry to maintain a system of exclusive dealerships, because vehicles require expert maintenance; state aid permitted as compatible with the overall interests of the Union amounted to 5 bn ECUs (1989–93); mergers with a Community dimension are subject to Commission approval.
- *Structural measures*   The industry benefits from structural fund expenditure, particularly training (under Objective 4), which focuses on adaptation to new production methods, and assistance to small and medium enterprises which act as subcontractors to major manufacturers. The Commission has initiated the ADAPT programme (with a budget of 1.4 bn ECUs) to promote adaptation of the workforce to industrial change, and improved competitiveness of enterprises.
- *Research and technological development*   The Community assists 'pre-competitive' research and development, and an estimated 550 m ECUs was granted between 1990 and 1994 to projects with potential application or benefit to the automobile industry. Research is continuing on transport technologies (including integrated transport, environment and safety), information technologies, energy efficiency, and clean manufacturing.
- *External trade policy*   The Community has negotiated voluntary export restraint by Japan up to 1999, tariff reductions in the General Agreement on Tariffs and Trade (GATT), and trade agreements with countries in central and eastern Europe. There are provisions to counter unfair trade practices such as dumping and subsidization. The Community has also sought to overcome non-tariff barriers to market access for Community exporters in the USA, Japan and Korea.

6.2.2   Policies for new technologies

One of the main concerns of Community industry policy is adaptation to technological developments. The Commission has highlighted the importance of Community leadership in the development and application of new technologies, and has identified two areas of particular significance: information and communication technologies, and biotechnology.

Table 6.2 Trans-European telecommunication networks: strategic project areas and investment expenditure requirements, 1944–1999

Project areas	Expenditure (bn ECUs)
High-speed network	20
Digital network	10
Electronic access	1
Electronic mail	1
Interactive video	10
Teleworking	3
Inter administration links	7
Teletraining	3
Telemedicine	7
Total	67

Source: European Commission, COM (93) 700, p. 95.

Trans-European communication networks are vital for the functioning of the single market and the cohesion of the Community. The EC Treaty (Article 129b) requires the Community to contribute to the establishment and development of such networks. With respect to electronic communications, there are three key facets: (1) the creation of infrastructure (for cable and radio communication, and digital networks), (2) development of services (including electronic images, databases and electronic mail), and (3) the promotion of applications (such as teleworking and teletraining). Strategic areas that the Commission has identified for development, and the estimated investment requirements, are set out in Table 6.2. The Community role is designed to be catalytic, to assist in the removal of obstacles such as market fragmentation, and to enable markets to achieve a critical mass.

Advances in information and communications technologies, and the prospective development of 'electronic superhighways', give rise to immense challenges and opportunities. The Commission's 1993 White Paper observed that 'production systems, methods of organizing work and consumption patterns are undergoing changes which will have long term effects comparable with the first industrial revolution' (COM(93)700, p. 20). Opportunities are foreseen for Europe to bolster its competitive position in the world economy if it can be among the leaders in adapting to the new technologies. The challenge for policy-makers is to facilitate the adjustment process and mitigate any adverse impacts.

The most problematical aspect is the effect on employment. On this count the White Paper is not altogether reassuring: it acknowledges that the new technologies may speed up the transfer of manufacturing activities to countries with lower labour costs, but suggests that technological change will generate productivity improvements that will 'save large numbers of jobs which would otherwise have been lost'. This of course assumes that output will expand to absorb the increased productivity and maintain employment—an outcome that is possible, but by no means self-evident.

The Commission has proposed a strategy for the 'information society'. This comprises measures to ensure diffusion of best practice, to combine a competitive environment with common standards, and to support training, research and development and pilot projects

(COM(93)700, p. 110). One essential element is the liberalization of telecommunications, that in many countries are operated by closely regulated monopolies. The Commission has drawn up a Proposal for liberalization in the single market (COM(92)47) that, despite support in principle, was rejected on procedural grounds by the European Parliament (see Sec. 2.4.3).

The Commission has characterized biotechnology as 'one of the most promising and crucial technologies for sustainable development', and has proposed a Community strategy for its development. This includes review of single market regulations in the light of scientific advances and potential risks; co-ordination of expert advice and research; focusing on key areas for research and development; creation of a science park network; measures to enhance investment incentives and improve public understanding; and clarification of ethical issues (COM(93)700, pp. 118–19).

6.3   SOCIAL POLICY

The Community's role in social policy originated with provisions in the original Treaties relating to terms and conditions of employment. Three motivations can be distinguished for the Community interest in this area:

1. A need to avoid the erosion of national provisions in the internal market (a process known as 'social dumping').
2. Removal of obstacles to labour mobility in the internal market.
3. Improvement in the quality of labour as a factor of production, for social and economic reasons.

The first of these was a prominent consideration when the Community was formed (see Sec. 1.2.3). France in particular feared that its industry would be at a disadvantage in competition with products from countries with less favourable conditions for workers. Consequently provisions were included in the EEC Treaty setting out a basis for Community legislation relating to terms of employment, health and safety, and equality of treatment.

The second motivation is of growing importance with the development of the single market. Differences—and indeed incompatibility—between employment regulations can impede labour mobility; for example workers moving across national frontiers may be disadvantaged by health and social security schemes that do not give credit for contributions made in other member states. Furthermore, there can be an inverse of 'social dumping' if workers are reluctant to move to countries with lower standards of social protection; the result would be a distortion of the labour market in the Community.

The quality of the labour force (the third motivation) is of great importance for economic competitiveness. The Community has emphasized the development of human resources in the single market, and particularly in the less prosperous regions: this has a major role both in mitigating inter-regional economic disparities and also in securing the Community's position in the world economy. There are provisions under the structural funds (see Sec. 3.4.2) for expenditure to meet social objectives, including training and integration of unemployed people into the labour market; the main vehicle for this expenditure is the European Social Fund (see Box 6.6).

Community social policy has—uniquely—two parallel legal bases: the EC Treaty, and the Agreement on Social Policy attached to a protocol to the EC Treaty. The provisions of both are summarized in Box 6.7. The UK is not a party to this Agreement, and is not (at least directly) subject to legislation enacted under it.

BOX 6.6
Objectives of the European Social Fund

- To improve employment opportunities
- To increase geographical and occupational mobility
- To facilitate adaptation to change

Source: EC Treaty Article 123.

6.3.1   Community social policy under the EC Treaty

Although a framework for social legislation was included in the original EEC Treaty (see Box 6.7), the Community for many years maintained a low profile in this area. The first substantial initiative was the *Social Action Programme* (1972–80), which included measures relating to employment protection, employee participation, equality in pay, access to employment, social security and health and safety.

BOX 6.7
Social legislation: the framework

EC Treaty

Article 118   The Commission must promote close co-operation between member states, particularly with reference to:

- employment
- labour law and working conditions
- vocational training
- social security
- occupational health and safety
- rights of association

Article 119   Men and women should receive equal pay for equal work.

[Added in 1987 by the Single European Act]   *Article 118a*   The Council must adopt Directives incorporating minimum requirements for the health and safety of workers.

Additional provisions in the Agreement on Social Policy (not applicable in the UK)

Article 2   The Community shall support and complement the activities of member states (in the areas listed in Article 118, plus provision for the information and consultation of workers [*sic*], and integration of persons excluded from the labour market) and may adopt Directives under the Co-operation Procedure. The Council shall act unanimously in the following areas:

- social security and protection of workers
- worker representation
- conditions of employment for non-EC citizens
- financing of measures to promote job creation

Article 3   The Commission must promote consultation at Community level between management and labour.

Article 6 (3)   This permits measures by member states to enable women to pursue careers.

BOX 6.8
The social charter: main elements

- Removal of obstacles to freedom of movement
- Rights to employment and 'fair' remuneration
- Improvement of living and working conditions
- Social protection: minimum wages and social assistance
- Rights to free association and collective bargaining
- Vocational training
- Equal treatment of men and women
- Employees' rights to information, consultation and participation
- Health and safety at work
- Rights of young and disabled workers and pensioners

Source: European Commission (1990), 'The Community Charter of Fundamental Social Rights for Workers', *European File* 6/90.

There followed a less interventionist phase, with many governments giving priority to deregulation. This was exemplified by the 1986 action programme on employment growth (Council Resolution (1986)), endorsed by the Council under the UK presidency, which emphasized efficient labour markets, the promotion of small and medium enterprises and training, for the long-term unemployed.

Social Policy was relaunched with the Charter of Fundamental Social Rights of Workers (the 'Social Charter'), which was adopted by the European Council, with the exception of the United Kingdom, in 1989. The Charter formed the basis for a Commission action programme comprising 47 initiatives, covering the areas listed in Box 6.8. This also marked the formal beginning of the UK's 'rejectionist' line in Community social policies, which led eventually to its non-participation in the Agreement on Social Policy.

The Charter was of course a political declaration, and did not in itself have any legal force. Commission Proposals pursuant to the Charter were brought forward in the framework of the EEC Treaty, so the UK participated in the legislative process and was subject to any eventual legislation.

The UK's 'dissident' stance highlighted the procedures for decision-making in the Council. Proposals subject to unanimity can be blocked by a single member state sufficiently determined to maintain its opposition, and prepared to bear the political cost of isolation. In contrast, qualified majority voting means that a single member state can be outvoted, since an alliance of at least three member states is required to block a Proposal (see Sec. 2.3.2); and a member state that is thought obstructive is not well placed to construct alliances.

Decision-making procedures for social legislation are a matter of some legal complexity. Depending on the specific Treaty provision, Proposals may be subject either to unanimity or to qualified majority voting. Measures relating to health and safety of workers are enacted under Article 118a by qualified majority under the Co-operation Procedure, while unanimity is required for legislation (under Article 119) on equal pay for men and women and (under Article 118) on other aspects of social policy. Moreover, in the context of the single market, the Treaty (Article 100a(2)) specifies that unanimity is required to enact 'provisions ... relating to the rights and interests of employed persons'.

There is evidently a potential conflict between Articles 118a and 100a(2). So legislation enacted under the former Article may in some circumstances be challenged in the Court of Justice, on the grounds that the original Proposal should have been based on Article

100a(2). By this means a member state that unsuccessfully opposed the legislation in question might secure its annulment. A recent instance is Directive 93/104 on working hours. This was enacted by qualified majority, and against UK opposition, as a health and safety measure under Article 118a; the UK then announced its intention to challenge the legality of the Directive on the grounds that Article 118a was not the most appropriate legal base, and so the Directive should have been subject to unanimous approval by the Council.

6.3.2   The Agreement on social policy

The provisions of the EC Treaty relating to social policy were not changed by the 1992 [Maastricht] Treaty on European Union. In the process of negotiation leading to the EU Treaty, it proved impossible to achieve a compromise between the UK's 'deregulatory' stance and the more interventionist position favoured by other member states. The UK was not prepared to accept Treaty amendments supported by the other member states which would have extended the Co-operation Procedure, and would have set up a Community framework for employee consultation and agreements between labour and management. Since Treaty amendments require unanimous agreement, it was therefore not legally possible to introduce the proposed amendments into the EC Treaty.

Instead, the proposed amendments were incorporated in an Agreement on Social Policy covering all member states except the UK. Legislation is enacted under the Agreement in the same way as under the EC Treaty, except that UK representatives do not normally participate in the Council's deliberations. Legislation under the Agreement is not applicable to the UK. The Agreement is linked to the EC Treaty by a Protocol on Social Policy agreed by all member states (including the UK). The Protocol has the status of an Annex to the EC Treaty, and it authorizes the use of the institutional framework of the EC Treaty for implementation of the Agreement on Social Policy. Confusion frequently arises over the terminology of social policy, which is due to the complicated structure that has developed from the lack of consensus between member states. For clarity Box 6.9 summarizes the status of the various framework documents.

BOX 6.9
Social Charter, Chapter, Agreement, Protocol

The Social Charter is a political declaration agreed in 1989 by the member states with the exception of the UK. It formed the basis for the *Social Chapter*, which was proposed for inclusion in the EC Treaty.

The UK did not agree to this, and so the other member states concluded the *Agreement on Social Policy*, to provide for further measures in the area of social policy.

Provisions enacted under this Agreement are given the status of Community legislation by the *Social Protocol*, agreed by all 12 member states and attached to the 1992 EU Treaty, which also provides that measures adopted are not applicable in the UK.

Legislation under the Agreement   Depending on the provisions of the EC Treaty and the Agreement, legislation may be enacted:

1. Under the EC Treaty by Council unanimity, or under the Agreement by qualified majority.

2. By qualified majority under either the EC Treaty or the Agreement.
3. Under the Agreement, by qualified majority.
4. Under the Agreement, by Council unanimity.

Policy areas included in Article 118 of the EC Treaty and Article 2(1) of the Agreement (listed in Box 6.7) generally fall into category 1, as does equal opportunities and treatment of men and women:[1] so the prospects for legislation in these areas are significantly greater under the Agreement than under the Treaty.

Category 2 comprises one of the most important areas, health and safety, which is subject to qualified majority voting under the EC Treaty (Article 118a). The Agreement offers a better chance than the Treaty for adoption of legislation in the face of opposition from the UK, but only if the opposition (including the UK) has between 26 and 35 votes: the arithmetic of this is explained in Box 6.10.

BOX 6.10
Health and safety legislation under the EC Treaty and the Agreement on Social Policy

A *qualified majority* is defined in the EC Treaty as 62 votes (out of 87), and in the Agreement on Social Policy as 52 votes (out of 77). The UK is not a party to the Agreement, and so its 10 votes are not included in the decision-making procedure of the Agreement.

A Proposal supported by the UK stands or falls on voting under the Treaty; the chances of adoption will be no better under the Agreement because the lowering of the 'threshold' by 10 votes (from 62 to 52) is exactly offset by the absence of the UK's 10 votes. If the UK is opposed, there are three possible outcomes, depending on the number of votes commanded by the countries which are in favour of the Proposal. If this number is:

- *at least 62 votes*, a qualified majority can be secured under the Treaty, so there is no need to have recourse to the Agreement;
- *between 52 and 61 votes*, there will be a qualified majority under the Agreement, but not under the Treaty;
- *less than 52 votes*, there will be no qualified majority, under the Treaty or under the Agreement

So only in the second scenario is the Agreement of critical importance. The possible outcomes are summarized in tabular form below.

| | Position of the UK | | Qualified majority under | |
	For	Against	the EC Treaty?	the Agreement on Social Policy?
Votes	at least 62	at least 62	Yes	Yes
in	less than 62	Less than 52	No	No
favour		between 52 and 61	No	Yes

Categories 3 and 4 comprise areas mentioned only in the Agreement. Worker consultation and integration of persons excluded from the labour market (Article 2(1) of the Agreement) are subject to legislation by the Consultation Procedure (category 3 above), while provisions relating to the rights and protection of workers, the employment of non-Community citizens and job creation measures are subject to unanimous decision (Article 2(3)).

The Commission has indicated a pragmatic approach to the Agreement as the basis for legislation, noting that the absence of unanimity (of the 15) cannot be 'an excuse for standing still', while hoping that 'social policy action will in the future once again be founded on a single legal framework' (COM(94)333, p. 6).

The formal isolation of a member state from an area of legislation under the Treaty is unprecedented; and not surprisingly, it raises some complex legal issues, which may eventually have to be resolved by the Court of Justice. It can for instance be argued that the exclusion of the UK conflicts with the rights of workers, and indeed of all European Union citizens, to equal protection before the Court, and there may also be conflicts with the competition provisions of the EC Treaty. Additional legal complexities may arise from the UK Act of Parliament (the European Communities (Amendment) Act 1993) providing for ratification of the EU Treaty, since the Treaty as defined by this Act specifically excludes the Social Protocol.

Although the United Kingdom is not a party to the Agreement, its implementation will nevertheless involve British (albeit not British *government*) participation. The Agreement does not constitute a separate 'European Social Community': the Social Protocol authorizes the other member states 'to have recourse to the institutions, procedures and mechanisms of the [EC] Treaty' in implementing the Agreement and legislation enacted under the Agreement. UK representatives may not participate in Council deliberations on legislation to be adopted under the Agreement; but other institutions—including the Commission, the Parliament, the Economic and Social Committee and the Court of Justice—continue to operate with British members, even when dealing with business arising exclusively from the Agreement. This rather anomalous situation may add to the legal complications, and may also cause political difficulties.

The financial aspects of the Agreement are also problematical. Administrative costs of Community institutions are borne by the Community budget; the Protocol provides for the use of the Community institutional structure in implementing the agreement, but (as noted above) the UK's ratification of the EU Treaty is based on an Act of Parliament which excludes the Social Protocol: so it is arguable whether the UK government is authorized to agree contributions from the Community budget to administrative costs associated with the Agreement. The UK is not liable to contribute to other types of expenditure—and this implies that funds must be established, separate from the Community budget, to finance measures taken pursuant to the Agreement. Complications are then liable to arise in demarcation between these funds and the European Social Fund (which is established under the EC Treaty and financed by the Community budget).

The effect of the Agreement depends on the policy measures that are adopted in the course of its implementation, and on the degree to which these measures go beyond those instituted under the EC Treaty. It is important to note that many of the policy areas included in the Agreement are already covered by the EC Treaty, although in some instances the procedural requirements for enactment of legislation under the Agreement are less formidable than those of the Treaty. This is because the Agreement provides for more extensive use of the Co-operation Procedure, with a modified system of qualified majority voting, whereby enactment of legislation requires 52 (rather than 62) votes in the Council.

6.3.3   Economic aspects of social policy

The objectives of Community social policy are set out in Article 117 of the EC Treaty (see Box 6.11). This Article is somewhat ambivalent: workers benefit from the functioning of the common market, but there is nevertheless a need for Community legislation to protect their interests. To a degree this reflects differences between the interests of employers and organized labour; and it also reflects tensions between a 'deregulationist' market orientation and

---

BOX 6.11
The objectives of Community social policy

Member states agree upon the need to promote improved working conditions and an improved standard of living for workers, so as to make possible their harmonization while the improvement is being maintained.

They believe that such a development will ensue not only from the functioning of the common market which will favour the harmonization of social systems, but also from ... the approximation of provisions laid down by law, regulation or administrative action.

Source: EC Treaty Article 117.

'interventionism', in which the key issue is the extent to which regulation is necessary or desirable to protect the interests of employees. It can be argued that workers benefit from the prosperity generated by minimally regulated markets, and that conditions of employment are primarily a matter for agreement between employers and employees. An 'interventionist' would contend that, unless the Community takes action to ensure high standards, competitive pressures in the single market would tend to devalue employee protection by a process of 'social dumping'.

The objectives of EC social policy are not always achieved through legislation. The EC Treaty provides for promotion of co-operation and securing agreement (Articles 118 and 118b respectively), while the equal pay provision (Article 119) has been held to have direct effect (Case 149/77). The Agreement on Social Policy emphasizes consultation with, and between, industry and employees; this consultation may lead to contractual arrangements or, in some instances, legislation—but this requires agreement between the parties concerned (Article 4).

Behind the legal provisions, there is a continuing tension between the 'deregulationist' and 'interventionist' perspectives. This is to some extent a right–left ideological division, but it is also a manifestation of differences in national traditions. In particular, regulation and state intervention in employment has tended to be less extensive in the UK than in continental member states, and this is reflected in the structure of industrial relations, and in legislation governing conditions of employment and employee representation. Thus, harmonization that approximates to procedures already followed in most member states is liable to require significant changes to existing practice in the UK.

The fundamental economic issue is the effect of social legislation on employment. Opponents of regulation argue that it has adverse effects on employment, through:

1. Increases (both direct and indirect) in costs borne by employers.
2. Reductions in flexibility and in workers' incentives.
3. The costs of 'voluntary' agreements which are concluded to avoid the threat of legislation.
4. Disincentives for investment.

The last point has influenced the UK government's decisions to opt out of the Social Charter and against participation in the Agreement on Social Policy (see above). It is argued that flexible, minimally regulated labour markets attract investment and thus stimulate employment, because potential investors seek to avoid restrictions and heavy additional costs in their use of labour. The UK's stance could also be characterized, in less complimentary terms, as encouraging 'social dumping'.

There are counter-arguments on the lines that:

1. The effects of cost increases are transitory, and are absorbed by employers without long-term increases in unemployment.
2. Security and the assurance of good conditions of employment are beneficial to worker productivity and the development of a skilled labour force.
3. A framework for co-operation between employers and workers representatives helps to facilitate economic restructuring.
4. The stability provided by social legislation promotes the wider interests of society.

These arguments are not altogether consistent with the concept of social dumping, because they suggest that social provisions yield direct economic benefits to the country concerned.

In addition to any ideological issues, there are practical questions concerning the influence on investment of the cost and quality of labour, and of employment regulations. There is in fact wide variation in labour costs between Community member states, as is shown in Table 6.3. Hourly labour costs in 1991 ranged from less than 4 ECUs to over 20 ECUs; and clearly, if the cost of labour is the prime consideration, new investment would be strongly attracted to Portugal and Greece. However, higher-cost countries are able to compete because their more expensive labour is more productive, as can be seen from the figures in the table for value added per employee.

Table 6.3   Labour costs and value added per employee in industry, European Union member states, 1991

	Hourly labour costs (ECUs)	Value added per employee (ECUs)
Germany	21.17	44 486
Belgium	18.66	48 088
Sweden	18.17	62 102
Netherlands	18.08	45 787
Denmark	18.01	41 761
Austria	17.74	45 202
Finland	17.57	54 740
UK	13.37	40 125
Ireland	12.29	40 247
Spain	12.15	37 069
Greece	7.02	14 794
Portugal	3.92	15 514

Note: The figures for Germany exclude the eastern Länder; figures for France, Italy and Luxembourg were not available.
Source: calculated from Eurostat (1994: Tables 2.1, 2.4, 3.17, 3.42).

Employment of labour involves direct costs (wages and salaries) and indirect costs (mostly employers' social security contributions). There are appreciable differences between member states in indirect costs as a proportion of total labour costs—see Table 6.4. If the burden of social provisions adversely affects employment, it would be expected that high percentages of indirect costs would be associated with high rates of unemployment; but on the evidence of the table there does not appear to be strong relation between the two.

Table 6.4 Indirect costs in proportion to total labour costs in industry, and rates of unemployment, European Union member states
Averages of 1984, 1988, 1991 figures

	Indirect costs (%)	Unemployment rates (%)
Belgium	28.1	10.1
Denmark	5.0	8.2
Germany[‡]	23.2	6.7
Greece	19.7	8.2
Spain[*]	24.9	20.0
France[*]	31.4	9.9
Ireland	17.7	16.8
Italy[*]	28.1	10.2
Luxembourg[*]	16.5	2.5
Netherlands	26.8	9.6
Portugal	25.5	6.1
UK	14.6	9.7
Austria	23.6	3.6
Finland[†]	22.8	4.0
Sweden	29.8	2.5

[*] Figures for 1984 and 1988 only.
[†] Figures for 1988 and 1991 only.
[‡] Excluding eastern Länder.
Source: calculated from Eurostat (1989 and 1994: Tables 3.22 and 3.43).

Nor is it self-evident that social legislation is generally a significant cause of unemployment. From the employer's perspective, the significant factor is the aggregate burden of costs, both direct and indirect, and restrictions on conditions, and the termination, of employment. Capital mobility and competition in global markets will tend to set the level of employers' aggregate unit labour costs, irrespective of the proportion that is 'indirect' cost. So the effect of social provisions must be a combination of lower wages and lower employment.

Consequently, the supply side of the labour market is critical in determining the effect of social provisions on employment. The employee's immediate concern is the perceived value of the 'remuneration package', comprising wages and any other benefits. If the labour market is uniformly regulated, workers will be subject to the regulations unless they withdraw from the labour market, work informally (the so-called 'black economy') or migrate. The last possibility is unlikely to be significant, particularly if social provisions are harmonized in the single market. So to prevent unemployment the main concern must be avoidance of disincentives for work—such as the so-called 'poverty trap', where potential workers can obtain higher incomes from benefits than from work.

To address this problem, the Commission White Paper on growth, competitiveness and employment calls for reductions in the relative cost of low qualified work. In most member states the aggregate indirect costs of skilled and semi-skilled labour should decrease by the equivalent of 1–2 per cent of GDP by the year 2000. Employment stimulated by this reduction would generate tax revenue, which according to the Commission would offset 30 per cent of the reduction in social contributions. The remaining need for social expenditure could be financed from other sources, notably environmental taxation (COM(93)700, p. 15); the scope for the latter is discussed in Sec. 7.5.1.

Critics of social protection measures have contrasted western Europe unfavourably with the United States, where, it is argued, a flexible labour market has produced a more dynamic economy with less unemployment. Such comparisons are complicated by cultural differences, so it is not self-evident that American-style deregulation would have the same results in Europe. Moreover, supporters of European practice stress the qualitative aspects of employment, arguing that a well-trained workforce is essential for enduring prosperity; they also draw attention to the polarization of the US labour market, with attendant social problems such as exclusion of underprivileged groups from the labour force.

Economic consequences of the Agreement on Social Policy   A certain amount of mythology has developed, particularly in the UK, around the Agreement attached to the Social Protocol, and as usual the myths have tended to obscure the reality. The disagreements between the UK and other member states focused on the economic impact of social policy, and in particular on the costs—and specifically indirect costs—of employing labour, and the flexibility of labour markets, i.e. the ease with which employees can be recruited and (especially) dismissed. In the negotiations leading up to the EU Treaty (the Maastricht Treaty), claims were made that measures envisaged in the Agreement on Social Policy would seriously weaken the competitiveness of industry within the Community, and exacerbate unemployment. So two questions arise:

1. Does social legislation actually have this effect?
2. Will the Agreement on Social Policy place a significant burden on employers?

The arguments advanced by the UK government imply that both questions are answered in the affirmative; but, if the answer to one or both is 'no', then these arguments are not valid.

6.3.4   The position of the United Kingdom

The implications of the United Kingdom's 'semi-detached' position are uncertain, and there is continuing debate as to whether it serves the UK's own interests. The United Kingdom's abstention from the Agreement on Social Policy has been presented as an attempt to enjoy the best of both worlds: optional participation in social measures, which enables the UK to insulate itself from any allegedly damaging measures. However, in practice it is very unlikely that the UK can stand aloof from, and remain unaffected by, developments in social policy under the Agreement.

The economic case advanced by the UK government is that the UK will attract a higher levels of investment—and particularly inward investment coming from outside the European Union—if its industry is not subject to the burden of measures enacted under the Agreement on Social Policy. However, this argument, even if valid in principle, loses some of its force if the total amount of investment is reduced. By its non-participation, the UK government has forgone the opportunity to exert what it would see as a moderating influence on the operation of the Agreement; so, by this logic, the burden would be appreciably greater, and investment and employment lower, than would have been the case with the UK's participation. But the rest of the European Union accounts for approximately half of the UK's foreign trade; and if the UK's main trading partners are in economic decline this will also affect investment, employment and living standards in the UK. By the same token, economic stagnation in the

European Union will tend to diminish the attractions of investment in the UK as a base to serve the European market.

Social policy measures are now developed in the context of both the Treaty and the Agreement; and the existence of two possible legislative frameworks is an important consideration for the enactment of social policy measures, in so far as it influences the negotiating stances of the various protagonists. For instance, Proposals will be advanced, and positions adopted, in the knowledge that the Agreement provides a 'fall-back' option if no agreement can be secured under the terms of the EC Treaty. This possibility tends to weaken the bargaining position of the United Kingdom; UK representatives in the Council know that if they are in an isolated position, or if they press too hard for changes to proposed legislation, the other 11 member states do not necessarily have to defer to the UK—they have the option of enacting legislation under the Agreement. By the same logic, the UK will have difficulty in withholding agreement pending concessions to its position as part of an overall compromise. In short, it will be easier for other member states to call the UK's bluff.

Conversely, member states most strongly opposed to the UK can afford to be intransigent, seeking to have proposed legislation adopted under the Agreement, rather than settling for a compromise under the EC Treaty. (And under the Agreement a qualified majority requires only 52 votes, rather than 62 under the EC Treaty.)

Although without legal force in the UK the Agreement is nevertheless potentially influential because it provides a focus for those who wish to raise standards of social protection, and for alignment of practice in the UK with standards in other member states. Legislation and other measures pursuant to the Agreement will be regarded as defining aspects of good practice in employment: and this perception will be promoted by organised labour in the UK, and by those British members of the European Parliament who favour the measures in question. Consequently UK employers will come under pressure to offer terms of employment equivalent to those prevailing under the Agreement. Multinational companies in particular will find it difficult to insulate their UK operations from standards prevailing across the rest of the European Union, and other employers may be expected to follow the multinationals' lead.

UK employers also have an interest in the consultative aspects of the Agreement. The Agreement (Article 3(1)) charges the Commission with 'promoting the consultation of management and labour at Community level' as a prelude to, and in the course of, developing legislative Proposals. Notwithstanding their formal exemption from any eventual legislation, the consultative process offers opportunities to UK employers, because it enables them to work in conjunction with their counterparts in other member states to influence developments that are, directly or indirectly, relevant to employment practice in the UK.

UK employers are also liable to be brought into formal processes established under the Agreement. Legislation enacted under the Agreement (Directive 94/45) requires Community-level committees for employee consultation in 'Community-scale' undertakings or groups of undertakings. To qualify as such, an undertaking must employ at least 1000 workers in member states that are party to the Agreement, and 100 or more in at least two of these member states. It is estimated that about 1000 multinational companies are affected, and of these approximately 100 are UK-owned (*Financial Times*, 20 April 1994); as a practical matter, it will be difficult (and probably counter-productive) to exclude UK employees from the consultative machinery.[2]

A future UK government may decide that participation in the Agreement is to the UK's advantage. Legally this would entail revision of the Protocol and, most probably, amendment of the EC Treaty to incorporate the Agreement, replacing—where appropriate—

existing Treaty provisions; legislation under the Agreement would then be based on the Treaty, and applicable in the UK. The UK would become subject to measures over which it had little influence; and the absence of a direct UK input would be manifested in the extent to which these measures reflected (or failed to reflect) the UK's interests and priorities.

6.3.5   The future of Community social policy

The Commission's vision of social policy emphasizes the synergy and mutual interdependence between economic and social policies in the maintenance and improvement of living standards. From this perspective, the dichotomy between labour market intervention and deregulation may appear somewhat outmoded.

The strategy set out in the Commission's 1994 White Paper on social policy emphasizes the Community's role as facilitator, rather than as a regulator. Acknowledging the importance of economic competitiveness, the White Paper notes that prosperity is the key to affordability of high levels of social protection. Conversely, social policy measures have a crucial role in ensuring that the Community has the 'well educated, highly motivated and adaptable working population' that is vital to ensure the continuing health of the economy (COM(94)333, p. 4). While the single market demands minimum standards of social provision to avoid 'social dumping', the Commission states its intention to respect national diversity and the coexistence of national systems, while seeking agreement on common objectives (p. 5).

Notwithstanding ideological differences, an emerging consensus on social policy is acknowledged even in British government circles (European Commission 1992: 49). Member states are facing similar social problems—such as ageing populations, declining birth rates, family breakdowns and structural unemployment—and have similar constraints on public expenditure. The resulting tension between social and budgetary pressures has given a powerful impetus for spontaneous convergence of policies.

6.4   EDUCATION, VOCATIONAL TRAINING AND YOUTH

The Community shall contribute to the development of quality education, by encouraging cooperation between Member States, and, if necessary, by supporting and supplementing their action.

(Article 126 EC)

The Community shall implement a vocational training policy which shall support and supplement the action of the Member States.

(Article 127 EC)

Education and training within the Community display considerable diversity between member states, in terms of structures, institutions and types of qualification. This is to some extent a reflection of contrasting national and cultural traditions; but there are also differences in priorities and resources devoted to education and training—as is shown by the wide variation between member states in levels of educational attainment in the workforce (see Table 6.5).

The Community's role in education and training is related both to the functioning of the single market and to the wider aspects of cohesion outlined above. Freedom of movement within the single market is facilitated by mutual recognition of qualifications and by wider

Table 6.5 Percentage of the labour force aged 25 and above with post-compulsory education, European Community member states (excluding France), 1991

Over 60%	Germany, Denmark, Netherlands
40–59%	Belgium, Ireland, Greece
20–39%	UK, Italy, Spain, Luxembourg
Under 20%	Portugal

Source: European Commission (1993: 103).

study of the languages of member states. Educational co-operation and exchanges are important in promoting cohesion, encouraging a mutual learning process and respect for cultural diversity.

These concerns are reflected in the priorities set out in the EC Treaty for Community policy with respect to education and training (see Box 6.12). Although the relevant provisions were inserted in the Treaty only in 1993, the Community's role in these areas began much earlier. The first Community action programme in the field of education was established in 1976 (Council Resolution (1976)): focusing on transnational co-operation, language teaching, and access to education, it set out a core agenda that has changed very little over the years.

BOX 6.12
Education and training policies: European Community priorities

Education (Article 126(2) EC)

- The European dimension in education, particularly the teaching and dissemination of languages
- Mobility of students and teachers, with academic recognition of diplomas and periods of study
- Co-operation between educational establishments
- Exchanges of information and experience
- Exchange programmes for youth and socio-educational instructors
- Development of distance education

Training (Article 127(2) EC)

- Adaptation to industrial changes
- Vocational integration and reintegration into the labour market
- Access to training; mobility of instructors and trainees
- Co-operation between educational and training establishments and firms
- Exchanges of information and experience

6.5   CULTURE

The Community shall contribute to the flowering of the cultures of the Member States, while respecting their ... diversity ... bringing the common cultural heritage to the fore.

(Article 128 EC)

Cultural matters have been the subject of numerous Council Resolutions and Community-sponsored programmes. The EC Treaty calls for Community action to encourage co-operation between member states, and to support or supplement national measures. This encompasses initiatives to improve and disseminate knowledge of culture and history, and to promote conservation, cultural exchanges and artistic creation. To achieve Community objectives, the Council may adopt 'incentive measures' and recommendations.

The single market has necessitated Community legislation on the export of cultural goods such as antiques. Export to a non-Community country must now be licensed by the member state in which the cultural good in question is *lawfully* located (Regulation 3911/92, Article 2); so a member state may not license the re-export of an antique that is unlawfully imported from elsewhere in the Community.

The Community has sought to promote—or defend—European culture by legislating on television programmes. Member states are required to ensure that, 'where practicable broadcasters reserve for European works a majority proportion of their transmission time' (Directive 89/552, Article 4). As a protectionist measure—directed primarily at imports from the USA—this runs counter to the free trade provisions of the GATT agreement (see Sec. 10.2.2), and the legislation may eventually have to be modified, or even abandoned.

6.6   PUBLIC HEALTH

The Community shall contribute towards ensuring a high level of human health protection by encouraging cooperation between the Member States and if necessary lending support to their action.... Community action shall be directed towards the prevention of diseases ... by promoting research into their causes and their transmission, as well as health information and education.

(Article 129 EC)

The Community's role in health policy can be traced to various facets of the single market. Harmonization and mutual recognition of product standards applies to health supplies, including blood. (The Community has sought to be self-sufficient in blood supplies—see Decision 91/317 on a plan of action against AIDS.) More generally, free movement for Community citizens implies a mutual commitment on the part of member states to combat infectious diseases and health risks, and to observe minimum standards of public health.

Community health ministers have agreed Resolutions on a number of issues, including a cancer action programme, a European health card, AIDS, tobacco, alcohol abuse (COM(93)559, para. 39). The Commission's public health action programme (set out in COM(93)559) includes a framework for exchange of information (para. 94), comparison and evaluation of preventive policies (para. 87), research (paras. 96–102), and training (paras. 103–4). It also envisages action to co-ordinate health information (para. 89), education (para. 90) and promotion (para. 91). In addition, the programme includes co-operation with countries outside the European Union and with international organizations (para. 105), and health protection requirements for, and health protection afforded to, persons from non-Community countries (para. 88). The development of specific Community health policies is illustrated by the programme to combat cancer (see Box 6.13) with a strategy combining prevention, information, training and research.

BOX 6.13
The European Community programme against cancer

Prevention: anti-smoking

- Upward alignment of tobacco taxes
- Harmonized health warnings
- Prohibition of high tar content
- Elimination of tax-free sales of tobacco products
- Protection of children
- Advertising restrictions

Prevention: nutrition

- Epidemiological research
- Better nutritional labelling
- Nutritional recommendations, health information and education campaigns

Prevention: protection against carcinogenic agents

- Inventory of carcinogenic chemical substances
- Protection of workers (e.g. against asbestos)
- Protection against ionizing radiation (e.g. maximum limits for foodstuffs)
- Exchanges of information on systematic screening programmes and early diagnosis

Information and education

- European Code Against Cancer (raising awareness of what people can do to reduce risks to themselves)
- Surveys of risk awareness
- Cancer prevention week (1–7 May 1988)
- Cancer Year 1989

Training

- Minimum training standards required for mutual recognition of qualifications
- Mobility of medical students and student nurses
- Exchanges of experience and teaching materials
- Development of expert systems for diagnosis and treatment

Research

- Exchange programme for researchers
- Research coordination and sponsorship

Source: 'European Community programme against cancer', *Official Journal*, 1986 C184

6.7   CONSUMER PROTECTION

The Community shall contribute to the attainment of a high level of consumer protection through ... action which supplements the policy of Member States to protect the health, safety and economic interests of consumers and to provide adequate information to consumers.

(Article 129a EC)

The principles underlying the Community's consumer protection policy are set out in Box 6.14. The main concerns are with technical standards for safety, to ensure that consumers are properly informed and consulted, and have sufficient right to redress when problems arise.

BOX 6.14
The five principles of consumer protection

1. *Protection of health and safety*:   consumer information on potential risks, product standards to avoid risk under normal conditions of use and to afford protection against injury.
2. *Protection of economic interests*, including measures to prohibit abusive selling practices, misleading advertising, and unfair contract and credit terms.
3. *Consumer rights to information and education* on features, prices, efficient and safe use, in order to make informed choices.
4. The *right to redress* for defective goods and unsatisfactory service, including rights to compensation for injury and damage, with simple, affordable and rapid procedures for dealing with complaints and settling compensation.
5. *Consumer representation and participation*:   consumer organizations to be consulted in the formulation of policies and legislation affecting consumer interests.

Source: European Commission (1993), *Consumer Rights in the Single Market*, Office for Official Publications, Luxembourg.

Consumer protection is an essential component of a market system. In many instances consumers are at a considerable disadvantage *vis-à-vis* producers in terms of the information available to them. Markets will function very inefficiently if nothing is done to compensate for this imbalance, because there will be a substantial cost in making transactions as consumers seek to protect themselves from the risks associated with defective products and services. The purpose of consumer protection measures is to ensure that purchasers of goods and services are not exposed to undue risk of injury or damage, and that they are properly informed about product characteristics and modes of use.

The Community has a longstanding interest in consumer policy. A 'Contact Committee' representing European consumer groups was established to advise the Commission in 1962. The Commission's Consumer Protection Service originated in 1968, and the first programme for consumer protection was adopted in 1975.

The Commission is now advised by a Consumers' Consultative Council, which includes representatives of European and national consumers' organizations, together with representatives of the disabled and senior citizens. The major European organizations are the European Office of Consumer Organizations (BUEC) the Committee of Family Organizations in the European Communities (COFACE), the European Community of Consumer Co-operatives (Euro-Coop), the European Trade Union Confederation (ETUC) and the European Inter-regional Institute for Consumer Affairs (EIICA).

Consumer protection standards were included in the single market legislative programme:

Article 100a(3)EC requires that 'the Commission, in its proposals … concerning … consumer protection, will take as a base a high level of protection'. Free movement of goods and services in the single market, with growth in cross-border sales and electronic and mail order shopping, requires a system of consumer protection which covers transactions across national frontiers. In this context the Community's consumer protection policies have focused on development of consumer information, harmonization of national provisions relating to product safety, and the contractual terms governing cross-border transactions. Community legislation now covers packaging requirements (quality ranges and unit pricing), misleading advertising, consumer contract terms and liability for defective products. Standards are set for food products, medicines, cosmetics and the marketing, packaging and labelling of dangerous substances. Safety requirements have been specified for products including toys, building materials and gas burning appliances. Safety standards may be combined with consumer information; for example, in the case of toy safety (Directive 88/378), the 'CE' mark confirms that the product meets the standard for safety established by the standardization body CEN.

Under Community law the manufacturer of a defective product is liable for damage suffered by consumers as a result of the defect. This liability is absolute, irrespective of any negligence on the part of the manufacturer, unless it can be shown that the defect is due to compliance with mandatory requirements imposed by the public authorities. However, it is for the consumer 'to prove the damage, the defect and the causal relationship between defect and damage' (Directive 85/374, Article 4).

However, legislation to strengthen the contractual position of consumers will be ineffective unless there are adequate mechanisms to enforce the rights that are conferred. If consumers can obtain redress more easily against suppliers in their own country than in other member states, there will be an impediment to cross-border trade in the single market. The Commission has envisaged a number of possible initiatives to improve and simplify the settlement of disputes involving consumers (COM(93)576, pp. 77–85). At present difficulties arise in bringing injunctions against unlawful commercial practices, such as misleading advertising or unfair contract terms; this problem could be mitigated by harmonization or the mutual recognition of national provisions. Legal aid could be provided, from national or Community funds, to assist consumers' organizations in taking legal action against suppliers in other member states. The Commission has also proposed a review of settlement procedures for transfrontier disputes, with a view to eventual simplification, and a dialogue between consumers' organizations and self-regulatory professional bodies, to examine possible ways to increase public confidence in the latter. In the end, much depends on the development of mechanisms for transfrontier co-operation involving all types of organization, to achieve a common approach to issues such as dishonest practices, misleading advertising, dispute resolution and credit assessment.

6.8   THE WIDENING POLICY AGENDA: KEY POINTS AND ISSUES

The process of European integration has led to policy-making at European Community level in a wide range of areas. The single market programme in particular has given a strong impetus to the widening of the Community policy agenda. The Community now has a basis in the EC Treaty for economic and social policies, and for policies in the fields of education, training, culture, public health and consumer protection.

The following issues can be identified as arising in connection with the widening of the policy agenda:

- The development of the single market has led to a deepening, and a broadening, of policy-making at Community level: why is this? To what extent is the process constrained by the subsidiarity principle?
- The EC Treaty specifies that policies must follow an integrated approach, taking account of environmental and consumer protection, health and safety, culture, and industrial competitiveness: what difficulties arise in maintaining the coherence of policy-making? How can these difficulties be overcome?
- The Commission's industrial strategy is to promote innovation, training and the functioning of markets: how is this strategy to be implemented?
- The ostensible purpose of Community social policy is to ensure that the single market does not erode social protection and working conditions: what measures have been adopted to achieve this objective? What is their economic rationale?
- The Protocol on social policy permits the UK to 'opt out' of some Community social legislation: what is the effect of this provision? Is the maintenance of the UK 'opt-out' feasible or desirable?
- The EU (Maastricht) Treaty gave a formal legal basis for Community action in the fields of education, culture and public health: to what extent is the Community's role in these areas consistent with the principle of subsidiarity?
- Community-level measures for consumer protection are justified with reference to growth in cross-border purchases in the single market: what difficulties arise in the enforcement of consumer rights in transactions across national frontiers? How are these difficulties resolved?

NOTES

1. Article 2(1). The Agreement (Article 6(1) and 6(2)) also reproduces verbatim the text of Article 119 EC, on the principle of equal pay, which the Court of Justice has held to have direct effect (Case 149/77).
2. An early instance is acceptance by United Biscuits that its UK employees may participate in its Community-level committee ('Multinational accepts works councils principle', *Financial Times*, 17 June 1994).

REFERENCES

European Commission (1992) 'The convergence of social protection objectives and policies', *Social Europe*, Supplement 5/92.
European Commission (1993) *Employment in Europe 1993*, Office of Official Publications, Luxembourg.
Eurostat (1989, 1994) *Basic Statistics of the Community*, 26th and 31st edns, Office of Official Publications, Luxembourg.

European Community legislation

Regulation 3911/92, on the export of cultural goods, *Official Journal*, 1992 L395/1.
Directive 85/374, concerning liability for defective products, *Official Journal*, 1985 L210/29.
Directive 88/378, concerning the safety of toys, *Official Journal*, 1988 L187/1.
Directive 89/552, on the co-ordination of certain provisions concerning the pursuit of television broadcasting activities, *Official Journal*, 1989 L298/23.
Directive 93/104, concerning certain aspects of the organization of working time, *Official Journal*, 1993 L307/18.
Directive 94/45, on the establishment of a European Works Council or a procedure in Community-scale undertakings and Community-scale groups of undertakings for the purposes of informing and consulting employees, *Official Journal*, 1994 L254/64.

Decision 91/317, adopting a plan of action in the framework of the 1991 to 1993 Europe Against AIDS programme, *Official Journal*, 1991 L175/26.

Council Recommendation 94/7, on the broad guidelines of the economic policies of the member states and of the Community, *Official Journal*, 1994 L7/9.

Council Resolution (1976), comprising an action programme in the field of education, *Official Journal*, 1976 C38/1.

Council Resolution (1986), on an action programme on employment growth, *Official Journal*, 1986 C340/2.

European Commission documents

COM (90)556, *Industrial Policy in an Open and Competitive Environment*, 19 November 1990.

COM(92)47, *Proposal for a European Parliament and Council Directive on the Application of Open Network Provision to Voice Telephony*, 29 August 1992.

COM(93)559, *Commission Communication on the Framework for Action in the Field of Public Health*, 24 November 1993.

COM (93)576, *Green Paper on the Access of Consumers to Justice and the Settlement of Consumer Disputes in the Single Market*, 16 November 1993.

COM(93)700, *Growth, Competitiveness, Employment: The Challenges and Ways Forward into the 21st Century*, 5 December 1993.

COM(94)49, *Communication on the European Union Automobile Industry*, 23 February 1994.

COM(94)333, *European Social Policy: A Way Forward for the Union*, 27 July 1994.

Court judgments

Case 149/77, *Defrenne v. Sabena* [1976] ECR 445.

Case C300/89, *Commission v. Council* [1991] ECR I-2895.

THREE

TOWARDS SUSTAINABLE DEVELOPMENT

The transition to the single market, and the consequent extension of policy responsibilities at the Community level, have coincided with growing concerns over the effects of economic activity, which have become symbolized by the expression 'sustainable development'.

Sustainable development is essentially a concept of long-run economic efficiency. Failure to take proper account of the costs of environmental resources leads to their profligate exploitation and the development of technologies dependent on this pattern of exploitation. This is ultimately self-defeating, because the costs of environmental damage will escalate over time until they can no longer be ignored, while the costs, and extent, of necessary remedial action also increase.

The objective must therefore be to change economic activity so that the use of resources is sustainable in the long term. The key to achieving this lies in the motivation of producers and consumers. In the past there have been strong incentives—for example—to produce agricultural surpluses, to generate 'greenhouse' gases and to increase motor vehicle usage. Progress towards the Community's original objectives—the single market, the common policies for agriculture and transport—has tended to magnify these incentives. Freedom of movement and harmonization of national transport regulations tends to increase traffic, particularly across frontiers, and to create demand for additional infrastructure provision. Agricultural policies have promoted intensive agriculture, with massive use of fertilizers and pesticides.

The Community has sought to respond to this situation by strengthening environmental policies and by integration of an environmental dimension in other policy areas. This integrated approach holds the key to sustainable development: it implies a reorientation of economic policies, to change the structure of incentives.

Once again, the single market and the common agricultural and transport policies have a central role. The Community has begun to contemplate policies that include reductions in agricultural prices, increases in energy prices and changes in land use and infrastructure planning. However, in taxation, which has a major influence on economic incentives, Community legislation has—thus far—done little to reflect the environmental dimension.

In short, the Community has begun to orientate its policies towards sustainability, but there is still a long way to go.

SEVEN

ENVIRONMENTAL POLICIES

In 1992 the European Commission published *Towards Sustainability* (COM(92)23 II), setting out a Community programme of action relating to the environment and sustainable development; this programme was subsequently adopted by the Council on 1 February 1993 (Council Resolution 1993). The main objective is to integrate into Community policies the concept of sustainable development, following from the 1987 report of the World Commission on Environment and Development (generally known as the 'Brundtland Report'). The basis for the programme was set out in June 1990 at the Community 'summit' meeting in Dublin, which made the following commitments:

As Heads of State and Government of the European Community, we recognise our special responsibility for the environment both to our own citizens and to the wider world. We undertake to intensify our efforts to protect and enhance the natural environment of the Community itself and the world of which it is part. We intend that action by the Community and its Member States will be developed on a coordinated basis and on the principles of sustainable development and preventive and precautionary action.

(European Council, 1990: 4)

To meet these requirements, the action programme sets out a strategy 'with the ultimate aim of transforming the patterns of growth' (COM(92)23 II, p. 25).

Although the action programme constitutes the framework for environmental policy, its objectives cannot be achieved solely by measures that react to environmental problems without reference to the economic activities that cause these problems to arise. Environmental policy in the conventional sense has been one among many, sometimes conflicting, Community interests; and the direct effects of environmental policies do not necessarily outweigh the side-effects on the environment of policy measures instituted for other purposes. In reality, the environment and the quality of life are influenced by a wide variety of Community policies, elements of which may appear inconsistent. For example, the Common Agricultural Policy has encouraged farmers to use fertilizers to increase output, while environmental legislation restricts fertilizer application, in order to reduce water contamination by nitrates. The motivations of Community policies are illustrated in Box 7.1, which shows incentives (and disincentives) implicit in the main items of revenue and expenditure in the Community budget. None of these is particularly favourable to sustainable development—indeed, some, particularly those concerning agriculture and infrastructure, can in some circumstances be positively harmful.

The action programme stresses the importance of integrating the environmental dimension into all areas of policy, as a precondition for the general sustainability of its policy role. The key

---

BOX 7.1
European Community budget: incentive and disincentive effects of revenue raising and expenditures

	% of EC budget in 1995	Main incentive effect
Revenue		
VAT	51%	Favours purchases of goods and services taxed at lower rate
Customs duties	17%	Disincentive to purchase goods which are imported from outside the EU and are subject to a tariff
Expenditure		
Agriculture (Guarantee Section)	50%	Incentive for high agricultural output through intensive farming
Regional development	20%	Incentive for expenditure on infrastructure projects in less prosperous regions

---

to sustainable development lies in an anticipatory and preventive approach: 'to focus on the agents and activities which damage the environment and deplete the natural resource stock rather than wait, as has been the tendency in the past, for problems to emerge' (COM(92)23 II, p. 19) Certain areas of economic activity—notably energy, transport and agriculture—are identified as 'target sectors', which have particularly significant environmental impacts, and which must play a crucial role if development is to follow a sustainable course (COM(92)23 II, Chapter 4).

7.1   THE COMMUNITY ROLE IN ENVIRONMENTAL POLICIES

The Community first set out a systematic body of environmental policies in 1974, although some environmental measures had been instituted before then in connection with the harmonization of product standards. Policies in this area were initially an *ad hoc* response to a perceived need: there was no specific legal basis for Community environmental action until 1987, when Articles 130r–t were added to the EC Treaty.

From this beginning environmental policy has grown in significance, so that the Community's objectives now include 'sustainable ... growth respecting the environment' (Article 2 EC). Meanwhile Community environmental policies have acquired a legal base, which specifies their fundamental objectives and principles (see Box 7.2), and requires that 'environmental protection requirements must be integrated into ... other Community policies' (Article 130r(2) EC).

7.1.1   The development of Community environmental policy

Community environmental policies have been developed in five successive action programmes. In addition to prospective legislative initiatives, these programmes have also presented the Commission's thinking on broader issues of policy, and particularly the interaction between environmental policies and economic conditions and priorities.

BOX 7.2
Community environmental policy: objectives, principles and other considerations

Objectives

- Preservation, protection and improvement in the quality of the environment and human health
- Prudent and rational utilization of natural resources
- Promotion of measures at international level to deal with regional or worldwide environmental problems

Principles

- Precautionary and preventive action
- Rectification of environmental damage at source
- The polluter should pay

Other considerations are:

- Available scientific and technical data
- Potential benefits and costs of action or lack of action
- Environmental conditions in the regions of the Community
- Economic and social development of the Community, and the balanced development of its regions

Source: adapted from Article 130r EC Treaty.

The Community's interest was stimulated by growing concern over environmental degradation, marked by the 1972 United Nations Stockholm conference on the human environment. The October 1972 meeting of Community heads of state or government declared that 'economic expansion ... should result in an improvement in the quality of life as well as in standards of living' (Council Declaration (1973) p. 5); following this declaration, the first Community environmental action programme was inaugurated at the beginning of 1974.

From an initial emphasis on pollution abatement, Community policies have come to focus on avoidance of environmental damage and eventually on the conditions for sustainable development. The first action programme (1974–7) emphasized the immediate need for legislative and administrative measures to deal with an environmental protection 'backlog' resulting from previous neglect of the environment. A further theme was the need to strengthen the basis for future development of policies, and for the assessment of policy measures, in terms of scientific justification and economic impact: to this end, emphasis was given to development of scientific criteria and methodologies and to research and development in the environmental field (Council Declaration 1973).

The second action programme (1977–81) reaffirmed the objectives and principles set out in the first (Council Resolution (1977); however, the economic context was very different, as economic growth stagnated in the aftermath of the 1973 oil crisis. Against this background, a perception developed that regulations instituted merely as a reaction to environmental damage could be costly and inefficient, in both economic and environmental terms; interest grew in alternative approaches, and specifically in possibilities for preventive or anticipatory policies for the rational management of resources (European Commission 1984: 13). One important outcome of this new thinking was the 1985 Directive (85/337) on environmental impact assessment (see Sec. 7.3.1).

The Community's third environmental action programme (1982–6) anticipated one of the key elements of sustainable development: the integration of an environmental dimension into other policies (Council Resolution 1983). The main features of environmental policy developed over the first three action programmes—anti-pollution measures, the anticipatory approach and policy integration—are reflected in the objectives and principles set out in the EC Treaty (see Box 7.2).

The fourth action programme (1987–92) developed further the Community's thinking on the implementation of policies, and specifically on the types of measure that may be used to achieve environmental objectives (Council Resolution 1987). A variety of policy instruments is available to provide incentives to avoid, or reduce, damage to the environment: these may be broadly categorized as:

1. *Regulation*:   controls over emission sources, substances or products, either based on what is technically feasible or geared to achievement of environmental quality standards which may be defined in terms of a single medium (for example water, or air) or multiple media.
2. *'Informational' measures*: environmental impact assessment, environmental auditing, product labelling.
3. *Economic incentive mechanisms*:   Including charges, taxes, subsidies, or liability for environmental damage.

The current (fifth) action programme has evolved from its predecessors, but its objectives are cast in much broader terms. The new element is an emphasis on changing patterns of human consumption and behaviour, to:

achieve full integration of environmental and other relevant policies through the active participation of all the main actors in society (administrations, enterprises, [the] general public) through a broadening and deepening of the instruments for control and behaviourial change including in particular greater use of market forces.

(COM(92)23 II, p. 19)

The effect of human activities on the quality of the environment is the result of a multitude of decisions, taken by individuals and in various types of organization—in government, in industry and in other bodies. These decisions are influenced by numerous factors, and represent the cumulative impact of the variety of incentives to which decision-makers are exposed. The function of the policy process is to modify the pattern of incentives, to favour the achievement of objectives established by the policy-maker, and to discourage actions that detract from achievement of these objectives.

7.1.2   Why Community environmental policy?

The original impetus for Community environmental measures came from two distinct sources: the single market, and a growth in environmental consciousness. The latter has prompted a wide range of policy initiatives geared to protection of the environment. Economic integration within the single market has increasingly focused policy measures at the Community, rather than national, level because (in accordance with the principle of subsidiarity) 'objectives ... cannot be sufficiently achieved by the Member States ... and can therefore be better achieved by the Community' (Article 3b EC).

The fifth environmental action programme seeks to promote 'shared responsibility' between public authorities, enterprises and the public, the 'actors' whose interplay influences economic activity and its environmental impacts (COM(92)23 II, pp. 26–7). The Community collaborates with these 'actors' to the extent that is appropriate in the light of the subsidiarity principle. The Community has a lead role particularly where measures affect the single market, or involve international agreements; in other instances it complements action that is primarily the responsibility of others; for example, environmental auditing (see Sec. 7.3.2) is undertaken by and for enterprises, while the Community and national authorities establish standards of good practice (COM(92)23 II, pp. 73–4).

The Community's involvement in environmental policy is to a great extent a consequence of the single market. As was shown in Sec. 3.1, free movement requires the elimination of barriers between member states, and this may be accomplished by mutual recognition of national standards, or—if necessary—by action at Community level. Environmental protection is clearly a legitimate objective, both for the Community (see Article 130r EC) and for member states. Many of the standards for products traded across national frontiers are specified for environmental reasons. At the same time, variations in these standards may constitute non-tariff barriers to trade; for example, if each member state were to have its own vehicle emission standards, there could not be a single market for motor cars.

The earliest Community legislation relating to environmental protection was concerned with removal of such barriers in order to facilitate the single market. The legal base of these measures was usually Article 100 EEC, which provides for 'approximation' of national measures. For instance, a 1970 Directive (70/220) harmonized vehicle emission standards: the preamble to the Directive called for member states to adopt the same requirements, specifically to supersede measures recently introduced in Germany and France which were liable to hinder the functioning of the single market. Another example of environmental legislation designed to overcome 'hindrance' to trade was the 1967 Directive (67/548) to harmonize the testing of chemicals: the Community testing procedure was not necessarily better than those of member states, but a single, generally recognized, procedure was preferable in order to avoid wasteful duplication of tests.

Community environmental measures also prevent economic distortions in the single market. The four freedoms of movement—of goods, services, capital and people—create opportunities, but may also compromise environmental protection. A country may seek a competitive advantage—say, to improve its terms of trade or to attract capital inflows—by setting low environmental standards (a process that can be characterized as 'environmental dumping') or by financial aid to industry. In either case there is a subsidy that may distort trade: a low-quality environment represents a burden on the population, as does the taxation necessary to provide financial support. To combat these forms of subsidy, the Community has in a number of instances legislated for minimum environmental standards, and has established procedures (under Article 93, EC) to limit state aid for environmental purposes. Minimum standards also ensure that Community citizens can exercise their freedom of movement under the EC Treaty (Article 7a) undeterred by the prospect of encountering a low-quality environment.

In many instances Community initiatives are prompted by national measures which have repercussions within the single market. One notable instance is the 1991 German legislation on packaging, which obliges producers and sellers of products to take back packaging materials for recycling. (This led to the establishment of the *Duales System Deutschland* (DSD), which has developed infrastructure—such as collection facilities at supermarkets—to channel waste for recycling.) One side-effect of the system was to stimulate exports of material for recycling, and to depress the prices of materials such as waste paper. This led to economic disruption in other member states, and pressure for Community action to prevent disorder in the market. In 1992 the Commission brought forward a Proposal for a Directive on packaging and packaging waste; in prolonged debate, the Council agreed a common position in 1994, setting a target for 50–65 per cent recovery of packaging waste within five years. This was agreed by qualified majority, against the opposition of three of the most environmentally conscious member states, Denmark, Germany and the Netherlands (Common Position (EC) No. 13/94 p. 78); in any event, the proposed targets were below the level of recycling being achieved in Germany. The eventual legislation incorporated the targets set out in the common position, while permitting Greece, Ireland and Portugal to set lower targets (in view of their economic and geographical circumstances), and allowing other member states to set higher targets, provided these do not distort trade or hinder compliance in other member states (Parliament and Council Directive 94/62, Article 6)

Free movement is not confined to goods: 'bads', in the form of pollution and other environmental impacts, have never respected national frontiers. Many of the most significant issues in environmental policy have required action at an international—and in some instances at a global—level. Pollution can arise from mobile sources (such as vehicles), it can be carried across frontiers, and it can affect the earth as a whole. The Community has an advantage in dealing with these problems since it has a transnational perspective, and—unlike other international organizations—can apply legal instruments to form a coherent policy framework. Two prominent instances of transfrontier impacts within the Community are pollution of the Rhine and damage caused by acid rain: these have strongly influenced Community legislation on aquatic discharges and atmospheric emissions, and it is very doubtful that effective action could have been taken by intergovernmental agreement alone. (There is indeed a long history of ineffectual efforts to co-operate in improving Rhine water quality.)

Threats to wildlife and their habitats also have implications beyond national borders. Co-ordinated action is necessary, especially to protect migratory species, but also to conserve species and habitats of general European—or global—significance. For example, the Mediterranean monk seal, the rarest in the world, used to inhabit several member states, but has suffered catastrophic decline, with the main surviving populations found in Greece; the Community has an interest in efforts to reverse the decline, in order to combat a loss of species diversity within its territory (European Commission 1987: 288). The main legislation relating to wildlife conservation in the Community are Directives on conservation of wild birds (79/409) and habitats (92/43).

Community environmental legislation has sometimes been criticized for breaching the subsidiarity principle, by impinging on matters that are properly the concern of member states—for example, on the lines that, 'if we choose to bathe in dirty water, that's our business' (*Financial Times*, 16 August 1994). Such arguments frequently combine (and occasionally confuse) two very distinct concepts: objection in principle to a Community standard, and criticism of the stringency of the standard. The justification of a Community *minimum* standard for bathing water lies in Treaty provisions for freedom of movement of people; so Community citizens should not be prevented from exercising this freedom by concerns over the quality of the environment. If member states believe the Community standard to be excessively high they can seek to have the relevant legislation amended. Member states can opt for standards higher than the Community minimum, provided this does not cause unacceptable distortion of trade within the single market (Article 130t EC). The Commission's 1993 review of subsidiarity concluded that, while some legislation (particularly that relating to water) required simplification, 'application of the subsidiarity principle must not be allowed to lower [environmental] standards' (COM(93)545, p. 17); the implication is that Community legislation might be amended, but that there would be no wholesale repeal.

7.1.3   Community expenditure on the environment

Expenditure in support of environmental policy has been consolidated under the LIFE financial instrument, which was established 'to contribute to the development and implementation of Community environmental policy' (Regulation 1973/92, Article 1). The amount of finance involved is a very small proportion of the Community budget—of the order of one-thousandth. LIFE has two main purposes: to support preparatory measures, demonstration schemes, awareness campaigns, and technical assistance (primarily a 'catalytic' function); and to contribute towards the cost of conservation measures.

Virtually all Community expenditure has some effect on the environment, which may or may not be benign. (Agricultural expenditure, in particular, has been criticized for causing environmental degradation—see Sec. 9.5.1.) Community expenditure with environmental objectives has been estimated at just over 1 bn ECUs in 1991, of which almost three-quarters came from the structural funds; however, such estimates should be treated with caution, because in many instances environmental effects are incidental to other objectives (Court of Auditors 1992: 3–5).

The Court of Auditors has identified several instances in which the environmental dimension of structural fund expenditures has been essentially cosmetic. Projects in protected coastal regions have been found to include environmentally damaging tourism developments; urban public transport investment has been—misleadingly—defined as purely for environmental purposes (Court of Auditors 1992: 14); and environmental expenditure for the protection of wetlands has included costs of purchasing lagoons constructed with the aid of structural fund resources to promote aquaculture (pp. 6–7).

In addition to expenditure from the Community budget, environmental projects are also supported by loans from the European Investment Bank (EIB). Loans for environmental purposes and urban development in 1993 amounted to 4.4 bn ECUs (approximately one-quarter of the financing provided within the Community); almost half of this (over 2 bn ECUs) was to support projects concerned with drinking water supply and waste water treatment (EIB 1994: 27–34). The latter is an area of particular need, because of the inadequacy of the existing infrastructure—particularly in the 'cohesion' countries—for compliance with new requirements that urban waste water should normally receive at least 'secondary' treatment before discharge to the environment (Directive 91/271, Article 4).

7.2   ENVIRONMENTAL POLICY: REGULATORY MEASURES

The Community's output of environmental legislation has been impressive: there are now over 200 items of legislation, concerning water quality, atmospheric pollution, noise, waste management, accident prevention and the use of chemicals. (The most significant pieces of legislation enacted up to 1991 are reproduced in European Commission 1992.) Most of Community law in this area is in the form of Directives, which are implemented by legislation in member states. Directives are inherently more flexible than Regulations, and for this reason can more easily be agreed by member states; this consideration is especially significant for environmental measures, which are often subject to legal and technical complexities.

7.2.1   Environmental legislation

The initial focus of Community environmental policy was on water pollution. With successive environmental action programmes and progress towards the single market, the Community's role has widened, particularly with respect to air pollution and waste management.

Water pollution   Directives have been enacted on water quality for specific purposes, including human consumption, abstraction for drinking water, bathing and to support shellfish and freshwater fish. These Directives do not specify standards for discharges into these waters: that is the responsibility of the authorities in member states, who must ensure achievement of the required water quality standards—without discriminating between national waters and waters that cross their frontiers.

A further set of Directives establishes pollution standards for discharges of dangerous substances. These have been enacted pursuant to the 'framework' Directive (76/464) which defines 'black' and 'grey' lists of substances: the former are toxic, persistent and bioaccumulative, while the latter have more localized polluting effects. Member states are required to regulate discharges of these substances. For those on the 'grey' list, discharge standards must be set to achieve environmental quality objectives (Article 7). For the 'black' list, discharge standards are specified, having regard to their environmental impact and the best technical means of pollution abatement; environmental quality objectives are also specified, and a member state may opt to achieve these, as an alternative to compliance with the discharge standards (Article 6).

Air pollution   Community measures to combat air pollution distinguish between mobile and non-mobile sources. The former—principally motor vehicles—circulate across national frontiers, and are products subject to standardization in the single market. Since 1970 the Community has had legislation on technical standards for motor vehicle emissions, and these standards have been periodically revised, to cover more substances and to introduce more stringent standards. A notable instance is the 1989 legislation on small car emission standards (Directive 89/458) which specifies emission levels achievable with catalytic convertors. (A high standard was set at the insistence of the European Parliament, acting under the Co-operation Procedure—see Box 2.5.)

Emissions from stationary sources are of concern to the Community because they can give rise to transfrontier pollution and also because differences between emission standards can distort competition in the single market. The main 'framework' legislation calls on member states to implement strategies to combat air pollution from large industrial plant, involving 'gradual adaptation . . . to best available technology' (Directive 84/360, Article 13). Subsequent legislation called for a reduction in emissions of sulphur dioxide and nitrogen oxides from large combustion installations (mostly power stations): requirements included conformity with specified emission limits for new plant (based on best available technology), and substantial abatement of emissions from existing plant—although exceptions were made for less developed member states with growing energy requirements (Directive 88/609).

Waste management   Community policies on waste management initially focused on disposal and transfrontier transport. Waste (although a 'bad' rather than a 'good') can circulate freely across frontiers in the single market (under the terms of the EC Treaty, Article 30—see Case 2/90); the Community has legislated for controls on hazardous waste transport (beginning with Directive 84/631) and on waste disposal, in order to prevent disparities in national legislation from causing distortions in the single market (Directives 75/442 and 78/319). As Community environmental policies developed, a three-fold approach evolved, comprising (in order of desirability) prevention, recycling and safe disposal (SEC(89)934, p. 7).

To prepare for the single market, the Community adopted a strategy for waste management, which called for provision of the necessary infrastructure so that waste disposal can be undertaken as close as possible to the location at which it is generated (Council Resolution 1990, para. 7). There is pressure on treatment and disposal capacity, particularly for waste incineration, which is likely to become more prevalent as alternative options (such as land fill or dumping at sea) are foreclosed (Task Force 1990: 120) The Commission has expressed concern that, without national frontier controls, differences between costs of disposal could lead to a 'flood' of waste to lower-cost facilities, exacerbating the already strong public opposition to movement of waste (SEC(89)934, pp. 21–2).

7.2.2 The effectiveness of environmental legislation

The quality of the environment, after approximately twenty years of Community environmental policies, presents a mixed picture. This is shown by Box 7.3 which is a very brief summary of the Commission's 1992 report on the state of the environment (COM(92)23 III).

The persistence of environmental problems does not imply that Community environmental legislation has necessarily been ineffective; on the other hand, there are clearly limits to what it can achieve. The regulatory approach defines problems in narrow—and unchanging—terms. For example, when the first Community environment programme was inaugurated, gross pollution of rivers by industrial and sewage discharges was very evident; and it has been

---

BOX 7.3
The state of the environment, after twenty years of Community policies

Atmospheric pollution Progress in reducing emissions of sulphur dioxide, particulates, lead and CFCs ... *but* serious problems of 'greenhouse' gases and urban air quality.

Aquatic pollution Progress in reducing discharges from point sources ... *but* increased pollution from diffused sources, surface water eutrophication, and overexploitation and pollution of groundwater; progress in reducing pollution from organic wastes, heavy metals and radioactive discharges ... *but* persisting pressures, especially in the Mediterranean, the Baltic and the North Sea.

Soil degradation Improvements as a result of Community legislation ... *but* contamination, acidification, desertification and erosion caused by over-intensive land use, excessive application of fertilizers, pesticides, herbicides and land drainage and clearance.

Nature conservation Community legislation and international conventions ... *but* intensified agriculture has increased pressures on biota and habitats; economic development and erosion are causing deterioration of the coastal environment; forest fires have devastated parts of the Mediterranean region; recreational and second-home developments have caused deterioration in upland and mountain regions.

The urban environment A desire for a good quality environment ... *but* the demands of commerce and transport lead to congestion, pollution, noise, deterioration of streets, public places and architectural heritage.

Waste management Extensive Community legislation ... *but* recycling and reuse are under-developed, and there are serious deficiencies in waste handling arrangements.

Source: adapted from European Commission, 'Towards Sustainability', COM(92)23 II and *Official Journal*, 1993 C138, Chapter 1.

countered by a series of Directives setting discharge and environmental standards. However, enforcement of these regulatory standards can be a complicated process, and their objectives can be frustrated by environmental and economic changes.

The effectiveness of Community Directives depends upon three factors:

1. Relevance of their provisions to the environmental concern that is addressed.
2. Full and prompt transposition into national legislation.
3. Enforcement of this legislation by national authorities.

The process of negotiating a Directive can be very time-consuming. Certain Directives have experienced particular difficulties; for example, a Directive (82/176) on mercury discharges by the chloralkali industry became a focus of controversy over the use of environmental quality objectives, and took three years from Commission Proposal to Council enactment. Another example is the Directive (80/778) on water for human consumption, which took five years; this was due primarily to the technical complexity of the Directive, which covers a large number of substances, subject to considerable scientific uncertainties.

Once enacted, Directives then require a considerable effort to secure implementation. The first step is enactment in national legislation; the normal period allowed is two years, and the Commission has the task of ensuring that this is done in a satisfactory manner. In some instances member states are required to designate the areas to which the Directive shall apply; where member states fail to do so—as for example with the Directive (79/923) on shellfish waters, where only three met the deadline—the Commission must act.

In most cases there are requirements for periodic reports on the implementation of Directives, on the part of the Commission and member states; and as the number of Directives has risen, the administrative burden has correspondingly increased. The reporting system has now been rationalized (Directive 91/692) so that implementation reports are submitted every three years; on average, the Commission has to receive more than 10 sets of reports per year. (Since each member state submits a report, the total number of reports each year is in the order of 150.)

Once enacted, the requirements included in the Directive must be enforced. The 'transmission' between Council decision and implementation at local level has a number of linkages, in which objectives and priorities may be obscured. This is particularly a problem in federal systems, where directives are agreed by national governments, but are implemented and enforced by local or regional administrations. In some cases inadequate administrative machinery may reflect a lack of commitment to the implementation of environmental measures; this has led the Commission to complain that 'the resources deployed by many of the member states for monitoring and performing the obligations imposed by Community legislation fall short of actual needs' (COM(93)320, p. 97).

Furthermore, implementation may be affected by change in legislative procedures following the 1992 EU (Maastricht) Treaty, which introduced qualified majority voting for Council decisions on environmental legislation (under Article 130s of the EC Treaty). This change was designed to facilitate enactment of legislation, and was supported by environmental pressure groups. However, it may be not be helpful for the enforcement of legislative requirements: while legislation enacted by unanimity will have had the support (or at least acquiescence) of all member states, decisions taken by qualified majority voting can leave member states in the minority with little commitment to the enforcement of the resulting legislation.

The Commission's ability to oversee enforcement is severely limited, since it 'has neither the means to investigate the facts of a specific case nor the power to impose periodic controls on the Member States' (COM(93)320, p. 101). Achievement of the objectives of Community legislation has been heavily dependent on complaints from the public and organizations in member states, which bring to the Commission's attention shortcomings in the application of Community legislation. The number of such complaints relating to environmental Directives increased dramatically in the 1980s—from 10 in 1982 to 460 in 1990 (European Commission 1991a: 226).

Complainants can seek information from national authorities under Directive 90/313, which sets out a public right of access to information on the state of the environment and on activities that affect the environment. This requires public authorities to make available information where it exists; but it does not specify the information that must be collected. The Directive (Article 3.2) also provides for exceptions to the right to information—notably where 'commercial and industrial confidentiality' are involved.

There is some scope for individuals or organizations to bring legal actions against member states where Directives are capable of having 'direct effect' (see Sec. 2.6.5). Such a Directive must set out precise and unconditional requirements, and it must immediately affect the interests of specific persons. Many environmental Directives meet the first of these preconditions, specifying requirements such as supply of information, achievement of environmental standards, or prohibitions on use or emissions of certain substances. The difficulty in applying the 'direct effect' doctrine lies in the second precondition, which requires plaintiffs to establish that failure properly to implement a Directive has infringed the rights of a specific person or group of people *vis-à-vis* the authorities. Thus for example individuals may bring a case on their own behalf if their drinking water supply does not conform to standards specified in Directive 80/778; but it is not possible to bring a case on behalf of fish and seals who suffer as a result of aquatic discharges that contravene the standards for dangerous substances set out in Directives derived from Directive 76/464.

The Commission has adopted a six-point programme to increase the effectiveness of environmental policy measures (see Box 7.4). This acknowledges that enactment of legislation achieves little unless there is a framework to ensure its enforcement. Nevertheless, implementation still depends heavily on member states: ultimately the Commission may take legal action if the national authorities do not respect deadlines, but this is of course a cumbersome and time-consuming process.

BOX 7.4
Environmental policy: measures to improve implementation and enforcement

1. *Improvement in legislation*: better preparation and consultation, enforceability assessment, enforcement provisions, follow-through (training, seminars, etc.)
2. *Implementation* national implementing legislation, programmes, plans, reports to be completed on schedule; effective institutions and procedures; transparency in implementation; review of fines and penalties; action under the EC Treaty (Article 171) to combat non-compliance.
3. *Integration of policies*: assessment of environmental implications of proposed Community and national legislation.
4. *Involvement of the public*: encourage participation, complaints facilities, access to the courts.
5. *Environmental liability*: mechanisms to ensure that environmental damage is remedied.
6. *Reports on implementation*: Commission reports to serve as a performance indicator and an incentive mechanism.

Source: adapted from European Commission, 'Towards Sustainability', COM(92)23 II, and *Official Journal*, 1993 C138, Chapter 9.

7.3 'INFORMATIONAL' MEASURES

The Community has supplemented its 'traditional' regulatory measures with a set of procedures that generate information on the environmental effects of economic activity. These procedures include environmental impact assessment, and voluntary schemes for environmental auditing and eco-labelling. Informational measures such as these can support the implementation of regulatory standards: environmental auditing examines conformity with relevant regulations, while eligibility for an eco-label is confined to products that comply with Community health, safety and environmental regulations. At the same time, good environmental performance is broadly defined, and this stimulates environmental protection beyond the minimum requirements specified in legislation.

The onus is placed on participating organizations to supply information to interested parties, who may then draw their own conclusions. Recipients of information are enabled, in various ways, to reward good environmental performance and penalize poor performance. Conversely, organizations stand to gain from a perception that they and their products are environmentally friendly.

Good environmental credentials can help enterprises to sell their products, to attract finance and to maintain a favourable image. The eco-label gives an advantage in the market through its appeal to environmentally aware consumers. Investors are reassured if environmental performance is subject to independent verification: risks of subsequent liability are minimized if it can be shown that all reasonable steps are taken to avoid environmental damage. Major projects are less likely to suffer disruption if preceded by thorough consultation based on independent assessment of their environmental impacts. Moreover, informative procedures can be reinforced by 'second round' effects: for example, environmental audits may be made a condition for favourable insurance rates; or procurement contracts may specify that products to be supplied should carry an eco-label.

7.3.1 Environmental impact assessment

Environmental impact assessment (EIA) consists of methods and procedures to incorporate environmental considerations into a decision-making process. Many member states have long established EIA systems (surveyed in Lee and Wood 1978) which predate the Community's framework legislation, Directive 85/337. Although EIA makes an important contribution to a preventive approach (which is one of the basic principles of Community environmental policy), the Directive was also needed to combat distortions of competition in the single market caused by differences between national regulations.

The difficulties of reconciling disparate systems have led to serious complications: by the end of 1992 (3½ years after the deadline) only two member states (France and the UK) had properly transposed the Directive into national law (COM(93)320, p. 100). The transposition process has also been complicated by the wide scope of the Directive: the projects involved come within the remit of different ministries—transport, energy and industry, as well as environment—and the authorization system may involve both central and regional tiers of government. Furthermore, compliance may require the use of different types of legislative instrument, and the development of new procedures, particularly for public consultation (COM(93)28, p. 64).

The Directive requires member states to ensure that prior assessment is made of the environmental impacts of certain categories of project (listed in Annex 1 of the Directive). These are large investment projects which, because of (*inter alia*) their nature, size or location, can be expected to have significant environmental impacts. Other types of project (listed in Annex 2) may be subject to assessment if member states consider that their characteristics justify this. A broad framework is specified for assessments, to include a description of the project and the environment likely to be affected, alternatives that have been assessed, significant environmental effects and mitigation measures (Article 5).

The main force of the EIA procedure is to create a presumption that information on environmental impacts of major projects will be available before project commencement. The requirements of Directive 85/337 are essentially procedural: an assessment must be made, and the public informed and consulted, before the public authorities give the necessary planning consent for the project (Article 6). There is widespread dissatisfaction with the implementation of these procedures. The Commission receives numerous complaints from individuals and organizations in member states concerning the authorization of projects without a proper assessment of the environmental impacts or with inadequate public consultation (COM(93)320, p. 103).

Complaints have also arisen over the poor quality of the assessments supplied by project promoters, and the relegation of environmental assessments to the status of a 'marginal consideration' in the decision-making process. In some instances there may be a misunderstanding of the scope of the Directive: it has no 'quality control' mechanism to ensure that assessments are of a high standard, nor is there any guidance as to how the information generated by the assessment should be weighed in appraisal of the project as a whole. So, provided that the procedural requirements are met, such complaints have to be addressed to the national authorities, rather than to the Commission.

The existing EIA procedure focuses on the analysis of variants of a specific scheme, prior to its authorization: there is little guidance on the initial (preliminary planning) and the final (post-authorization) stages of a project. To be meaningful, project appraisal should begin with an open-minded identification of all options (including that of doing nothing) and should avoid premature narrowing of choices; however, with respect to this essential preliminary stage the requirements of Directive 85/337 are very limited, specifying only that assessments should include 'where appropriate an outline of the main alternatives studied by the developer and an indication of the main reasons for his choice, taking into account the environmental effects' (Annex III(2)). Moreover, the Directive does not acknowledge the need for continuing appraisal, and has no provision for monitoring to ensure compliance with the terms of a project's authorization and to identify any modifications that may prove to be necessary to mitigate adverse impacts. The Commission has recognized some of these criticisms, and has brought forward a Proposal (European Commission 1994b) designed to strengthen the preliminary screening of projects, to broaden the scope of information to be included in EIAs, and to reinforce the influence of EIAs in project decisions.

Environmental assessment is relevant not only for individual projects, but also at a strategic level. (For example, while a project assessment would compare the environmental impacts of various options for a highway project, the strategic assessment could consider alternative forms of transport provision.) A strategic assessment, although inevitably less precise in some respects, offers an opportunity to introduce the environmental dimension at an earlier stage in the planning process, and to take account of environmental impacts at a broader level than is possible in a project assessment. In this way synergies between impacts can be identified, and it will be possible to streamline project assessments by establishing a framework at the strategic level for assessment of project impacts.

Strategic assessment is incorporated in the planning of Community structural fund expenditure programmes under Objectives 1, 2 and 5b (concerning respectively regional development, recovery of declining industrial regions, and rural development—see Sec. 3.4.2). Outline expenditure plans submitted by member states must include appraisals of the existing environmental situation and the environmental effects of proposed strategies and operations (Regulation 2081/93, Articles 8(4), 9(8) and 11a(5)). However, there is a gap between this general outline assessment and the detailed assessment of individual projects. To fill this gap, the Commission has indicated that it will submit a Proposal for a Directive requiring systematic assessment of plans, policies and programmes (Court of Auditors 1992: 23).

Environmental assessment procedures have thus far concentrated on the assembly of information; perhaps less attention has been given to the operational use of this information in decision-making. Further consideration may be given in future to the role of environmental assessment procedures in the definition of issues and as an integral part of the decision framework. This would then emphasize optimal solutions with an environmental dimension, rather than the limitation of environmental damage resulting from decisions taken according to other criteria.

One possible line of approach is the development of decision frameworks that take account of the economic value (broadly defined) of environmental resources. Another important issue is the incidence of costs: if a project causes damage to the environment, then the polluter-pays principle (see Sec. 7.4) suggests that the person responsible—the project developer—should bear the full costs of this damage.

7.3.2   Environmental management and auditing

The concept of 'good environmental practice' has been developed primarily by organizations and industry associations, to demonstrate that their activities are not inconsistent with care for the environment. (One example is Winter (1988), which sets out a checklist for 'environmentalist business management'.) The objective typically is to integrate an environmental dimension into management decisions (at all levels), and to demonstrate sound environmental performance to stakeholders, public authorities and the public.

Recent years have seen a considerable growth in environmental auditing, notably by large multinational enterprises. This has been undertaken on a voluntary basis by managements that have appreciated the benefit to their own organization. The benefit to the enterprise may take a number of forms, including:

- an enhanced corporate image, with employees and the public
- improved working relationships with regulatory authorities
- reduced exposure to litigation and adverse publicity
- improvements in employee training
- potential cost savings—for example by reduction in waste
- information to assist in investment planning
- lower risks of emergencies, and better emergency planning

The Community has acted to formalize, and to structure, the environmental management procedure (and there have been similar initiatives in member states, for example the British Standard BS7750—see Gilbert 1993). Regulation 1836/93 establishes a Community eco-management and audit scheme for industrial companies. Participation in the scheme is voluntary, and without prejudice to any requirements of Community or national law. Participating companies must adopt environmental policies and management systems, conduct environmental reviews and audits at their sites of operation, set objectives for environmental performance and prepare environmental statements for each site. At each stage the procedure is subject to independent validation, and the validated statements are disseminated 'as appropriate' to the public (Article 3).

Areas covered by the auditing procedure include:

- present performance of environmental management, systems and equipment
- compliance with legal and regulatory requirements
- compliance with corporate standards and policies
- risks of damage to the environment or human health
- shortcomings in performance or compliance

Environmental auditing disseminates information, and its influence on management depends upon the use that is made of the information. Success in this respect crucially depends upon the ability of the public, and interested bodies, to assess the results of the audit. There are some analogies with the auditing of financial management; however, there is also a crucial difference, inasmuch as environmental audits are—at present—entirely voluntary. Nor is there a convenient summary measure of environmental performance which is comparable with 'bottom line' financial performance.

7.3.3   Eco-labelling

An 'eco-label' identifies products that conform to specified environmental criteria: its purpose is to encourage the manufacture and use of 'environmentally friendly' products. In Germany the 'Blue Angel' scheme for eco-labelling (inaugurated in 1978) has achieved wide coverage and consumer recognition, although non-German companies, while free to participate, have made relatively little use of the scheme. Following the success of the German scheme, the Commission brought forward Proposals for a Community scheme, pre-empting moves to establish national eco-labels in other member states (COM(91)37, p. 3). A Community-level initiative was desirable, because the German experience of low participation by foreign companies suggests that national schemes could constitute a non-tariff barrier to competition in the single market.

The Community eco-labelling scheme was introduced in 1992 (Regulation 880/92). Participation is entirely voluntary. Companies may apply for the award of a label to a specific product; if the application is successful the label may be displayed on, and used to advertise, the product. Refusal of the label does not in itself imply any restriction on marketing a product.

The standard for award of the label is a relative rather than absolute concept: this is clear from the original Commission Proposal (COM(91)37), which stated that products should have 'an overall environmental impact significantly less than that for other products *in the same product group*' (Article 1; emphasis added). The Regulation defines product groups as 'competing products which serve similar purposes and which have equivalence of use' (Article 5). Environmental impacts vary—in nature and in magnitude—between product groups, and some product categories are inherently more damaging than others. For example, even the 'cleanest' motor vehicle emits more pollutants and noise than a bicycle; so, while consumers may help to improve the environment by choosing cars with relatively low environmental impacts, they could do even more by switching to transport modes that are more environmentally benign.

Product groups, and criteria for award of the label, are defined by the Commission, in collaboration with a committee representing member states, with advice from a 'consultation forum', comprising representatives of industry and commerce, and consumer and environmental organizations (Article 7). Labels are awarded to specific products by 'competent bodies' designated by member states (Article 10). Criteria and awards have a limited life; this allows for changes over time in concepts of 'environmental friendliness', as technology develops and as environmental perceptions and priorities vary.

The eco-label represents a simplification of a complex reality. It tells the consumer that a product is judged to be environmentally friendly in comparison with its close substitutes. The experts' judgement is a synthesis of a mass of diverse information. The award criteria are defined with reference to the entire life cycle of a product, including its manufacture, distribution and utilisation, and its eventual recycling or disposal as waste. Assessments must be made of environmental impacts that take various forms, including energy consumption, noise, waste generation, contamination of land, air and water, and impacts on natural resources. These environmental effects must then be weighed; and complex choices can arise; for example, if a product is energy-intensive but in other respects benign, is it better or worse than an alternative that consumes little energy but generates moderate to severe air and water pollution?

7.4 ECONOMIC INCENTIVES AND THE POLLUTER PAYS PRINCIPLE

The Community action programme 'Towards Sustainability' stresses the role of economic incentives in the 'shared responsibility' for sustainable development (COM(92)23 II, p. 67). The authorities should ensure that appropriate incentives exist, and are properly understood; and it is for enterprises to respond to these incentives. There are three main types of mechanism which provide a direct financial incentive for 'environmentally friendly' economic behaviour:

1. Subsidies.
2. Legal liability.
3. Taxes and charges.

7.4.1 The polluter pays principle

The EC Treaty (Article 130r(2)) states that one of the fundamental principles of Community environmental policy is that 'the polluter should pay'. In economic terms, the purpose of the polluter pays principle (PPP) is to guide the allocation of resources in a way that takes proper account of requirements for environmental protection. These requirements are determined by judgements with respect to the costs of environmental damage, and the costs and benefits of avoiding damage.

The PPP provides a framework for incentives to take proper account of the environmental dimension in economic activities. Theoretically, the environment could be fully protected by *cost internalization*, with a full monetary valuation of all costs of environmental damage, and the charging of these costs to those responsible for the damage (or potential damage). A system on these lines would ensure that all decisions took full account of the consequences for the environment. Any intensification in environmental pressures would be reflected in an increase in environmental damage costs, which would in turn raise the incentive to avoid environmental damage.

This represents an idealized model. In practice, the valuation of environmental damage, and potential damage, is—unavoidably—very imperfect, and in some instances impracticable (COM(92)23 II, p. 67). (Estimated valuations of environmental damage drawn from various studies are presented in COM(92)23 III, pp. 80–1.) Moreover, the effects of preventive action, in terms of the resulting environmental quality, are in many instances uncertain, and may vary over time. The Commission has outlined a number of measures to improve understanding of this relationship (see Box 7.5), so that economic mechanisms can be instituted 'to internalize all

BOX 7.5
Measures required to determine environmental costs

- Economic evaluation of natural resource stocks
- Renewable resource indicators, showing rates of depletion and renewal
- Development of environmental economic statistics, and modification of economic indicators (such as GDP), to reflect the value of, and damage to, environmental resources
- Development of cost–benefit analysis to include environmental impacts
- Redefinition of accounting methodologies to show costs of consumption and use of environmental resources

Source: European Commission, 'Towards Sustainability', COM(92)23 II, and *Official Journal*, 1993 C138, Section 7.4.

external environmental costs incurred during the whole life-cycle of products' (COM(92)23 II, p. 67); it remains to be seen how far this can be achieved in practice.

The objectives of environmental protection can be—and usually are—achieved without cost internalization. As has been seen, Community environmental policies have hitherto relied heavily on regulatory standards, and in practice the main requirement for observance of the PPP has been that those responsible for emissions to the environment should cover the costs of compliance with regulatory standards (see Box 7.6).

BOX 7.6
The polluter pays principle

The EC Treaty (Article 130r(2)) states that one of the fundamental principles of Community environmental policy is that 'the polluter should pay'. Guidance on implementation of this principle is given in Council Recommendation 75/436, the annex to which includes the following definitions:

1. *Who is 'the polluter'?* 'someone who directly or indirectly damages the environment, or creates conditions leading to such damage. [paragraph 3]
2. *What is to be paid for?* 'the costs of such measures as are necessary to eliminate ... pollution, or to reduce it so as to comply with ... standards or equivalent measures laid down by the public authorities. [paragraph 2]

This conception of the principle falls well short of a requirement that polluters (or potential polluters) cover *all* the costs arising from their activities. Point 2 excludes costs relating to damage to the environment, such as expenditures on remedial measures, payment of compensation to those who suffer from pollution and penalties for damage where there is no financial cost (such as effects on wildlife habitats). Nor is there any provision whereby charges are levied for the use of the assimilative capacity of the environment, which is a scarce resource.

The main thrust of the 1975 Recommendation is to restrict payment to polluters of subsidies which may distort competition within the single market. To achieve this, the Commission (using its powers to regulate subsidies under Article 93 EC Treaty) has issued guidelines to member states concerning state aid for environmental purposes. The Commission initially envisaged that state aid would be phased out over a period of transition (between 1974 and 1980) to 'full implementation' of the polluter pays principle. Following repeated extensions of the transition period, the objective of 'full implementation', defined as the absence of subsidies, appears to have been abandoned: guidelines issued in 1994 conceded that subsidies, albeit 'a second best solution', nevertheless 'have their place' (European Commission 1994a, p. 3).

Moreover, subsidy payments to polluters—the antithesis of cost internalization—can give incentives for environmental protection. The Commission now accepts that such payments can, in some circumstances, be a valid policy instrument when linked to investments needed for the achievement of environmental standards.

The existing concept of the PPP does not include any obligation to pay for the use of the absorptive capacity of the environment—which is an increasingly scarce (and valuable) resource. There is not even a general requirement that polluters should meet the costs of damage which they cause to the environment, although the Commission has been considering mechanisms for strengthening civil liability for such damage (see Sec. 7.4.3).

7.4.2   Subsidies for environmental protection

The Community's original objective in adopting the polluter pays principle (PPP) was to ensure that polluters bear the full costs of compliance with environmental standards prescribed by Community or national regulations. Conversely, governments should not use environmental protection as a justification for subsidies that distort competition and investment in the single market.

The EC Treaty (Article 92(1)) generally prohibits financial assistance from public authorities which may distort competition and affect trade between member states. Exceptions may be made 'to facilitate the development of certain economic activities or certain economic areas' (Article 92(3)(c)). The Commission is responsible for regulating state aid payments (Article 93) and has since 1974 issued guidance on the types and amounts of aid for environmental purposes which it regards as normally permissible under the Treaty. Subsidies to cover operating costs are generally prohibited, but investment aid is permitted in certain circumstances. The Commission originally intended to phase out state aid, as a prelude to 'full implementation' of the PPP, but it now regards subsidies as a legitimate, albeit 'second-best', policy instrument to facilitate environmental improvements (European Commission 1994a: 3).

The prohibitions of Article 92(1) apply 'except as otherwise provided in this Treaty'. The Commission's initial guidance on state aid predates the Treaty provisions for environmental policy (Articles 130r–t and 100a(3) and (4), which were added to the EC Treaty in 1987). These provisions specify various requirements and objectives, the achievement of which may be facilitated by the use of financial instruments. Hence, while these Articles do not mention the use of state aids (or indeed Community financial instruments) for environmental purposes, inclusion of a set of objectives in the Treaty must imply some provision for measures necessary for the attainment of these objectives.

Moreover, environmental protection is a dynamic process. The Treaty provisions on competition derive from an essentially static concept of economic efficiency, which fails to take account of the continuing evolution of economic activity, and its environmental impacts. Considerations of short-term competitive efficiency must be balanced against the long-term benefit of subsidies as an instrument to accelerate environmental improvements and facilitate adjustment to new policy measures. The changing preoccupations of environmental policy are starkly illustrated by comparison of the Community's first and fifth environmental programmes (See Council Declaration (1973) and COM(92)23 II): the latter is strongly concerned with climate change, and sets out proposals for stabilization of CO_2 emissions and a phasing out of CFCs. None of this figured in the first programme, because in 1974 the significance of the problem had yet to be recognized.

The institution of higher environmental standards may be retarded if governments regard the costs of adjustment as unacceptably high; but these costs can be mitigated by financial support to the industrial sectors that are affected. Hence the 1994 guidance on state aids for environmental protection (European Commission 1994a) states that authorization will normally be given for financial support towards investment necessary for compliance with *new* environmental standards: eligibility is restricted to industrial plant that has been in operation for at least two years (p. 6). The purpose of the two-year limit is to confine assistance to investment necessary for compliance with *unanticipated* environmental regulations—so allowance is made for a 'lead time' prior to the enactment of policy measures, within which it is possible to anticipate the eventual regulatory requirements. The value of assistance is limited to 15 per cent of the extra investment expenditure necessary to meet environmental objectives, although higher limits apply for small and medium-sized enterprises. There is no theoretical basis for this 15 per cent limit: it is simply the final point on a degressive scale in force between 1974 and 1980, which was originally designed to phase out state aid altogether.

A more generous limit—of 30 per cent of qualifying investment expenditure—applies to state aid that is designed to encourage firms to improve on mandatory standards, or to improve on their environmental performance in the absence of such standards. There is no restriction on aid to support environmental information campaigns or purchases of environmentally friendly products, if this does not confer a financial benefit on a specific firm (European Commission 1994a: 7–8).

7.4.3   Liability for environmental damage

A legal liability for damage to the environment contributes to the implementation of the polluter pays principle. Hitherto this has been of greatest value in cases in which damage occurs as a result of fault on the part of the polluter; it has been less effective for damage that was due to *force majeure*, or for chronic damage arising from continuing emissions (which are in any case usually subject to prior authorization by pollution control authorities).

The legal systems in Community member states include provisions for compensation for environmental damage. Persons who suffer financial losses may obtain redress by taking legal action against the polluter(s) whose actions gave rise to the losses in question. In general, it is necessary to establish fault on the part of the polluters.

This legal mechanism is therefore restricted in its application: if the damage, or its sources, are diffused over space or time, or if the polluter is not judged to be at fault, there is little chance of compensation for environmental damage. Thus for example fishery undertakings may be able to claim compensation from an oil tanker operator for financial losses resulting from reduced catches following an oil spill; but there is no provision for compensation to future generations for the effects of climate change, or species extinctions.

The Commission has published a Green Paper on civil liability for environmental damage, which concludes that it can be a valuable instrument for environmental protection under certain conditions. Specifically, its usefulness depends on the existence of a party with a legal interest who can bring an action for damage, and on the extent to which damage is measurable and immediate, and is caused by a finite act on the part of identifiable parties (COM(93)47, p. 24).

The environmental effectiveness of polluters' liability may be increased in future by an extension of strict liability. This would ease the burden of establishing that environmental damage was caused by the fault of the defendant, although it would still be necessary to establish that it was caused by the *actions* (or lack of action) of the defendant. The Green Paper concludes that such a system would give a better incentive for risk management to avoid environmental damage. The Commission has already devised a plan for strict liability in a Proposal for a Directive on environmental damage caused by wastes (European Commission 1991b).

A strict liability regime would reinforce incentives for avoidance of environmental damage, because risks are borne not only by those who cause damage but also by the financial institutions that support their activities. (Under the waste damage Proposal (Article 32), insurance cover for civil liability would be compulsory.) So banks and insurers would have a direct incentive to identify the risks to the environment, and to oblige their clients to take action to limit these risks (see COM(92)23 II, p. 27). 'Passive' measures to avoid actions that could be construed as fault would no longer be sufficient: instead an 'activist' approach would be required, to anticipate and prevent the possibility of environmental damage.

Where liability cannot be enforced—because the damage is diffuse, or its cause cannot be identified—the Green Paper recommends a 'joint compensation' system to cover the costs of environmental restoration, financed by 'the economic sector most closely connected to the presumed source of the damage' (COM(93)47, pp. 27–8).

7.4.4   Environmental charges

Charges are levied in all member states for environmental services such as waste water treatment and solid waste collection and disposal. Where these services are performed for commercial or industrial enterprises, charges should equate to a market price for the service being performed: a charge below this level may contravene the Community state aid regulations (Article 91 EC).

Several member states have systems of charging for emissions to the environment. There are well established schemes in France, the Netherlands, Germany and Italy under which charges are levied for discharge into watercourses; the charges generate revenue to finance environmental protection measures, and—in some instances—give an incentive to limit emissions. (The various charging schemes are detailed in OECD 1989.)

In principle, variations in the coverage and structure of charging systems could distort competition within the single market. For example, enterprises might be at a disadvantage if their competitors in other countries pay lower charges for the same level of effluent discharge, and this would amount to a competitive distortion unless the variation in charges could be related to objective factors such as pressures on the capacity of the receiving environment.

The Community has long been aware of the potential for distortion of competition, and of the case—in principle—for harmonization of charging. In 1975 the Council recommended that 'the Community should endeavour to standardize the methods of calculation used by the Member States to set charges' (Council Recommendation 75/436, Annex Paragraph 4). In 1992 the fifth environmental action programme envisaged that 'intervention at Community level may be necessary to ensure that charging systems are designed in a transparent and comparable way, and to ensure that distortions of competition within the Community are avoided' (COM(92)23 II, p. 67). However, little has actually been achieved in this direction—largely owing to the technical complexity of the subject, and to the reluctance of member states to modify established national systems.

7.5   INTEGRATION OF ENVIRONMENTAL AND ECONOMIC POLICIES

The new emphasis on sustainable development implicitly broadens the scope of the EC Treaty requirement (Article 130r(2)) concerning integration of the environmental dimension in Community policies. Sustainability cannot be assured solely by reactive environmental protection measures which mitigate the 'side-effects' of economic activity. It is necessary instead to consider the nature and context of the economic system, the factors that determine its growth path, and the policy measures that may influence its sustainability—favourably or otherwise.

Both environmental and economic policies now envisage a mobilization of economic incentives to change the development path of the Community. The environmental action programme advocates 'getting the prices right', so that 'market forces ... reflect the full costs of production and consumption, including the environmental costs' (COM(92)23 II, Sec. 7.4). The Commission's 1993 White Paper on growth, competitiveness and employment sets out 'thoughts on a new development model', envisaging changes in the technological base to permit economic growth with less environmental degradation—for example by increasing energy efficiency, product lives and recycling, and by reducing the generation of wastes (COM(93)700, p. 178).

Action by the Community can stimulate these changes. One possible initiative is a restructuring of the tax system (see Sec. 7.5.1). More generally, policy-making in all areas can give greater weight to environmental considerations. In this context the Community environmental action programme has identified transport and agriculture as key areas for the integration of economic and environmental policies (COM(92)23 II, Sec. 4). Policies and measures to promote sustainable development in these areas are considered in Chapters 8 and 9.

7.5.1   Taxation and the environment

The White Paper on growth, competitiveness and employment identifies two fundamental economic problems: 'insufficient use of labour resources and ... excessive use of natural resources' (COM(93)700, p. 178). This is the result of incentives that generate high unemployment and over-exploitation of natural resources: taxes are levied on 'goods'—products and the labour input to produce them—whereas 'bads' are usually untaxed, notwithstanding the damage they cause to the environment and the quality of life. The solution is to tax 'bads'; this would tend to discourage over-exploitation of the environment and permit reduced taxation of 'goods'.

As noted in Sec. 6.3.3, serious economic difficulties arise from the pressure of social expenditure on government budgets. The White Paper argues that a switch from taxation of employment to taxation of environmentally damaging activities could alleviate this problem. Incentives would be generated for increased employment, which would tend to reduce expenditure needed to pay for unemployment benefits; furthermore, environmental taxes would provide an economically efficient means of financing the remaining social expenditure (COM(93)700, p. 15).

A restructuring of taxation on such lines would enhance the environmental dimension in fiscal policy, which is very much in accordance with the EC Treaty (Article 130r) requirement for an integrated approach. Although there have been extensive deliberations over 'green' taxes, and a number of instances in which member states have introduced such taxes (see OECD 1993), the Community's record in this respect is not wholly impressive.

The Community enacted extensive fiscal legislation in connection with the programme establishing the framework for the single market, which was completed in 1992 (see Sec. 3.1.2). If this was an opportunity to extend the environmental dimension of fiscal policy, it was largely missed. There is—thus far—only one major instance in which the Community has explicitly taken account of environmental considerations in product taxation: this is the tax differential between leaded and unleaded petrol. The minimum excise duty on leaded petrol is 50 ECUs per 1000 litres (approximately 17 per cent) above the minimum rate for unleaded petrol (Directive 92/82, Articles 3–4).

There are only three product areas (alcoholic beverages, tobacco and mineral oils) subject to Community legislation on excise taxes. Some member states have introduced environmentally related product taxes (see OECD 1993: 44), but they are constrained to avoid trade distortions and the use of frontier controls in the single market.

Value added tax (VAT), the general tax on products and services, has at present little environmental dimension. Indeed, Community VAT legislation appears to preclude incentives for the consumption of environmentally friendly products, or disincentives for the consumption of products that damage the environment. Member states are required to apply a 'standard' rate of tax, which must be not less than 15 per cent (Directive 92/77, Article 1(1)). Some categories of goods and services may be taxed at one or two reduced rates (which must be at least 5 per cent); the only reduced-rate category with an environmental connection is 'services supplied in connection with street cleaning, refuse collection and waste treatment'. Exemptions from VAT in a few member states are permitted to continue, although this provision is not used for environmental purposes; indeed, in the UK it has had an 'anti-environmental' effect, since fuel for domestic heating (previously exempt from VAT) is subject to a special 8 per cent VAT rate (under the Finance Act 1993 (Section 42)), while home insulation materials are subject to tax at the standard UK VAT rate of 17½ per cent.

Fiscal incentives can be used to encourage environmentally friendly production processes, but the difficulties of operating at national level are even greater than in the case of product taxes. For instance, tax concessions for the use of recycled materials are difficult to administer, because discrimination must be avoided against products imported from other member states. One example involved a reduced rate of tax for 'regenerated' mineral oil (which is technically indistinguishable from the primary product): eligibility was confined to oil regenerated under the supervision of the national authorities—thus excluding imports. The Court of Justice held that the member state must either abolish the tax concession or extend it to regenerated oil imported from other member states (Case 21/79). So the tax incentive would not be viable in the absence of a system for certification that imported oil was actually regenerated—and such a system would require Community-wide mutually recognized supervision of the regeneration process.

There would appear to be a case for Community initiatives to co-ordinate environmental taxes, on the same grounds that originally led to the introduction of VAT because it was 'in the interest of the common market to achieve such harmonisation of legislation concerning turnover taxes as will eliminate ... factors which may distort competition' (Directive 67/227).

7.5.2   The 'carbon/energy tax' Proposal

The main Commission initiative on taxation for environmental purposes is its 1992 Proposal for a carbon-cum-energy tax (COM(92)226). This was designed to promote energy efficiency and to meet the Community's objective of stabilization of carbon dioxide emissions in the year 2000 at 1990 levels (Council Decision 94/69). (Some member states—notably Germany and Denmark—have set themselves targets involving a substantial reduction in emissions: see Skjærseth 1994.) The Commission's tax Proposal has an element of conditionality, designed to ensure that it does not put Community industry at a competitive disadvantage: it is dependent on the introduction of similar or equivalent measures by other OECD member states (COM(92)226, Article 1(3)).

The proposed carbon and energy tax would provide incentives for a more efficient use of energy, and to reduce consumption of high carbon fuels. There would be a two-part fiscal mechanism combining an energy tax with a tax based on the carbon content of fuels: the latter would give an incentive to reduce the consumption of fossil fuels with a high carbon content, while the energy tax would deter increased use of nuclear energy as a substitute for fossil fuels.

The Commission estimated that the tax would initially raise energy costs by the equivalent of $3 per barrel of oil, rising to $10 per barrel by the end of the century (COM(92)226, p. 11). It is envisaged that the tax should be 'budget-neutral', offset by reductions in other taxes, and that the revenue would accrue to the authorities in member states. The tax is not intended to be a Community 'own resource' (see Sec. 2.3.3), although there is no reason in principle why it could not be used as such, and supplant revenue requirements from existing own resources such as VAT; indeed, such a development would be entirely consistent with the philosophy of the 1993 White Paper (COM(93)700) in switching the tax burden from 'goods' to 'bads' (see Sec. 7.5.1).

The Commission Proposal is subject, as a fiscal measure, to unanimous decision-making in the Council (Article 99 EC), and it is by no means assured of enactment. The United Kingdom has expressed opposition on grounds of subsidiarity, and has proposed that the tax be 'optional'; and suggestions have been made to exempt the 'cohesion' countries (ENDS 1993: 35). Such modifications would appear inconsistent with the spirit of the single market. The purpose of the proposed tax is to utilize the market mechanism, so that increases in energy efficiency and emission abatement are concentrated in areas where they can be achieved at lowest cost. Since climate change has a global effect, the environmental impact of emissions does not depend on their location—so a lower tax rate for 'cohesion' countries cannot be justified on environmental grounds. A more rational approach (see Skjærseth 1994: 39) is to share the burden by financial transfers through instruments such as LIFE (see Sec. 7.1.3) and the Cohesion Fund (see Sec. 3.5).

7.6 ENVIRONMENTAL POLICY: KEY POINTS AND ISSUES

Much of the European Community's interest in environmental protection arose in the context of single market legislation. Many national regulations with ostensibly environmental objectives were in need of harmonization. The Community has also had a significant role in measures to combat transfrontier and global environmental impacts. As the single market developed, and as the international dimensions of environmental problems became more apparent, it became increasingly clear that policy measures at national level had their limitations. So—in accordance with subsidiarity—environmental problems call for action at Community level.

Community environmental policies have deployed various types of measure—regulation, 'voluntary' instruments and (to a limited extent) economic instruments. Their success, as reflected in the state of the environment, has been mixed.

The declared objective of the Community is now to pursue sustainable development, through the integration of an environmental dimension in all policy areas. The Commission has envisaged a new development model, which would, *inter alia*, shift the burden of taxation on to environmentally damaging activities. Practice has not—thus far—matched these aspirations: existing Community fiscal legislation has taken little account of environmental considerations.

In the context of Community policies, the following key issues may be identified:

● The Community has instituted environmental measures in order to prevent distortion of the single market, and as a policy response to concerns for environmental protection: to what extent is Community action in this area consistent with the principle of subsidiarity?
● The EC Treaty calls for integration of the environmental dimension in Community policies: how far is this principle observed in practice? What are the obstacles to its implementation?
● There is now a substantial body of Community environmental legislation: what has it achieved? What are the limitations of the regulatory approach embodied in much of this legislation?

- The Community has also developed 'informational' environmental measures including impact assessment, auditing and eco-labelling: what factors influence the success of these measures?
- The Community has adopted the polluter-pays principle and has declared its support for economic incentives to achieve environmental objectives: to what extent do Community policies reflect this commitment?

REFERENCES

Court of Auditors (1992) 'Special Report No 3/92 concerning the environment', *Official Journal*, 1992 C245.

EIB (1994) *Annual Report 1993*, European Investment Bank, Luxembourg.

ENDS (1993) 'Ministers agree air pollution rules, but row again on climate change', *Environmental Data Services Report* no. 221, p. 35.

European Commission (1984) *Ten Years of Community Environment Policy*, European Commission, Brussels.

European Commission (1987) *The State of the Environment in the European Community 1986*, 2nd edn, Office of Official Publications, Luxembourg.

European Commission (1991a) 'Eighth annual report on the monitoring of the application of European Community legislation', *Official Journal*, 1991 C338.

European Commission (1991b) 'Amended Proposal for a Council Directive on civil liability for damage caused by waste', *Official Journal*, 1991 C192/6.

European Commission (1992) *European Community Environmental Legislation* (6 vols), European Commission, Brussels.

European Commission (1994a) 'Community guidelines on state aid for environmental protection', *Official Journal*, 1994 C72/3.

European Commission (1994b) Proposal for a Council Directive amending Council Directive 85/337/EEC', *Official Journal*, 1994 C130/8.

European Council (1990) *Declaration on the Environment*, European Council, Dublin.

Gilbert, M. J. (1993) *Achieving Environmental Management Standards: a Step-by-Step Guide to Meeting BS7750*, Pitman, London.

Lee, N. and Wood, C. (1978) 'The assessment of environmental impacts in project appraisal in the European Communities', *Journal of Common Market Studies*, 16(3) 189–210.

OECD (1989) *Economic Instruments for Environmental Protection*, Organisation for Economic Co-operation and Development, Paris.

OECD (1993) *Taxation and the Environment: Complementary Policies*, Organisation for Economic Co-operation and Development, Paris.

Skjærseth, J. B. (1994) 'The climate policy of the EC: too hot to handle', *Journal of Common Market Studies*, 32(1).

Task Force (1990) *'1992': The Environmental Dimension*, Task Force Environment and the Internal Market, Brussels.

Winter, G. (1988) *Business and the Environment*, McGraw-Hill GmbH, Hamburg.

Community legislation

Regulations

Regulation 880/92, on a Community eco-label award scheme, *Official Journal*, 1992 L99/1.

Regulation 1973/92, establishing a financial instrument for the environment (LIFE), *Official Journal*, 1992 L206/1.

Regulation 1836/93, allowing voluntary participation by companies in the industrial sector in a Community eco-management and audit scheme, *Official Journal*, 1993 L168/1.

Regulation 2081/93, amending Regulation 2052/88 on the tasks of the structural funds, *Official Journal*, 1993 L193/5.

Directives

Directive 67/227, on the harmonization of legislation of member states concerning turnover taxes, *Official Journal*, 1967 71/1301.

Directive 67/548, on the approximation of provisions relating to dangerous substances, *Official Journal*, 1967 196/1.

Directive 70/220, on measures against air pollution by motor vehicles, *Official Journal*, 1970 L76/1.

Directive 75/442, on waste, *Official Journal*, 1975 L194/39.

Directive 76/464, on pollution caused by certain dangerous substances discharged into the aquatic environment, *Official Journal*, 1976 L129/23.

Directive 78/319, on toxic and dangerous waste, *Official Journal*, 1978 L84/43.

Directive 79/409, on the conservation of wild birds, *Official Journal*, 1979 L103/1.

Directive 79/923, on the quality required of shellfish waters, *Official Journal*, 1979 L281/47.

Directive 80/778, relating to the quality of water for human consumption, *Official Journal*, 1980 L229/11.

Directive 82/176, on discharges of mercury by the chloralkali industry, *Official Journal*, 1982 L81/29.

Directive 84/360, on the combating of air pollution from industrial plants, *Official Journal*, 1984 L188/20.

Directive 84/631, on the supervision and control of transfrontier shipments of hazardous waste, *Official Journal*, 1984, L326/31.

Directive 85/337, on the assessment of the effects of certain public and private projects on the environment, *Official Journal*, 1985 L175/40.

Directive 88/609, on the limitation of emissions of certain pollutants into the air from large combustion installations, *Official Journal*, 1988 L336/1.

Directive 89/458, amending, with regard to cars below 1.4 litres, Directive 70/220, *Official Journal*, 1989 L226/1.

Directive 90/313, on the freedom of access to information on the environment, *Official Journal*, 1990 L158/56.

Directive 91/271, concerning urban waste water treatment, *Official Journal*, 1991 L135/40.

Directive 91/692, standardizing and rationalizing reports on the implementation of Directives relating to the environment, *Official Journal*, 1991 L377/48.

Directive 92/43, on the conservation of natural and semi-natural habitats and of wild flora and fauna, *Official Journal*, 1992 L206/7.

Directive 92/77, supplementing the common system of value added tax, *Official Journal*, 1992 L316/1.

Directive 92/82, on the approximation of the rates of excise duties on mineral oils, *Official Journal*, 1992 L316/19.

Parliament and Council Directive 94/62, on packaging and packaging waste, *Official Journal*, 1994 L365/10.

Recommendations, Declarations, Resolutions, Decisions and Common Positions

Council Recommendation 75/436/Euratom, ECSC, EEC, regarding cost allocation and action by the public authorities on environmental matters, *Official Journal*, 1975 L194/1.

Council Declaration (1973), on the programme of action of the European Communities on the environment, *Official Journal*, 1973 C112.

Council Resolution (1977), on the continuation and implementation of a European Community policy and action programme on the environment, *Official Journal*, 1977 C139.

Council Resolution (1983), on the continuation and implementation of a European Community policy and action programme on the environment, *Official Journal*, 1983 C46.

Council Resolution (1987), on the continuation and implementation of a European Community policy and action programme on the environment, *Official Journal*, 1987 C328.

Council Resolution (1990), on waste policy, *Official Journal*, 1990 C122/2.

Council Resolution (1993), on a Community Programme of Policy and Action in relation to the Environment and Sustainable Development, *Official Journal*, 1993 C138/1.

Council Decision 94/69 concerning the UN framework Convention on climate change, *Official Journal*, 1994 L33/11.

Common Position (EC) No. 13/94, on the amended Proposal for a Directive on packaging and packaging waste, *Official Journal*, 1994 C137/65.

European Commission documents

SEC(89)934, *A Community Strategy for Waste Management*, 18 September 1989.

COM(91)37, *Proposal for a Council Regulation (EEC) on a Community Award Scheme for an Eco-label*, 11 February 1991.

COM(92)23 II, *Towards Sustainability: a European Community Programme of Policy and Action in relation to the Environment and Sustainable Development*, 27 March 1992 (reproduced in, *Official Journal*, C138, 17 May 1993).

COM(92)23 III, *The State of the Environment in the European Community: Overview*, 27 March 1992.

COM(92)226, *Proposal for a Council Directive Introducing a Tax on CO_2 Emissions and Energy*, 30 June 1992.

COM(93)28, *Report from the Commission on the Implementation of Directive 85/337*, 12 April 1993.

COM(93)47, *Green Paper on Remedying Environmental Damage*, 14 May 1993.

COM(93)320, *Tenth Annual Report on the Monitoring of the Application of Community Law*, 28 April 1993.

COM(93)545, *Commission Report to the European Council on the Adaptation of Existing Legislation to the Subsidiarity Principle*, 24 November 1993.

COM(93)700, *Growth, Competitiveness, Employment: the Challenges and Ways Forward into the 21st Century*, 5 December 1993.

Court judgments

Case 21/79, *Commission v. Italy* [1980] ECR 1.

Case 2/90, *Commission v. Belgium*, Judgment 9 July 1992, not yet reported.

EIGHT

TRANSPORT POLICY

The Community's founders regarded transport as a vital economic sector, since its development was essential for the success of the single market. This remains the case, but transport now has comparable significance in the Community's strategy for sustainable development; and policy-makers face a challenge to reconcile the benefits of mobility with measures to mitigate the environmental impacts of transport.

Consequently the transport policy of the Community has two main themes: promotion of the single market, and safeguarding the environment. The Commission in 1992 published a wide-ranging White Paper (COM(92)494) setting out a framework for transport policies following the inauguration of the single market: the main objectives were provision of adequate infrastructure, and the harmonization, where necessary, of regulations governing transport. Several key issues were identified, among them regulation, infrastructure charging, technological development, harmonization of standards and Community responsibility for external transport relations.

With respect to infrastructure, the EC Treaty (as amended by the 1992 EU (Maastricht) Treaty) calls for Community action to promote interconnection and inter-operability of national transport networks (Article 129b). Specifically, the Community has to establish guidelines and implement technical standardization measures; it may also provide interest subsidies and loan guarantees for national projects with importance for the Community (such as transfrontier highway schemes), and give financial support from the Cohesion Fund (see Sec. 3.5) for infrastructure projects in Greece, Spain, Portugal and Ireland (Article 129c).

8.1 THE COMMON TRANSPORT POLICY AND THE SINGLE MARKET

The EC Treaty provides for a Common Transport Policy, to be implemented 'taking into account the distinctive features of transport'. The identification of transport as a key sector shows its fundamental importance for attainment of the objectives of the Treaty. Freedom of movement, and achievement of a single market, was for many years impeded by restrictive national regulations and the primarily national focus of transport networks. Community transport policies therefore had to focus on the elimination and avoidance of discriminatory regulation, and on the development of infrastructure to transcend national borders.

In order to ensure that regulations governing transport between member states do not operate in discriminatory manner, the Treaty provides for:

1. common rules for international transport to or from, or between, member states (Article 75);

2. conditions under which carriers may operate transport services in another member state (Article 75);
3. prevention of discrimination depending on the country of origin or destination, with respect to rates and conditions for carriage of goods (Article 79; the ECSC Treaty has a similar provision—Article 70);
4. restriction of national measures to protect transport undertakings from competitive pressures (Article 80).

8.1.1 The late development of the Common Transport Policy

Transport, along with agriculture, was specifically identified in the original 1957 EEC Treaty as a key policy area for the common market. However, in marked contrast to the Common Agricultural Policy, the Common Transport Policy for years made little progress. The Commission developed action programmes and legislative Proposals, but usually the Council failed to act. In 1985 the Court of Justice censured the Council, in an action brought by the Parliament, for its failure to enact legislation to fulfil Treaty obligations (Article 75(1)(a) and (b) EC) relating to free circulation and cross-border provision of transport services (Case 13/83).

In the absence of Community policies, transport remained subject to national regulations, price controls and quantitative restrictions on market entry, which were largely incompatible with a single market. Some forty years after the EEC Treaty, movement and operation of vehicles throughout the Community was still partly restricted, and competition was considerably distorted, by different national regulations on capacity and access to the road haulage industry, and by controls on haulage charges (European Commission 1988: 96). Transfrontier road haulage was restricted by bilateral and multilateral quotas, so that hauliers required special licences to move goods between member states. There is evidence that limited availability of quotas led to black markets—one study found that in the UK the price of an annual EC haulage permit in 1986 was in the region of £12 000 (Cooper *et al.* 1987: 24). There was also a general prohibition of 'cabotage' (the possibility for non-resident hauliers to collect and deliver loads within the boundaries of another member state), which caused a large number of journeys without loads: a 1987 study for the Commission estimated that regulatory restrictions increased the number of 'empty' movements across national frontiers by approximately 20 per cent (Ernst & Whinney 1987: Annex III).

Air transport was similarly restricted by bilateral agreements between national governments. These agreements imposed capacity restrictions, excluded non-designated carriers, regulated conditions of service and limited the scope for price competition. On almost all routes designation was limited to no more than one airline per country; in many cases there were pooling agreements, whereby revenue was shared between carriers. In 1987 only one route between two Community countries was operated (under so-called 'fifth freedom' rights) by an airline from a third member state (European Commission 1988: 97).

The Common Transport Policy was eventually 'relaunched' in the mid-1980s, as the Council was prompted to take action by the 1985 Court judgment and the advent of the single European market. In the approach to the 1992 single market deadline, the Council adopted a large amount of legislation to harmonize or—where appropriate—eliminate national regulations.

8.1.2 Single market measures for transport

Removal of national restrictions on transport has significant effects. Traffic is stimulated by reductions in transport rates, prompted by increased productivity and competition. On the other hand, deregulation, and (eventually) unrestricted cabotage permits a more efficient utilization of capacity, and thus tends to *reduce* traffic. The latter effect may be significant for air transport, when the industry is eventually rationalized, but perhaps not for road haulage, where most empty running was due to imbalances in trade between countries (a demand-side effect) rather than to cabotage restrictions (Cooper *et al.* 1987: 9).

Road Transport   At present, and until 1998, Community regulations on transfrontier road haulage services make a distinction between journeys *between* member states and journeys *within* a single member state. The former may be operated by any Community haulier; the latter is restricted by quotas limiting market access for operators registered elsewhere in the Community.

Hauliers who fulfil the necessary technical conditions under the Community licensing scheme may operate without restriction between member states; licensing conditions are set out in Regulation 881/92 Article 3; quota restrictions on international journeys were abolished from the beginning of 1993 by Regulation 1841/88. Rates charged for road haulage between member states were officially deregulated in 1990, and are now set by agreement between the parties to the contract (Regulation 4058/89, Article 2).

Road haulage services within member states remain subject to restriction. A cabotage authorization is required by operators carrying goods between points within a member state but licensed elsewhere in the Community. Authorizations are valid for two months, and are issued to road hauliers by the authorities in the member state in which they are licensed. In the approach to the 1992 single market deadline, the total number of cabotage authorizations was fixed at 15 000 from July 1990, with provision for subsequent annual increases of at least 10 per cent (Regulation 4059/89, Article 2).

At the end of 1992, notwithstanding the inauguration of the single market, cabotage restrictions, although liberalized, were not abolished. The Council eventually agreed to continue the system of authorizations until June 1998. The total number of authorizations for 1995 is 46 296, rising to 54 091 in the first half of 1998. From July 1998, Community hauliers will be allowed to operate freely within the member states (Regulation 3118/93, Article 2).

Within the overall total, quotas are allocated between member states, depending on the size of the country and the capacity of its haulage industry to exploit opportunities for cabotage. Countries—particularly the larger ones—around the geographical centre of the Community tend to have higher allocations than smaller and peripheral countries; the largest shares are given to Germany (16 per cent in 1995), the Netherlands (14 per cent), France and Italy (13 per cent each), while Finland, Ireland and Greece have 4 per cent each.

Restrictions also remain on transfrontier road passenger services. Unrestricted cabotage is to be allowed for 'non-regular' road passenger transport services only after 1995; until then it is restricted to 'closed door' tours, where the same vehicle is used to carry the same group of passengers along the entire route, and to services for workers and students in frontier zones (Regulation 2454/92, Article 3).

The prospective growth in transfrontier provision of transport services raises the issue of payment for the use of infrastructure. Road haulage imposes substantial costs in the country through which a vehicle travels. These include costs of provision and maintenance of infrastructure—such as highways and bridges—and impacts on the environment, in the form of pollution, congestion and intrusion. On the other hand, operators of vehicles using the highway system of their own country contribute to government revenue, in the form of vehicle licence fees.

Complications arise because licence fees (vehicle excise duty in the UK and Ireland, and equivalent charges elsewhere) are paid to the authorities in the member state of registration

(Directive 93/89, Article 5), so that (for example) a vehicle registered in the Netherlands pays the licence fee in that country, even if it travels mostly on German roads. Thus, vehicles have access to the roads of other countries without being required to pay additional licence fees; conversely, a country must bear the costs imposed by vehicles for which it does not receive any licence revenue. This system has tended to favour smaller countries at the centre of the Community—such as the Benelux countries—over larger countries (with more extensive road networks) such as Germany and France.

Concern was felt—particularly in Germany—over disproportionate use of the highway system by vehicles from other member states, causing an imbalance between licence revenue and infrastructure costs. To compensate for this, the German authorities imposed a tax on all heavy goods vehicles using German federal highways; the tax amounted to DM9000 for access to the highway system for one year. The tax was ruled unlawful by the Court of Justice in 1992 (Case 195/90), on the grounds that it was discriminatory, since payments by German hauliers were offset by a reduction in their motor vehicle tax.

The Council eventually in 1993 agreed a 'package' linking the liberalization of cabotage with a system of vehicle taxes and charges. National authorities may levy annual charges (of up to 1250 ECUs per year) on vehicles registered in their own country for the use of the highway network; otherwise user charges are to be in proportion to the duration of use of highways, while tolls are to be related to costs of construction, operation and development of infrastructure. There is also provision for member states to group together to establish a common system of annual user charges, so that revenue can be allocated in proportion to highway usage in the participating countries (Directive 93/89, Articles 7–8). An agreement has now been concluded between Germany, Denmark and the Benelux countries for a common system of user charges, with maximum rates of 1250 ECUs per year and 6 ECUs per day (van Vreckem 1994).

Rail transport   Community transport policy now gives priority to the development of railways, as a means of accommodating transport demand and mitigating environmental pressures. Recent trends are not promising: the share of rail in freight and passenger transport declined by almost half in the two decades between 1970 and 1990 (COM(92)494, Annex 1). Moreover, Community railways have not been orientated towards the single market: they have developed primarily as national networks operated by national monopoly undertakings, and transfrontier linkages have been impeded by differences between national standards.

The Community is pursuing technical harmonization, with a Commission Proposal designed to promote inter-operability (see Sec. 8.2); rail projects also figure among the links for development in the 'trans-European networks' (see Table 8.1 below). Legislation has been enacted to ensure that users are properly charged for use of the rail system, notwithstanding the monopolistic structure of the rail industries in member states: rail undertakings are required to account separately for service operations and infrastructure management (Directive 91/440). The Commission has declared its intention to propose further legislation concerning access to, and charging for, rail infrastructure (COM(92)494, p. 103).

Railways are potentially competitive in long-distance freight transport and high-speed inter-city passenger services; realization of their advantages in these areas can be environmentally beneficial, inasmuch as traffic is diverted from highways and airlines. The Community has sought to encourage the 'combined transport' of freight, using rail for long-distance haulage integrated with road transport modes (Directive 92/106).

Air transport   As the single market develops, the airline industry, and governments, face a huge challenge of restructuring in the wake of fundamental changes in the regulatory framework. This comes at a time when pressures are growing on capacity at certain locations, amid an awareness of the environmental impact of air transport.

During the industry's formative period following the Second World War, Europe's leading airlines—such as British Airways, Air France, Lufthansa—were conceived as 'flag carriers'. Their commercial role was subject to the direction of their governments, whose priorities included national prestige, support for the country's aircraft industry, foreign currency earnings and provision of uneconomical services for social and/or strategic reasons. Operation of international scheduled services (including those within the European Community) was subject to bilateral intergovernmental agreements which restricted competition and protected the position of national airlines.

Deregulation—and particularly the opening of routes to competition—began to affect European airlines in the late 1970s, as their governments negotiated air traffic agreements with the USA. The first agreement to incorporate significant deregulation was the US/UK Bermuda 2 agreement in 1977, which was followed by the US/Netherlands agreement in 1978. Later, some bilateral agreements between Community member states were liberalized, beginning with the UK/Netherlands agreement in 1984 (for a history of these developments, see Doganis (1991), Chapters 3 and 4).

The impetus for development of Community policies increased following the 1986 *Nouvelles Frontières* case, in which the Court of Justice held that the competition rules of Articles 85–90 EC apply to air transport (Joined Cases 209–13/84). This judgment had far-reaching implications, because widespread practices such as price fixing, revenue pooling and capacity-sharing were liable to be found unlawful. In a subsequent case the Court ruled that airlines were acting unlawfully in fixing ticket prices (Case 66/88, which concerned parallel imports into Germany of air tickets to destinations outside the Community). In 1987 the Council enacted Regulations for application of the Treaty provisions on competition (Regulations 3975/87 and 3976/87), and the following year exemption of inter-airline agreements from the competition rules (under Article 85(3) EC) was made subject to conditions designed to avoid abuse of market power (Commission Regulation 2671/88).

The Community adopted two 'packages' of measures, in 1987 and 1990, which liberalized bilateral agreements to allow more flexibility in fare setting, capacity sharing and service provision. However, bilateral arrangements, even when liberalized, are not generally compatible with the single market provisions for freedom of movement (Article 7a EC), because they involve restrictions on the supply of a service (air travel) across national frontiers (they also constitute discrimination on grounds of nationality, contrary to the EC Treaty, Article 6). So even if (for example) an air service agreement between the UK and France allowed British airlines free access to the London–Paris route, it would not permit them to operate a service between Paris and Rome.

Eventually in 1992 a third package was agreed, involving a phased transition to a single market in air services. Community airlines may now—in principle—serve any route *between* two member states, but access to routes *within* a single country is still restricted: up to 1 April 1997 member states are not required to authorize cabotage within their territory by carriers licensed by other member states unless it is the extension of a service to and from the state of registration, with less than 50 per cent of the capacity of the service that is extended (Regulation 2408/92, Article 3(2)). Airlines have discretion over the fares they charge, although excessively high (or low) fares may be disallowed by agreement between the member states concerned (Regulation 2409/92, Article 6).

The remaining substantial anomaly in Community air transport policy is the persistence of bilateral air service agreements between member states and countries outside the Community:

there are in all more than 700 such agreements (COM(90)17 p. 8). Moreover, agreements permitting non-Community airlines to serve routes between member states (under so-called 'fifth freedom' rights) are negotiated by the member states concerned. The result is somewhat paradoxical: Community legislation limits cabotage rights for Community airlines, but not for third-country airlines (COM(90)17, p. 39). The logic of the single market, and the EC Treaty provision for a common commercial policy (Article 113), suggest that such agreements should—at least—be co-ordinated at Community level. The Commission presented a Proposal for legislation in 1990 (COM(90)17), pointing out that 'it is in the Community interest to avoid a situation where third countries exploit the lack of Community unity' (p. 31), but the Council has thus far failed to act.

As the Community single market framework developed, the airline industry was undergoing far-reaching structural changes which were originally prompted by liberalization of bilateral air service agreements. Observing the dominance of a small number of large carriers in the deregulated US market, the major European airlines have sought to extend their market base through mergers and alliances. Their strategies have involved:

- ensuring a dominant position in their home markets (for example Air France's 1990 acquisition of UTA)
- entry into other European markets (examples include SAS's 40 per cent shareholding in British Midland, and British Airways' major stakes in Deutsche BA and the French regional carrier TAT)
- establishing a global presence through collaboration with non-European airlines—for instance, British Airways and Iberia have purchased shareholdings in a number of foreign airlines (Doganis 1994: 17).

Recent developments within the European airline industry, and more extensive US experience, suggest that deregulation will not necessarily lead to a pro-competitive structure. Independent airlines have survived in 'niche' markets, but in challenging the erstwhile flag carriers they have generally been unsuccessful: most of those that attempted to do so either collapsed (for example Air Europe in 1991) or were taken over by the majors (as with Air France's acquisition of UTA and Air Inter, and British Airways' takeover of British Caledonian (in 1987) and Dan Air (in 1992)). This experience suggests that air transport in Europe is not characterized by contestable markets: entry and start-up costs are high, established operators have substantial marketing advantages, and high exit barriers cause unsuccessful airlines to continue operating unprofitably (Doganis 1994: 22–5). If this is indeed the case, a few major airlines will continue to dominate the industry, and the Commission will need to monitor their conduct closely, having regard to Article 86 EC which prohibits abuse of a dominant position.

In the immediate future the prospect appears to be an intensified rivalry between the major airlines, as governments seek to ensure the survival of their country's flag carrier in the face of pressures for rationalization of the industry. Their motivation is both commercial and sentimental; for example, the government of Greece has given substantial financial support to Olympic Airlines' unprofitable services to the USA and Australia, in order to maintain cultural links and to boost trade, and because Greeks resident in those countries are seen as a source of investment in Greece and influence abroad (*Financial Times*, 29 July 1994). So the observation that 'Europe's state owned airlines occupy the same place as flags, languages and national anthems in the hearts of Europe's citizens' (*Financial Times*, 29 July 1994) may be an overstatement, but it has an element of truth. The problems this poses for Community policy-makers are succinctly expressed in Box 8.1.

BOX 8.1
The problem of national airlines: a Commission insider's view

The biggest barrier to air transport liberalisation in Europe is this crazy idea that every Member State has to have its own airline ... People still assume there is something glamorous about flying, but airlines are just glorified bus companies ... Everybody knows the contraction of the airline industry is inevitable in Europe. Governments are trying to make sure that when the fight finally comes, their national carriers will be the ones that survive.

Source: An (anonymous) Commission official, quoted in 'Flying the flag crowds the air', *Financial Times*, 29 July 1994.

Moves towards deregulation, and privatization, of air transport pose a challenge to airlines facing extensive rationalization and restructuring. Governments are concerned to ensure that their flag carriers are among the survivors of the rationalization process; and where privatization is on the agenda, this concern is reinforced by a desire to boost the sale price of the airline.

Protectionist measures persist in various guises. One of these is the discriminatory allocation of traffic between airports, an instance of which arose in 1994 when the airline TAT (in which British Airways has a substantial stake) was denied access to Paris Orly Airport. Member states are permitted to regulate the distribution of traffic between airports within an airport system and to limit traffic where there are serious congestion and/or environmental problems (Regulation 2408/92, Articles 8 and 9), but this must not involve discrimination to favour national airlines. The French authorities' strategy of concentrating international traffic at Charles de Gaulle airport, and excluding new airlines from routes serving Orly, was found by the Commission to be unfair to airlines wishing to serve Orly (Cases VII/AMA/II/93 and VII/AMA/IV/93).

Discrimination can also arise in the allocation of take-off and landing slots at congested airports. The Community has a procedure whereby slot allocation is, as far as possible, agreed between the parties involved, and slots can be exchanged between airlines. Carriers are entitled to retain the slots they use (under so-called 'grandfather rights'), and this can limit the scope for competition from new or expanding airlines (Regulation 95/93, Article 8(1); see also Comité des Sages 1994: 20).

Several member states have sought to secure the future of their major airlines with substantial infusions of state aid. This requires the approval of the Commission under Article 93 EC, which prohibits aid that is 'incompatible with the common market'. Government aid programmes are ostensibly to facilitate adjustment to a more competitive environment, although critics have argued that they distort competition in the airline industry and perpetuate inefficiencies.

With a large number of member states concerned to ensure the survival of their airlines, the Commission has come under strong political pressure to approve state aid payments. Clearance was given for substantial amounts of state aid for Sabena in 1991 (Commission Decision of 24 July 1991), Iberia in 1992 (COM(93)162, p. 291), Aer Lingus in 1993 (Commission Decision 94/118) and Air France, Olympic Airways, and TAP in 1994 (Commission Decisions 94/653, 94/696 and 94/698).

These payments were—purportedly—on a 'one time, last time' basis, as the Commission has sought to limit aid programmes to the amount, and duration, necessary to complete the restructuring process. When this process is complete, a restructured—and possibly privatized—airline will then have to compete without the benefit of subsidies. Conditions imposed by the

Commission typically require airlines to reduce costs and capacity, to refrain from the use of aid for the financing or acquisition of interests in other airlines, and not to obstruct the opening of routes to competing airlines (*Financial Times*, 9 June 1994; see also Commission Decision, 94/118). For example, following the massive FFr20 bn capital injection into Air France, the French government undertook to privatize the airline, and to 'adopt the normal behaviour of a shareholder' (Commission Decision 94/653, pp. 78–9).

8.2   TRANS-EUROPEAN NETWORKS

To accommodate the economic growth induced by the single market, and to realize its full potential, requires infrastructure—such as highways, airports and energy transmission systems. Capacity must be expanded, especially in peripheral regions whose full participation in the single market requires good access to the rest of the Community. There is also a need for a refocusing of communications, to integrate a set of primarily national systems into European networks.

The historical inheritance consists of structures developed and planned at national level—often by governments—with transfrontier linkages sometimes having the appearance of an 'afterthought'. The national railway systems that developed in nineteenth-century Europe provide a good example. Lines in Britain mainly ran to and from London; similarly, the French and Belgian systems were centred on Paris and Brussels respectively. This led to differences in standards and technical specifications, which have tended to impede the development of long-distance rail services across national frontiers. Thus, for example, mainline services have a wide range of electrical systems with different voltages: 25 kv a.c. (France and Britain), 15 kv a.c. (Germany and Switzerland), 3 kv d.c. (Belgium and Italy), 1.5 kv d.c. (the Netherlands and France).

The link between infrastructure provision and economic activity is both obvious and frequently overlooked. Numerous studies of the economic impact of the single market have concluded that economic growth will accelerate, with a marked increase in linkages and movement across national frontiers. There is an implicit assumption that infrastructures will be available to accommodate these developments. For example, vehicles require roads; so, when it is predicted that transfrontier road freight will increase by up to 50 per cent (Task Force 1990: 100), there is a presumption that highway capacity will also increase; if capacity does not expand sufficiently, traffic growth will be constrained.

Thus, there is a need for a strategic perspective at Community level, and for integration of national infrastructure projects into a coherent system. These requirements are addressed in Title XII of the EC Treaty (summarized in Box 8.2), which provides for measures to integrate communications infrastructure in 'trans-European networks'. The Community participates in the development of transport, energy and telecommunications networks, and is empowered to identify and support projects that contribute to these networks.

The Community's role includes measures to promote technical harmonization, in order to avoid a repetition of problems such as those caused by the multiplicity of electrical standards in national railway systems. In this particular instance, the Commission recently submitted proposals for common technical standards for the European high-speed train network, including a 'technical specification for interoperability' (European Commission (1994), Article 5).

According to Commission estimates, expenditure requirements for communications infrastructure up to the end of the century amount to 250 bn ECUs for transport and energy, and 150 bn ECUs for telecommunications. Within these totals, costings have been made for individual priority projects of 'common European interest' identified pursuant to Article 129c EC (COM(93)700, pp. 82–95).

> **BOX 8.2**
> **Trans-European networks: provisions of the EC Treaty**
>
> *Article 129b* 'To derive full benefit from ... an area without internal frontiers, the Community shall contribute to the establishment and development of Trans European networks in the areas of transport, telecommunications and energy infrastructures.'
>
> *Article 129c* Community action should promote 'interconnection and interoperability of national networks, as well as access to such networks', taking particular accounts of the needs of island, landlocked and peripheral regions.
>
> Community initiatives may include:
>
> - guidelines relating to objectives and priorities, and (subject to the approval of member states(s) concerned*) identifying projects of common interest
> - measures to ensure inter-operability, particularly technical standardization
> - financial support for projects by sponsorship of feasibility studies, loan guarantees or interest rate subsidies, and (in the case of transport infrastructure projects) financing through the Cohesion Fund
>
> * Article 129d.

8.2.1   Transport infrastructure

The transport projects have an estimated total cost in excess of 80 bn ECUs (mostly for rail projects): the rail, road and water transport projects are listed, with indicative cost estimates, in Tables 8.1, 8.2, and 8.3 respectively. In addition to specific transport links, the lists also include projects to develop traffic management systems, including air traffic control (indicated expenditure 8 bn ECUs), road and waterway systems (1 bn ECUs each) and a multimodal satellite positioning system (1 bn ECUs).

Table 8.1   Trans-European transport network: indicative list of rail projects and their costs

Project	Countries involved	Indicative cost (bn ECUs)
Brenner Axis trans Alpine connection	Italy, Austria, Germany	10
Fehmarn Belt fixed link	Denmark, Germany	4.5
Rotterdam–Cologne–Frankfurt–Karlsruhe–Switzerland–Italy	Netherlands, Germany, Switzerland, Italy	12.7
Paris–Brussels–Cologne–Amsterdam–London	Belgium, Netherlands, UK	8.5
Madrid–Barcelona–Perpignan	Spain, France	6.8
Paris–Strasbourg	France	4
Karlsruhe–Frankfurt–Berlin	Germany	8.5
Lyon–Turin	France, Italy	6.2

Source: European Commission, COM(93)700, pp. 90–1.

Table 8.2   Trans-European transport network: indicative list of highway projects

Project	Countries involved	Indicative cost (bn ECUs)
Nürnburg–Prague	Germany, Czech Republic	1
Berlin–Warsaw	Germany, Poland	3.2
Patras–Thessaloniki	Greece	1.5
Lisbon–Valladolid	Portugal, Spain	2
Holyhead–Felixstowe/Harwich	UK	1
Bari–Otranto	Italy	1

Source: European Commission, COM(93)700, p. 91.

Table 8.3   Trans-European transport network: indicative list of waterway projects

Project	Countries involved	Indicative cost (bn ECUs)
Rhine–Rhone canal	France	2.5
Seine–North canal	France	1.5
Elbe–Oder link	Germany	0.6
Danube upgrading Straubing–Vilshofen	Germany	0.7

Source: European Commission, COM(93)700, p. 92.

8.2.2   Energy transmission

There is considerable scope for investment in energy networks both within the Community and—particularly for gas—in connections with non-Community countries. Links requiring development are listed in Table 8.4; the Commission has estimated the expenditure requirements for priority projects at 13 bn ECUs (COM(93)700, p. 34). The Commission has identified administrative constraints—such as exclusive contracts and monopolies—as the main impediment to investment in this area, and has called for deregulation and increased competition. This would in turn enhance efficiency in the use of resources, and would encourage the more widespread use of less polluting forms of energy.

There are however limits to deregulation. The administrative constraints are to some degree related to concerns over security, and the possible interruption of energy supplies for political reasons—as happened in 1973, when Europe's oil imports were disrupted following the outbreak of war in west Asia. Heavy dependence on imports from politically less stable regions has an element of risk, particularly in the case of gas supplied by pipeline from Russia and Algeria. The integration of networks within western Europe will tend to spread these risks.

8.2.3   Telecommunications

The development of 'electronic highways' in telecommunications is widely seen as critical for the economic future of the Community into the next century. In this context the Commission

Table 8.4   Trans-European electricity and gas networks: requirements for new or improved connections within the European Union and with non member countries

Electricity	Gas
Ireland–UK	Ireland–UK
Greece–Italy	UK–Continental Europe
Germany–Denmark, Netherlands, Belgium	Germany–Belgium
France–Belgium, Germany, Italy	Spain–France
Belgium–Netherlands, Luxembourg	Portugal–Spain
Germany–Sweden, Poland, Norway, Austria	Belgium, Netherlands, Germany, Denmark–Norway
Italy–Switzerland, Austria, Tunisia	Spain, France, Italy–Algeria
Greece–Balkan countries, Turkey	European Union—Russia
UK, Netherlands–Norway	
France–Switzerland	
Spain–Morocco	

Source: European Commission COM(93)700, pp. 93–4.

has devised a strategy to promote trans-European networks, calling for Community action to facilitate infrastructure development, service provision and the application of new technologies (see Sec. 6.2.2).

8.3   SUSTAINABLE TRANSPORT

In 1992, as the single market legislative programme advanced, the Commission published a Green Paper (COM(92)46), followed by a White Paper (COM(92)494), on the future of the Common Transport Policy. The focus, particularly of the former, was on sustainable development and its implications for transport policies. These papers signify a new agenda for Community transport policy, as the single market has extended the scope of Community responsibilities and has generated additional demand for transport services, and pressure on transport capacity.

8.3.1   The single market: spatial effects

As the Community's founders foresaw, transport has a vital role as the single market leads to accelerated economic growth and industrial restructuring. The result is pressure for a substantial increase in demand for transport, and in particular growth in transfrontier traffic. The single market gives opportunities for firms to shift production to lower-cost locations, to adopt 'just-in-time' production techniques, and to develop Community-wide strategies. One effect is a spatial concentration of production in order to realize economies of scale; and this necessarily involves transport of inputs and final products from fewer centres and over greater distances.

There is a pronounced contrast within the Community between the 'core' and the 'peripheral' regions. The former are centrally located, relatively prosperous and densely populated; while the latter are isolated at the geographical fringes, economically disadvantaged and more sparsely populated. One definition of the 'core' is the Benelux countries and adjacent regions (south-east England, Nordrhein–Westfalen (Germany), and Ile de France, Bassin Parisien, and Nord–Pas-de-Calais (France)), which generate 30 per cent of Community's GDP and account for 25 per cent of its population and 17 per cent of its land area. In contrast, the four 'cohesion' countries (Greece, Ireland, Spain and Portugal) at the periphery of the Community, although accounting for 34 per cent of its land area, have only 18 per cent of the Community's population, and generate only 11 per cent of Community GDP.

There is evidently a potential divergence of interest here. In and around the 'core' there are problems associated with congestion, as accelerated economic growth places additional pressure on transport facilities. In contrast, isolated regions in the periphery of the Community do not suffer from the problems of economic success: they require improved transport links to ensure full participation in the single market.

These differences are liable to be exacerbated by a concentration of economic growth in the 'core' regions. This may well turn out to be the initial effect of the single market, since the more prosperous and centrally located regions are well placed to increase trade between themselves: it has been estimated that the single market will cause an increase of 35–50 per cent in transfrontier road freight traffic, in addition to increases resulting from 'normal' economic growth, and that initially most of this increase will be concentrated in the 'core' regions (Task Force 1990: 100). On the other hand, the peripheral regions are handicapped by deficiencies in their infrastructure, which must as a priority be remedied; the purpose of the Community Cohesion Fund and large elements of the structural funds (see Secs 3.4 and 3.5) is precisely to enable the less prosperous countries to develop their infrastructure with a view to the requirements of the single market.

8.3.2   Surface transport: environmental implications of future growth

Road transport has shown vigorous growth in recent years. Over the two decades between 1970 and 1990, car and road freight mileage doubled (COM(92)494, p. 17). Private cars accounted for 84 per cent of surface transport passenger-kilometres in 1990; corresponding figures for buses and coaches and for rail were, respectively 9 and 7 per cent. Approximately 70 per cent of freight tonne kilometres was carried by road in 1990 (COM(92)494, Annex I).

Rates of car ownership vary markedly across the Community. Table 8.5 shows that the numbers of private cars per 1000 inhabitants in the 'cohesion' countries (Greece, Ireland, Portugal and Spain) are well below the European Union average (the low figure for Denmark is explained by high rates of tax); the rate of car ownership in Greece would have to be more than doubled to reach the EU average. Commission projections suggest that the 'saturation' rate of car ownership is in the region of 500 cars per 1000 inhabitants (European Commission 1990: 154); at this level, the stock of cars in the European Union would be some 25 per cent above the 1991 level.

Transport is a major source of environmental impacts of various types, especially atmospheric pollution, noise and land use changes. In many instances, these effects are particularly acute in urban areas where traffic is heavily congested; within the Community, large cities in the south—such as Athens and Naples—are worst affected, owing in large part to the pressures on their infrastructure from a rapidly growing population (COM(90)218, p. 17).

Table 8.5   Private cars per 1000 inhabitants, EU member states, 1991

Luxembourg	498
Italy	488
Germany	458
France	419
Sweden	419
European Union	404
Belgium	398
Austria	394
Finland	380
United Kingdom	374
Netherlands	371
Spain	322
Denmark	310
Portugal	281
Ireland	235
Greece	176

Source: Eurostat (1994: Table 7.10); the EU figure was calculated by the authors.

Air pollution   Transport sources are responsible for various types of polluting effects—localized and global, short and long-term. Transport accounts for approximately two-thirds of the Community's nitrogen oxide emissions (European Commission 1992: 153), and for 17 per cent of emissions of volatile organic compounds (VOCs) (COM(92)23 III, p. 15). The overall environmental impact of these pollutants is complicated by synergistic effects, such as the formation of ground-level ozone from nitrogen oxides and VOCs. Proportions of pollutants emitted depends upon the flow, speed and composition of traffic.

Noise   Studies in Germany have found that transport is the main source of noise disturbance. Estimates in the 1980s suggested that over half the population was significantly disturbed by traffic (COM(92)23 III, p. 41).

Land use impacts   Transport developments have a variety of effects on land use. The most obvious is the loss of land for other purposes, such as farming or recreation, and damage to wildlife habitats; other impacts, particularly in urban areas, include severance of communities, and visual intrusion.

The *'greenhouse' effect*, leading to global warming and hence climate change, has become a major environmental concern. Transport is an important source of 'greenhouse' gases: one-quarter of the carbon dioxide emissions in the EU come from transport (European Commission 1992: 45); and of the transport emissions over half come from cars, and almost one-quarter from road freight vehicles (COM(92)494, p. 13). Carbon dioxide emissions are a function of fuel consumption; indeed, the use of catalytic convertors and unleaded petrol has an energy penalty, which may increase fuel consumption by as much as 10 per cent.

   Commission projections suggest that, with existing policies, car traffic will increase by approximately 25 per cent between 1990 and 2010, while fuel efficiency will improve by 12 per cent: the result would be a 10 per cent increase in total fuel consumption, and hence in carbon dioxide emissions. An alternative 'sustained high growth' scenario assumes restrictions on car usage, and a switch in passenger and freight traffic to railways, so that car traffic is eventually stabilized at around the 1990 level; an emphasis on energy efficient technology permits a one-third reduction in vehicle fuel consumption, so that carbon dioxide emissions decline by the same proportion (European Commission 1992: 156–9).

8.3.3   Air transport: environmental implications of future growth

Air travel has grown dramatically in the past two decades, and as the airline industry adapts to the single market the overall volume of air traffic is likely to rise still further. The development of the single market will generate additional cross-border travel, although on some short routes between major centres (such as London, Brussels and Paris) competition from high-speed rail services may cause a decline in air travel. Furthermore, deregulation tends to increase air traffic as additional services are introduced, and as airlines compete on frequency, operating more flights with smaller aircraft. (Thus, the average number of seats per aircraft on services within Europe declined from 139 in 1982 to 133 in 1992—Doganis 1994: 21.)

This has various implications for the quality of life for Community citizens: air transport and airports have significant environmental impacts, including noise, greenhouse gas emissions and land use impacts.

Noise   Aircraft noise can be an extreme form of transfrontier environmental impact, inasmuch as aircraft operating international flights conform to the standards of their country of registration. Commission efforts to raise noise standards for Community-registered aircraft are liable to be resisted by the industry on competitive grounds (Comité des Sages 1994: 39–40). Technological progress can be expected to lead to development of quieter aircraft, but it remains to be seen how far growth in air traffic offsets the abatement of noise emissions.

Greenhouse gas emissions   Aviation accounts for approximately $2\frac{2}{3}$ per cent of Community carbon dioxide emissions. As with motor vehicles, reduction in emissions depends on increased fuel efficiency.

Land use impacts: Airports, and associated transport infrastructure, have environmental impacts including noise, effects on wildlife and loss of agricultural land. Airport projects are subject to the Community's environmental impact assessment procedures (Directive 85/337), but investment decisions are ultimately a matter for the authorities in member states.

As air traffic increases, there is a danger that congestion will grow, reducing fuel efficiency and exacerbating environmental impacts. These effects can be mitigated to some extent by a pricing regime that recognizes that slots at congested airports are a scarce resource, and takes full account of environmental damage. The Commission's carbon/energy tax Proposal, designed to stimulate energy efficiency and thus reduce greenhouse gas emissions, is a first step; but there may be a case for more explicit economic incentives in the slot allocation procedures at Community airports.

Congestion can also be mitigated through improvements in infrastructure, especially the integration of air traffic management. Member states have hitherto been reluctant to compromise sovereignty over their air space, and have reserved substantial areas for military use. The result has been economic inefficiency: air traffic control is provided from 52 different centres, and it is estimated that the resulting congestion causes up to 70 additional aircraft to be in the air at any given time (Comité des Sages 1994: 23–4).

Traffic growth is likely to be concentrated at certain airports. Deregulation in the USA saw the emergence of a pattern of 'hub' airports, linked by the main trunk routes, with 'feeder' services to smaller centres. Liberalization of air transport in the Community will facilitate this process in Europe, as airlines are now generally free to provide services across national frontiers. The use of connecting services for travel from points outside the Community has been eased by the reform of customs procedures, so that checked-in baggage is examined at the ultimate destination within the Community (Commission Regulation 1823/92).

The design and planning of airports will be simplified to some degree as a result of the relaxation of frontier controls. For travellers between member states, systematic customs checks were abolished in 1993, and duty-free purchases are to be phased out by 1999 (Directive 92/12, Article 28). Immigration controls have been removed between the 'Schengen' countries (see Sec. 3.2.4), and may eventually be eliminated within the Community altogether.

8.3.4   Sustainable transport: the Community policy response

The Commission's 1992 Green Paper (COM(92)46) set out a strategy for the promotion of sustainable mobility which comprised the following main points:

1. land use planning, to reduce the need for mobility and to exploit alternatives to road transport;
2. infrastructure planning, incorporating environmental costs and benefits;
3. measures to improve the competitive position of environmentally friendly transport modes;
4. improvement in urban public transport;
5. technical improvement in vehicles and fuels;
6. measures to induce behavioural changes in car usage, and driving (including speed limits).

This was not a matter for Community policy alone. Policy-making in transport is very much a matter of shared responsibility, with inputs at different levels, in accordance with the subsidiarity principle. Decisions taken at Community level establish the parameters for national and local measures. Where environmental impacts are localized, and there is no danger of distortion of the single market, policy measures are primarily a matter for authorities in member states, at national, regional or local level. At the same time, Community policies are generally a compromise between the varying priorities of—and in—member states.

For example, vehicle specifications, including environmentally related standards, are determined at Community level. There is now provision for a uniform 'type approval' system, and member states cannot require vehicles to conform to standards higher than those specified in Community regulations. The Community standards for exhaust emissions are determined in the light of available technologies (for example Directive 89/458 anticipates the use of catalytic convertors) and the environmental benefit. The latter of course varies: cars meeting the Community specification will be used both in thinly populated rural areas and also in urban areas with high concentrations of cars. Since the Community standard is a compromise, it may not be sufficient to achieve desired air quality standards in some cities: if this is the case, local transport policies must include action (such as traffic management schemes, and support for public transport) in order to alleviate the problem. This is essentially a matter for local and regional authorities, although the Community has a role in co-ordinating information and support for research and development, and in the promotion of standards to ensure technical compatibility (for example in the development of electronic road pricing systems).

Charging for environmental costs   The Commission's 1992 White Paper advocates the 'internalization' of costs, in accordance with the polluter pays principle outlined in Sec. 7.4.1 (COM(92)494, p.58). This means that transport users should be charged for the use of infrastructure, at a rate sufficient to cover *all* the costs arising from their activities, including the costs to society associated with pollution and congestion. Charges, particularly for the use of highways, have been a contentious matter (see Sec. 8.1.2): use of charges to frustrate the transfrontier provision of transport services within the single market is against Community law, and so national authorities must ensure that charging is non-discriminatory and also transparent, in the sense that it is linked to costs. There is evidently a need for co-ordination at Community level, possibly going beyond the type of 'voluntary' arrangements between member states provided for in Directive 93/89 (see Sec. 8.1.2).

Environmental assessment   The Community clearly has an interest in infrastructure development, particularly in the context of trans-European networks. From the perspective of the Community's wider policy objectives, expenditure should be assessed in terms of its contributions to the single market and also to sustainable development.

At the level of individual *projects*, Community legislation provides for environmental impact assessment (EIA). Such assessment is mandatory for construction of motorways, express roads, long-distance railway lines, major airports, trading ports and large-capacity inland waterways and their port facilities; member states may also require assessments to be made for other roads, harbours, airfields, tramways, elevated and underground railways (Directive 85/337, Annexes 1 and 2).

There is no corresponding assessment framework for infrastructure development *programmes*, although it is arguably decisions at this level that are more important for sustainable development. Usage of individual links within a network has a high degree of interdependence, so that, while for a specific link the transport benefits may appear to outweigh the environmental impact, assessment of the programme to which the link contributes may identify economically viable alternative strategies which cause less environmental damage.

Economic and environmental priorities vary across the Community, and especially between the 'core' and 'peripheral' regions. Projects may be of Community or national importance, but much of the environmental impact is local. For example, the rail link between London and the Channel Tunnel—an important component of the European high-speed rail network—will run through one of the most prosperous and densely populated regions of the UK; hence it has encountered opposition on environmental grounds (which has caused its cost to increase). However in other, less prosperous, regions the environmental impacts associated with the original project might have been regarded as an acceptable price to pay for the economic benefit of improved transport links with the core of the European Community.

The Commission has indicated its intention that strategic environmental assessment should be integrated in the decision process for transport infrastructure policies, programmes and investment decisions, in conjunction with a recommended standard methodology for cost–benefit analysis, 'in order to provide a level playing field for investment decisions' (COM(92)494, pp. 111–12). Nevertheless, priorities, and hence costings of *localized* environmental impacts, may legitimately vary (in the same way that land prices vary).

Strategy for sustainable transport   The environmental impacts of transport can to some extent be mitigated through technological developments leading to improvements in fuel consumption and noise emissions. However, sustainable mobility depends to a large degree on changes in transport usage, which may be encouraged in various ways. Administrative and regulatory constraints can be removed. For example, the Community has taken steps to facilitate the switching of traffic to railways: licensing provisions must not be a disincentive to the use of combined transport, whereby road freight carriers are transported over long distances by rail (Directive 92/106).

Land use planning can enable people to live closer to their work and the services they require, while traffic management and support for public transport can reduce pressures on the urban environment. Charges that include the full costs of environmental damage and congestion give incentives to use transport modes for which these costs are lower (COM(90)218, pp. 40–4).

The Commission has foreseen an important role for electronic technology in transport and communications (COM(94)469). The application of new technologies to traffic management can increase efficiency in the use of infrastructure; there can also be safety benefits, in the monitoring of operator fitness, warning of dangers and aids to navigation. These technologies can contribute to environmental protection, through monitoring and control of emissions, avoidance of congestion and surveillance of transport of hazardous substances. Furthermore, development of electronic communications may reduce the need to travel—so for example environmental considerations might indicate a higher priority for 'electronic highways' in the trans-European network programme (see Sec. 6.2.2).

Electronic technologies can also be used to implement sophisticated charging systems to reduce traffic flows and consequent environmental impacts. Charges could, for example, be varied by area and by time of day, to give a strong disincentive to the use of motor vehicles in polluted and congested urban areas. Such systems have been developed at the pilot stage, but their political acceptability remains problematical.

In some instances there is a clear motivation to take action at local level to promote sustainable mobility; for example, cities have an economic incentive to relieve congestion and pollution, in order to be more attractive business locations. Where measures are liable to distort the single market, the Community has to intervene, as has happened in the case of infrastructure charging (see Sec. 8.1.2); and if electronic road pricing systems come into general use, it will be necessary to ensure the compatibility of the technologies employed. Community action is also called for in the case of transfrontier and global environmental impacts; one example is the proposed carbon/energy tax designed to promote energy efficiency in order to combat the 'greenhouse' effect (see Sec. 7.5.2).

8.4   TRANSPORT: KEY POINTS AND ISSUES

The Common Transport Policy, after making slow progress initially, was given a strong impetus by the single market programme. The success of the single market (and of economic and monetary union) depends upon economic cohesion, and hence convergence, between member states. Achievement of these objectives is facilitated by the freedom to provide transport services throughout the Community, and by the availability of adequate infrastructure. The Community legislation has derestricted transport between member states, and provides for a phased relaxation of restrictions on cabotage. The Community has undertaken to promote a massive programme of investment in transport infrastructure, to improve transfrontier links; this is likely to be of particular benefit to the peripheral and less prosperous member states.

Transport is also a key policy area for the integration of economic and environmental policies in order to ensure sustainable development. In principle, charges for the use of infrastructure should reflect the costs of environmental resources, although as yet there is no agreed methodology for assessment of these costs across the Community. Infrastructure projects are subject to environmental assessement, although more could be done to impart an environmental dimension to infrastructure development strategies.

Transport is a major source of emissions of 'greenhouse' gases, and as such must make a major contribution to meeting targets for reduction in these emissions. This is an important facet of the Community strategy for sustainable mobility, which envisages a combination of improved energy efficiency, increased use of transport modes that are relatively environmentally friendly, and land use measures to reduce the demand for transport.

Community transport policy, and the growing emphasis on sustainable development, give rise to a number of issues. These may be identified as follows:

- The single market programme has greatly liberalized cross-border provision of transport services, and remaining restrictions are being phased out: what impact will this have on Community transport industries and on the Community economy?
- Community air transport policies do not cover air service agreements with non-member countries, which remain a matter for member states: what are the implications of this division of responsibility? What are the obstacles to an extension of the Community's role?
- The Commission has identified massive requirements for investment in infrastructure to facilitate economic cohesion: what can be done to ensure that such investments correspond with Community (as distinct from national) priorities?
- Projections of economic growth in the single market imply a substantial increase in demand for transport: how far can this demand be accommodated without compromising the objective of sustainable development?

REFERENCES

Comité des Sages (1994) *Expanding Horizons. Civil Aviation in Europe: an Action Programme for the Future*, Report by the Comité des Sages for Air Transport to the European Commission, January.

Cooper, J., Browne, M. and Gretton, D. (1987) *Freight Transport in the European Community: Making the Most of UK Opportunities*, Transport Studies Group, Polytechnic of Central London.

Doganis, R. (1991) *Flying Off Course: the Economics of International Airlines*, 2nd edn, Harper Collins, London.

Doganis, R. (1994) 'The impact of liberalization on European airline strategies and operations', *Journal of Air Transport Management*, 1(1).

Ernst & Whinney (1987) *Costs of 'Non Europe': Illustrations in the Road Haulage Sector*, Study for the European Commission, November.

European Commission (1988) 'The economics of 1992', *European Economy*, No. 35, March.

European Commission (1990) 'Energy for a new century: the European perspective', *Energy in Europe*, July.

European Commission (1992) 'A view to the future', *Energy in Europe*, September.

European Commission (1994) Proposal for a Council Directive on the interoperability of the European High Speed Train network *Official Journal*, 1994, C134/6.

Eurostat (1994) *Basic Statistics of the Community*, 31st edn, Office of Official Publications, Luxembourg.

Task Force (1990) *'1992': The Environmental Dimension*, Task Force Environment and the Internal Market, Brussels.

van Vreckem, D. (1994) 'European Union policy on taxes and charges in the road transport sector', in ECMT, *Internalising the Social Costs of Transport*, European Conference of Ministers of Transport, Paris.

European Community legislation

Regulations

Regulation 3975/87, laying down the procedure for the application of the rules on competition to undertakings in the air transport sector, *Official Journal*, 1987 L374/1.

Regulation 3976/87, on the application of Article 85(3) of the Treaty to certain categories of agreements and concerted practices in the air transport sector, *Official Journal*, 1987 L374/9.

Regulation 1841/88 on the Community quota for carriage of goods by road, *Official Journal*, 1988, L163/1.

Commission Regulation 2671/88, on the application of Article 85(3) to certain categories of agreements, decisions and concerted practices in the air transport sector, *Official Journal*, 1988 L309/9.

Regulation 4058/89, on the fixing of rates for the carriage of goods by road between member states, *Official Journal*, 1989 L390/1.

Regulation 4059/89, laying down the conditions under which non-resident carriers may operate national road haulage services within a member state, *Official Journal*, 1990 L390/3.

Regulation 881/92, 26 March 1992, on access to the market for carriage of goods by road, *Official Journal*, 1992 L95/1.

Commission Regulation 1823/92, laying down detailed rules concerning the elimination of controls and formalities applicable to the cabin and hold baggage of persons taking an intra-Community flight and the baggage of persons making an intra-Community sea crossing, *Official Journal*, 1992 L185/8.

Regulation 2408/92, on access for Community air carriers to intra-Community air routes, *Official Journal*, 1992 L240/8.

Regulation 2409/92, on fares and rates for air services, *Official Journal*, 1992 L240/15.

Regulation 2454/92, laying down the conditions under which non-resident carriers may operate national road passenger transport services within a member state, *Official Journal*, 1992 L251/1.

Regulation 95/93, on common rules for the allocation of slots at Community airports, *Official Journal*, 1993 L14/1.

Regulation 3118/93, laying down the conditions under which non-resident carriers may operate national road haulage services within a member state, *Official Journal*, 1993 L279/1 (as amended by Regulation 3315/94, *Official Journal*, 1994 L350/9).

Directives

Directive 85/337, on the assessment of the effects of certain public and private projects on the environment, *Official Journal*, 1985 L175/40.

Directive 89/458, amending, with regard to cars below 1.4 litres, Directive 70/220, *Official Journal*, 1989 L226/1.

Directive 91/440, on the development of the Community's railways, *Official Journal*, 1991 L237/25.

Directive 92/12, on the general arrangements for products subject to excise duty and on the holding, movement and monitoring of such products, *Official Journal*, 1992 L76/1.

Directive 92/106, on combined transport, *Official Journal*, 1992 L368/38.

Directive 93/89, on the application by member states of taxes on certain vehicles used for the carriage of goods by road and tolls and charges for the use of certain infrastructures, *Official Journal*, 1993 L279/32.

Commission decisions

Commission Decision of 24 July 1991, on aid to be granted by the Belgian government in favour of the air carrier Sabena, *Official Journal*, 1991 L300/48.

Commission Decision 94/118, concerning aid to be provided by the Irish government to the Aer Lingus group, *Official Journal*, 1994 L54/30.

Commission Decision 94/653, concerning the notified capital increase of Air France, *Official Journal*, 1994 L254/73.

Commission Decision 94/696, concerning aid to be provided by the Greek government to Olympic Airways, *Official Journal*, 1994 L273/22.

Commission Decision 94/698, concerning aid to be provided by the Portuguese government to TAP, *Official Journal*, 1994 L279/29.

European Commission documents

COM(90)17, *Communication on Community Relations with Third Countries in Aviation Matters*, 23 February 1990.

COM(90)218, *Green Paper on the Urban Environment*, 27 June 1990.

COM(92)23 III, *The State of the Environment in the European Community: Overview*, 27 March 1992.

COM(92)46, *Green Paper on the Impact of Transport on the Environment: a Community Strategy for Sustainable Mobility*, 20 February 1992.

COM(92)494, *The Future Development of the Common Transport Policy: A Global Approach to the Construction of a Community Framework for Sustainable Development*, 2 December 1992.

COM(93)162, *XXIInd Report on Competition Policy*, 5 May 1993.

COM(93)700, *Growth, Competitiveness, Employment: the Challenges and Ways Forward into the 21st Century*, 5 December 1993.

COM(94)469, *Commission Communication on Telematics Applications for Transport in Europe*, 4 November 1994.

Court judgments

Case 13/83, *Parliament v. Council* [1985] ECR 1513.
Joined cases 209–13/84, *Ministère public v. Asjes and others* [1986] ECR 1457.
Case 66/88, *Ahmed Saeed v. Zentrale* [1989] ECR 803.
Case 195/90, *Commission v. Germany*, [1992] ECR I. 3141.

Legal actions

Case VII/AMA/II/93, TAT Paris Orly–London: Commission Decision of 27 April 1994 on a procedure relating to the application of Regulation 2408/92, *Official Journal*, 1994 L127/22.
Case VII/AMA/IV/93, TAT Paris Orly–Marseille and Paris Orly–Toulouse: Commission Decision of 27 April 1994 on a procedure relating to the application of Regulation 2408/92, *Official Journal*, 1994 L127/32.

POLICIES FOR AGRICULTURE AND RURAL DEVELOPMENT

Of all sectors of economic activity, agriculture has been most influenced by the European Community, and until the inauguration of the 1992 single market programme it was generally the most 'high-profile' area of Community intervention. The cost and administrative complexity of the Common Agricultural Policy (CAP) has been a regular subject of political controversy, and a frequent source of difficulty in setting the Community budget and controlling expenditure.

When the Community was established, there was a real concern over security of food supplies in Europe. The CAP was designed to consolidate, and supersede, previous national agricultural support schemes, and to secure a high degree of self sufficiency in agricultural products. In this respect the CAP proved an extravagant success: its price support mechanism gave incentives for farmers to produce at levels that went beyond self sufficiency, generating massive agricultural surpluses. The effect was to encourage farming practices that emphasized quantity, rather than quality, of output, and in many respects were damaging to the environment and ultimately unsustainable.

The combined weight of budgetary difficulties, environmental concerns and international pressures led the Community to take the first serious steps towards reform of the CAP in 1992. If agricultural policies are to become consistent with sustainable development this process must continue, so that farmers have incentives to reorientate their production techniques to avoid environmental damage.

Opposition to reform has to a large extent been based on fears about the future of rural society in the European Union. However, it is questionable whether the traditional agricultural support mechanisms are a cost-effective means of securing the economic viability of rural areas. This objective may be better achieved by measures to develop the infrastructure required for the development of new industries.

9.1 THE COMMON AGRICULTURAL POLICY

In industrialized countries, free trade in agricultural products has been the exception rather than the rule: the late nineteenth-century period of general free trade in agricultural products lasted little more than 30 years (Economist 1992: 3). Long before the CAP, European agricultural markets had been subject to intervention to stabilize agricultural prices and to secure supplies of agricultural products. The CAP has superseded a variety of agricultural policy mechanisms deployed at national level. These mechanisms included price supports, import levies and quotas, production quotas, income supplements, and subsidies for agricultural inputs (El-Agraa 1990: 195–6).

The CAP was established by the original EEC Treaty in 1957. Article 38 of the Treaty provides that 'the common market shall extend to agriculture and trade in agricultural products'; but it also stipulates that 'the common market for agricultural products must be accompanied by the establishment of a common agricultural policy among the member states'.

The objectives of the CAP as specified in the EC Treaty (Article 39) are as follows:

- To increase agricultural productivity
- To ensure a fair standard of living for the agricultural community
- To stabilize markets
- To assure the availability of supplies
- To ensure that supplies reach consumers at reasonable prices.

This is a highly interventionist agenda. Agriculture is unique among Community policy areas in the extent to which markets are managed in order to determine prices and levels of production—the Common Transport Policy, for instance, does not involve massive subsidies from the Community budget to ensure the availability of transport services. In only one other sector—coal and steel—are the provisions for Community intervention comparable to those of the CAP; but it requires a 'manifest crisis' before the Commission can invoke its powers to set production quotas for these industries (Article 58 ECSC).

The implementation of the CAP has followed three guiding principles:

1. *A single market*   The market is managed by common rules which prevail across the Community, including fixed currency exchange rates, harmonized administrative and health regulations and common external trade policies.
2. *A high degree of self sufficiency*   Community markets have been protected from import competition, and Community production has been encouraged by prices well above world market levels.
3. *Financing from the Community budget*   As a Community-level policy, the CAP's support for agriculture has been financed from Community resources, and for years has taken up well over half the total Community budget. (In Community terminology this is known as *financial solidarity*.)

9.1.1   The working of the CAP

The CAP is implemented through 'market organizations' which cover more than 90 per cent of the Community's agricultural production. Market organizations are categorized by the type of mechanism used to manage the market and subsidize producers. There are four main types of organization:

1. *Intervention with import protection*   Products have 'intervention' prices, at which the authorities will purchase all the produce offered to them. Community prices are kept higher than world market prices with levies on imports into the Community (and subsidies for Community exports). Approximately 60 per cent of Community agricultural output is covered by arrangements of this type, including cereals, sugar, milk, beef and sheepmeat.
2. *Import protection*   Although there is no intervention purchasing, prices are influenced by import levies and export subsidies; this type of organization accounts for some 25 per cent of Community output, principally in the poultry sector.
3. *Supplementary price support*   In sectors with little or no import protection, subsidies are given for the processing of agricultural produce originating in the Community: less than 5 per cent of Community output is covered by this type of organization.

4. *Direct support for producers*   Subsidies are given per hectare of land under cultivation, or per unit of output: such support was in the past confined to a few specialized sectors, with less than 1 per cent of Community agricultural output. The 1992 CAP reforms extended direct support for farmers' incomes (see Sec. 9.2.4).

Measures to implement the CAP are financed from the European Agricultural Guidance and Guarantee Fund (EAGGF). This has two sections: the Guarantee section covers the costs of market organization, which mainly comprises expenditure on intervention purchasing, while the Guidance section is one of the Community's three structural funds (see Sec. 3.4).

The system of intervention prices (see Box 9.1) has been the mainstay of the CAP, and the source of many of its difficulties. The basic principle of the system is simple enough: the authorities administering the CAP purchase and sell agricultural output in order to prevent excessive variations in market prices. This process—known as intervention buying—should support prices, and hence farm incomes, when output is high, and sales from stockpiles can restrain prices when output is low. It is possible in this way to offset the effects of good and bad harvests, so that producers and consumers do not face severe fluctuations in prices. If the system is working properly, stockpiles, and the budgetary impact of the CAP, should vary cyclically. Expenditure on intervention in periods of surplus should be offset by revenue from sales of stockpiled produce in periods of low output, so that in some years the CAP would earn positive net revenue for the Community.

BOX 9.1
The EC agricultural price support system

The price intervention procedure begins with the setting of a *target* price. Any output not purchased by consumers can be sold by farmers at the *intervention* price, which is slightly lower than the target price—for example by 10 per cent in the case of cereals. So intervention purchases effectively set a minimum price, below which farmers will not sell on the open market; any output they do not sell in the market at or above the intervention price could be sold to the intervention stockpile.

Imported agricultural products are sold in the Community at a *threshold* price, which is slightly above the target price (in the case of cereals it is 10 per cent higher). Community prices are usually well above world market prices, so imports are subject to *levies* amounting to the threshold price minus the world market price; the addition of the levy raises the price of imports to the threshold level. Therefore the threshold price is the minimum price at which imports into the Community are economically viable.

The reality, as is well known, has been very different. Expenditure on the EAGGF (Guarantee Section) has consistently been well in excess of half the total Community budget. Stockpiles have reached levels at which there is no prospect of significant depletion through sales at realistic prices, giving rise to talk of 'butter mountains' and 'wine lakes'. Old stock has been sold at low prices to the former Soviet Union, whose agricultural system was beset by chronic inefficiencies; and some Community output has been exported with the aid of subsidies (a form of dumping, since the export prices are well below Community prices), with disruptive effects on agriculture particularly in developing countries.

CAP market organization strained budgetary controls, because it involved 'open-ended' commitments: expenditure on intervention purchasing could not be predicted in advance, since purchases depended on the amount of produce that farmers offered for sale at the intervention price. These two factors—the amount and the unpredictability of expenditure—gave rise to serious budgetary pressures in the 1980s. Indeed, prior to the launch of the single market programme, the Community was in many quarters associated mainly with excessive expenditures leading to massive agricultural surpluses.

9.1.2   Achievements of the CAP

Despite the problems of surplus production and budgetary pressures, the CAP can nevertheless be judged a success in terms of its three guiding principles—a single market, self sufficiency and financial solidarity.

Agricultural policy and the single market   Over the years, the CAP developed a large body of legislation designed to protect plant and animal health, to ensure the safety of food, to maintain breeding standards and to safeguard animal welfare. Measures to implement this legislation relied to a great extent on veterinary and plant health examinations which were performed at national frontiers. So the Community-level common policy was actually implemented by controls that were inconsistent with a single market.

Since the removal of frontier controls at the end of 1992, agricultural standards have been enforced by systems of mutually recognized certification, based on the 'country of origin' principle. Plants and animals, and products derived from them, are certified at their point of origin as complying with Community standards. This has required legislation to harmonize national regulations, and to ensure that the certification procedure covers essential requirements and that the personnel responsible for its implementation are properly trained.

This system severely limits the scope for member states to restrict imports, and calls for a high degree of mutual trust. Health protection can be invoked under the EC Treaty (Article 36) as legitimate grounds for national measures to restrict trade (see for example Case 74/82), but this does not apply if the necessary protection is afforded by Community regulations. Tensions can of course arise between national perceptions and priorities and the requirements of Community law. This was illustrated by pressure in Germany for the prohibition of imports of beef from the UK: concerns were raised over infection of British cattle with BSE (bovine spongiform encephalopathy—popularly known as 'mad cow disease') and the adequacy of control measures, notwithstanding the compliance of these measures with Community requirements.

Agricultural self sufficiency   The Community has become largely self sufficient in a wide range of agricultural products (although it remains a big importer of tropical produce and animal feedstuffs). This is illustrated in Table 9.1, which shows the extent of the Community's self sufficiency in the main temperate agricultural products. Self sufficiency, and the accumulation of agricultural stockpiles, has ensured the security of food supplies, minimizing any risk of food shortages.

Financial solidarity   The CAP pricing regime has stabilized Community agricultural markets and—on average—has sustained farm incomes. Although prices may have been excessive inasmuch as they have led to excess supply, and hence agricultural surpluses, they have not risen as rapidly as the general price level. From 1980 to 1992 consumer prices overall approximately doubled, as did food prices; in contrast, producer prices for agricultural output increased by only two-thirds. The difference between the rates of growth in consumer and producer prices is explained by increases in processing and distribution costs, which accounted for a growing proportion of the cost of food to the consumer.

Table 9.1   Degree of self sufficiency in agricultural products, European Community, 1991

	%[*]
Grain	129
Potatoes	101
Sugar	123
Meat	105
Cheese	105
Butter	111

[*] 100% denotes EC self sufficiency.
Source: Eurostat (1994: Table 5.14).

9.1.3   The mixed success of the CAP

The CAP's very success in achieving its original objectives has led to a questioning of these objectives, and to calls for the redefinition of the purposes of Community agricultural policy. In the years since the CAP was inaugurated, increases in productivity have been sufficient to offset the effect of declining prices; consequently farm incomes have been sustained—in aggregate—and output has increased to levels at which massive surpluses accumulated.

A major factor in this achievement has been the growing intensification of agriculture, with 'agro-industries' comprising of 'factory farms'. The crucial disadvantages, apart from the direct costs of surplus production, have been the social and environmental impacts.

The benefits of the CAP to farmers have been very uneven, and the price support system has tended to favour larger farmers. By 1992, 80 per cent of Community expenditure on the CAP accrued to only 20 per cent of the farmers, largely because small farms were not in a position to benefit fully from new technologies and more intensive production measures. The outcome has been a continuing attrition of small farmers, particularly in marginal agricultural areas. Over the 30 years 1960–90, the total number of farmers and farm workers declined by one-half in the territory of the six original member states (European Commission 1993a: 15).

The increase in agricultural productivity has been very uneven. In some areas output increased as land was over-exploited with intensive use of fertilizers and pesticides. In marginal farming areas with little scope for intensification of production, farmers' living standards declined and many left the land.

The population in general, as taxpayers and as consumers, benefits from assured supplies and stable prices; but these benefits come at a cost. Agricultural price support places a heavy burden on the Community budget, and prices charged to consumers exceed world market prices (see Table 9.2). Apart from questions of equity, the system is economically inefficient inasmuch as the aggregate cost to consumers and taxpayers exceeds the benefit to producers (according to some estimates, by as much as 50 per cent); the overall cost of the CAP has been estimated at approximately 0.5 per cent of Community GDP. (The estimates are surveyed in Dimitrios *et al.* 1988.)

9.2 REFORM OF THE CAP

Dissatisfaction with the CAP has a long history, and proposals for reform have been discussed since the 1960s. The general objectives were to rein back price support and promote structural adjustment in order to curb the industry's propensity for excess production. There was however continual difficulty in securing agreement to radical reform—it was always easier to secure agreement on increased financial support. (For an account of this period in the history of the CAP, see Warley 1969.)

As pressures mounted, various expedients were introduced to curb increasing expenditure and agricultural surpluses. Initially these concentrated on the abatement of surplus production, but did not fundamentally modify the system of incentives that led to the surpluses; in a sense, this amounted to treatment of the symptoms rather than the cause of the ailment. A more fundamental reform was instituted in 1992, which began to limit the price incentives for excess production, and switched resources from price guarantees (which linked payments to output) to income support and to structural measures designed to encourage more environmentally friendly farming.

9.2.1   Market stabilizers and supplementary measures

In order to contain budgetary pressures and excess production, the Community introduced a system of 'market stabilizers', which reduced market support when output rose beyond specified threshold levels, together with measures to promote structural changes in agriculture which would reduce excess production (see Regulations 1097–1115/88, *Official Journal*, 1988 L110). Whatever their other effects, the undeniable consequence of these reforms has been to complicate the system, and to generate terminology, a sample of which is set out in Box 9.2.

BOX 9.2
Common Agricultural Policy jargon

Maximum guaranteed quantity: the level of production at which measures to reduce excessive output are activated.
Co-responsibility levies: a charge paid by producers, which is refunded if output does not exceed the maximum guaranteed quantity.
Reference quantities: the quantities that may be sold through different channels within overall production quotas.
Set-aside: withdrawal of land from agricultural production, with compensation paid to farmers for loss of income.
Green currencies: agricultural expenditures and prices are expressed in ECUs and converted into national currencies at special 'green' exchange rates; the original purpose was to insulate farmers from the effects of movements in exchange rates in the currency markets.
Monetary compensation amounts: payments made to, or levied on, exporters of agricultural products at frontiers between member states, in order to offset differences between green rates and market exchange rates for currencies; this practice was discontinued at the end of 1992.
Switch-over mechanism: in the event of a realignment of currencies, the green ECU was revalued upwards in proportion with the national currency that appreciated the most; farm prices expressed in that currency remained the same, while in other currencies prices increased.
Livestock unit (LU): bovine and equine animals aged over two years and six months respectively; bovines between six months and two years are 0.6 LUs, and sheep and goats 0.15 LUs (see Regulation 2328/91, Annex 1).

The stabilizers typically specified maximum quantities for which price support was guaranteed, and various measures were adopted in order to restrain output within these maximum limits. Co-responsibility levies (see Box 9.2) were instituted for cereals and milk. For butter and beef, prices for intervention purchases above the guaranteed maximum were fixed by competitive tendering. Intervention prices (for tobacco, fruits and sheepmeat) or aid for production (in the case of olive oil and oilseeds) were reduced when the guaranteed maximum output was exceeded.

The stabilizers were supplemented by incentives to modify farming practices. Schemes were established to provide financial aid to farmers in order to promote restructuring: member states had considerable latitude with respect to the detailed organization of the schemes, and were mainly responsible for their financing. The objectives were to reduce excess supply, to support farmers' incomes during the adjustment process, and to promote 'environmentally friendly' farming. Measures were instituted in 1988 to provide financial support for:

1. *set-aside schemes*, which provide financial compensation for farmers who take land out of production;
2. *extensification*, with a reduction in output per hectare of at least 20 per cent;
3. *production conversion*, such that farmers diversify into products not subject to surpluses;
4. *early retirement of farmers*, with their farmland either used to enlarge other farms or assigned to non-agricultural uses.

The stabilizers and supplementary measures were not a conspicuous success. In the period 1988–92 stockpiles of cereals and beef increased, by approximately 150 and 70 per cent respectively. The only substantial stockpile that was significantly reduced was that of wine (European Commission 1993b).

9.2.2   The 1992 reform package

In the early 1990s the need for further reform of the CAP became increasingly evident. In 1992 the Council enacted a series of Regulations (published in the *Official Journal*, 1992 L180, L181 and L215) designed to curtail incentives for overproduction and to encourage diversification, while maintaining the Community's position as a major agricultural producer.

The most radical feature of the reforms was a shift from price intervention to direct support for farmers' incomes, with phased reductions in the target prices (and hence threshold and intervention prices) of agricultural commodities. This signified a fundamental change in the CAP, after years of continuous increases in the index of producer prices (although *effective* levels of price support had declined, because agricultural prices had increased less than the general price level).

9.2.3   Price reductions and measures to limit output

The cut in prices was most severe in the case of cereals (the sector in which intervention stocks had grown most in the period 1988–92): the target price was reduced by approximately 15 per cent (from 130 to 110 ECUs/te) over three years between 1993/4 and 1995/6. (The threshold and intervention prices were fixed respectively 45 ECUs above and 10 per cent below the target price.)

Prices for milk and butter were reduced over the period 1992/3 to 1994/5 by approximately 2½ and 5 per cent respectively. Although co-responsibility levies (see Box 9.2) were discontinued from April 1993, milk production remained severely constrained by quotas (see Box 9.4).

Sel
pg 280 for enlargement & CAP.

Production in excess of quotas attracts a levy of 115 per cent of the guide (target) price. (This applies to milk delivered to dairies; for direct sales the levy is 75 per cent.)

Intervention prices for beef are determined by competitive tendering, with limits on the amount of intervention purchases (750 000 te in 1993, reducing to 350 000 te by 1997), subject to a 'safety net' if market prices fall below 84 per cent of the intervention level. Market support for sheep and goat meat, in the form of a premium to compensate for differences between the base (target) price and the market price, is now subject to a production ceiling, beyond which the premium is reduced by 50 per cent.

9.2.4   Income support and structural measures

Change of emphasis

The reforms are designed to switch expenditure from market intervention to payments that directly support farm incomes. These payments are not linked directly to the individual farmer's output, and so do not give an incentive for production. In the case of cereals, income support takes the form of 'compensatory payments', which are determined with reference to the 'base area yield' (defined by regional average output): these payments were set to increase from 25 to 45 ECUs/te between 1993/4 and 1995/6. Large cereal producers (with annual output over 92 te) must set aside at least 15 per cent of their productive land, in return for a payment of 45 ECUs per tonne of output forgone (as calculated from the 'base area yield'); this scheme is optional for smaller producers.

Beef producers receive premiums to encourage less intensive farming. (They also benefit from reductions in the cost of animal feed arising from lower cereal prices.) Premiums are payable where animal densities on open grazing land are below prescribed levels: 3.5 LU/ha (livestock units per hectare) in 1993, declining to 2 LU/ha 1996. (An LU is one cow, or its equivalent—see Box 9.2.)

The aid scheme for early retirement from farming was continued with a new Regulation. The purpose of this scheme is to provide income for farmers who decide to retire, to improve the viability of agricultural holdings, and to reassign farmland that is not viable to non-agricultural uses (Regulation 2079/92, Article 1(1)).

The reforms were complemented by schemes to promote the use of agricultural land for forestry (Regulation 2080/92) and to encourage environmentally friendly agricultural practices (Regulation 2078/92). The latter Regulation (Article 2) provides for financial assistance to farmers who undertake to:

- reduce fertilizer usage
- change to, or to maintain, extensive production methods
- reduce the number of sheep or cattle per hectare
- use production methods compatible with protection of the environment and natural resources and maintenance of the countryside,
- rear local breeds in danger of extinction
- ensure the upkeep of abandoned farm or woodland
- set aside farmland for environmental purposes for at least 20 years
- manage land for public access and leisure activities.

The last item on this list was not in the original Commission Proposal. It can include activities that actually damage the environment, for example recreational use of land which may give rise to damage to wildlife habitats.

9.3   AGRICULTURE: THE INTERNATIONAL DIMENSION

The European Community is not alone in the support and protection it gives to agriculture. Agriculture is also heavily subsidized elsewhere in western Europe and in the United States. Levels of subsidy are shown by the figures in Table 9.2, which measure the divergence between producer prices and world prices in the European Community, the United States, and (on average) OECD member states. The levels of support were on the whole higher in the late 1980s than in the period 1979–86, although in all cases the overall divergence between domestic and world prices was highest in 1987.

Table 9.2   Agricultural subsidies: producer prices in relation to world prices, European Community, United States and OECD member states, averages 1979–1986 and 1987–1993

	1979–86	1987–93
All products		
EC	1.57	1.87
USA	1.24	1.29
OECD	1.47	1.69
Crops		
EC	1.53	2.14
USA	1.23	1.36
OECD	1.49	1.92
Livestock products		
EC	1.58	1.78
USA	1.26	1.24
OECD	1.46	1.58

Note: The figures given above are producer nominal assistance coefficients, which measure the ratio of effective producer prices to world prices. In the absence of agricultural subsidies, price supports, tariffs and import quotas, this ratio would be 1. The ratio is expressed by the formula $(P + P_s)/P$, where P is the implicit reference (border) price, which approximates to the world price, and P_s is the producer subsidy equivalent, representing the value of transfers to farmers from consumers or taxpayers, mainly through price support.
Source: © OECD (1994) *Agricultural Policies, Markets and Trade: Monitoring and Outlook 1994*, Annex Table III. Reproduced by permission of the OECD.

Agricultural policies have involved substantial barriers to trade, so that prices and output diverge significantly from the levels that would prevail if there were no subsidies or market intervention. For some major commodities substantial producers and markets have been excluded from the scope of free trade; for instance, the European Community and the United States together account for approximately one-quarter of world production of wheat, and almost one-third of all cereal production and meat production. With only a small proportion of output traded freely and subject to market forces of supply and demand, the result has been a distortion of prices in world markets, which has been exacerbated by the dumping of European Community surpluses which are subsidized by export rebates.

9.3.1   Implications of the GATT Uruguay Round

Agreement was reached in 1993—after years of difficult negotiation—to reduce agricultural subsidies world-wide. For years, agriculture had been excluded from the scope of the GATT agreement (see Sec. 10.2.2), but this omission appeared increasingly anomalous as the effects of agricultural subsidies on the world trading system became apparent. At the conclusion of the Uruguay Round negotiations, it was agreed that agricultural price support should be reduced by one-fifth, and subsidized exports reduced in value by 36 per cent and in volume by 21 per cent; these reductions are based on 1991–2 levels, and are phased over six years.

The GATT agreement on agriculture will affect the European Community in several ways. The most evident consequence is a restriction on price and income support, although the severity of this limitation depends on the relative levels of Community and world market prices. World prices, free of the distorting effects of dumped surpluses, are likely to increase, thus moderating the degree of adjustment required, while Community agricultural prices are already set to decline following the 1992 CAP reforms. The effect on the Community of reductions in income support is mitigated by exemptions for some direct payments to farmers, including support to ease structural adjustment.

The reduction in subsidies required by the GATT agreement can thus be seen as broadly consistent with the direction of Community agricultural policy following the 1992 reforms. Closer alignment of Community and world prices will ease the burden of price support on the Community budget. The GATT rules will, in principle, encourage the 'targeting' of income support in areas where it is most effective in facilitating structural change.

Liberalization of trade following the Uruguay Round will limit the Community's discretion in setting technical standards that act as non-tariff barriers to trade, and may require the abandonment of measures that the Community has instituted in the name of health protection. For example, Community legislation has forbidden the use of animal growth hormone and BST (bovine somatotrophin), which is used to increase milk yields (Decision 94/363); apart from any health risks, these prohibitions were expedient in preventing additional growth in agricultural surpluses. However, with the advent of free trade, the Community may be unable to restrict imports of products made from animals treated with these substances, which are permitted in the United States. The solution would appear to lie in agreement on harmonized standards, specifying what is necessary to protect health and the environment.

The GATT agreement also calls into question the objective of self sufficiency, which has been one of the fundamental tenets of the CAP. Restrictions in subsidies, together with trade liberalization, limit the Community's ability to restrain imports in favour of its own production.

9.4   THE COMMON AGRICULTURAL POLICY: AN ASSESSMENT

The problems of the CAP are well documented. Its tendency to generate surplus production and budgetary burdens has been severely criticized. Attempts to limit the adverse effects while retaining the original concept of the CAP have added additional layers of complexity. The result has been a system that is virtually impossible to manage efficiently, and is extremely vulnerable to fraud (see Box 9.3).

Nevertheless, the survival of the CAP in the face of such severe difficulties is evidence that it has served some purposes. There is a strong political motivation to maintain the social and economic structures of rural areas, and to avoid the damaging effects of rural depopulation and increasing urbanization. The CAP has been perceived as a means to achieve this objective, since agriculture is seen as the mainstay of the rural economy. Support for agriculture has been

Fraud.

BOX 9.3
Fraud and mismanagement in the Common Agricultural Policy

The Court of Auditors has characterized the CAP as a set of 'complex mechanisms, the very complexity of which has created an environment which is favourable to irregularities and fraud'. The management of the CAP has been found seriously deficient: 'Member States and the Commission have failed in their duty by adopting a somewhat minimal approach to monitoring and combating agricultural fraud.' The Court has criticized monitoring procedures as 'superficial and ineffective', especially in relation to concerns which operate in more than one member state; and, in the absence of agreed definitions of fraud and irregularities, sanctions are not applied in a uniform fashion, so that conduct which would be punishable by a fine or even imprisonment in one member state might attract no sanction in another. Between 1972 and 1991 5775 cases of fraud had been detected, involving 725.5 bn ECUs (of which only 77.7 bn has been recovered).

One-third of CAP expenditure is used to subsidize exports. The Court has criticized member states' procedures for administering these expenditures, and especially their failure to recover export subsidies erroneously paid. For example, a consignment of cheese was exported, with the benefit of export subsidy, to the USA, but rejected on arrival as sub-standard; it was then re-exported from the Community, again with a subsidy, so that subsidies were paid twice for the same consignment.

Sources: Court of Auditors Special Report No. 7/93, concerning controls of irregularities and frauds in the agricultural area, *Official Journal*, 1994 C53/1; Court of Auditors Special Report No. 1/94, concerning follow-up to the Court's special report No. 2/92 and continuation of the Court's audit of major beneficiaries of export refunds accompanied by the replies of the Commission, *Official Journal*, 1994 C75/1. (For previous reports see *Official Journal*, 1992 C101, and 1990 C133.)

pport for
rural
areas.

justified on the grounds that declining agricultural incomes would weaken the economic condition both of farms and the industries that depend on them. This in turn would lead to a vicious circle of falling employment and population, as rural settlements lose the essential services that make them viable centres of population. There is an implicit assumption that the farming sector, and the rural economy generally, cannot be restructured to ensure a viable future in which agriculture is unsubsidized.

Through the CAP, agriculture has received support not available to other economic sectors. In addition to price guarantees and import protection, farming has been shielded from risks and liabilities that are borne as a matter of course by firms in other industries. For instance, the 'green' currency system, with the 'switch-over' mechanism (see Box 9.2), has insulated agriculture from adverse effects of exchange rate movements, and indeed has enabled farmers to receive price increases in proportion to the devaluation of their country's currency. The system has now been modified to permit upward revaluation of 'green' currencies, but with provision for state aid to farmers in the event of an 'appreciable' revaluation; the Community is to contribute half of this aid, and three-quarters in the less prosperous 'objective 1' regions (Regulation 150/95). There remain strong political pressures to avoid upward revaluations of 'green' currencies which reduce agricultural support. Apart from a lack of even-handedness between industries, the effect is to impart an upward bias to agricultural prices, tending to counter the effects of reductions in the target prices expressed in ECUs.

Subsidization permeates the CAP to a far greater extent than other areas of policy. Schemes provide financial assistance for services to agriculture, such as farm modernization, training and diversification. Aid is given for cessation of farming, as for example with the early retirement scheme, designed 'to provide an income for elderly farmers [and] improve the viability of agricultural holdings' (Regulation 2079/92). There are few comparable industry-specific schemes applying to other sectors of economic activity. This prompts a question as to whether expenditure on agricultural restructuring might be used more effectively to increase the competitiveness of other industries within the Community.

What about other Inds [margin note]

Reforms of the CAP have sought to adhere to its original framework, including market intervention and a high degree of self sufficiency. The 'market stabilizers' introduced in the 1980s qualified the 'open-ended' guarantees of the intervention purchasing system, but agricultural surpluses persisted nevertheless. The complexity and administrative problems of the CAP increased, as is illustrated by the difficulties that have arisen in implementation of the milk quota scheme (see Box 9.4).

BOX 9.4
Complexities of the milk quota system

The Community scheme of production quotas for milk is administered by member states, in conjunction with national measures. The result, according to the Court of Auditors, is a system 'often tailored by each Member State to suit its own requirements' incorporating measures which in some cases 'serve more to skirt round the Community objectives than to achieve them'. Moreover, national variation 'singularly complicates the management, assessment, supervision and monitoring [of quotas]'.

One consequence is that 'milk producers are treated differently from one Member State to another by the same Community programme or measure'. Another is extensive litigation: in addition to national court judgments, the Court of Justice has ruled on approximately 30 cases involving milk quotas.

Source: Court of Auditors Special Report No. 4/93 on the implementation of the quota system intended to control milk production together with the Commission's replies, *Official Journal*, 1994 C12/1.

The 1992 reform set up a progressive reduction in prices, which is compensated by increased income support. In principle this is to be welcomed, since it increases the transparency of agricultural subsidies, and enables support to be targeted on restructuring and on support for marginal farms on the fringe of viability. In practice, the reforms largely maintain the practice of indiscriminate support, which has given the most support to the wealthier farmers.

The switch to income support may facilitate a decline in subsidization. While price support requires farmers to deliver their output for purchase, income support is, in contrast, a pure subsidy: recipients are not necessarily required to perform any service to society, such as measures to diversify production or improve the environment. The level of such support cannot be determined on an objective basis, and budgetary and political pressures may lead to its curtailment in the future.

The CAP is in a continuing state of tension. Even with the 1992 reforms, and reductions in support following the GATT Uruguay Round, agriculture is set to remain a substantial burden on the Community budget. However, continuing support from the taxpayer does not appear to induce in farmers a sense of well-being—as is evidenced by widespread political discontent.

The general explanation of this apparent paradox may lie in the ultimate distribution of the benefits of subsidies. The poorer, marginal, farms generate very modest incomes, even with support from the CAP—as noted in Sec. 9.1.3, the CAP has tended to favour the larger, wealthier farmers who are better able to increase their productivity over time. However, the larger farmers also face difficulties, as reductions in CAP expenditure cause land prices to decline. This is because land prices tend to reflect the availability of financial support, both at present and (in terms of expectations) in the future, so that the ultimate beneficiaries of subsidies are landowners rather than farmers. (In economic terms, the flow of subsidy payments becomes capitalized in the price of land.) Subsidies therefore do not in the long run affect the operating finances of farms—but declining land values can leave farmers exposed financially, having to cover the costs of purchasing land that has subsequently fallen in value.

9.5   A SUSTAINABLE FUTURE FOR THE RURAL ECONOMY

In the past, farmers responded to the incentives of the CAP price support mechanism by intensifying production; this has proved to have been environmentally damaging. Reform of the CAP has effected some changes, so that there is now a complex mixture of incentives which in some instances appear inconsistent. The main priority for agriculture must be to continue the reform process, so that there is a consistent pattern of incentives for the development and adoption of farming techniques compatible with sustainable development.

It is also necessary to separate the issues of agricultural support and the future of the rural economy. Although agricultural expenditure does benefit the wider economy, the CAP cannot be justified on this basis: much of the expenditure on agricultural support occurs in areas where other types of industry, not dependent on agriculture, are prospering. Rural areas in economic decline are more likely to be assisted by measures that address their problems directly, and that support training and infrastructure for the development of economically viable industries.

9.5.1   Environmental impacts of intensive agriculture

Increases in agricultural output under the CAP have been achieved primarily through intensification of production. Yields of cereal crops in the European Community Member States increased on average by approximately two-thirds from 1972 to 1992 (Eurostat 1994: Table 5.3). Production has become geographically concentrated, so that 5 per cent of the Community's agricultural land accounts for one-third of its cereal production (COM(92)23 III, p. 57).

Intensive livestock rearing has developed in regions where agriculture has become industrialized. This is particularly the case in the Netherlands, where the pig population almost doubled between 1973 and 1990, when it reached 13.8 m (Eurostat 1992, Table 11.1.5)—compared with a human population of some 15 m. With less than 2 per cent of the European Community's agricultural land area, the Netherlands in 1989 accounted for 15 per cent of its pork production, 9.2 per cent of egg production and 7.2 per cent of poultry production (Commission Decision 1992). Economic integration within the single market will tend to accelerate intensification, following the removal of trade barriers and restrictions on capital movements between member states. This effect may be particularly marked in the less developed regions of the Community, where agriculture has hitherto been less intensive: there, the single market affords opportunities for vertical integration by food processing companies taking over farms (Task Force 1990: 109).

The intensification process has had significant implications for farm management and agricultural production processes. Agriculture has become more 'industrialized', with 'factory' farms and increasing use of fertilizers and pesticides. This has tended to change the balance between farming and nature, as pressure is put on the capacity of the environment to recycle wastes and absorb agricultural inputs.

BOX 9.5
The environmental consequences of intensive agriculture

Agricultural practice	Environmental impact
Systematic use of pesticides	Resistance to pesticides, increasing frequency and costs of subsequent treatments, soil and water pollution problems
Excessive use of nitrogenous and phosphate fertilizers	Eutrophication in surface waters, ecological damage, water rendered less suitable for human consumption and recreation
Imprudent land management	Soil erosion
Genetic uniformity of plants and livestock	Plant and animal diseases
Concentration of livestock	Soil and water pollution from animal wastes
Ground clearance and drainage	Depletion of wetlands and reduced biodiversity

Source: European Commission, 'Towards Sustainability', COM (92)23 II, and Official Journal, 1993 C138, Sec. 4.4.

A number of practices associated with intensive agriculture, and their consequences for the environment, are summarized in Box 9.5. Over-use of fertilizers and pesticides, and poor land and stock management, can lead to a degradation of soil, water and natural resources.

Factory farms, like other types of factory, generate wastes. While the manure generated by grazing animals in open fields at low density has value as a natural fertilizer, the manure from intensively farmed livestock has a negative value. It is produced in quantities that far exceed the absorptive capacity of the land, and is liable to cause pollution of water as its phosphate content gives rise to eutrophication. In the Netherlands a massive increase in manure processing capacity is proposed—from 420 000 te in 1989, capacity is planned to rise to 20 million te by 2000 (Commission Decision 1992).

As the Community has made progress in the control of water pollution from 'end-of-pipe' sources such as industrial plant and sewage works (see Box 7.3), attention has increasingly focused on pollution from diffuse, 'non-point' sources. The most important such source is agriculture, and the greatest concern is over concentrations of nitrates in surface and underground water, the main cause of which is the leaching of fertilizers from fields into water courses. Usage of nitrogen fertilizers in the Community rose by approximately 50 per cent between 1972 and 1988 (COM(92)23 III, p. 57). Similar increases have been observed in concentrations of nitrates in river water: monitoring points on the Rhine in Germany and the Netherlands recorded increases in nitrate concentrations of approximately 50 per cent between 1970 and 1985; even greater increases were recorded on the Rhone (France) and the Po (Italy) (Eurostat 1990: 134, Table 8.4.3).

9.5.2   Farmers' incentives

In 1988 the Commission submitted a Communication to the Council on agriculture and the environment. The opening sentence began: 'European agriculture is traditionally an ally of the environment', and went on to observe that farmers 'have depended ... for their livelihood ...

AP
x
ihre
dog

upon fertile soils, clean water and a stable ecological balance'. Where farmers have deviated from this traditional role, the main explanation was 'a technological revolution which has led to more intensive farming practices' (COM(88)338, p. 1)

This begs a question: why did technological changes take this course? Technology develops in response to needs, and in the case of agriculture it is necessary to look to the CAP, and the pattern of incentives it incorporates, as the driving force for technological change.

Price incentives As the CAP has grown in complexity, it has presented farmers with a profusion of incentives, which in many cases have not been mutually consistent. Historically, the main incentive came from price guarantees: farmers found it profitable to generate surplus output because they were assured that their production could be sold to the intervention stock, and that the price would exceed the level indicated by consumer demand.

The stabilizers introduced in the 1980s qualified this open-ended guarantee, and added to the complications of the CAP. Some of these measures, such as co-responsibility levies and tendering for intervention sales, were designed to introduce price flexibility in response to excess supply. The result was to create an element of uncertainty for the individual farmer, without fundamentally altering the price support system. Other measures, including milk quotas and the 'set-aside' system, introduced quantitative restrictions to prevent farmers from responding fully to price incentives; but incentives were created to operate the system (for example in the allocation of milk quotas) to circumvent output constraints.

The price incentive for surplus production was eventually curtailed in the 1992 reforms, with progressive reductions in agricultural prices and a switch of CAP expenditure from price to income support. Income support is 'neutral' with respect to the level of production, inasmuch as it is paid irrespective of the individual farmer's actual output. However, it is not certain that the process that induced excessive output can easily function 'in reverse', to bring about a decline in production in response to lower prices. The critical factor is the extent to which costs vary as output is reduced. If a large proportion of their costs are fixed, farmers can be to some extent 'locked in' to their existing levels of output: this situation can result from high loan payments (reflecting the capitalization of subsidies described in Sec. 9.4), or a lack of alternative employment.

Subsidies Some critics of the CAP have argued for fundamental reform, and have identified subsidization as the basic cause of the problems confronting agriculture in the Community. For example, *The Economist* (1992) characterized agricultural polices as 'grotesque', and concluded that 'farming subsidies have reached absurd proportions.... Gradual reform does not work. Radical reform might.'

Agricultural policy is indeed unique in the European Community (and elsewhere) in its emphasis on subsidy as the primary instrument of policy. For instance, the EC Treaty (Article 130r(2)) specifies that 'environmental damage should ... be rectified at source and ... the polluter should pay'. Industrial enterprises are expected to bear the costs of measures that are necessary to limit the environmental impact of their activities (Council Recommendation 75/436). Agriculture is ostensibly subject to similar rules; thus for example the 1985 Commission Green Paper on the CAP observed that 'agriculture ... like other sectors with potentially harmful activities should be subject to ... controls designed to avoid deterioration of the environment. In general the principle of "polluter pays" would apply, and it would not be normal for farmers to expect to be compensated by the public authorities for the introduction of such rules' (COM(85)333, p. 50).

However, in agriculture, practice does not generally correspond with this principle.

Massive subsidization has contributed to environmental problems, as described above, associated with intensive farming and overproduction, and in many instances the Community has sought to mitigate these problems with further subsidies. For example, the 1992 reforms sought to promote environmentally friendly agricultural practices by means of financial assistance to farmers adopting these practices (see Sec. 9.2.4). In other economic sectors, subsidies to promote cleaner technologies are generally limited to support for pilot or demonstration programmes: if agriculture were treated similarly, environmentally *un*friendly processes and products would be *dis*couraged, by regulations, liability for environmental damage and (possibly) taxation, and also by pressures from consumers (such incentives are discussed in Chapter 7). Quality products can command a premium price, but the CAP has tended to obscure the incentive effect of such price differentials.

In principle, subsidies are inefficient. They burden the Community budget and divert resources from alternative—possibly more effective—uses. Subsidies can also be wasteful, inasmuch as they may pay farmers to do things that they might have done in any case. For example, the Commission's 1988 paper on environment and agriculture points out that farmers have depended on nature for their livelihood, and so have 'played a key role in maintaining the soil, preventing rural pollution and defending rural ecology' (COM(88)338, p. 1). So when the Community makes payments to farmers who engage in afforestation and conservation, a question arises as to how far they would have engaged in these activities purely in their own interest, without subsidy.

Economic incentives in a reformed CAP   The present situation is the outcome of continuing incentives over many years for higher production, which have caused agricultural developments to be geared mainly to raising output. As the objectives of the CAP have changed and widened, various incentive mechanisms have been added on; but piecemeal measures do not amount to a coherent policy. Beef producers, for example, face complex decisions—should they tender for intervention sales, and if so at what price? What account should they take of the 'safety net' that is activated when market prices reach low levels? Is it worth while to reduce animal densities in order to qualify for the extensification premium?

Conflict between policy measures is nothing new. For instance efforts to promote conservation may be countered by agricultural support measures; a notable example is identified in the Community's environmental action programme, which observes that 'efforts to protect heatherland and combat erosion ... can fail because of overgrazing as a result of the headage payment scheme (COM(92)23 II, p. 36).

Nevertheless, the reforms appear to have exacerbated inconsistencies within the CAP. For example, set-aside may hinder extensification, if farmers seek to offset the loss of output from set-aside land by more intensive cultivation of their remaining land. Another instance is the early retirement scheme for farmers: if the productivity of their land increases under new management, this will tend to increase agricultural surpluses.

The challenge now is to reorientate agriculture and to promote technologies designed to improve product quality and protect the environment; and this requires that farmers have appropriate incentives. One example is the use of pesticides and fertilizers. In the past there was little reason to develop and use more efficient methods for application to crops, since these inputs constitute a very small proportion of farmers' production costs, while ensuring high yields. However, with restrictions on fertilizer use in nitrate-sensitive areas (Directive 91/676), there is now more of an incentive to develop technologies for efficient application, to ensure that a higher proportion of the fertilizer will be taken up by the crops rather than contaminating surface and underground water.

Consumer preferences can also generate strong incentives. In the past the CAP price mechanism has tended to obscure the qualitative aspects of products. A reformed CAP could deploy informative measures (on the lines described in Sec. 7.4) and facilitate producers' responses to demand for variety and for 'environmentally friendly' products.

After many years of intensification and excess production, it is unrealistic to expect that agriculture will be reorientated instantly and painlessly. Nevertheless, just as price supports motivated increased output, farmers can be expected eventually to respond to new incentives for quality rather than quantity. There is clearly scope for improvement in this respect through better management of inputs—for example by use of integrated crop management techniques.

9.5.3   Prospects for the rural economy

As food shortages ceased to be a realistic possibility, the future of the CAP came to be judged more in terms of its contribution to the maintenance of rural society. This became a key point in the context of the GATT Uruguay Round negotiations. Opponents of cuts in farm subsidies argued that support for farmers was essential for the survival of rural communities. Populations of rural settlements have a 'critical size' below which they are not viable as centres providing services for their hinterland. Without the support of the CAP, it was argued, marginal farms would be uneconomic; and this would lead to land abandonment, with undesirable environmental effects, and would undermine the rural enterprises that provide services for farms. The consequence would be unemployment and depopulation as rural settlements became unviable.

However, the CAP is a rather blunt instrument for the maintenance of rural society. Even with the support of the CAP, the economic importance of agriculture has diminished over time: it accounted for 5.4 per cent of European Community GDP in 1970, but for only 2.9 per cent in 1991. Moreover, agriculture has been a declining source of employment: between 1965 and 1991, the full-time agricultural labour force in the Community (excluding Spain and Portugal) fell by approximately 60 per cent.

So if agriculture is in relative decline, the survival of the rural economy must in the main depend on other industries. It is doubtful whether there is any single prescription for rural economic development, such is the diversity of the Community and its regions. For instance, in Greece agriculture contributed 16.3 per cent of 1991 GDP, and 21.9 per cent of the workforce was engaged in farming in 1992; in contrast, the corresponding figures for the UK were only 1.5 and 2.2 per cent (Eurostat 1994: Tables 2.5 and 3.18).

In 1988 the Commission issued a paper on the future of rural society, which set out the following three-fold classification of rural areas (COM(88)501, p. 19):

1. *Areas under development pressure close to conurbations*: these include south-east England, the Paris–Brussels–Bonn triangle, Flanders and some Mediterranean coastal regions.
2. *Areas in decline*, suffering depopulation, land abandonment, soil erosion, failure to maintain woodlands and fire risk; these problems arise particularly in Greece, Portugal, southern Italy and central and southern Spain.
3. *Marginal areas*, mostly in mountainous regions and outlying islands: these suffer the problems of declining areas in an even more acute form.

Regions in the first category do not suffer from depopulation or economic decline: on the contrary, their small towns have become development 'subpoles' with concentrations of infrastructure and amenities (COM(88)501, p. 18). These regions have attracted dynamic developing enterprises, and 'reverse' migration from cities back to rural areas by people in search of a better quality of life (COM(88)501, p. 12).

Declining and marginal areas do not have the economic advantages of proximity to conurbations; but nor do they gain greatly from the 'traditional' support mechanisms of the CAP. The CAP has taken account of the difficulties of farming in areas in which there are natural handicaps such as slope, altitude or infertile land, through measures including exemption from the milk co-responsibility levy, and higher premiums for sheep. Member states are empowered to provide compensatory allowances to support farmers' incomes in these regions (European Commission 1993c: 9; allowances are paid pursuant to Article 17 of Regulation 2328/91); however, there is no requirement to pay these allowances, and Denmark does not do so. Farmers in less favoured areas (LFAs) gain proportionately more from direct income subsidies than from price support measures,[1] and so, in principle, they should gain from the switch in CAP expenditure to income support.

If the maintenance of rural society is to be the main focus of agricultural support, then this support logically should be concentrated in less favoured areas in which the viability of the rural economy is threatened. However, rural areas are not wholly dependent on farming—indeed, more than half the farmers in LFAs spend less than 50 per cent of their time working in agriculture (European Commission 1993c: 18). Commission studies suggest that income support has given sufficient incentive for part-time or older farmers to continue farming, but is not adequate to attract and retain younger farmers in LFAs (European Commission 1994: 132).

So agricultural policies are not self-evidently the best means of supporting the rural economy, even if they have an important role in conjunction with other policy measures. The Community is able to contribute to rural development through several of the policy areas discussed in Chapters 3 and 6 above, such as infrastructure development and training (under structural fund objectives 1, 3 and 6), industry policies (and especially support for small and medium-sized enterprises), and research and development (including information and communication technology).

9.6 AGRICULTURE: KEY POINTS AND ISSUES

Although the Common Agricultural Policy has manifest defects, it is to a large extent the victim of its own success in achieving its original objectives of market stabilization and security of supply. The problematical aspects of the CAP are well known: pressures on the Community budget, disposal of agricultural surpluses, and excessive intensification of farming. Successive reforms have sought to mitigate these effects: price support is being cut back, and there is a growing emphasis on structural measures and income support for farmers. These developments have received further impetus from the agreement concluding the GATT Uruguay Round negotiations.

Agriculture has been treated very differently from other economic sectors, and to some degree has been insulated from economic realities; in particular, subsidization has become deeply ingrained. Farmers have responded to incentives that encouraged intensification and over-production, and they now face the need for adjustment to other incentives, as the system has become increasingly complex.

Political support for agriculture remains strong, as is shown by the tortuous progress of the CAP reform process and the GATT Uruguay Round negotiations. Opponents of reform have raised legitimate concerns over the future of rural societies; but it is not clear that continued subsidization of agriculture is the most effective means of ensuring the viability of economic activity in rural areas.

Arising from the Community's agricultural policies, the following key issues may be identified:

- The Common Agricultural Policy (CAP) was designed to stabilize agricultural markets and to ensure a high degree of self sufficiency for the Community: how far can the existence of the CAP now be justified with reference to these objectives?
- Reforms of the CAP have sought to ease budgetary pressures with a combination of market stabilization and structural measures: how far do the gains from these measures offset the additional complexity they have brought to the CAP?
- A key feature of the reforms is a switch from price support to income support for farmers: to what extent can a system of income support be justified with reference to the fundamental objectives of the CAP?
- Agricultural support has been restrained by the GATT Uruguay Round agreement, and faces further reduction to accommodate new member states in eastern Europe: how can the Community best make the necessary adjustment to lower levels of support?
- Defenders of the CAP have suggested that agricultural support has an important role in maintaining the viability of rural societies: how far is this true? What alternative measures can be used to achieve this objective?

NOTE

1. European Commission (1994: 131); the share of income subsidies in farm net value added (FNVA) is approximately equal (at 20 per cent) in less favoured areas (LFAs) and 'normal' areas, while income subsidies are proportionately much higher in LFAs. (They range from approximately 10 per cent (in the south of the EU) to 30 per cent (in the north-west) of FNVA in LFAs; the corresponding average figure for 'normal' areas is 5 per cent.)

REFERENCES

Dimitrios, G. *et al.* (1988) 'The effects of the CAP on the EC: a survey of the literature', *Journal of Common Market Studies*, 27(2).

Economist, The (1992), 'Survey of Agriculture', *The Economist*, 12 December.

El-Agraa, A. M. (1990) *Economics of the European Community*, 3rd edn, Philip Allan, Oxford.

European Commission (1993a) *Our Farming Future*, Office for Official Publications, Luxembourg.

European Commission (1993b) *The New Regulation of the Agricultural Markets Vademecum 1/93*, Office of Official Publications, Luxembourg.

European Commission (1993c) 'Support for farms in mountains, hills and less favoured areas', *Green Europe*, 2/93.

European Commission (1994) *The Agricultural Income Situation in Less Favoured Areas of the European Community*, Office for Official Publications, Luxembourg.

Eurostat (1990) *Environment Statistics 1989*, Office for Official Publications, Luxembourg.

Eurostat (1992) *Environment Statistics 1991*, Office for Official Publications, Luxembourg.

Eurostat (1993) *Basic Statistics of the Community*, 30th edn, Office for Official Publications, Luxembourg.

Eurostat (1994) *Basic Statistics of the Community*, 31st edn, Office for Official Publications, Luxembourg.

OECD (1994) Agricultural Policies, Markets and Trade: Monitoring and Outlook 1994, OECD, Paris.

Task Force (1990) '*1992': The Environmental Dimension*, Task Force Environment and the Internal Market, Brussels.

Warley, G. (1969) 'Economic integration of European agriculture', in G. R. Denton (ed.), *Economic Integration in Europe*, Weidenfeld & Nicolson, London.

European Community legislation

Regulations

Regulation 2328/91, on improving the efficiency of agricultural structures, *Official Journal*, 1991 L218/1.

Regulation 2078/92, on agricultural production measures compatible with the requirements of the protection of the environment and the maintenance of the countryside, *Official Journal*, 1992 L215/85.

Regulation 2079/92, instituting a Community aid scheme for early retirement from farming, *Official Journal*, 1992 L215/91.

Regulation 2080/92, instituting a Community aid scheme for forestry measures in agriculture, *Official Journal*, 1992 L215/96.

Regulation 150/95, on the unit of account and the conversion rates to be applied for the purposes of the CAP, *Official Journal*, 1995 L22/1.

Directives

Directive 91/676, concerning the protection of waters against pollution caused by nitrates from agricultural sources, *Official Journal*, 1991 L375/1.

Decisions and recommendations

Commission Decision (1992), concerning aid envisaged by the Netherlands government in favour of an environmentally sound disposal of manure, *Official Journal*, 1992 L170/34.

Decision 94/363, concerning the placing on the market and administration of bovine somatotrophin (BST), *Official Journal*, 1994 L366/19.

Council Recommendation 75/436/Euratom, ECSC, EEC, regarding cost allocation and action by the public authorities on environmental matters, *Official Journal*, 1975 L194/1.

European Commission documents

COM(85)333, *Perspectives for the Common Agricultural Policy: Green Paper of the Commission*, 13 July 1985.

COM(88)338, *Environment and Agriculture: Commission Communication*, 8 June 1988.

COM(88)501, *The future of rural society: Commission Communication*, 23 September 1988.

COM(92)23 II, *Towards Sustainability: a European Community Programme of Policy and Action in relation to the Environment and Sustainable Development*, 27 March 1992 (reproduced in *Official Journal*, 1993 C138).

COM(92)23 III, *The State of the Environment in the European Community: Overview*, 27 March 1992.

Court judgment

Case 74/82 *Commission v. Ireland* [1984] ECR 317.

FOUR

THE EXTERNAL DIMENSION

Since the foundation of the European Community, there have been far-reaching political changes both in Europe and across the globe. The Community was established in a divided Europe, at the 'front line' in a global confrontation between 'East' and 'West'; and several of the member states had strong colonial links—the vestiges of an earlier form of economic integration. In the 1990s the world economy has seen increasing globalization and moves to liberalize world trade—together with tensions in trading relations and the development of regional groupings of states for the purpose of trade and economic co-operation. Although the ideological division of Europe has ended, the continent remains divided economically between the relatively prosperous West and the post-communist East which is now in the throes of economic restructuring. Almost all western European countries are now Community members, while to the east the economies of the former communist countries are in transition to a market economy, and striving to prepare for eventual accession to the Community.

These changes have occurred in parallel with the development of the European Community's role in international economic relations, the result of increasing integration within the single market. The Community is an economic 'superpower', accounting for one-fifth of world trade, and as such has taken a prominent role in international trade negotiations. Community trade policy is ostensibly in favour of liberalization, with some similarities—at a global level—to the single market framework. The commitment in principle to free trade coexists with trade restrictions in practice, notably in relation to the Common Agricultural Policy, but also including restrictions on 'sensitive' trade with eastern Europe, limitation of imports from east Asia (particularly Japan), and continuing preferential trade arrangements with the former colonies of Member States. To some extent these restrictive measures reflect tensions within the Community, in some instances exacerbated by economic restructuring in the single market; so in a sense trade policies represent an opportunity to 'externalize' economic problems within the Community.

A growing recognition of global interdependence has led international economic co-operation to reflect the agenda of sustainable development. Environmental standards feature in many of the Community's international agreements, including those with eastern European countries aspiring to Community membership and beset by an inheritance of environmental degradation. International economic relations have a growing environmental dimension, reflecting concerns over issues such as climate change, species conservation and management of hazardous waste. As a major presence in the world economy, the Community has taken a prominent role in these areas, and is a party to a number of international conventions with environmental objectives.

THE EUROPEAN COMMUNITY'S EXTERNAL RELATIONS

The European Community has become very much the focus of economic integration within the continent of Europe. Almost all of western Europe is now within the single market, and most of the countries of central and eastern Europe are aspirants to membership of the European Union and are linked to the Community by association agreements.

The European Community now has a major presence in the world, as the single market has developed against a background of growing interdependence in the global economy. Integration of national economies within a single entity has enhanced the role of the Community in economic relations with non-Community countries and within international organizations. Thus, policies with respect to trade and international economic co-operation are to a large extent determined at Community level; and, even where policies remain formally a national responsibility, there has to be a high degree of co-ordination within the Community.

This extension of the Community's role has coincided with an increasing recognition of the importance of international co-operation to secure sustainable development. The Community supports international action for technical co-operation in the environmental field. As a major economic power, the Community is a party to numerous international conventions providing for the use of trade policy instruments to achieve environmental objectives: examples include measures to conserve endangered species, to protect the ozone layer and to control the movement of hazardous waste. The Community is also a signatory to the 1992 Conventions on Biodiversity and on Climate Change.

10.1 ENLARGEMENT OF THE COMMUNITY

Judged by its attraction of membership applications, the Community has been a great success—so much so that it now encompasses almost all of western Europe. The EU Treaty (Article O) provides that 'any European state may apply to become a member of the [European] Union' (and hence of the European Community), and most non-member countries in Europe are now contemplating Community membership as a long-term aspiration, if not an immediate possibility.

The recent history of membership applications is summarized in Table 10.1. The composition of the Community was previously influenced very strongly by political considerations. The accession of Greece, Spain and Portugal, despite their relative economic weakness, constituted a recognition of their restoration of democracy; conversely, Austria, Finland and Sweden are economically strong but until 1995 remained outside the Community because of their neutrality in the East–West division of Europe.

Table 10.1   Applications for European Community membership up to 1993

Country	Date of application	Entry date (if decided)	GNP per capita, 1992 ($EC^* = 100$)
Turkey	1987		10
Austria	1989	1995	115
Cyprus	1990		50
Malta	1990		39
Sweden	1991	1995	139
Finland	1992	1995	113
Norway	1992	1995†	133

* The European Community of 12 member states.
† Norway did not ratify the Treaty of Accession, and so did not join the European Union.

With the end of the East–West division, economic considerations have become more prominent in the criteria for membership. The three newest member states were accorded a 'fast track' to Community membership (as was Norway, which eventually rejected membership). In contrast, other (earlier) applications have proceeded much more slowly, which suggests that any political advantages for the Community are outweighed by the relatively low economic prosperity of the applicant countries. The Community recently agreed to open negotiations for the membership of Cyprus and Malta after the conclusion of the 1996 Intergovernmental Conference, while Turkey has only secured agreement to a customs union with the Community (*Financial Times*, 7 March 1995). Countries of central and eastern Europe are also seeking eventual membership of the Community, but their economic position would seem to rule out any immediate prospect of this.

10.1.1 The European Economic Area

The Community in 1972 concluded agreements with neighbouring countries in western Europe establishing free trade in industrial goods, and including provisions on competition, agriculture and fisheries. Closer relations were instituted within the European Economic Area (EEA), which came into being on 1 January 1994, with membership comprising the European Community (which at that time had 12 member states), Austria, Finland, Norway, Sweden and Iceland.[1] Following enlargement of the Community in 1995, the only remaining EEA member states are Iceland, Norway and Liechtenstein.

The EEA in practice entailed 'quasi-membership' of the European Community with participation in the single market. The EEA Agreement (European Community 1994) closely follows the EC Treaty in establishing freedom of movement for goods (Pt II) and persons, services and capital (Pt III), competition regulations (Pt IV), provisions on transport, economic and monetary co-operation (Pt III), social policy, consumer protection, the environment, company law and statistical systems (Pt V). The general effect is that Community legislation prevails throughout the EEA.

The EEA institutional structure also mirrors that of the Community. There is a Council, comprising representatives of the European Commission and EEA member states (EEA Agreement, Article 90), a Joint Committee to oversee the implementation of legislation (Article 92), and a Joint Parliamentary Committee with a consultative role (Article 93). In the development of Community legislation, other EEA members are consulted where their interests are affected (Article 99 *et seq.*), and in these circumstances Commission Proposals are identified on publication as texts 'of EEA relevance'. However, the final decisions on enactment remain with the Community Council of Ministers, and the final arbiter remains the Community Court of Justice. (An earlier proposal for an EEA court, including representatives of the Court of Justice and the courts of EEA member states, was rejected by the Court (Opinion 1/91) because it would have compromised the integrity of the Community legal system.)

10.1.2 Political and economic changes in central and eastern Europe

The European Community came into being in a Europe divided into opposing blocs. Up to 1989 this division had an impression of permanence (which is easily forgotten in the light of subsequent events), as the wall dividing the city of Berlin came to symbolize the wider division of Europe. The unexpected collapse of the wall in 1989 led to the unification of Germany, and was followed by the emergence of democratic governments in eastern Europe and the disintegration of the Soviet Union and Yugoslavia (and, later, the orderly separation of the Czech and Slovak Republics).

Economic restructuring   As this transition began, problems inherited from the communist regimes became very evident. Compared with western Europe the economies of central and eastern Europe, (CEE) were extremely inefficient, because priority had been given to heavy industry, with little regard to the endowment of natural resources. The legacy of economic inefficiency and environmental degradation is illustrated by Table 10.2, which compares energy consumption and carbon dioxide emissions in the CEE countries, the former Soviet Union, the (then) 12 member European Union and the EFTA (European Free Trade Area) countries (three of which are now in the European Community). The table shows that, compared with the European Union average, more than three times the energy was required to produce one unit of output in the CEE countries; and in the former Soviet Union the figure was almost five times. Eastern Europe nevertheless had lower energy consumption per capita, but this was only because output per capita—and hence economic prosperity—was *much* lower.

Products manufactured in central and eastern Europe were, by western standards, unsophisticated, of low quality and obsolescent. The principal trading partner of the CEE countries was the Soviet Union, which was the main export market for manufactures, from which energy and raw materials were imported. Trade within the eastern bloc was generally transacted in non-convertible currencies, and much of it took the form of barter.

After 1989 the CEE countries were faced with the prospect of radical, and rapid, reorientation of their economies. The market system replaced the planned economy as the dominant model; substantial investments were required to modernize productive capacity; foreign trade was to be in hard currencies at world market prices; in order to be competitive, product quality had to be improved.

The initial effect was severe economic disruption. In Poland, Hungary and Czechoslovakia, the period 1989–92 saw drastic declines in industrial production (approximately 30 per cent), and GDP (approximately 20 per cent), and rapid inflation; in the most extreme case—Poland—prices increased more than twenty-fold in the two years 1989–90 (Myant 1993: 16–17). In the Balkan region—Romania, Bulgaria and Albania—the decline in industrial output was even more severe, of the order of 50 per cent (European Commission 1994: 35). This economic decline, in conjunction with a reorientation of trade towards the West, led to a dramatic decline in the balance of trade with the European Community (COM(94)361, p. 19).

Table 10.2 Energy consumption relative to gross domestic product and population and carbon dioxide emissions per head, Europe, 1991

	Energy consumption/ GDP	Energy consumption per capita	CO_2 emissions per capita
EU[*]	303	3.52	8.9
EFTA[**]	282	4.76	7.7
CEE[†]	1088	2.44	6.4
ex-USSR	1490	4.50	12.3

Note: Energy consumption is in gross terms, and measured in tonnes of oil equivalent. GDP is measured in millions of ECUs at 1985 prices. Carbon dioxide (CO_2) emissions are measured in tonnes.
[*] The 12 member states comprising the European Union up to the end of 1994.
[**] Austria, Finland, Iceland, Norway, Sweden and Switzerland.
[†] Albania, Bulgaria, Czech Republic, Hungary, Poland, Romania, Slovakia and ex-Yugoslavia.
Source: European Commission (1993).

Economic reforms Economic transformation proceeded most rapidly in the countries with closest links to western Europe—Poland, Hungary, and the Czech Republic—which pursued 'shock therapy' market liberalization, followed by the privatization of industries. Controls were eased on prices and imports, and restrictive fiscal and monetary policies were adopted accompanied by partial currency convertibility and exchange rate devaluation. Privatization has had a key role in the economic restructuring strategies: the most rapid progress was seen in the Czech Republic, where citizens were able to buy (for a small fee) vouchers entitling them to shares in state owned enterprises. (Many of these shares were subsequently sold to large investment funds.) The voucher system has a crucial advantage inasmuch as it permits privatization to go ahead even in the absence of well-developed capital markets.

Nevertheless, capital markets are essential for the efficient operation of the private sector. Share prices provide an indicator of company and management performance, and pressures from shareholders and bankers exert discipline on managers. The markets also have an important role in the efficient allocation of capital: poorly performing companies have difficulty in raising funds, and are vulnerable to predators.

Privatization has not been a panacea. Since it could not be achieved instantly, there remained a need for improved management of state-owned enterprises, and a need to avoid the danger of paralysis while managements battle over ownership arrangements, neglecting investment, modernization, and long-term planning. One expedient was the 'enterprise pacts' adopted in Poland, which involved workers and managers in planning for the future of state-owned enterprises.

If the old state monopolies live on after privatization, little is achieved. The new owners need to take hard decisions; and provision needs to be made for bankruptcy and the reorganization of unsuccessful enterprises. In this context policy initiatives are needed to encourage a culture of commercialization, in order to enable the new ownership patterns to assert themselves.

A further aspect of the reform strategies has been an opening of the economies to foreign investment, so that in some instances privatization has led to takeover by western companies. Investment from the west enables the CEE countries to improve their management and access to advanced technology, while the inward investors benefit from relatively low labour costs. By far the largest amount of investment has taken place in Hungary, followed by the Czech Republic: these countries received approximately $6½ bn and $3 bn respectively in the period 1990–94 (COM(95)71, p. ii).

Much of the investment in Hungary has come from US companies. In contrast the Czech Republic has drawn substantial investment from German companies, including Volkswagen, Siemens, and Mercedes—investors attracted by the location (close to Germany, but with access to Eastern Europe), the low cost of labour (wages approximately one-tenth of German levels) and the availability of industrial skills.

Community economic assistance to central and eastern Europe   As their transition to democracy and a market system began, the CEE countries looked to the European Community, initially for aid in the process of economic restructuring. The Community responded with assistance channelled through the PHARE programme of technical assistance,[2] loans from the European Investment Bank (EIB), and Community participation in the European Bank for Reconstruction and Development (the EBRD); these forms of aid are summarized in Box 10.1.

BOX 10.1
Community assistance for countries of central and eastern Europe

Expenditure from the Community budget for economic co-operation with countries of eastern and central Europe amounted to some 521 m ECUs in 1993 (European Parliament 1994: 1342).

As of 1993, EIB loans to CEE countries amounted to 1.7 bn ECUs; this was just over one-quarter of the amount of loans to non-Community countries, but only 1.76 per cent of total EIB loans. Less than 300 m ECUs of the loans to CEE countries had actually been disbursed (EIB 1994: 77).

The EBRD was founded in 1991; the Community and the EIB both subscribed 3 per cent of its capital, and Community member states a further 45 per cent. Its public sector lending is limited to 40 per cent of total investment, which tends to constrain its role in infrastructure financing. Up to the end of 1994, loans and equity commitments amounted to 5.8 bn ECUs, half of which went to the six countries associated with the European Community through the Europe Agreements.

The annual disbursements of assistance in grants and loans to eastern and central Europe are small compared with structural expenditure within the Community (see Sec. 3.4.3): the former is measured in millions per annum, whereas the latter amounts to billions of ECUs.

10.1.3 Towards membership of the European Union and Community

With the end of the East/West division of Europe the CEE countries began to aspire to membership of the European Community. However, as the Community contemplated the prospect of enlargement to the east, political support was tempered by an awareness that progress was subject to severe economic constraints.

In balancing the political and economic considerations the Community has developed institutional links with the CEE countries, while avoiding any commitment to a timetable for accession to membership. Thus trade agreements with the CEE countries were followed by association under 'Europe Agreements' (see below), which will—in principle—lead to eventual Community membership provided that certain specified pre-conditions are met.

By 1994 six CEE countries (Hungary, Poland, Bulgaria, Romania, and the Czech and Slovak Republics) had concluded association agreements with the European Community. Poland and Hungary made formal applications for membership of the Union (and hence of the Community) in April 1994, while the Czech Republic has indicated that it will seek membership along with these two countries.

Pre-conditions for European Union and Community membership In 1993 the European Council agreed that associated countries of central and eastern Europe could eventually become members of the European Union. The final Declaration of the Copenhagen meeting of June 1993, after welcoming their 'courageous efforts ... to modernise their economies ... and to ensure a transition to a market economy' stated that associated countries may accede to membership as soon as they are 'able to assume the obligations of membership by satisfying the economic and political conditions required'. These 'conditions' require:

- institutional stability, guaranteeing: democracy, the rule of law, human rights, and respect for and protection of minorities
- the existence of a functioning market economy
- the capacity to cope with competitive pressure and market forces within the Union.

The first two conditions are sufficient to qualify for participation in the two intergovernmental political 'pillars' of the European Union. The third condition is a necessary prerequisite for membership of the Community. Although there is no precedent, it is conceivable that democratic countries with weak economies could be members of the European Union but not of the Community—a form of political, but not economic membership.

Association with the European Community: 'Europe Agreements' The 'Europe Agreements' establish a framework for association of the CEE countries with the Community. These Agreements were devised as a means of accommodating political pressure from the CEE countries for closer integration with the Community, without raising any immediate prospect of their accession to full membership. The Agreements are concluded bilaterally between the Community and the country concerned, but in each case the terms are very similar: the main features of the Agreements are summarized in Box 10.2. Agreements with Czechoslovakia (now superseded by agreements with the Czech and Slovak Republics), Poland, and Hungary, came into force on 1 March 1992, followed by Agreements with Romania and Bulgaria.

The Europe Agreements typically provide for free trade in industrial products within ten years, and the phasing out of Community trade barriers over five years. In the transitional period the Community is able to maintain barriers to imports from the CEE countries; and there are particularly strong pressures for protection in 'sensitive' sectors, which include iron and steel, textiles, chemicals, and glass. These sectors are sensitive for two reasons: because of difficulties that have arisen for EC enterprises in these sectors (for the case of the steel industry, see Box 6.2), and because of the competitiveness of exporters in the associated countries. Consequently, the Europe Agreements have an element of ambiguity: the associates' freedom to trade is most restricted in sectors in which their competitive position is strongest, and their potential benefit is therefore greatest.

These trade restrictions might appear paradoxical when there has been general acceptance of economic restructuring in the single market (see for example Rollo and Smith, 1993: pp. 165–66). However, a sense of caution in a time of economic recession may have rendered additional upheavals unwelcome; moreover the single market programme was presented as a 'package'

Box 10.2

Association of central and eastern European countries with the European Community: the 'Europe Agreements'

In 1991 the European Community negotiated association agreements (known as 'Europe Agreements') to foster economic co-operation with Czechoslovakia, Hungary and Poland; further agreements were concluded in 1994 with Romania and Bulgaria. These Agreements were concluded on a bilateral basis between the Community and each country separately. The associate status fell a long way short of membership of the Community—it did not for example give any formal role in the Community's decision-making process or institutional structure—but it was regarded by the associated countries as a stepping stone to eventual Community membership.

The Agreements provide for a phased relaxation of trade barriers, so that there will be free movement of goods and free trade in services within ten years, and for removal of associated countries' controls on capital movements. There is also provision for freedom of establishment for businesses from Community member states in the associated countries (and vice versa). There is no provision for freedom of movement of workers, although workers from the associated countries who are legally employed in the Community are entitled to equal treatment with workers from Community member states.

Three sectors are covered by special arrangements:

1. *Aricultural products* This is characterized as an area of 'particular sensitivity', and while the Community undertook to abolish quantitative trade restrictions, tariffs remain. In cases of 'serious disturbance' in agricultural markets, the Agreements permit unilateral action pending consultation.
2. *Textile products* Customs duties are to be phased out, but quantitative trade restrictions continued.
3. *Coal and steel* Duties are to be phased out; quantitative restrictions are to be abolished; state aid is restricted.

---

with a positive overall benefit, in which Community legislation and financial support could be mobilized to mitigate adverse impacts.

Trade in agricultural products is restricted, and will remain so until the Common Agricultural Policy (CAP) is drastically reformed, or the CEE countries become full members of the Community. The CAP has been historically protectionist, raising the prices of imported produce to Community levels by means of levies, so that it is not at present compatible with free trade with non-member countries. Moreover, integration of the CEE countries into the CAP in its present form would place intense pressures on the Community budget (see Sec. 10.1.4).

The Europe Agreements, like the EEA Agreement, involve a form of quasi-membership of the Community, inasmuch as Community standards will be phased in along with free trade. However, unlike the participants in the EEA Agreement, the CEE countries in many cases do not meet Community standards, and have no immediate prospect of doing so. Thus, for instance, the environmental provisions of the Europe Agreements call for 'approximation of laws to Community standards' (see, for example, the Europe Agreements with Hungary (Council and Commission, 1993a, Article 79(3)) and Poland (Council and Commission, 1993b, Article 80(3)), but the Agreements do not explicitly acknowledge that the requisite environmental measures may require extensive resources (see p. 279). Although there is a framework for collaboration in areas such as environmental monitoring, training and research, there is no provision for financial assistance to the CEE countries to support the investment expenditures necessary for achievement of Community standards.

Once within the Community the CEE countries would be eligible for structural expenditure in accordance with the prevailing criteria. However, first they must make sufficient economic progress to qualify for membership, thus—paradoxically—diminishing their requirements for assistance.

There are precedents for aid to prepare weak economies for accession to the Community. For instance, in the period 1981–84, Portugal received 175m ECUs in grant aid and 375m ECUs in EIB loans (Nicholson and East, 1987: 249). However, the problems of economic integration of the CEE countries are more formidable than those arising from previous enlargements of the Community. The prospective new member states have an aggregate population approximately one quarter of that of the Community, and following their accession they would constitute a substantial bloc of low-income countries. Consequently, their net contribution to the Community budget would be heavily negative.

Integration with the European Community   For the CEE countries preparation for Community membership represents a massive investment aimed at securing their future prosperity. Eventual participation in the single market, and access to Community structural funds, hold out the prospect of substantial economic benefits. However, the necessary economic restructuring in the transitional period has its costs.

Before they can accede to the Community, the CEE countries must fulfil certain preconditions so that their economic systems become compatible with those of existing member states. In principle, membership of the European Community implies acceptance of the entire body of Community law. (This is known as the *acquis communautaire*.) The provisions of the law may differ between member states—notably in the context of social policy and the single currency—but measures necessary for freedom of movement must be applied evenly in order to ensure the integrity of the single market.

The essential preconditions for a properly functioning market economy are secure property rights and a transparent and trusted legal system (see, for example, Olsen, 1992). Hence much of the Community's technical assistance to the CEE countries has been concerned with institutional strengthening—putting in place the 'building blocks for a market economy' (European Commission 1995: para. 4.30). This has involved extensive reforms of administrative machinery, judicial structures and the tax system, together with appropriate regulatory frameworks for financial services and capital markets. Alignment with the Community also requires adoption of technical standards compatible with those which prevail—either as a result of legislation or of voluntary agreement—within the single market. The effectiveness of these reforms is heavily dependent on the availability of staff with the appropriate expertise to ensure the proper functioning of the institutional structure; the Community has provided assistance for training to develop relevant skills (European Commission, 1995: para. 4.31, and COM(95)71, p. 15).

To gain unrestricted access to EU markets, the CEE countries have to adopt, and implement, policies on competition and public procurement that are consistent with Community legislation. Thus, the Europe Agreements provide for adoption by the CEE countries of provisions similar to those in the EC Treaty, and for surveillance and regulation of state aid. (For a survey of progress in this respect see Hoekman and Mavroidis, 1995.) In the area of public procurement legislation is in place, but it has had limited effectiveness because tendering practices have been slow to change (European Commission, 1995, para. 4.34).

The Commission has also called for harmonization with the Community where this is necessary to permit freedom of transactions between the CEE countries and EU member states. In this context social, consumer, and environmental protection have been identified as priority areas (European Commission 1995: paras 3.7–10, 4.24–26). The CEE countries have to balance the economic advantages of access to the single market against the costs associated with adoption of Community standards. Fears have been expressed that premature introduction of institutional structures on the Community model—such as the Agreement of Social Policy— might inhibit competitiveness, and thus act as an obstacle to integration with the Community (Csaba, 1995: 71–2).

In the longer term integration with the Community requires the development of communication links between East and West (the inadequacies of which are a legacy of the Cold War division of Europe), and also between the CEE countries themselves (COM(95)71, pp. 12–13). The eventual objective is integration of the CEE countries within the European Community system of Trans-European Networks (see Sec. 8.2), although the financing of the necessary transport infrastructures raises problems that have yet to be wholly resolved even within the Community. Steps have also been taken to integrate the energy networks throughout Europe with the European Energy Charter, which encompasses the European Community, the CEE countries and the former Soviet Union. The Charter's objectives include development of energy resources, access to markets, liberalization of trade in energy, and the promotion of energy efficiency and environmental protection (COM(94)405).

As the reform process began, much attention focused on the CEE countries' inheritance of environmental degradation. Under the previous regimes, there had undoubtedly been profligate exploitation of environmental resources (as is illustrated by the figures for energy consumption in Table 10.2). The result has been a legacy of soil contamination, industrial dereliction, water pollution and hazardous industrial activities; and the necessary remedial action clearly represents a substantial cost burden for the national economies. There is also a need for expenditure to update previously neglected environmental infrastructures, such as waste and waste-water treatment facilities. The Community has made this area a priority in its technical assistance programmes, including training and demonstration projects (COM(95)71, p. 14), but substantially larger resources are required if the problems are to be satisfactorily resolved.

On the other hand, economic restructuring has been beneficial in environmental terms, with the closure of inefficient and grossly polluting industrial capacity, and investment in modern, cleaner, technology. This new productive capacity is geared to the achievement of higher standards, with products that conform to the requirements of the European Union market. Moreover, the new owners of industrial enterprises have no direct liability for the costs of inherited environmental degradation (although their taxes contribute to the financing of remedial measures).

10.1.4 Implications of enlargement for the European Community

Existing member states will derive little immediate economic benefit from admission of the CEE countries to the Community. The economies of the CEE countries are comparatively small, and in the throes of reconstruction, so they will add little to the Community single market. Their levels of prosperity, as measured by per capita GNP, are well below the Community average (see Table 10.3). The more prosperous Community member states will face demands for additional resources to finance structural expenditure in the CEE region, while the less prosperous of the existing member states are likely to see reductions in Community funding as expenditures are channelled towards the new member states.

In the overall context of the European Union, enlargement to the east is primarily a matter of *political* concern, particularly with respect to stability in the region, relations with Russia and the situation in the former Yugoslavia. As an *economic* issue it is of lower priority, although for the CEE countries economic relations with the Community are of great importance, and they

Table 10.3   Potential member states in Central and Eastern Europe:
per capita GNP relative to the European Community,[*] 1992

	Per capita GNP
Bulgaria	7
Czech Republic	13
Estonia	14
Hungary[†]	15
Latvia	10
Lithuania	7
Poland[†]	10
Romania	6
Slovak Republic	10
Slovenia	34
EC[*]	100

[*] The European Community of 12 member states.
[†] Formally applied for membership in April 1994.

give high priority to aligning their economies with the Community. Nevertheless membership remains a fairly distant prospect, and the Community in its trade and aid policies has yet to show a firm commitment to accelerating the process.

As the Community contemplates enlargement, attention has focused on changes which would be needed to accommodate new member states. This has tended to highlight tensions in the Community's existing arrangements, which would have to be resolved before enlargement. Two areas of particular concern in this respect are institutional reform and the future of the Common Agricultural Policy.

Enlargement and the Common Agricultural Policy   The accession of new member states is unlikely to be feasible without radical changes in the Common Agricultural Policy (the CAP). Membership of the Community centres on the single market, and once national frontiers are removed it would not be practicable to exclude the new member states from the CAP, or significantly to vary the provisions of the CAP in the CEE countries.

The prospective incorporation of the CEE countries raises serious doubts as to the viability of the existing CAP, even when modified by the 1992 reform package and the GATT Uruguay Round (see Secs. 9.3.1 and 10.2.2). This is because extension of the CAP in its present form is likely to result in unsustainable pressures on the Community budget. If the existing system of agricultural price guarantees were to be instituted in the CEE countries, there would be a massive increase in the cost of the CAP. Meanwhile the new member states would in any case absorb expenditure well in excess of their contribution to revenue, since they would qualify for substantial assistance from the structural funds while generating only modest amounts of Community own resources.

When the Europe Agreements were inaugurated, agricultural prices in the CEE countries were generally in the region of half the level prevailing under the CAP. Most CEE countries had an inheritance of inefficient collectivized agriculture, although in Poland and Hungary there were fragmented small farms (Buckwell 1994: 43 and 38). There is evidently scope for considerable growth in output, facilitated by restructuring and stimulated by higher prices. The consequence for the CAP, in the absence of fundamental reform, would be massive over-production at an insupportable cost.

Institutional implications of enlargement The progress of economic and political integration has led to changes in the Community's institutional structure and decision-making procedures; possible further changes are to be discussed at the Intergovernmental Conference scheduled for 1996 (see Sec. 2.5.2). In this context it will be necessary to consider the implications of growth in the Community's membership, which has risen from the original six member states to 15 in 1995, and of the further enlargement which is now in prospect.

The enlargement process could ultimately lead to a European Union with twice the present number of member states. There are six countries associated through the Europe Agreements, and other plausible candidates for eventual membership including Slovenia, Malta, Cyprus and the Baltic states. With the exception of Poland, all are 'small' countries, which under present arrangements would nominate only one member of the Commission; but even so this would imply an enlargement of the Commission to over 30 members, which is likely to compromise its viability. Enlargement on this scale would also call into question the existing system of Council presidencies: each country would hold the presidency less frequently, while the burden of the presidency would increase to such an extent that smaller countries might find difficulty in meeting the required commitments with their limited resources of administrative manpower. If a qualified majority in Council decision-making were to remain at two-thirds of the national votes (as at present), the power of member states would be diluted: eventually the blocking minority could require more than the combined votes of four large member states.

The institutional implications of enlargement will have to be considered by the Community in due course. This process is likely to demonstrate both the unviability of the existing constitutional arrangements with an expanded membership, and also the difficulties of securing unanimous agreement on radical change.

10.2 THE EUROPEAN COMMUNITY IN THE WORLD

The European Community has become a major presence in the global economy. As a legal entity, it is empowered to negotiate, and conclude agreements, with non-member countries, to participate in multilateral international agreements, and to contribute to the work of international organizations.

Community trade policy is a major factor in international economic relations. With free circulation of goods in a frontier-free single market, the trade policies of individual member states have been superseded by policies at Community level. Thus, the Community has the main responsibility for trade negotiations, for measures to restrict imports and for preferential trading arrangements with the former colonies of member states.

10.2.1 The Community as an economic superpower

The European Community, along with the United States and Japan, is one of the world's three 'economic superpowers' which between them account for over half of total world trade. Of the three, the Community has the largest aggregate GDP and external trade (see Table 10.4).

Much of the impetus for the Community's development stems from a realization that individual European countries are ill-equipped to compete with the economic might of the USA and Japan. Economies with small fragmented markets must accommodate in international

Table 10.4 The European Community, the United States and Japan: gross domestic product and share of world trade, 1992

	GDP (bn ECUs)	Share of total world trade (%)
EC	5421	21
USA	4586	18
Japan	2834	10

Note: Share of world trade is the average of import and export shares; trade between EC countries is excluded.
Source: calculated from Eurostat (1994: Tables 2.1, 6.1 and 6.2).

trade and investment to the policies and priorities determined by large trading blocs. In these terms, the economies of Community member states can generally be characterized as 'medium-sized': the average GDP of the 15 member states amounted to 389 bn ECUs in 1992, and the largest GDP—Germany's—was 1498 bn ECUs (approximately one-quarter of the Community total). Industrialized economies of this size cannot match the influence of the economic superpowers; but on the other hand, they are clearly too large to fit into 'niche' roles—such as offshore financial centres—complementing larger economies.

The European Community has extensive responsibilities with respect to external trade policy. The EC Treaty (Article 113) provides for a Common Commercial Policy, covering tariffs, trade agreements, measures to counter dumping and the distorting effects of subsidies. The scope for trade policies at national level is very limited: member states may take protective measures (under Article 115) in case of 'economic difficulties', but only with the authorization of the Commission.

As a practical matter, a common policy is unavoidable, since member states' tariffs were long ago superseded by the Community's system of common external tariffs, and the existence of a single market without frontiers inhibits Community member states from using policy instruments that make use of trade barriers.

Policy responsibilities are shared between the Community and member states with respect to trade in services and trade-related aspects of intellectual property. In these areas, the allocation of responsibility in external relations depends upon the extent of relevant Community legislation. There has been only limited harmonization of immigration regulations which affect transfrontier trade in services, and of measures to protect intellectual property, so that trade policies in these areas remain largely a matter for member states (see Opinion 1/94, p. 5417).

Under the Common Commercial Policy, the Council of Ministers authorizes the Commission to enter into negotiations with non-Community countries, and the negotiations are conducted in consultation with a special committee appointed by the Council. Any agreements resulting from these negotiations require the approval of the Council (acting by qualified majority), which in this particular instance is *not* required to consult the European Parliament (Article 228(3)).

In the Uruguay Round negotiations on the General Agreement on Tariffs and Trade (GATT—see Box 10.3), member states were represented within the Community delegation. The Community negotiating position was worked out at preliminary co-ordination meetings; in the absence of an agreed position, the Community reserved its position. The Agreement establishing the World Trade Organization, which concluded the Uruguay Round, provides (Article IX)

BOX 10.3
The General Agreement on Tariffs and Trade (GATT) and the World Trade Organization

The *General Agreement on Tariffs and Trade (GATT)* is a multinational treaty to which more than 100 countries subscribe. The GATT came into existence, with 23 original signatories, in 1948: its principal objective was a substantial reduction in tariffs and other barriers to trade. The GATT, like the European Community, began with a strong desire to avoid a repetition of the great depression of the 1930s, when escalating protectionism led to a collapse of world trade.

Membership of the GATT involves three basic principles:

1. *Non-discrimination*, which requires that a tariff reduction in favour of one country must be extended to all other GATT members (the *most favoured nation (MFN) rule*).
2. *Transparency*, which requires that restrictions on imports should be only in the form of tariffs, the magnitude of which is evident: other types of restriction, such as import quotas and (possibly obscure) provisions relating to product specifications, should be avoided.
3. *Reciprocity*, which requires that a country that receives tariff concessions must offer comparable concessions in return (and these concessions are then generalized through the MFN rule).

Following the Uruguay Round negotiations, the GATT came under the auspices of the *World Trade Organization (WTO)*, inaugurated in January 1995. Parties to the Agreement establishing the WTO must subscribe to a 'package' of Agreements: the revised GATT (GATT 1994), the General Agreement on Trade in Services (GATS), and the Agreement on Trade Related aspects of Intellectual Property Rights (TRIPS). WTO members may also choose to participate in four 'plurilateral' agreements, on government procurement, trade in civil aircraft, the dairy sector and bovine meat.

The WTO has a standard procedure for settlement of trade disputes by an arbitration panel, and may authorize reprisals against parties that do not abide by the panel's rulings.

---

that the Community has a vote for each of its member states. The Commission has proposed that it should deploy the Community votes in a block (COM(94)143, Explanatory Memorandum); this is clearly appropriate for matters coming within the Common Commercial Policy, but in other areas member states may act independently. The Court of Justice has emphasized that, whatever the strict demarcation of responsibilities, the Community and member states have a duty to co-operate in external relations (Opinion 1/94, pp. 5419–21).

10.2.2 The European Community and world trade

The considerations that motivated the founders of the European Community are also relevant to the world economy. Specifically, the benefits from free trade were highlighted by experience of the great depression (described in Sec. 1.2.1), with escalating tariffs and a collapse of world trade; and this concentrated minds on the need for international economic co-operation to combat barriers to trade.

The basic economic theory of trade states that there are general advantages to be derived from each country specializing in areas in which it is most competitive with its available resources: this is known as the doctrine of *comparative advantage*. Conversely, the introduction of artificial barriers—such as import tariffs—tends to reduce the amount of trade, and thus detracts from the benefit of international specialization, as countries switch resources away from areas in which they have a comparative advantage to make up for the reduced availability of imports.

This suggests that all countries stand to benefit from a liberal trading system; and indeed, free trade between nations is generally accepted as a desirable objective in principle, albeit with considerable differences of view with respect to its implementation, and permissible exceptions.

Trade liberalization has been pursued since the Second World War in successive rounds of negotiation under the auspices of the General Agreement on Tariffs and Trade (GATT—see Box 10.3). The GATT has had considerable success in securing tariff reductions: average levels of tariffs on industrial products declined from approximately 40 per cent in 1947 to roughly 13 per cent by the early 1960s, and to around 4 per cent by the late 1980s. There has been much less success in reducing non-tariff barriers, until the conclusion of the Uruguay Round in 1993 (see below).

In parallel with the GATT negotiations, there has been a trend towards the regionalization of trading arrangements. The European Community is the most prominent (and successful) regional trading bloc; the North American Free Trade Agreement (NAFTA) has recently been concluded; and proposals have been made for similar organizations in east Asia, Latin America and Africa. As explained in Sec. 1.3.2, customs unions such as the European Community represent only a limited form of free trade, and indeed are not *necessarily* a step towards the realization of the benefits of global free trade: in some circumstances, the main effect might be a diversion of trade. Although Community member states have unimpeded access to one another's markets, trade with other countries remains subject to tariff and other barriers.

The Community itself is not consistent with the GATT requirement of non-discrimination, which includes the most favoured nation principle (see Box 10.3). The Community makes use of an exception to the general GATT rules, which permits a customs union to eliminate barriers with respect to substantially all the trade between its members, *provided that* barriers to trade with non-members are not on the whole higher or more restrictive than they were prior to the formation of the customs union (GATT Article XXIV).

In general, trade negotiations must reconcile multiple interests and objectives. In this connection, it should be emphasized that mutual gain from comparative advantage is a static concept, which assumes that resource endowments are given. In practice, countries pursue strategic objectives, seeking to *change* their resource endowment (for example by technological development), to dominate key market sectors, or to insulate themselves from risks of economic disruption (for example by agricultural self sufficiency). These motivations have given rise to conflicts in which trade policy measures have been used to seek a strategic advantage.

GATT: The Uruguay Round The most recent round of trade negotiations (the Uruguay Round), concluded in 1993, led to the 1994 agreement to establish the World Trade Organization (see Box 10.3). The success of previous rounds has reduced the significance of tariffs, and the focus in the Uruguay Round has been on non-tariff barriers, relating in particular to technical standards, administrative and procedural requirements, import quotas, subsidies (especially in the agricultural sector), restrictions on trade in services and inadequate safeguards for intellectual property rights.

In addition to the European Community, the main protagonists in the Uruguay Round were the United States, Japan, the 'Cairns' group (comprising exporters of agricultural products with low or zero subsidies) and the developing countries. The main concerns for the Community were the protection of intellectual property, the liberalization of trade in services and a lowering of tariffs and subsidies, particularly the demands by the USA and the Cairns group for radical reduction in agricultural subsidies (see Sec. 9.3.1). By 1993 the successful resolution of the Uruguay Round had come to hinge on agreement between the Community and the United

States to limit agricultural subsidies. The Community's Common Agricultural Policy has involved massive subsidies, primarily through the price support mechanism, whereby prices paid to Community producers are usually well above world market prices. In recent years Community prices have been on average almost twice the world market price, and some 30 per cent above the level in the United States (OECD 1994: Annex Table III).

Agreement was eventually reached after eight years of negotiation. The benefits of the Uruguay Round are similar to those of the Community single market: gains from specialization in areas of comparative advantage, increased competition, realization of scale economies and a stimulus to innovation, with faster dissemination of new technologies and products. It has been estimated that by the year 2005 aggregate world income will be $500 bn greater than it would have otherwise been (*Financial Times*, 4 October 1994); this is approximately one-fortieth of the world's aggregate GDP at present, or in other words of a magnitude similar to the GDP of China.

The main benefit is to consumers; among producers there is a mixture of gains and losses. Apart from agriculture, the sensitive points for the European Community have been the effects of subsidy reductions on the aerospace industry and a perceived threat to the audiovisual industry from unrestricted American imports (which prompted Community legislation on television programmes (see Sec. 6.5)): in the event, neither of these was fully resolved in the Uruguay Round. Of greater long-term significance are the likely gains to Community industry from liberalization of trade in services (particularly in financial services, telecommunications, shipping and aviation), and government procurement.

10.2.3 European Community trade policy

The Community's trade policies manifest a degree of tension between a professed belief in free trade and numerous manifestations of protectionism. The argument for worldwide trade liberalization is essentially the same as that enthusiastically adopted by the Community as the basis for the single market programme: indeed, the case is stronger in a global context because there is no possibility of trade diversion.

Tariff barriers to trade have diminished. On completion of the Community's customs union in 1968, its common external tariffs averaged 10.4 per cent, compared with member states' average tariffs of 13 per cent in 1958 (Sapir 1992: 1500); and since then Community tariffs have been reduced with successive GATT rounds.

However, the Community has maintained numerous non-tariff barriers. Its agricultural sector has been subject to import quotas and levies and export subsidies which give rise to massive trade distortions. The Community has sought to protect its industry from competition from Japan and the newly industrializing countries by means of 'voluntary' export restraint (VER) and anti-dumping actions. The Europe Agreements with CEE countries, while ostensibly liberalizing, include protectionist provisions for 'sensitive' sectors. Community trade policy has often deployed selective concessionary exemptions from trade barriers, which can have a discriminatory trade diverting effect; traditionally, such arrangements have been applied to trade with member states' former colonies, and they are now seen in the Europe Agreements with countries in central and eastern Europe.

Anti-dumping measures Dumping can occur when products are sold in export markets at prices below those that are (or should be) charged in the exporter's home market. The main economic objection to this practice lies in its potential adverse effects on industry in the importing country. The exporter may for example use high profits earned in a protected home market to subsidize export sales. This will tend to weaken competitors in the export market, and possibly force them out of the market. The exporter can thereby gain market share, exploit additional economies of scale, and ensure monopoly profits in the longer term. Not all dumping is of this predatory type; low prices may be charged:

- because demand is depressed (giving rise to excess production capacity) in recession;
- in order to enter (or to expand product range in) export markets; or
- to earn additional hard currency (particularly in the case of exporting countries with non-market economies and/or non-convertible currencies).

The most obvious instance of dumping in world trade is the Community's subsidization of agricultural exports to offset the difference between prices established under the Common Agricultural Policy (CAP) and world market prices. The practice is of course inherent in the CAP as it now operates, and reflects the extent to which agriculture has been isolated from the world trading system.

Anti-dumping measures are (or should be) designed to offset export subsidies, whether these subsidies are financed by governments or by consumers who pay higher prices in other markets. The Community has enacted legislation under the EC and ECSC Treaties (Articles 113 and 74 respectively), empowering the Commission to implement anti-dumping measures provided that certain conditions are met (Regulation 3283/94 and Commission Decision 2424/88/ECSC). These conditions are summarized in Box 10.4. The Commission has to be satisfied that dumping has occurred, and also that the dumping has caused significant injury to Community industry and to the overall interests of the Community.

In the period 1981–93, the Commission initiated on average 37 anti-dumping investigations per year, and definitive anti-dumping duties were imposed in 13 cases per year. Three east Asian countries—China, Japan and South Korea—accounted for one-third of the investigations between 1987 and 1993 (calculated from COM(95)16, Table 2 p. 5, and Annex G, p. 107).

BOX 10.4
Anti-dumping measures: essential preconditions

Community legislation permits the Commission to institute anti-dumping measures, provided it is established that three conditions are met:

1. *Exports to the Community have actually been dumped* According to the GATT (Article IV), dumping is deemed to occur when the price of a product in the export market exceeds a 'normal' value. In implementing the European Community Anti-Dumping Regulation, the Commission bases its estimates of this value either on the selling price in the exporter's domestic market or, if domestic sales are unprofitable or insignificant, on the estimated cost (including a 'representative' profit margin) of serving the domestic market.

2. *The dumping has caused or threatened material injury to Community industry, or will materially retard the establishment of a Community industry* Injury is established essentially by comparisons between indicators in the existing situation and in a hypothetical 'without dumping' scenario. Although Community legislation includes numerous possible indicators, the most significant—and most frequently used—are the prices, market shares and profitability of Community producers.

3. *The application of anti-dumping measures is in the interests of the Community* The legislation does not define assessment criteria, and this requirement has rarely prevented the adoption of anti-dumping measures when conditions 1 and 2 are met.

The existence of dumping (the first condition) is not always easy to determine. Comparison between prices in Community markets and estimated 'normal' values in the importer's home market is not straightforward when prices are influenced by extraneous factors, and when there is variation between segments of the market. For example, the features and specifications of advanced technology products can vary between manufacturers and between markets, so that a 'like with like' comparison is exceedingly difficult. Comparisons can also be distorted by differences in prices charged to different types of purchaser; for example, high-volume users tend to get keener prices, and prices are lower for direct sales than for sales through dealers.

The Commission's practice is to compare prices including costs of distribution. This tends especially to penalize exporters from Japan, where the relative complexity and high costs of the distribution system impose a high mark-up on costs of production (and allegedly impede the market access of European Community exporters). Apart from retaliation against such impediments, it is difficult to see a rationale for the Commission's procedure, since high distribution costs represent a burden, and not a source of profit, to Japanese manufacturers.

Injury to Community industry—the second condition—is assessed in terms of the degree of price undercutting by imports, and the effect on prices charged by Community producers who compete directly with dumped imports. This implicitly assumes that a reduction in profitability is injurious—which may not be the case if high profits breed complacency which is damaging to competitiveness in the longer term. The procedure also implies a disincentive to profit-making, inasmuch as reduced profitability increases the chances of gaining protection from import competition.

The third—and little used—requirement is in principle the most critical, since the interests of the Community as a whole are wider than those of any particular industrial sector. The EC Anti Dumping Regulation does not specify criteria for assessment of the wider interest, but presumably it should encompass effects on consumers, suppliers, employment, Community exporters and implications for the broader policy interests of the Community, such as technological development, training, the environment and health and safety.

Assessment of the impact of anti-dumping duties involves the weighing of different interests: the duties benefit producers at the expense of those who purchase their products (households and/or industrial purchasers). Important issues in this context are the motivation of the importer and the structure and future prospects of the Community industry. If the importer is seeking to dominate the Community market by predatory dumping, thus threatening the viability of Community enterprises, then anti-dumping action may safeguard a competitive market structure. On the other hand, if dumping is transitional, in order to facilitate the importer's entry into a hitherto uncompetitive Community market, anti-dumping measures will work against the interests of greater competition.

Furthermore, measures to safeguard a particular sector of Community industry can be justified only if the sector in question has a long-term future. Difficulties in competing with low-priced imports can be symptomatic of a fundamental lack of competitiveness, so that anti-dumping duties can be only a short-term palliative. In these circumstances a better policy may be to facilitate restructuring of the industry, to shift resources into areas in which the Community has a better prospect of remaining competitive.

10.2.4 Economic relations with the United States

The main economic preoccupation of the United States in recent years has been the trade deficit with Japan, although disagreements have arisen with the Community in relation to specific issues. In the past decade, there have there have been two instances in which the possibility has arisen of 'trade war' between the United States and the Community: in 1986, on the accession of Spain and Portugal, when US fruit exporters allegedly suffered from loss of Community markets to the new member states, and in 1992, when difficulties arose over Community subsidies for oilseed exports. Trade wars, involving escalating tariffs, would have been mutually damaging, and on both occasions the threat was averted.

There are continuing disagreements over a number of issues, notably the following:

1. *Civil aircraft subsidies* The USA has objected to Community financial support for the Airbus project, while the Community has maintained that this merely offsets aid that the US industry receives through military aircraft programmes.
2. *Public procurement* Both sides have objected to restrictions on procurement tenders: a bilateral agreement has been concluded on opening US electricity supply projects to Community contractors (and vice versa), but both sides have restricted each other's contractors access to telecommunications projects (COM(94)342, p. 4).
3. *Steel* In the midst of general over-capacity, Community producers agreed to a 'voluntary' restraint of exports to the United States of America.

In general, relations with the US have shown the benefit of solidarity that the Community confers. Where there is no common policy, as for example in air transport, the United States of America has been able to gain considerable leverage in negotiating individually with the member states (see Sec. 8.1.2).

10.2.5 Economic relations with Japan

The European Community has not suffered from general trade deficits with Japan on the same scale as has the United States (although its overall deficit grew in the late 1980s to reach $85 bn by 1991). Nevertheless, the Community, like the USA, has had substantial imbalances in its trade with Japan: in 1992 this amounted to approximately two-thirds of the Community's aggregate trade deficit, and was concentrated in key manufacturing sectors. Electronic goods and motor vehicles accounted for almost three-quarters of the deficit with Japan in 1992, this is clear from Table 10.5, which shows the balance of trade with all countries and with Japan, both in aggregate and in four specific sectors: office machines, ADP equipment, telecommunication and recording apparatus and motor vehicles. The Community's trade in services, in contrast, has a substantial surplus with Japan, which amounted to 10.5 bn ECUs in 1992 (COM(95)73, p. 8)

Table 10.5 European Community balance of trade with all countries and with Japan, 1992 ($bn)

	Balance with all countries	Balance with Japan
Office Machines, ADP Equipment	−21.21	−8.81
Telecommunication and Sound Recording Apparatus	−10.28	−8.42
Road Vehicles	16.71	−13.39
Other commodities	−48.96	−11.56
Total trade	−63.74	−42.18

Source: calculated from © OECD (1994) *Foreign Trade by Commodities 1992*. Reproduced by permission of the OECD.

The European Community, like the United States, has followed a strategy of seeking to restrain imports from Japan, while negotiating for better access to the Japanese market. The Commission has noted a 'unity of purpose' between the Community and the USA in seeking market openings, despite 'disagreement over how to achieve results'. The European strategy has been to press the Japanese authorities to pursue more active competition policies (particularly in the distributive sector), deregulation and openness to foreign investment. At the same time, encouragement has been given for the development of links between European and Japanese enterprises (COM(95)73, p. 6, pp. 10–13).

The principal weapons deployed by the Community to limit imports are anti-dumping duties and voluntary import restraint. The instances of anti-dumping duties against Japan constitute a catalogue of advanced technology products: EPROMs (Eraseable Programmable Read Only Memory) (duties imposed 1991), DRAMs (Dynamic Random Access Memory) (1990), compact disc players (1991), video cassette recorders (1989), photocopiers (1987) and electronic typewriters (1985). In the case of audio cassettes, anti-dumping measures were justified on the grounds that, under pressure from allegedly dumped imports, the Community industry had to lower its prices and consequently was able to spend less on advertising its products, leading consumers to develop 'a lower perception of the quality of Community products' (European Commission 1992: 12)

Voluntary export restraint: the case of motor vehicles   Exports of Japanese motor vehicles to western Europe have for many years been restrained, ostensibly on a voluntary basis. Some (but not all) Community member states used these 'voluntary' arrangements to limit imports until 1993, when the advent of the European single market rendered the system of national import quotas unviable. The single market has a common external frontier and no barriers between member states: vehicles (like other products) can be sold freely across national frontiers within the Community, and national restrictions can be circumvented by routing imports through countries in which imports are not subject to quotas. Consequently, the 'voluntary' import restraint could be maintained only by the institution of a quota system for the Community as a whole. The system is explained in Box 10.5.

Matters were further complicated by the development of Japanese manufacture in Europe—the so-called 'transplant' operations, mostly located in the United Kingdom. The output of these operations increased rapidly in the early 1990s, and has projected to reach 500 000 cars by the middle of the decade. There were strong differences of view between member states as to whether this output should be included in the Community quotas for Japanese vehicles subject to 'voluntary' restraint: were they primarily European or Japanese? Did they represent a resurgence of car manufacturing in Europe (as was claimed in the UK) or a 'Trojan horse' to maintain Japanese competitive advantage at the expense of European manufacturers? After some uncertainty, it was declared that this agreement 'took into account' transplant production, so that, although it was not formally included in the quota, higher than forecast growth in transplant output might be offset by reductions in import quotas (*The Economist*, 12 June 1993).

10.2.6 Economic relations with developing countries

The Community has numerous agreements with developing countries, covering trade, development assistance and technical co-operation. These were initially with neighbouring countries in the Mediterranean area and with former colonies of member states, but they now extend to most countries of Asia, Africa and Latin America.

BOX 10.5
Voluntary export restraint: Japanese cars in European markets

For many years imports of Japanese cars have been subject to quota restrictions in France, Italy, Spain, Portugal and the United Kingdom. These restrictions have taken the form of 'voluntary' restraint on the part of the exporter (and so were not contrary to GATT rules). The effect of the quotas is apparent from the table, which shows Japanese imports as a percentage of new car registrations in EC member states in 1992. There is a clear division between countries with import restrictions and those without, and in three of the former countries (France, Spain and Italy) the Japanese market share is very small indeed, and well below the Community average of 9.6 per cent. In countries where their car exports are unrestricted, Japanese manufacturers have a sizeable market share, particularly in Ireland, Greece and Denmark, which have no indigenous automobile industry.

Japanese imports: percentage of registrations of new cars in EC member states, 1992

Countries with restrictions on Japanese imports		Countries without restrictions on Japanese imports	
France	3.9	Belgium	21.3
Italy	3.0	Denmark	36.0
Portugal	10.4	Germany	12.5
Spain	3.7	Greece	28.9
United Kingdom	10.4	Ireland	43.4
		Luxembourg	15.2
		Netherlands	27.0

Source: derived from Society of Motor Manufacturers and Traders, World Automotive Statistics 1993, Table 34, p. 92; presentation or format by authors.

In 1991 the Commission negotiated an agreement with the Japanese government, whereby car imports into the Community would be subject to 'voluntary restraint' over a seven-year transitional period between 1993 and 1999. It was envisaged that Japanese imports would amount to 1.23 m vehicles out of a total EC market of 15.1 m in 1999 (Financial Times, 5 August 1991); the output of Japanese transplant operations was forecast to reach 2–3 m by that year, mostly from the UK.

Relations with its southern neighbours are of increasing political concern for the Community, and particularly for the southern member states. The Community has adopted a strategy to promote political stability in the Mediterranean region through economic reform and development of trade. There are some similarities with the Community's policies for central and eastern Europe, although in the case of the Mediterranean countries there are very limited possibilities for enlargement of the Community. The longer-term prospect is for a free trade area encompassing the Community and its southern neighbours.

In the Mediterranean region there are great economic disparities between countries, not to mention political instability and demographic pressures in the southern and eastern countries. The Community has a direct political interest in avoiding upheavals on its own doorstep, and also in moderating the economic incentives for immigration into the Community. Risks of instability are mitigated by increased prosperity in the neighbouring countries. Thus, the co-operation agreements with Mediterranean countries are designed to promote economic development through trade and—in some instances—technical and economic assistance, including loans from the European Investment Bank. Industrial products from these countries are allowed duty-free access to the Community, while their agricultural exports are subject to concessions on an individual basis.

The Community economic strategy for the Mediterranean region seeks to encourage the private sector, to attract private investment from member states, and to assist improvement of infrastructures. There is also a strong emphasis on political and economic co-operation, both with the Community and its member states, and also between countries within the region (COM(95)72).

Development co-operation with former colonies has been the subject of a series of conventions between the Community and its member states and African, Pacific and Caribbean (ACP) countries. The present agreement, the fourth Lomé Convention, was concluded in 1989 and has 69 ACP signatories. The main principles (set out in Part 1, Chapter 4, of the Convention) are:

1. free access to the Community market for ACP exports, but with special provisions for agricultural products;
2. most-favoured nation treatment for Community exports;
3. Community technical assistance for ACP countries;
4. improved access for ACP countries to private capital markets; and
5. stabilization of ACP export earnings.

The Community's policies towards developing countries reflect a conflict of objectives, so that a general commitment to assist development coexists with policies that tend to frustrate the development process. For instance, developing countries need to expand their trade, but if their exports are competitive they can meet with protectionist pressures. A good example is the textile sector, in which developing countries' exports are restricted under the Multi Fibre Arrangement (MFA); the MFA is now being phased out, but over a period of ten years.

Similarly, agricultural exports are restricted by special provisions in the development co-operation agreements. For example, Article 168 of the Lomé Convention provides that certain ACP exports to the Community may have more favourable treatment than exports from other countries which—purportedly—receive most-favoured nation treatment. Such restrictions are implicit in the Community's Common Agricultural Policy (CAP), which in its present form is incompatible with free trade. (In the course of the GATT Uruguay Round pressure for reform of the CAP came from the Cairns Group (see Sec. 10.2.2) which includes a number of developing countries such as Fiji, Indonesia and the Philippines.)

The advent of the single market has enhanced the Community role in trade policy, and this in turn has highlighted the discriminatory effects of development co-operation agreements. These agreements have developed in an *ad hoc* manner, and the most extensive (with the ACP countries) arose from the heritage of colonial links, mainly of France and the UK, but also of Belgium, Italy, Spain and Portugal. Preferential trade arrangements with former colonies can divert trade from other developing countries, and this has led to friction with member states that do not have colonial ties.

In the single market, without frontier controls to regulate movement of goods within the Community, individual member states can no longer maintain bilateral trade arrangements with other countries; so such arrangements have been either superseded by Community measures, or abolished. The problems that arise in these circumstances are well illustrated by the case of the Community banana import regime, which was instituted to replace the preferential access of former colonies in the French and UK markets; this was strongly opposed by Germany, which has no ex-colonial special relationships, and which faced an increase in the price of its bananas (see Box 10.6).

BOX 10.6
Bananas

The Community market for bananas was traditionally segmented between member states with import restrictions and higher prices, and those with unrestricted imports and lower prices. Some member states (notably France and the UK) have given preferential market access to their 'traditional' suppliers: these are mostly their former colonies, heavily dependent on banana cultivation and unable easily to diversify their economies. They also tend to be relatively high-cost producers, at a competitive disadvantage in unrestricted markets.

Member states with preferential arrangements restricted imports from non-'traditional' sources, including imports coming via other Community countries. Following the removal of frontier controls between member states, market segmentation was no longer possible, and the Community instituted an import regime to replace the systems operated by member states. Quotas corresponding to amounts 'traditionally' imported are allocated between ACP countries (Regulation 404/93, Article 15); there is a further 2 mte quota for non-'traditional' imports from ACP countries (with a tariff of 100 ECUs/te). Imports in excess of the quotas are subject to levies: 750 ECUs/te ('non-traditional' ACP) and 850 ECUs/te (other countries) (Article 18).

The new import regime fulfils a commitment in the Lomé Convention (Protocol 5, Article 1) that the Community will safeguard the position of 'traditional' suppliers. However, other suppliers are prevented from exploiting their cost advantages (in contravention of the GATT non-discrimination principles), and member states with hitherto unrestricted markets face an increase in prices due to tariffs and import quotas. One member state in this position subsequently took legal action (unsuccessfully) seeking annulment of the Regulation instituting the Community import regime (Case C-280/93).

10.3 INTERNATIONAL CO-OPERATION FOR SUSTAINABLE DEVELOPMENT

The pursuit of sustainable development has given rise to a number of policy issues with a strong international dimension, some of which involve matters of global concern. International co-operation in these areas is to some extent analogous, on a wider scale, to action by the Community to harmonize national measures, and to provide essential safeguards in the single market. In some instances, such as transfrontier movement of waste or trade restrictions for environmental purposes, the issues arising at a global level have already been addressed within the Community.

The Community's economic integration has enhanced its international role, and has stimulated the development of environmental policies at Community level. Meanwhile, growing environmental concerns have led to the conclusion of several major international agreements relating to the environment and sustainable development. The Community is party to many of these agreements because they relate to matters in which it has assumed policy responsibilities.

10.3.1 International trade: the environmental dimension

There are numerous instances in which product standards are specified for environmental reasons, and importation of products that do not conform to these standards are restricted or prohibited. Conversely, an environmental justification is sometimes offered for measures that are designed mainly to protect industries from import competition, and so to interfere with free trade.

The balance between free trade and environmental protection is an issue that has arisen in various contexts in the European single market. The doctrine of 'mutual recognition' is tempered by permitted grounds for trade restrictions, which include environmental protection (see Sec. 3.1.1). Where the Community has not adopted policy measures, national restrictions may be maintained (although they must not be enforced by frontier controls, or cause unacceptable distortions of trade in the single market). However, if Community measures ensure a minimum standard of environmental protection, member states would have more difficulty in justifying import restrictions. This is illustrated by the apparent paradox that member states may restrict imports from elsewhere in the Community of non-hazardous waste but not of hazardous waste, since the latter (unlike the former) is the subject of Community legislation (see Case 2/90).

Similar issues arise in international (as distinct from intra-Community) trade. The GATT agreement commits its signatories to the principle of free trade, although contracting parties may be permitted to take action involving restriction of trade if this is 'necessary to protect human, animal or plant life or health' (Article XX(b)), or relates to 'the conservation of exhaustible natural resources' (Article XX(g)); there is a general proviso that the measures in question are 'not applied in a manner which would constitute a means of arbitrary or unjustifiable discrimination ... or a disguised restriction on international trade'.

This falls short of a comprehensive exemption for environmental measures that have incidental effects on trade. There have been instances of import restrictions purportedly justified on environmental grounds, despite their doubtful compatibility with the GATT. A well-known case concerned a US measure to conserve dolphins: imports of tuna fish from Mexico, and from countries that import Mexican tuna, were prohibited on the grounds that nets used by Mexican fisherman caused an unacceptably large number of dolphins to be killed. The Community was affected as an importer of Mexican tuna, and brought a successful action against the secondary embargo in a GATT disputes panel. (For details of this and similar trade and environment cases, see Esty 1994: Appendix C.)

Within the Community (and within individual countries), conflicts arising from divergence between environmental perspectives can be resolved by legislation.[3] Where such conflicts involve countries outside the Community, they must be settled by intergovernmental negotiation, in the absence of a supranational legal structure governing environmental protection measures. (A Global Environmental Organization, as proposed by Esty (1994: Chapter 4), would prevent such conflicts by establishing a system of environmental management on a world scale.)

Countries (and the Community) set environmental standards in accordance with their own priorities and the availability and cost of technology. Nevertheless, developments elsewhere, and international co-operation and economic competitiveness, are important influences. Exporters ultimately have to comply with the specifications of their export markets; and legitimate environmental standards can serve as a stimulus to the development and transfer of technology geared to improved environmental performance. For example, a US prohibition on disposal of industrial waste to landfill stimulated exports of process technology by European companies with experience in this area. On the other hand, Japanese companies gained a technological lead in catalytic reduction processes as a result of high standards for nitrogen oxide emissions in their own country, and were then able to export the technology to Europe when the Community later adopted higher emission standards (European Commission 1990: 138–9).

10.3.2 The Convention on International Trade in Endangered Species

There are international agreements under which trade restrictions are deployed as an instrument of environmental protection. Perhaps the best known is the 1973 (Washington) Convention on International Trade in Endangered Species (CITES), for which the Community enacted implementing legislation in 1982 (Regulation 3626/82). CITES regulates trade in species in danger of extinction, or at risk of becoming endangered. Imports of such species require a permit, and are not allowed for commercial purposes. Specimens may be exported only if the authorities in the exporting state are satisfied that an import permit has been issued, and that the specimen was not obtained unlawfully. Scientific authorities in both the exporting *and* the importing state must certify that the trade will not be detrimental to the survival of the species.

In the single market, with no frontier controls between member states, the trade restrictions of CITES must be implemented for the Community as a single entity. There is mutual recognition of import and export permits issued by member states, and these are checked at the external frontier of the Community (which is not necessarily the frontier of the member state issuing the permit).

10.3.3 Protection of the ozone layer

Trade restrictions also figure prominently in international co-operation to protect the ozone layer. The 1987 Montreal Protocol sets limits leading to a phased decline in production and consumption of ozone depleting substances (Article 2); it also prohibits trade in these substances with non-signatory countries (Article 4).

The Community and member states are parties to the Protocol (Decision 88/540), and the production and consumption limits apply to member states collectively (Protocol Article 8a). The Community has established a system of quotas and licensing for imports of ozone-depleting substances from signatory countries (Regulation 594/91, Articles 3 and 4). There is a general prohibition on trade with non-signatory countries, both in ozone depleting substances and in products containing them (Articles 5 and 6). Lawful imports enter into free circulation within the Community single market, but producers, importers and exporters must supply the Commission with detailed information on production, use, recycling and trade with respect to individual substances.

10.3.4 Controls on the international movement of hazardous waste

Under the 1989 Basle Convention, international movement of hazardous wastes is permitted only with the informed consent of the importing state. The Community has ratified this Convention (Decision 93/38), which does not apply to movement between Community member states; in the single market there are no frontier controls to enforce national restrictions, and movement of hazardous wastes is governed by Community legislation in the framework of the Community waste management strategy (see Sec. 7.2.1).

The provisions of the Convention have similarities with the Community strategy: Article 4 calls for generation and transfrontier movement of wastes to be minimized, while Article 8 sets out principles for sound management of waste. The Convention also requires that illegal exports, once discovered, should be returned to the country from which the waste was exported.

The Lomé IV Convention goes beyond the restrictions of the Basle Convention: it prohibits export of hazardous and radioactive waste from the Community to ACP countries, and commits ACP states to refrain from importing such waste from whatever source (Article 39).

10.3.5 The Lomé IV Convention: environmental provisions

The Lomé IV Convention includes a number of other provisions to promote sustainable development. These include environmental impact assessment of projects 'as appropriate' (Article 37), exchange of information on the safety of pesticides and other chemical products (Article 40), and technical co-operation on measures to combat desertification (Articles 54–57).

10.3.6 Climate change

The 1992 (Rio) Conference on Environment and Development agreed a Convention with the objective of securing reductions in emissions of 'greenhouse' gases which may lead to climate change. The Convention provides for co-operation—including transfer of technology—in measures to reduce anthropogenic emissions of carbon dioxide, and in the management of 'carbon sinks', such as forests and the oceans.

The Community is a party to the Convention, and has affirmed its objective of stabilization of carbon dioxide emissions in the year 2000 at 1990 levels (Decision 94/69). The proposed carbon/energy tax (see Sec. 7.5.2) would constitute a Community-level initiative for achievement of this objective. The Commission has also participated in a pilot project on conservation of the Brazilian rain forests, and has called for regulation through the International Timber Organization of trade in tropical timber (COM(92)23 II, p. 84).

10.3.7 Biodiversity

The Rio conference also agreed a Convention for the preservation of diversity of species. This establishes a financial mechanism to support conservation in developing countries (which account for most of the world's species), and commits 'developed countries' (including the Community) to providing the necessary financial resources. The Community ratified the Convention in 1993 (Decision 93/626).

10.4 EXTERNAL RELATIONS: KEY POINTS AND ISSUES

The Community now encompasses almost all of western Europe, and may eventually double its membership with the accession of countries to the east and to the south. Six countries in central and eastern Europe have 'associate' status, which gives access to the single market (except with respect to mobility of labour, and trade in the 'sensitive' areas of agriculture, textiles, coal and steel). There is strong political pressure for eastern enlargement of the European Union, but there is also an economic constraint because the potential new member states are at present unable to meet the full requirements for membership of the European Community.

The Community is ostensibly committed to global free trade, although in practice this commitment has been heavily qualified. The most notable instance has been in agriculture, where the objective of self sufficiency has been pursued under the Common Agricultural Policy, implemented by systems of import quotas and levies, and export subsidies. Imports have also been restricted in other sectors, mainly through 'anti-dumping' actions and 'voluntary' import restraint. Trade with developing countries has been affected by preferential arrangements which tend to favour the former colonies of member states.

The Community, as a major economic and trading entity, has become closely involved in international co-operation for sustainable development, and is a party to several international agreements which regulate trade in the interest of environmental protection. The Community also participates in international environmental conventions, including those concluded in 1992 on climate change and biodiversity, following the World Conference on Environment and Development.

In the context of the Community's external relations, the following key issues may be identified:

- The Community has concluded 'Europe Agreements' with countries in central and eastern Europe, providing for partial liberalization of trade: what is the purpose of these agreements—to ease the transition to full Community membership, or to postpone difficult decisions concerning membership applications?
- Under the Europe Agreements, trade restrictions are maintained for 'sensitive' sectors: to what extent does this negate the ostensible purposes of the Agreements?
- The Community has provided financial assistance for economies in transition, but the amounts are much less than structural fund expenditures in the Community's less prosperous regions: how much assistance for eastern Europe is desirable? How much is feasible?
- Enlargement to the east will incorporate new member states with large agricultural sectors and relatively low levels of prosperity: what are the implications for Community agricultural and regional policies, and for the Community budget?
- The Community has made extensive use of anti-dumping actions, and maintains a system of restraint on Japanese car imports: how far can these be reconciled with a professed commitment to free trade?
- The advent of the single market has highlighted the influence of ex-colonial ties on Community trading arrangements with developing countries: what is the future for such arrangements?
- The Community is a party to a number of international environmental co-operation agreements: to what extent are these compatible with free trade?

NOTES

1. Switzerland and Liechtenstein (which are joined in a customs union) were to have been founder members, but Switzerland failed to ratify the original Agreement establishing the EEA; this also made Liechtenstein's membership impracticable pending revised arrangements (which have now been agreed).
2. The PHARE programme (Poland and Hungary: Aid for Economic Reconstruction of Economies) was originally confined to those two countries, but now covers the entire CEE region.
3. This is indeed a matter of controversy in the Community, with calls by environmentalists to strengthen restrictions on drift net fishing (Financial Times, 19 July 1994).

REFERENCES

Buckwell, A. (1994) *The Feasibility of an Agricultural Strategy to Prepare the Countries of Central and Eastern Europe for European Union Accession*, Report to the European Commission, Brussels.
Council and Commission (1993a) Decision on the Europe Agreement with Hungary, *Official Journal*, 1993 L347.
Council and Commission (1993b) Decision on the Europe Agreement with Poland, *Official Journal*, 1993 L348.
Csaba, L. (1995) 'The political economy of trade regimes in central Europe', in L. A. Winters, ed. *Foundations of an Open Economy: Trade Laws and Institutions for Eastern Europe*, Centre for Economic Policy Research, London.
EIB (1994) *Annual Report 1993*, European Investment Bank, Luxembourg.
Esty, D. C. (1994) *Greening the GATT: Trade, Environment and the Future*, Institute for International Economics, Washington DC.
European Commission (1990) *Panorama of EC Industry*, Office of Official Publications, Luxembourg.
European Commission (1991) *Ninth Annual Report on the Community's Anti-Dumping and Anti Subsidy Activities*, Office of Official Publications, Luxembourg.

European Commission (1992) *Tenth Annual Report on the Community's Anti Dumping and Anti Subsidy Activities*, Office of Official Publications, Luxembourg.

European Commission (1993) *Energy in Europe: Annual Energy Review*, Office of Official Publications, Luxembourg.

European Commission (1994) *Panorama of EU industry*, Office of Official Publications, Luxembourg.

European Commission (1995) *White Paper: Preparation of the Associated Countries of Central and Eastern Europe for Integration into the Internal Market of the Union*, European Commission, Brussels.

European Community (1994) 'Agreement on the European Economic Area', *Official Journal*, 1994 L1.

European Parliament (1994) Final adoption of the general budget of the European Union for the financial year 1995, *Official Journal*, 1994 L369.

Eurostat (1994) *Basic Statistics of the Community*, 31st edn, Office of Official Publications, Luxembourg.

Hoekman, B. M. and Mavroidis, P. C. (1995) 'Linking competition and trade policies in central and east European countries', in L. A. Winters, (ed.), *Foundations of an Open Economy: Trade Laws and Institutions for Eastern Europe*, Centre for Economic Policy Research, London.

Myant, M. (1993) 'Problems of transition in eastern Europe: should we seek alternatives?', *British Review of Economic Issues*, 15: 9–32.

Nicholson F. and East R. (1987) *From the Six to the Twelve*, Longman, Harlow, Essex.

OECD (1994a) *Agricultural Policies Markets and Trade: Monitoring and Outlook*, Organisation for Economic Co-operation and Development, Paris.

OECD (1994b) *Foreign Trade by Commodities 1992*, Vol. 5, OECD, Paris.

Olsen, M. (1992) 'The hidden path to a successful economy', in C. Clague and G. C. Rausser (eds.), *The Emergence of Market Economies in Eastern Europe*, Basil Blackwell, Oxford.

Rollo, J. and Smith, A. (1993) 'The political economy of eastern European trade with the European Community: why so sensitive?', *Economic Policy*, 16: 139–201.

Sapir A. (1992) 'Regional integration in Europe', *Economic Journal*, 102: 1500.

European Community legislation

Regulations

Regulation 3626/82, on the implementation of the Convention on international trade in endangered species of wild fauna and flora, *Official Journal*, 1982 L384 31/1.

Regulation 594/91, on substances that deplete the ozone layer, *Official Journal*, 1991 L67/1.

Regulation 404/93, on the common organization of the market in bananas, *Official Journal*, 1993 L47/1.

Regulation 3283/94, on protection against dumped imports from countries not members of the European Community, *Official Journal*, 1994 L349/1.

Decisions

Decision 88/540, on the Vienna Convention for the protection of the ozone layer and the Montreal Protocol on substances that deplete the ozone layer, *Official Journal*, 1988 L297/8.

Commission Decision 88/2424/ECSC, on protection against dumped or subsidized imports from countries not members of the European Coal and Steel Community, *Official Journal*, 1988 L209/18.

Decision 93/38, on the Convention on the control of trans boundary movements of hazardous wastes and their disposal, *Official Journal*, 1993 L39/1.

Decision 93/626, on the Convention on biodiversity, *Official Journal*, 1993 L309/1.

Decision 94/69, concerning the UN framework Convention on climate change, *Official Journal*, 1994 L33/11.

European Commission documents

COM(92)23 II, *Towards Sustainability: a European Community Programme of Policy and Action in relation to the Environment and Sustainable Development*, 27 March 1992 (reproduced in *Official Journal*, 1993 C138).

COM(94)143, *Proposal for a Council Decision concerning the results of the Uruguay Round of Multilateral Trade Negotiations*, 15 April 1994.

COM(94)342 *Report of the Commission concerning Negotiations regarding Access to Third Countries' Markets in the Fields covered by Directive 93/38/EEC*, 7 September 1994.

COM(94)361, *Follow up to Commission Communication on the Europe Agreements and Beyond*, 27 July 1994.

COM(94)405, *The European Energy Charter*, 21 September 1994.

COM(95)16, *Twelfth Annual Report on the Community's Anti Dumping and Anti Subsidy Activities*, 15 February 1995.
COM(95)71, *Industrial Co-operation with the Countries of Central/Eastern Europe*, 14 March 1995.
COM(95)72, *Strengthening the Mediterranean Policy of the European Union*, 8 March 1995.
COM(95)73, *Europe and Japan: the Next Steps*, 8 March 1995.

Court judgments

Opinion 1/91, *Opinion on the European Economic Area Treaty* [1991] ECR I-6084.
Opinion 1/94, *Opinion pursuant to Article 228(6) of the EC Treaty* [1994] ECR I-5267.
Case 2/90 *Commission v. Belgium*, judgment 9 July 1992, not yet reported.
Case C-280/93 *Germany v. Council*, 1994. ECR I-4973.

IN CONCLUSION

The European Community is different from other international organizations. Its supranational institutions, and its legal identity distinct from the member states, provide a framework for policy-making and legislation. Decision-making in the Community, unlike in most other public international bodies, does not always require unanimous agreement between governments of member states: governments can—and do—find themselves being called upon to implement decisions they have opposed.

The Community was formed in the aftermath of a world war that had caused massive economic damage in Europe, and had left the continent dominated by opposing blocs, led by two superpowers. There was a determination not to repeat the disastrous experience of the world economy after the First World War, when a lack of international co-operation led to the great depression of the 1930s, and contributed to the political instability that led to the Second World War.

The priority in these circumstances was economic regeneration with a high degree of co-operation to secure growth in international trade and investment. For the European nations, independent action at national level had little to offer in these economic and political circumstances; consequently governments were obliged to collaborate in the formulation, and implementation, of common policies.

So the Community was a product of its times: it represented a historic opportunity to overcome past animosities, and, specifically, to integrate Germany with its former enemies and thus avoid a repetition of the past.

From the original six countries, membership of the Community has grown to 15, with more countries seeking membership. Successive enlargements have rendered the membership increasingly heterogeneous, in terms of living standards, and also in terms of economic structures, political concerns and cultural diversity.

The original purpose of the European Economic Community founded in 1957 was to raise living standards through the development of a common market, which is now known as 'the single market'. This involved a large number of measures to remove barriers that impeded the movement of goods, services, money and people between member states. The Community legal system played a vital role in ensuring that national regulations inconsistent with the single market could be overridden.

The Community's legislative framework for a single market is, with a few exceptions, now in place. National legislation implementing single market measures remains incomplete, and the effectiveness of these measures ultimately depends on the enforcement of laws and regulations. This in turn depends on action by the Commission, as 'guardian' of the Treaties establishing the

Community, and by the authorities in member states. Individuals and non-governmental organizations also have an important role: they may make complaints to the Commission, and may in some circumstances invoke European law in defence of their rights.

The single market gives rise to opportunities for accelerated economic growth, and also to numerous challenges, to ensure that the opportunities are taken in a way that is genuinely beneficial to the Community's citizens. In response to these challenges, the Community has developed policies in a number of areas which are essential to complement the single market programme. These include:

- *structural and cohesion funds*, the purpose of which is to counter disadvantages—mainly in the form of inadequate infrastructure—which impede participation in the single market and access to its economic benefits; the funds also act as an 'insurance policy' in regions that face heavy costs of economic restructuring;
- *competition regulation*, in order to combat distortions of the market by the anti-competitive practices of enterprises, or by subsidies given by public authorities;
- *social policy*, which includes provisions relating to health and safety, to combat discrimination, and for workers' representation.

The single market is the cornerstone of the Community: it requires, and has induced, a degree of economic integration such that the Community's role has broadened into a wide range of policy areas not mentioned in the original Treaties.

National governments are naturally anxious to safeguard their own positions, and have insisted that Community intervention must in every instance be justified under the principle of subsidiarity. Nevertheless, the integration process has also caused member states to share, and in some instances to cede, policy responsibilities. The single market has been a powerful influence, directly and indirectly, in the development of the Community dimension in policy-making.

To pass the test of subsidiarity, Community policy measures must serve objectives 'which cannot be sufficiently achieved by the Member States and can therefore ... be better achieved by the Community' (Article 3b EC). In some instances policy *objectives* are best defined at Community—or higher—level. For example:

- *Transport policy* by its nature concerns movement within the single market; the working of the single market depends on the availability of the necessary transport infrastructure; hence the Community has defined its own priorities for the development of transport networks, which do not necessarily coincide with those of member states.
- *Environmental objectives* established by the Community apply irrespective of the source or incidence of environmental impacts. Intergovernmental co-operation has had limited success in combating transfrontier pollution, but the Community, with its supranational policy-making structure, is able to take effective action.
- *Community agriculture policy* arose from concerns over self sufficiency in the aftermath of wartime food shortages: rather than each member state attempting to be self sufficient, it made more sense to pursue this objective for the Community as a whole.

Even where objectives are defined in national terms, Community action may nevertheless be justified under the subsidiarity principle because the objectives are pursued using *policy instruments* which affect the functioning of the single market. For example:

- *Consumer protection* measures instituted by member states may involve product specifications, but these must not be applied to imports from elsewhere in the Community in a way that disrupts the single market. In general, member states must accord mutual recognition to one another's product standards: hence in the landmark 'Cassis de Dijon' case Germany could not block imports of a French liqueur, even though it did not conform to the German definition of a liqueur.

- *Industrial policy* in several member states has included measures to shelter the domestic motor industry from Japanese competition; but national import controls cannot be maintained in the single market—so these were superseded by a Community import regime.
- *Cultural policies* promote objectives that are defined mostly at national or local level; but the removal of frontiers within the single market has necessitated Community intervention, including measures to control export of works of art, and to promote the European content of television programmes.

The single market, and associated developments, have tended to change the Community's role. In the past this was seen primarily as the co-ordination and harmonization of national policies, but now, to an increasing extent, policies are formulated at Community level. If for example there is concern to improve vehicle safety, recourse must be had to Community-type approval regulations, rather than any measures at national level. Similarly, pressure for action to counter alleged dumping is addressed primarily to the Commission: member states cannot enact their own trade policy measures independently of the Community.

Economic integration has made the Community a major entity in the world. Other regional trade blocs—for example the European Free Trade Area, or the North American Free Trade Agreement—have been a significant factor in the world economy, but thus far none has been accorded a legal status distinct from its member states. The Community has such a status, and was a very active participant in the negotiations on world trade which led to the conclusion of the GATT Uruguay Round in 1993. The Community's common commercial policy is an essential complement to the single market: goods imported from non-member countries enter into free circulation within the single market, and member states cannot restrict imports—whatever their original source—coming from elsewhere in the Community.

The Community's own trade policies manifest a degree of tension between a commitment to free trade in principle and an extensive range of exceptions in practice. The most obvious of these is the Common Agricultural Policy: import levies and export rebates are a consequence of a price support system that insulates the Community from world markets. There are in addition preferential trade arrangements, mostly with former colonial territories of member states, which are inconsistent with the non-discrimination principles of the GATT.

This uncertain commitment to free trade has also been manifested in relations with the countries of central and eastern Europe. The Community has supported economic restructuring in these countries, both politically and with some financial assistance: but this support falls short of allowing their exports completely free access to Community markets. Special provision is made for 'sensitive areas', including agriculture, textiles and steel—and these are 'sensitive' at least in part because they are sectors in which the Community's eastern neighbours can be competitive.

As the Community's role of policy-maker has evolved, changes have occurred in the policy agenda, and these changes have been reflected in the Community's own priorities. There are essentially three broad lines for the future development of Community policies: a widening of Community membership with the accession of additional member states, a 'deepening' of economic integration, and the formulation of policies in response to new concerns. The first of these is mainly a response to the political developments and economic transition in central and eastern Europe. The 'deepening' process is a continuation of the single market programme, both in terms of implementation of established measures and of further objectives, notably the achievement of monetary union with a single currency. The new direction of economic policies is manifested in the Community's commitment to sustainable economic growth, which potentially is a major influence on a wide range of policies.

There is now a political commitment to eventual Community membership for many of the countries of central and eastern Europe. Their 'Europe Agreements' with the Community require economic alignment, and the adoption of Community standards, with a view to their eventual participation in the single market and other policies of the Community. In this respect the position of these countries has some similarity with that of the Community's peripheral member states which face extensive economic restructuring in the single market; the difference is that the latter benefit from structural and cohesion fund expenditure amounting to billions of ECUs per year, while Community aid to countries of central and eastern Europe is measured only in millions.

The single (or common) currency objective is a logical continuation of the single market programme: there is an element of paradox in a single economic entity with a multiplicity of currencies. Currency exchange has a cost, which constitutes a non-tariff barrier between member states.

Notwithstanding its advantages for the single market, there is opposition to a single currency on the grounds of a perceived sacrifice of national sovereignty in economic and monetary policy. On the other hand, it is not evident that governments have much to lose in this respect: in an era of global financial markets and closely co-ordinated policy-making, both in the Community and world-wide, no country has an independent monetary policy. In any event, countries that (necessarily or by choice) remain outside the currency area will be constrained, simply because of the magnitude of trade and financial flows, to align their policies closely with those of the single currency 'bloc'.

It is conceivable that a single currency will lead to a collective gain in sovereignty which exceeds the sum of the losses to individual countries. This would be the case if in the financial markets Community policy-makers were to have more influence than the present combination of national authorities.

Perhaps the most problematical aspect of the single currency is adjustment to relative economic changes. If a country within the system loses competitiveness, it does not have the option of a currency devaluation to reduce its relative costs. There is little scope for adjustment through outward migration of labour, and it will be difficult to reduce wages to maintain employment. Regions in difficulty could obtain some support from the Community resources, but this is unlikely to have any significant impact—total expenditure under the Community budget is only of the order of 1 ½ per cent of the aggregate GDP of member states.

The objective of sustainable development calls for a reorientation of many of the existing policies of the Community (and also of its member states) to safeguard the environment and natural resources. The Community has had environmental policies for over twenty years; its intervention in this area (as in others) was prompted initially by the need to harmonize national regulations in the single market. A large amount of environmental legislation has been enacted; despite difficulties in implementation, this has had some success in alleviating gross pollution. The regulatory approach is now being complemented by other instruments, such as environmental impact assessment, environmental labelling of products, and auditing of environmental performance.

Sustainable development cannot be assured by environmental policy in the traditional sense: it can be achieved only if considerations of sustainability are instilled into all policy areas. The Community is, in principle, committed to an integrated approach, to take account of the environmental dimension in all areas of policy-making (EC Treaty, Article 130r), but the reality shows a somewhat uneven observance of this principle.

Policy measures have effect by influencing motivation and incentives. Mechanisms may involve persuasion, sanctions or rewards. The reorientation of policy objectives must therefore involve a change in the pattern of incentives: in the case of sustainable development, this means emphasizing protection of the environment and natural resources.

Judged in this light, Community policies still do not altogether satisfy the requirements for sustainable development. For instance:

- *Fiscal policy* in the single market acquired an environmental dimension with the introduction of a differential in the excise duty on leaded and unleaded petrol, but the differentials provided for in legislation on value added tax do not appear to have any environmental rationale. The Commission has envisaged fiscal reform to shift the burden of taxation on to the use of environmental resources; however, the principal measure to implement this approach at Community level—the proposed carbon/energy tax—has encountered strong opposition in the Council.

- *Agricultural policy*, primarily through the price support mechanism, has generated strong incentives for intensive, non-sustainable, farming practices. Some structural measures have been designed to promote environmental protection, but their incentive effect is comparatively small.

- *Transport policy* has been concerned mainly with single market measures and with infrastructure planning; individual projects have been subject to environmental assessment (in accordance with Community law), but in the past less account was taken of environmental factors at a strategic level. This is now changing, with a new emphasis on sustainable transport, and initiatives to encourage transfer of traffic to rail. The effectiveness of the new approach remains to be seen.

The Community's institutional structures and decision-making procedures have evolved to accelerate the legislative process and to address the developing policy agenda. The Community was for many years after its foundation an essentially intergovernmental arrangement, albeit with a supranational structure; all important decisions required unanimous agreement between the member states. When it became clear that this system was inadequate to ensure progress towards the single market, qualified majority voting was extended (under the 1986 Single European Act) to facilitate the passage of the necessary measures. At the same time, the powers of the European Parliament were extended, through the Co-operation Procedure. The process was continued with the 1992 EU (Maastricht) Treaty, which further extended the Co-operation Procedure, and also introduced the Co-Decision Procedure, whereby the Parliament enacts legislation jointly with the Council under certain articles of the EC Treaty.

These moves have gone some way to address the problem of the Community's so-called 'democratic deficit'. The Parliament is directly elected by the Community's citizens, and to this extent has democratic legitimacy, although this is somewhat diluted by low electoral turnouts, and the tendency of elections to focus on national, rather than Community, issues.

One expedient to improve democratic legitimacy is greater involvement of national legislators in Community decision-making. Declarations attached to the EU Treaty provide for co-operation between national and European parliaments. The effect of this process on policy formulation is constrained by the already full agendas of national parliaments; also, national legislators are liable to see themselves primarily as national representatives, possibly duplicating the role of government representatives in the Council. On the other hand, national parliaments do have an important role in the oversight of Community expenditure, most of which is actually administered by authorities in member states.

The most important step to improve the Community's democratic credentials would be greater openness in the Council. Deliberation behind closed doors may be appropriate for intergovernmental negotiations, but it does not serve the democratic legislative process. The objection is sometimes made that, if the Council were to meet in public, bargaining between governments would continue, but outside the Council chamber; nevertheless, the outcome of any private negotiations would be exposed to public debate, rather than—as at present—obscured by self-serving statements made outside the Council meeting.

The prospective enlargement of the Community raises a number of issues concerning the institutional structure. The Commission now has 20 members: there are two Commissioners from each of the five largest member states, while the rest have one each. If the Commission were to be constituted in the same way after the accession of further member states from eastern Europe, there would be around 30 Commissioners. This would be unviable—indeed, its present size may well be excessive. A reduction (or containment) of its membership would have to involve a departure from the principle of at least one Commissioner per country—and this would of course pose political difficulties, inasmuch as countries are unlikely to volunteer to go unrepresented.

These and other issues are to be addressed by an intergovernmental conference in 1996, which will review and amend the Community Treaties. A key issue for that conference will be the extent to which the homogeneity of the Community structure is maintained. Until the EU (Maastricht) Treaty, the Community had a single coherent body of law, notwithstanding variation in legislative provisions to take account of differences in the circumstances of member states. However, the EC Treaty now permits two member states (Denmark and the UK) to opt out of the single currency, and provides for social legislation to be enacted under an Agreement (linked to the Treaty by a Protocol) to which all member states except the UK are parties.

Although these developments represent an important legal innovation, their practical importance may turn out to be somewhat limited. Critics of the Agreement on social policy have claimed that it will lead to burdensome legislation, such that compliance costs will tend to increase unemployment. This argument may be ill founded, for two reasons. First, the Agreement, and the Commission's policy planning, emphasize agreement and consultation, so that a substantial extension of labour market regulation is unlikely. Second, if the cost burden is increased it is likely to fall mostly on labour, which, as the less mobile factor of production, has less scope for avoidance of the cost.

Ultimately there can be only limited scope for an *à la carte* system of Community membership. Membership must involve participation in the single market, which is the centrepiece of the Community, and is what distinguishes it from a free trade area; and the single market implies common standards and policies in a wide range of areas. This is the case even for the 'quasi Community membership' of participants in the European Economic Area. Divergence in social policy between the UK and other member states might conceivably disrupt the single market, either by diverting investment to the UK or by interfering with the free movement of labour. It is conceivable that if the disruption were to become sufficiently serious, the UK's membership of the Community could eventually become untenable.

Although economic integration requires common policies, it is not a precondition for political co-operation. So a separation could be visualized between EC membership and participation in intergovernmental co-operation in foreign policy and home affairs under the auspices of the European Union. The latter could involve agreement on economic measures—for example where trade sanctions are deployed as an instrument of foreign policy—but without the obligation of compliance with EC law.

The eventual shape of any new arrangements depends on the resolution of two contrasting lines of argument. One of these accentuates the heterogeneity of Europe, and points to a looser form of co-operation between a larger number of countries. The other emphasizes the shared experience and outlook of Europeans, and advocates intensified integration, to include further countries when they can fulfil the economic preconditions for membership of the Community. The future course, between these defining positions, remains to be seen: but it can be anticipated that the European Community will remain less than a 'superstate', and more than a free trade area.

FURTHER READING

A vast amount of material is published on the European Community. Listed below are some works (among many) which may be consulted to explore in greater depth the issues discussed in this book; these are in addition to the works cited in the text. There is also a steady stream of publications by the European institutions: particular mention may be made of the annual *Panorama of EU industry*, and the *European Economy* series; recent issues of the latter include *The Climate Challenge* (No. 51, 1992), *The European Community as a World Trade Partner* (No. 52, 1993) and *Stable Money—Sound Finances* (No. 53, 1993).

Anderson, K. (1992) *The Greening of World Trade Issues*, Harvester Wheatsheaf, Hemel Hempstead.

Bangemann, M. (1992) *Meeting the Global Challenge: Establishing a Successful European Industrial Policy*, Kogan Page, London.

Barro, J. R. and Grilli, V. (1994) *European Macroeconomics*, Macmillan, Basingstoke.

Brouwer, F. *et al.* (eds.) (1994) *Economic Policy Making and the European Union*, The Federal Trust, London.

De Grauwe, P. and Papademos, L. (1990) *The European Monetary System in the 1990s*, Longman, Harlow.

Dyker, D. (ed.) (1992) *The European Economy*, Longman, Harlow.

Dyson, K. (1994) *Elusive Union: the Process of Economic and Monetary Union in Europe*, Longman, Harlow.

Ernst & Young (1990) *A Strategy for the ECU*, Kogan Page, London.

European Commission (1994) *Science and Technology Policy: the European Community and the Globalization of Technology and the Economy*, Office of Official Publications, Luxembourg.

European Commission (1994) *Public Procurement: the Directives*, Office of Official Publications, Luxembourg.

European Commission (1994) *European Consumer Guide to the Single Market*, Office of Official Publications, Luxembourg.

Faini, R. and Portes, R. (1995) *European Union Trade with Eastern Europe: Adjustment and Opportunities*, Centre for Economic Policy Research, London.

Fennell, R. (1987) *The Common Agricultural Policy of the European Community*, 2nd edn, BSP, Oxford.

Gold, M. (ed.) (1993) *The Social Dimension: Employment Policy in the European Community*, Macmillan, Basingstoke.

Haigh, N. (1989) *EEC Environmental Policy and Britain*, 3rd edn, Longman, Harlow.

Hansen, J. D. *et al.* (1992) *An Economic Analysis of the EC*, McGraw-Hill, Maidenhead.

Ishikawa, K. (1990) *Japan and the Challenge of Europe 1992*, Pinter, London.

Johnson, S. and Corcelle, G. (1989) *The Environmental Policy of the European Communities*, Graham and Trotman, London.

Lynch, R. (1994) *European Business Strategies: the European and Global Strategies of Europe's Top Companies*, 2nd edn, Kogan Page, London.

Meehan, E. (1993) *Citizenship and the European Union*, Sage, London.

Michalski, A. and Wallace, H. (1992) *The European Community: the Challenge of Enlargement*, Centre for Economic Policy Research, London.

Molle, W. (1990) *The Economics of European Integration*, Dartmouth, Aldershot.

National Consumer Council (1988) *Consumers and the Common Agricultural Policy*, HMSO, London.

Nicolas, F. (1995) *Common Standards for Enterprises*, Office of Official Publications, Luxembourg.

O'Keeffe, D. and Twomey, P. M. (eds.) (1994) *Legal Issues of the Maastricht Treaty*, John Wiley, Chichester.

Preston, J. (1991) *EC Education, Training and Research Programmes: an Action Guide*, Kogan Page, London.

Rose, V. (ed.) (1993) *Bellamy and Child Common Market Law of Competition*, 4th edn, Sweet and Maxwell, London.

Westlake, M. (1994) *A Modern Guide to the European Parliament*, Pinter, London.

Williamson, J. and Milner, C. (1991) *The World Economy: a Textbook in International Economics*, Harvester Wheatsheaf, Hemel Hempstead.

Winters, L. A. (1992) *Trade Flows and Trade Policy After '1992'*, Centre for Economic Policy Research, London.

Young, S. and Hamill, J. (1992) *Europe and the Multinationals*, Edward Elgar, Aldershot.

INDEX